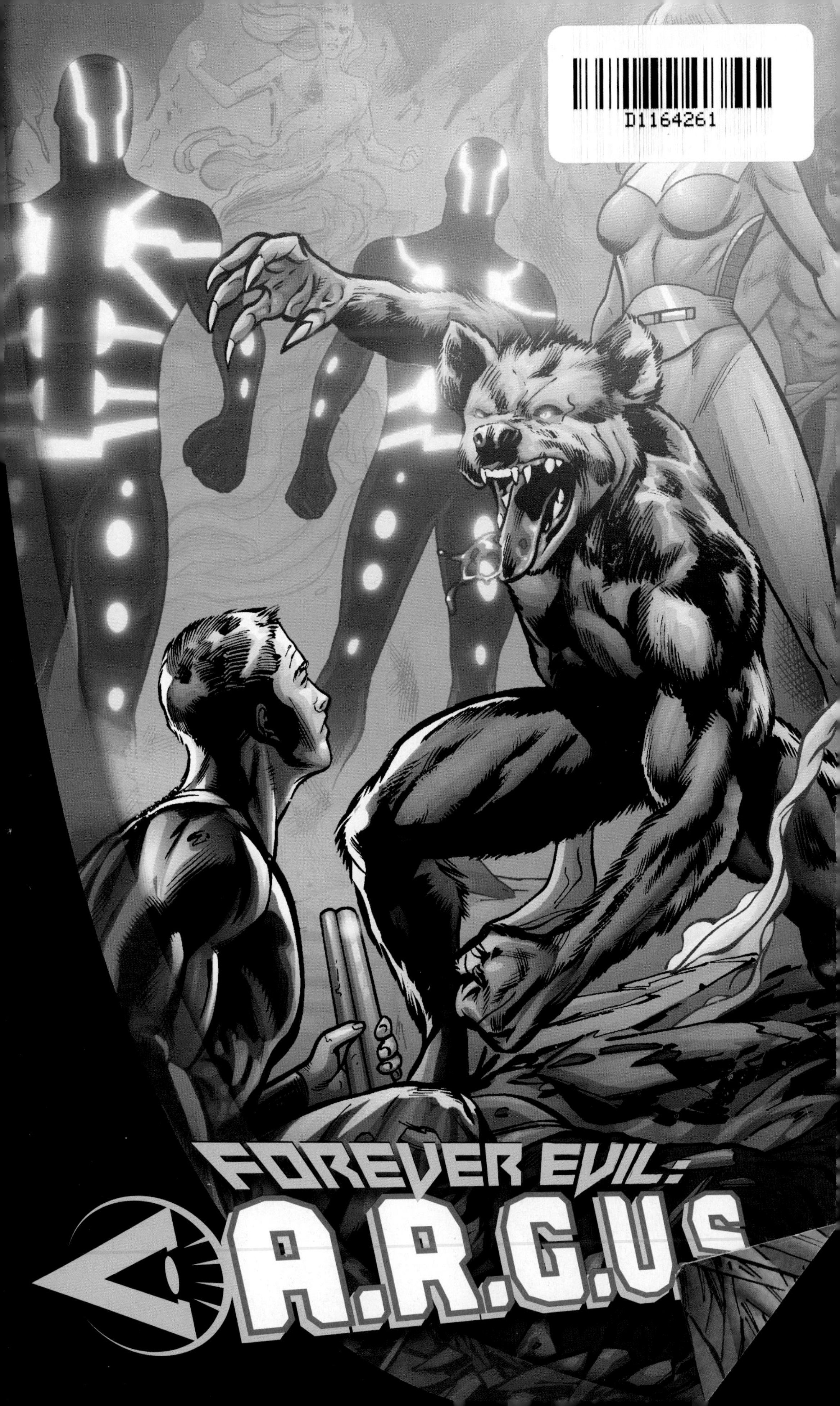
FOREVER EVIL:
A.R.G.U.

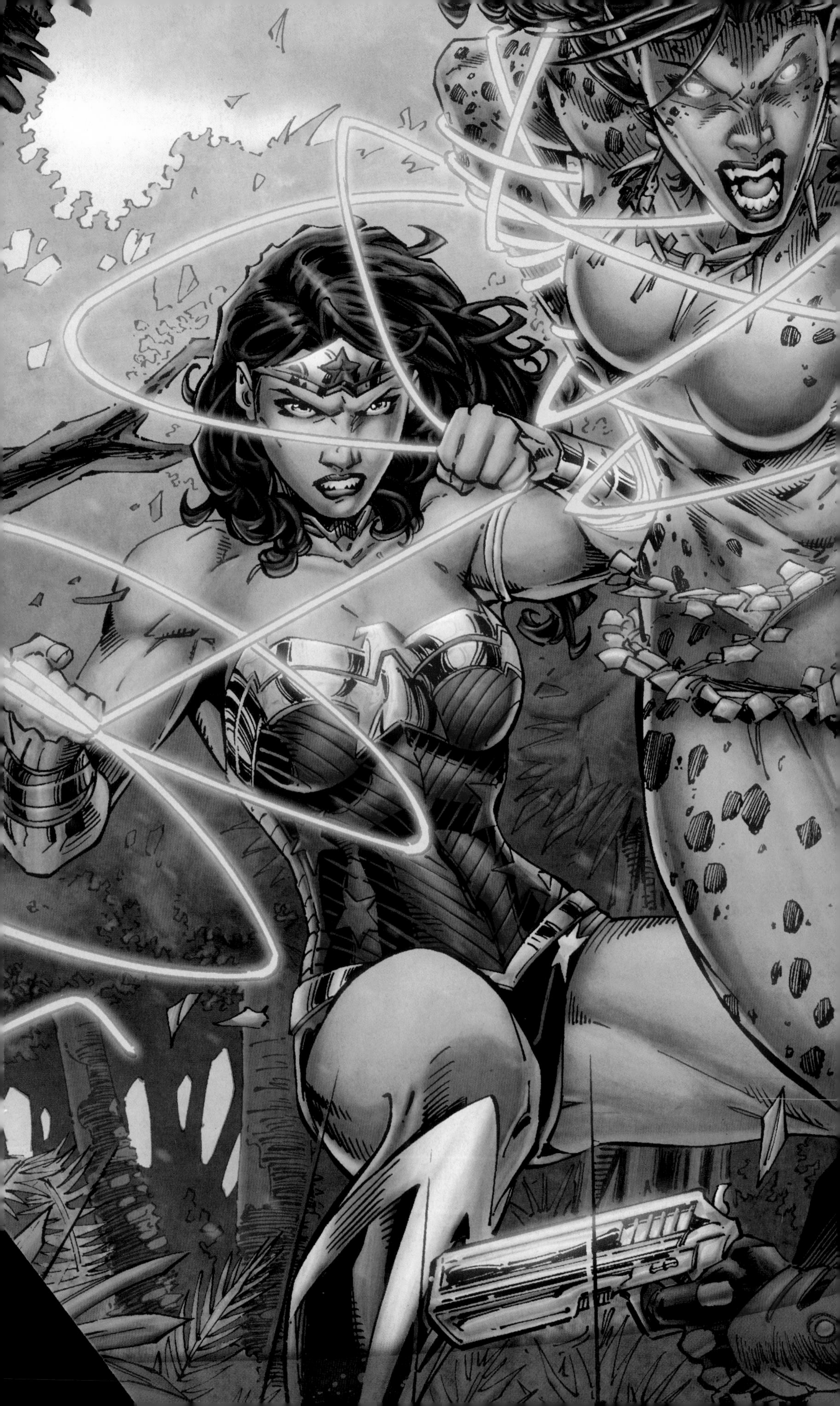

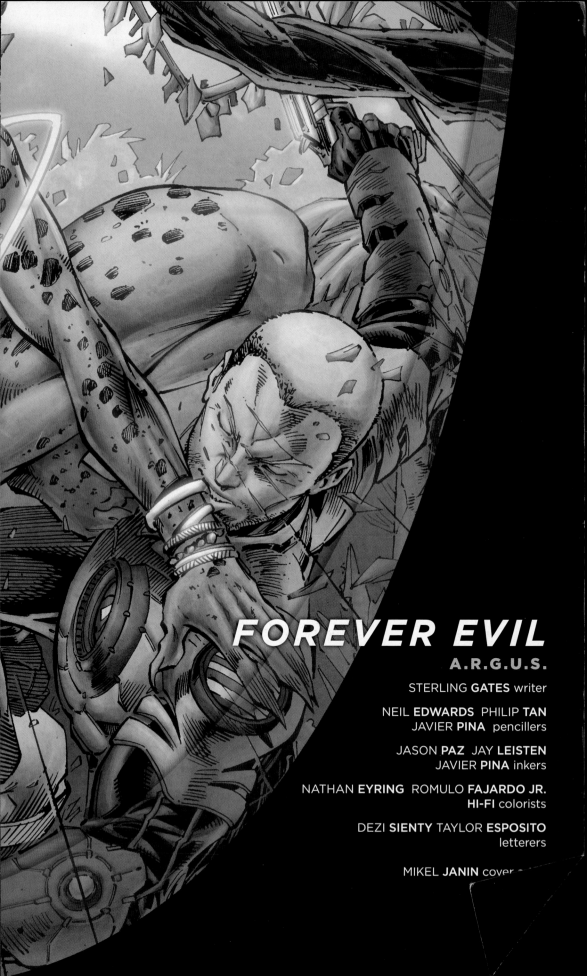

FOREVER EVIL
A.R.G.U.S.

STERLING **GATES** writer

NEIL **EDWARDS** PHILIP **TAN**
JAVIER **PINA** pencillers

JASON **PAZ** JAY **LEISTEN**
JAVIER **PINA** inkers

NATHAN **EYRING** ROMULO **FAJARDO JR.**
HI-FI colorists

DEZI **SIENTY** TAYLOR **ESPOSITO**
letterers

MIKEL **JANIN** cover

BRIAN CUNNINGHAM Editor – Original Series KATE DURRÉ Assistant Editor – Original Series
PETER HAMBOUSSI Editor ROBBIN BROSTERMAN Design Director – Books

BOB HARRAS Senior VP – Editor-in-Chief, DC Comics

DIANE NELSON President DAN DIDIO and JIM LEE Co-Publishers GEOFF JOHNS Chief Creative Officer
AMIT DESAI Senior VP – Marketing & Franchise Management AMY GENKINS Senior VP – Business & Legal Affairs
NAIRI GARDINER Senior VP – Finance JEFF BOISON VP – Publishing Planning
MARK CHIARELLO VP – Art Direction & Design JOHN CUNNINGHAM VP – Marketing
TERRI CUNNINGHAM VP – Editorial Administration LARRY GANEM VP – Talent Relations & Services
ALISON GILL Senior VP – Manufacturing & Operations HANK KANALZ Senior VP – Vertigo & Integrated Publishing
JAY KOGAN VP – Business & Legal Affairs, Publishing JACK MAHAN VP – Business Affairs, Talent
NICK NAPOLITANO VP – Manufacturing Administration SUE POHJA VP – Book Sales
FRED RUIZ VP – Manufacturing Operations COURTNEY SIMMONS Senior VP – Publicity BOB WAYNE Senior VP – Sales

FOREVER EVIL: A.R.G.U.S.

DC Comics, 1700 Broadway, New York, NY 10019
A Warner Bros. Entertainment Company.
Printed by RR Donnelley, Salem, VA, USA. 8/22/14. First Printing.

Library of Congress Cataloging-in-Publication Data

Gates, Sterling, author.
Forever Evil : A.R.G.U.S. / Sterling Gates, Philip Tan, Jason Paz.
pages cm. — (The New 52!)
Originally published in single magazine form as Forever Evil: A.R.G.U.S. 1-6
ISBN 978-1-4012-4939-7 (paperback)
1. Graphic novels. I. Tan, Philip, 1978- illustrator. II. Paz, Jason, illustrator. III. Title. IV. Title: A.R.G.U.S.
PN6728.F63G38 2014
741.5'973—dc23
2014011704

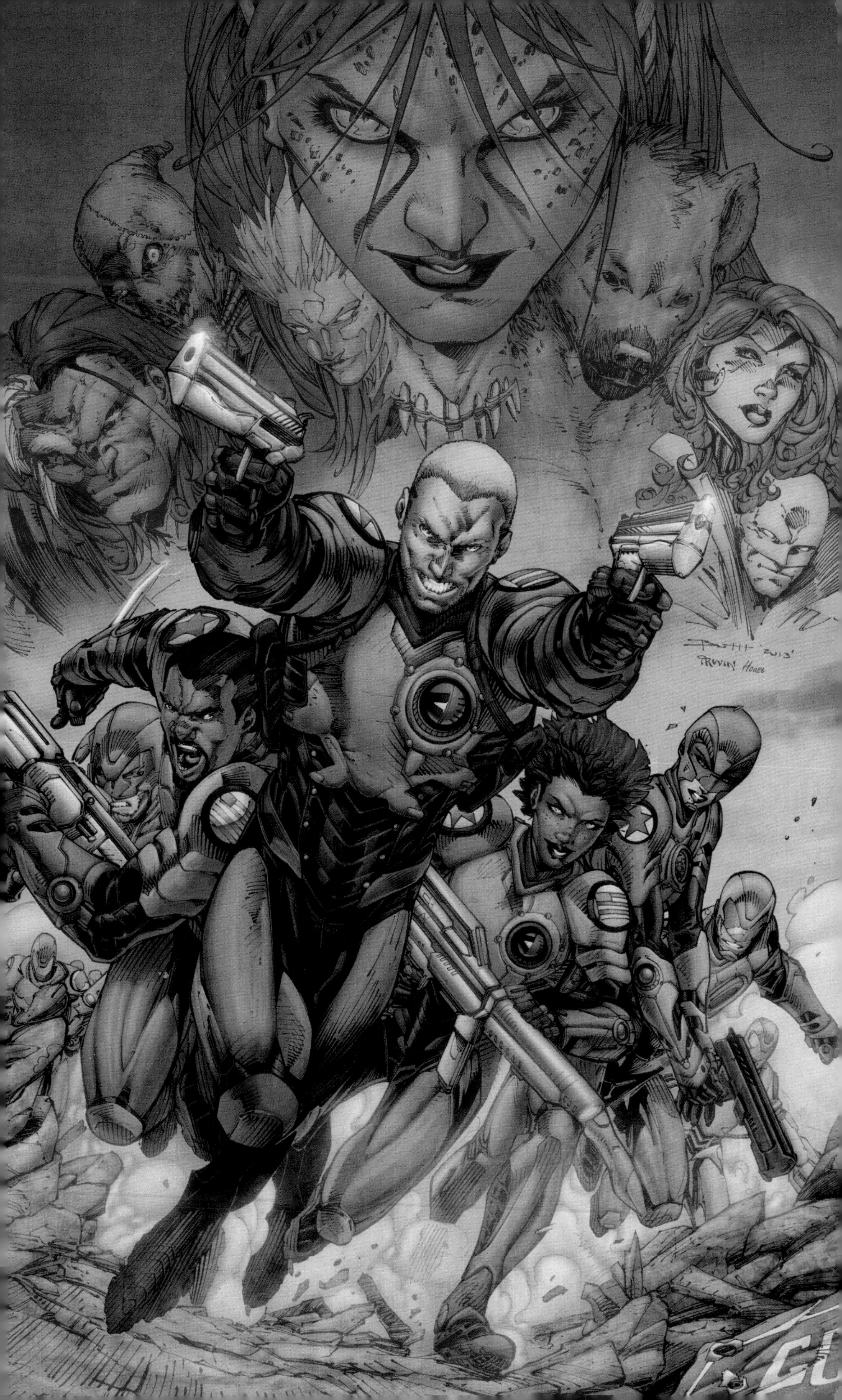
'2013'
House

PART ONE: ISSUES OF TRUST

STERLING GATES Writer **PHILIP TAN NEIL EDWARDS JAVIER PINA** Pencillers **JASON PAZ JAY LEISTEN JAVIER PINA** Inkers
NATHAN EYRING ROMULO FAJARDO JR. HI-FI Colorists **DEZI SIENTY** Letterer
Cover Art by **BRETT BOOTH, MARK IRWIN** and **ANDREW DALHOUSE**

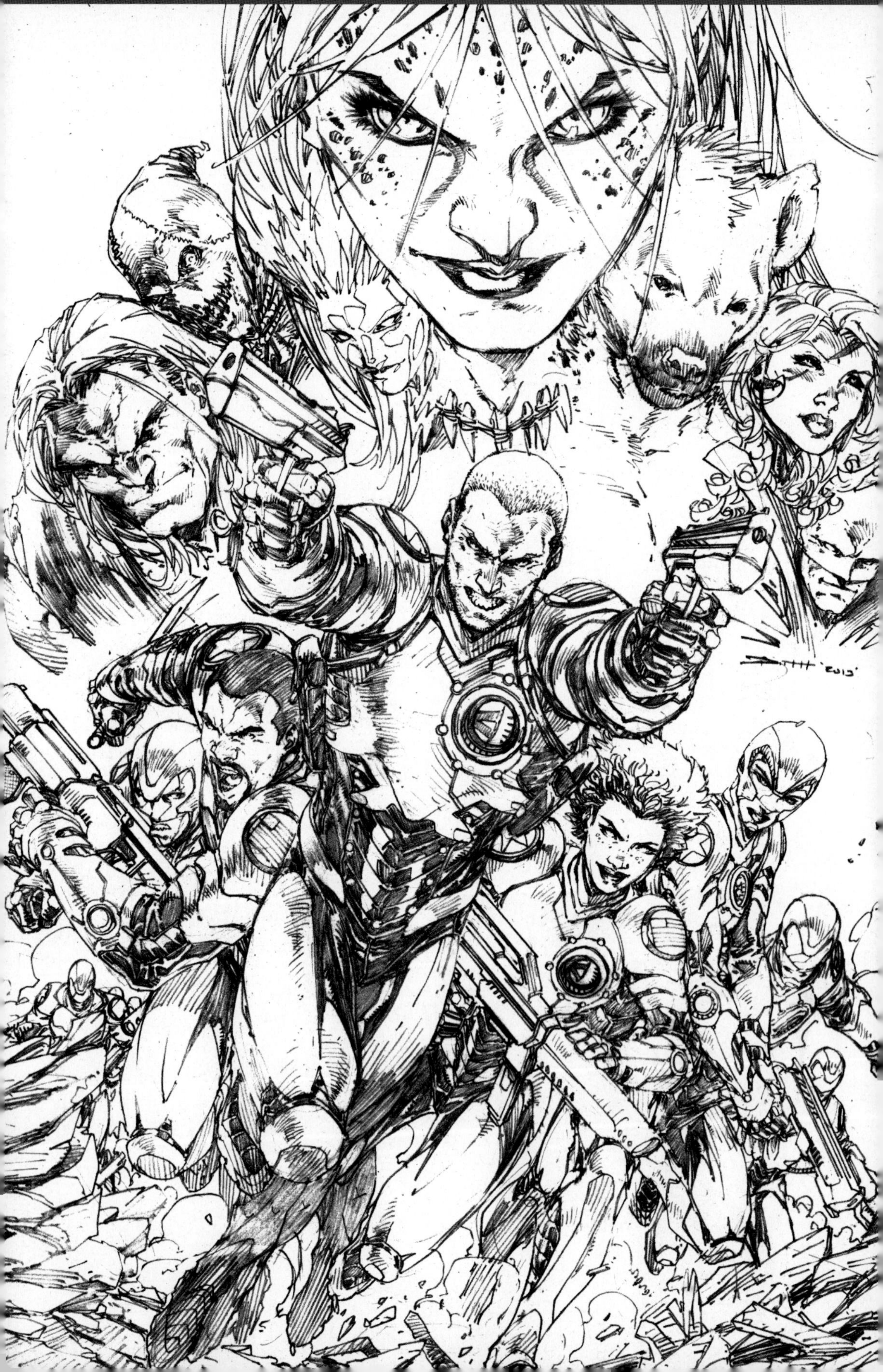

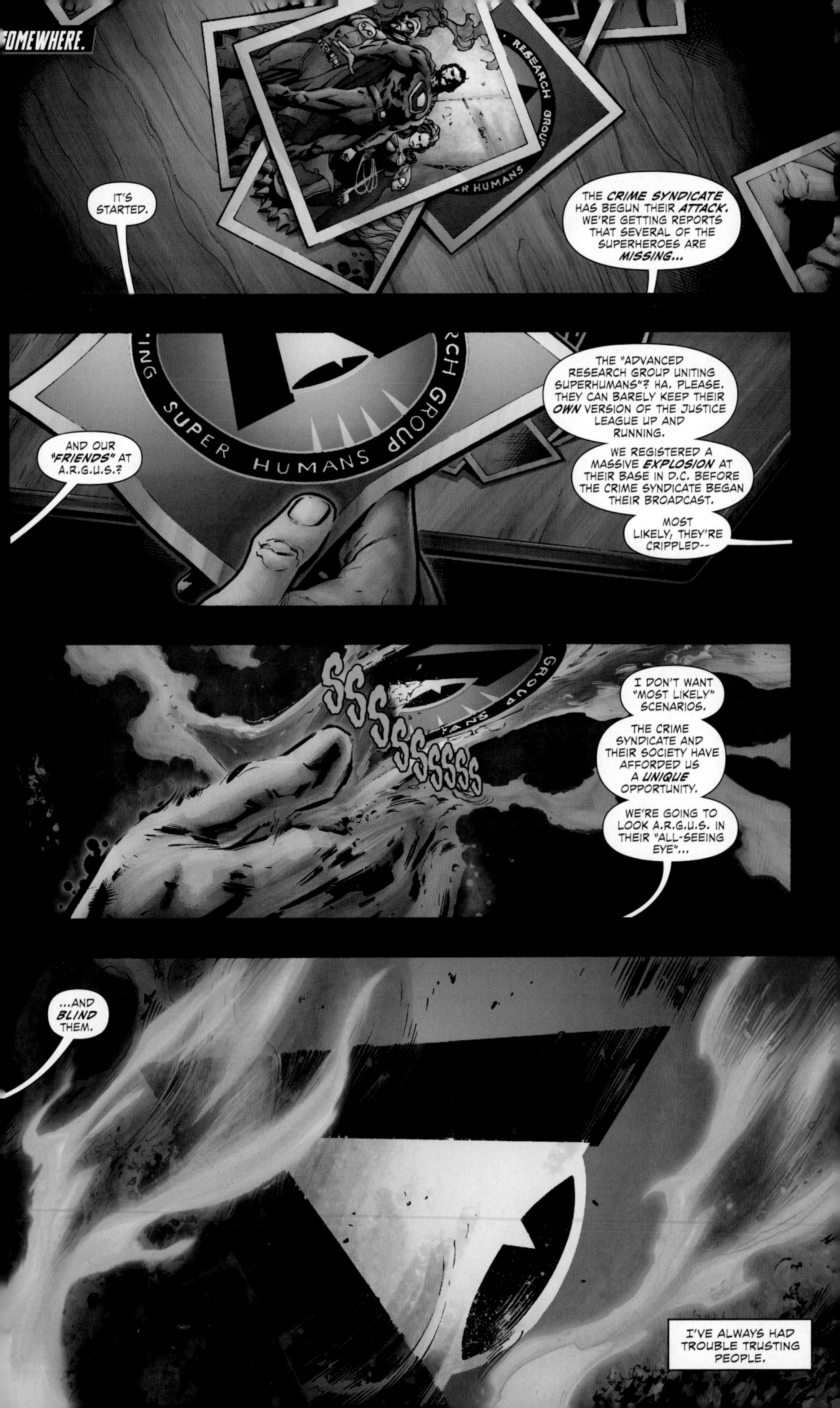

SOMEWHERE.
RESEARCH GROUP
SUPER HUMANS
IT'S STARTED.
THE CRIME SYNDICATE HAS BEGUN THEIR ATTACK. WE'RE GETTING REPORTS THAT SEVERAL OF THE SUPERHEROES ARE MISSING...
ING SUPER HUMANS RESEARCH GROUP
AND OUR "FRIENDS" AT A.R.G.U.S.?
THE "ADVANCED RESEARCH GROUP UNITING SUPERHUMANS"? HA. PLEASE. THEY CAN BARELY KEEP THEIR OWN VERSION OF THE JUSTICE LEAGUE UP AND RUNNING.
WE REGISTERED A MASSIVE EXPLOSION AT THEIR BASE IN D.C. BEFORE THE CRIME SYNDICATE BEGAN THEIR BROADCAST.
MOST LIKELY, THEY'RE CRIPPLED--
SSSSSSSSSS
I DON'T WANT "MOST LIKELY" SCENARIOS.
THE CRIME SYNDICATE AND THEIR SOCIETY HAVE AFFORDED US A UNIQUE OPPORTUNITY.
WE'RE GOING TO LOOK A.R.G.U.S. IN THEIR "ALL-SEEING EYE"...
...AND BLIND THEM.
I'VE ALWAYS HAD TROUBLE TRUSTING PEOPLE.

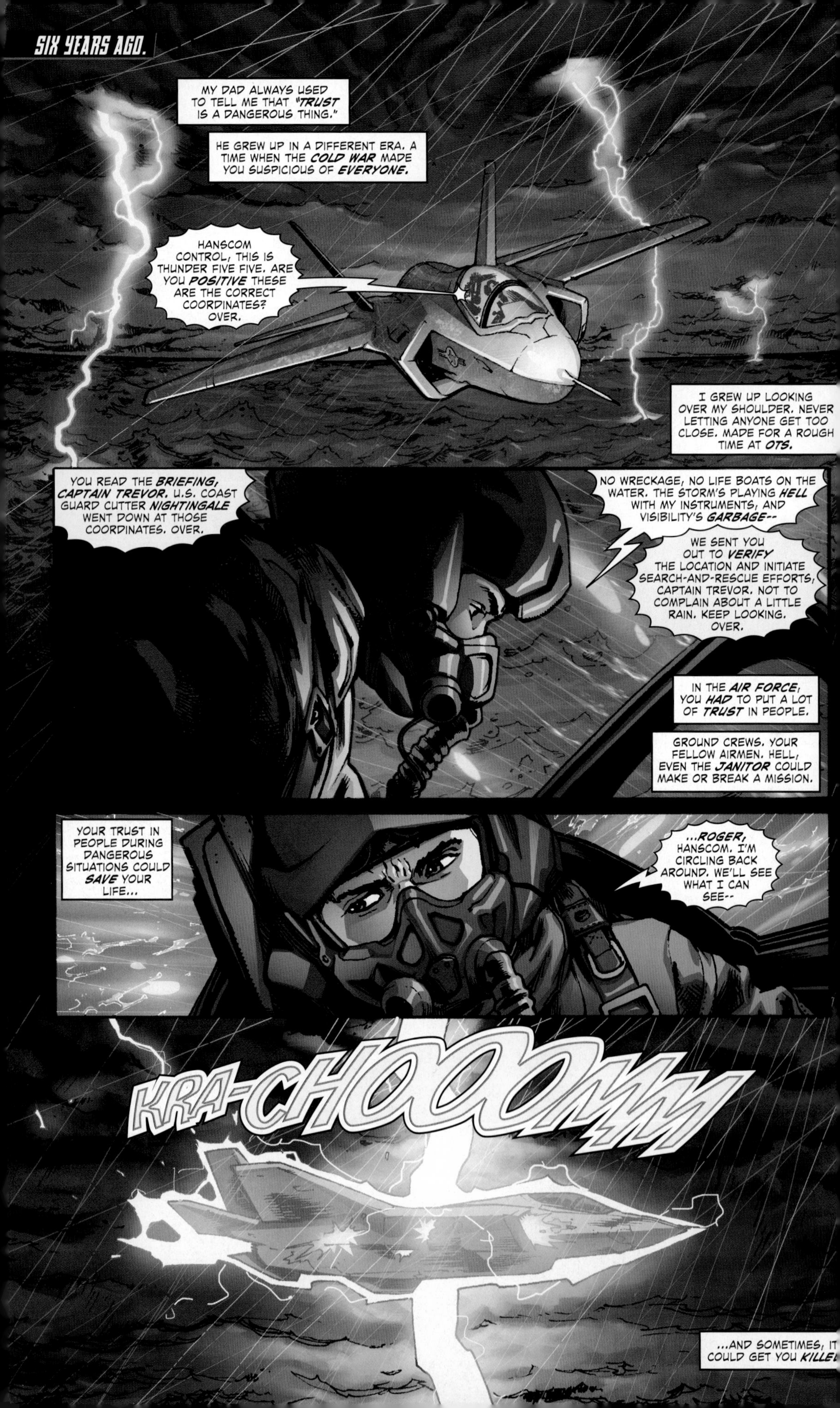
SIX YEARS AGO.
MY DAD ALWAYS USED TO TELL ME THAT "TRUST IS A DANGEROUS THING."
HE GREW UP IN A DIFFERENT ERA. A TIME WHEN THE COLD WAR MADE YOU SUSPICIOUS OF EVERYONE.
HANSCOM CONTROL, THIS IS THUNDER FIVE FIVE. ARE YOU POSITIVE THESE ARE THE CORRECT COORDINATES? OVER.
I GREW UP LOOKING OVER MY SHOULDER. NEVER LETTING ANYONE GET TOO CLOSE. MADE FOR A ROUGH TIME AT OTS.
YOU READ THE BRIEFING, CAPTAIN TREVOR. U.S. COAST GUARD CUTTER NIGHTINGALE WENT DOWN AT THOSE COORDINATES. OVER.
NO WRECKAGE, NO LIFE BOATS ON THE WATER. THE STORM'S PLAYING HELL WITH MY INSTRUMENTS, AND VISIBILITY'S GARBAGE--
WE SENT YOU OUT TO VERIFY THE LOCATION AND INITIATE SEARCH-AND-RESCUE EFFORTS, CAPTAIN TREVOR. NOT TO COMPLAIN ABOUT A LITTLE RAIN. KEEP LOOKING. OVER.
IN THE AIR FORCE, YOU HAD TO PUT A LOT OF TRUST IN PEOPLE.
GROUND CREWS. YOUR FELLOW AIRMEN. HELL, EVEN THE JANITOR COULD MAKE OR BREAK A MISSION.
YOUR TRUST IN PEOPLE DURING DANGEROUS SITUATIONS COULD SAVE YOUR LIFE...
...ROGER, HANSCOM. I'M CIRCLING BACK AROUND. WE'LL SEE WHAT I CAN SEE--
KRA-CHOOOMM
...AND SOMETIMES, IT COULD GET YOU KILLED.

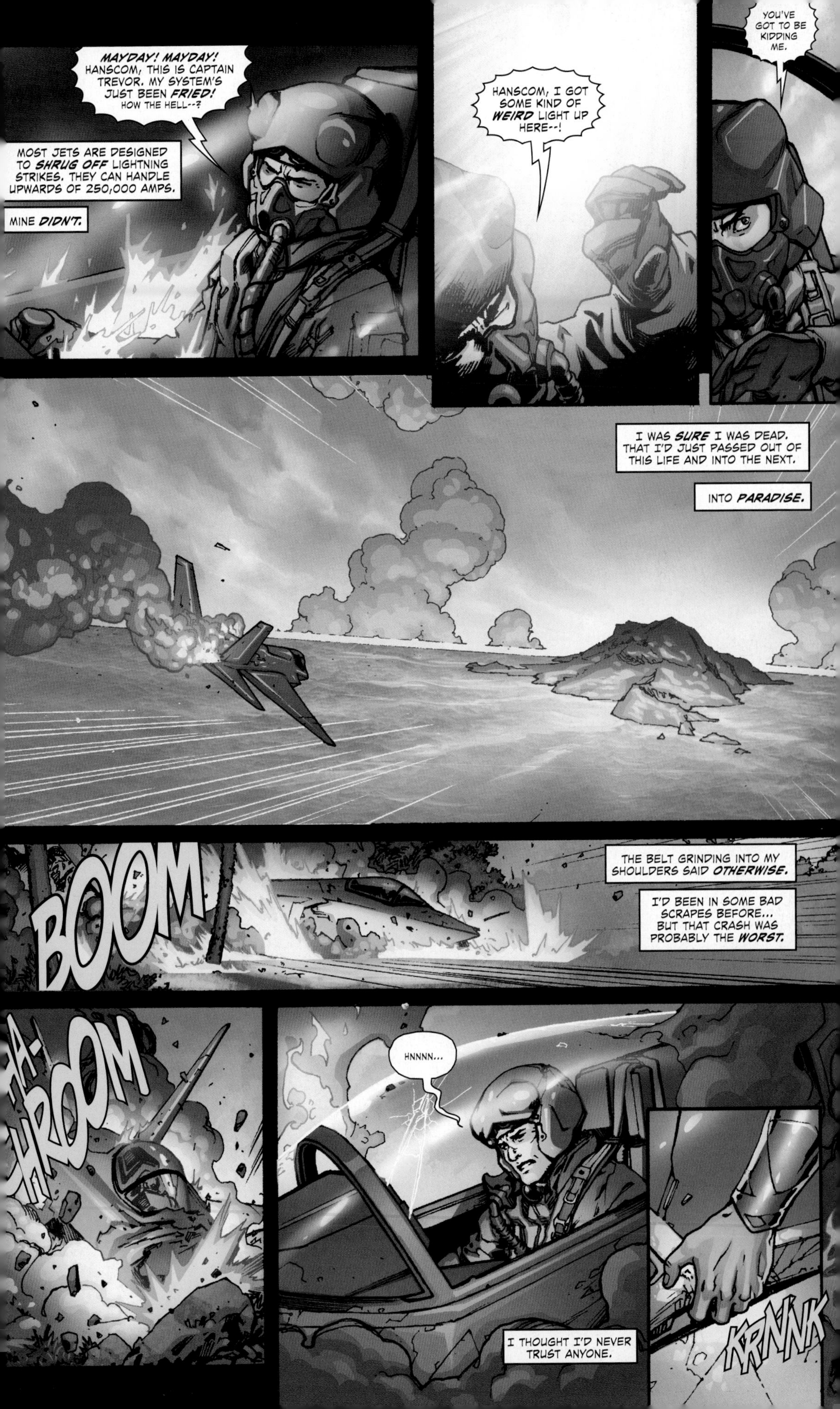
MAYDAY! MAYDAY! HANSCOM, THIS IS CAPTAIN TREVOR. MY SYSTEM'S JUST BEEN FRIED! HOW THE HELL--?
MOST JETS ARE DESIGNED TO SHRUG OFF LIGHTNING STRIKES. THEY CAN HANDLE UPWARDS OF 250,000 AMPS.
MINE DIDN'T.
HANSCOM, I GOT SOME KIND OF WEIRD LIGHT UP HERE--!
YOU'VE GOT TO BE KIDDING ME.
I WAS SURE I WAS DEAD. THAT I'D JUST PASSED OUT OF THIS LIFE AND INTO THE NEXT.
INTO PARADISE.
BOOM
THE BELT GRINDING INTO MY SHOULDERS SAID OTHERWISE.
I'D BEEN IN SOME BAD SCRAPES BEFORE... BUT THAT CRASH WAS PROBABLY THE WORST.
KA-THROOM
HNNNN...
I THOUGHT I'D NEVER TRUST ANYONE.
KRNNK

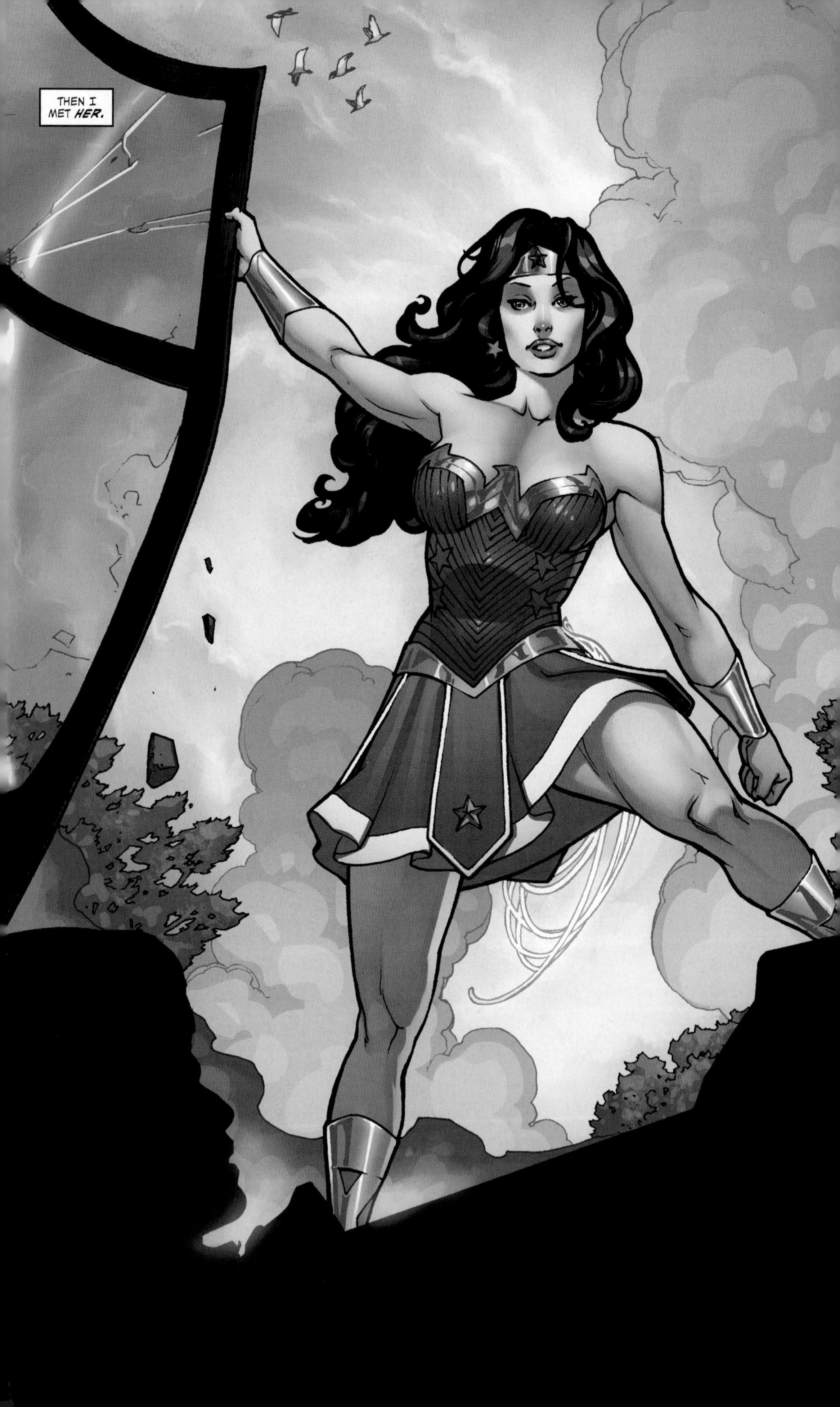
THEN I MET HER.

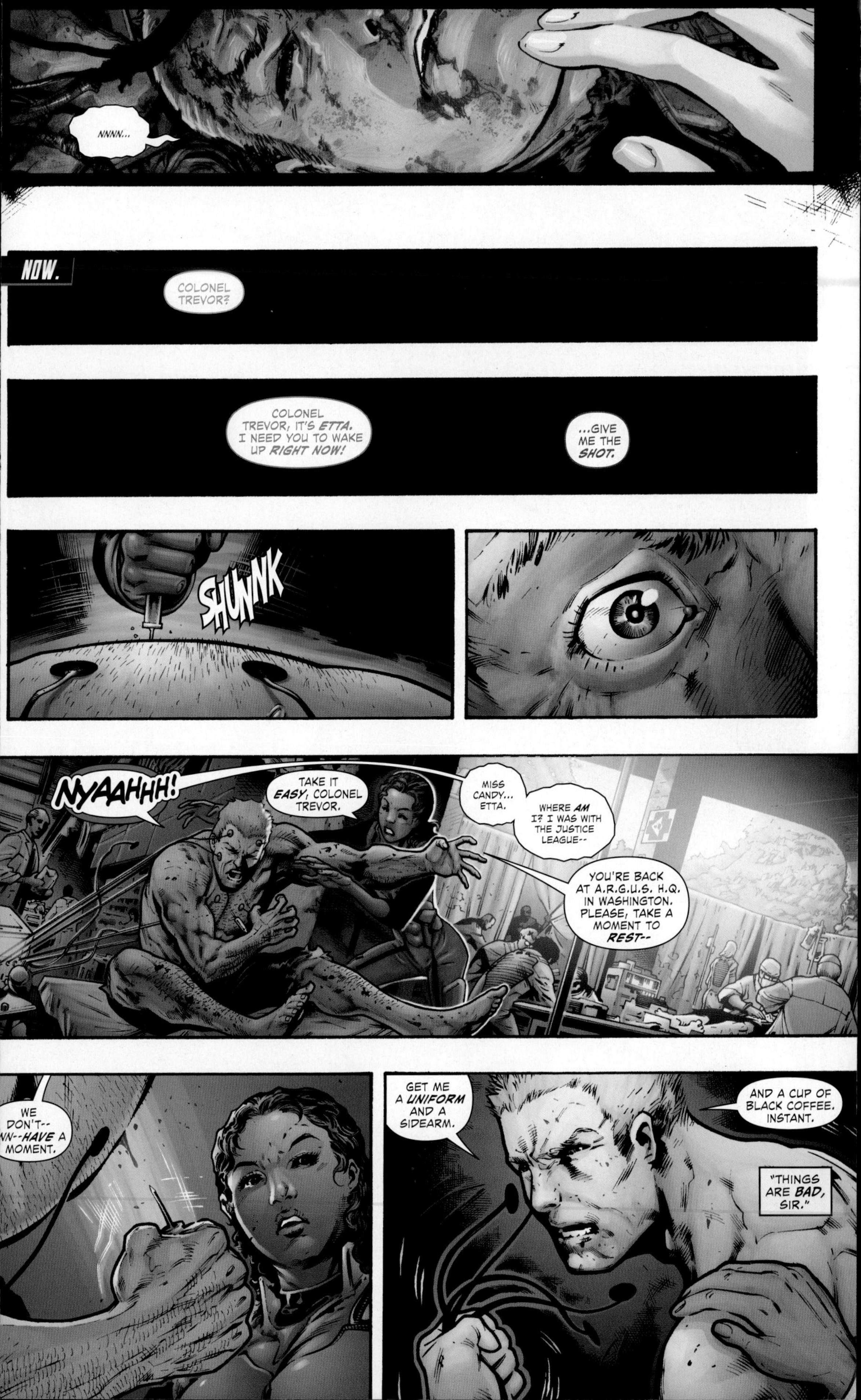
NNNN...
NOW.
COLONEL TREVOR?
COLONEL TREVOR, IT'S ETTA. I NEED YOU TO WAKE UP RIGHT NOW!
...GIVE ME THE SHOT.
SHUNNK
NYAAHHH!
TAKE IT EASY, COLONEL TREVOR.
MISS CANDY... ETTA.
WHERE AM I? I WAS WITH THE JUSTICE LEAGUE--
YOU'RE BACK AT A.R.G.U.S. H.Q. IN WASHINGTON. PLEASE, TAKE A MOMENT TO REST--
WE DON'T--NN--HAVE A MOMENT.
GET ME A UNIFORM AND A SIDEARM.
AND A CUP OF BLACK COFFEE. INSTANT.
"THINGS ARE BAD, SIR."

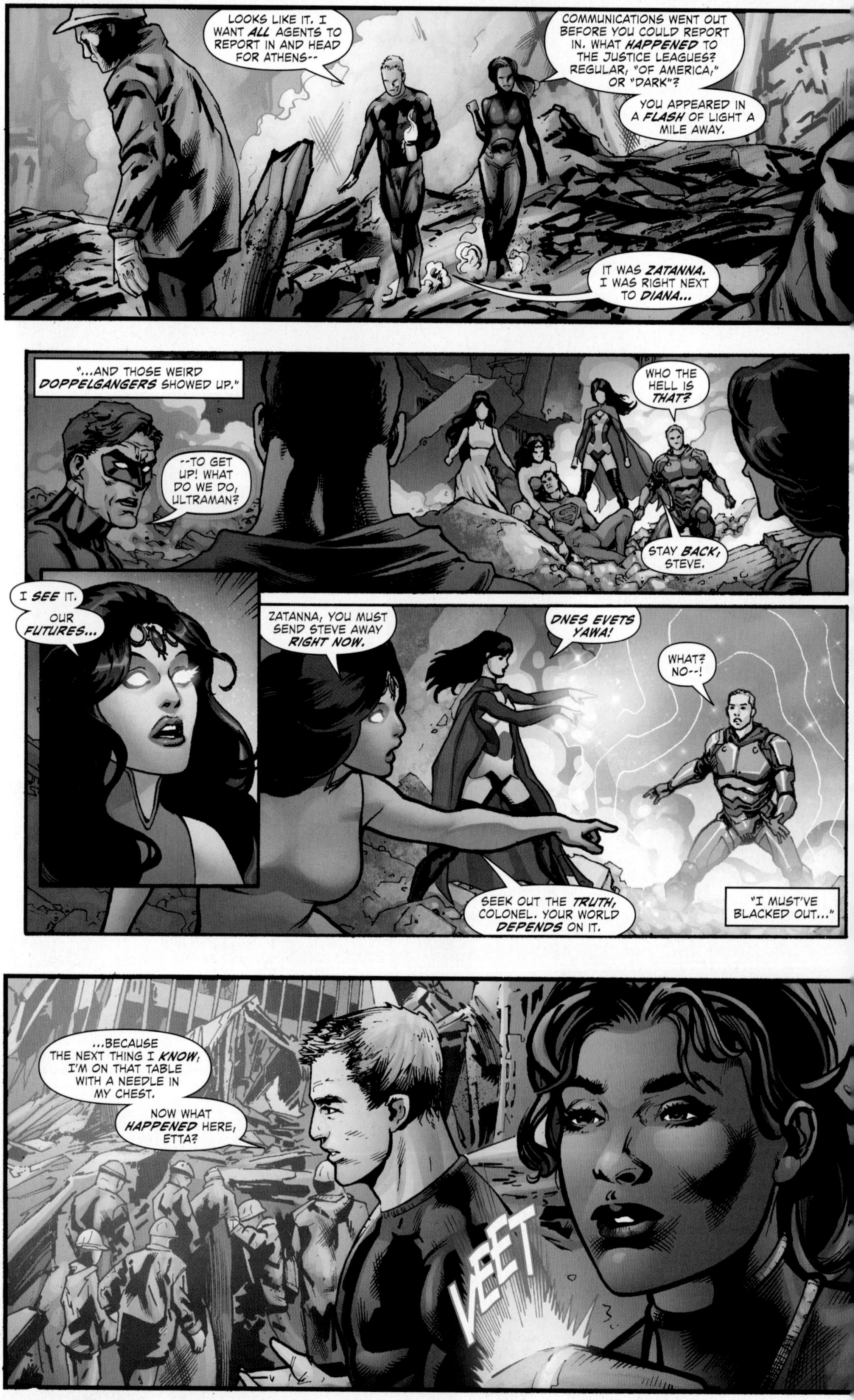
LOOKS LIKE IT. I WANT ALL AGENTS TO REPORT IN AND HEAD FOR ATHENS--
COMMUNICATIONS WENT OUT BEFORE YOU COULD REPORT IN. WHAT HAPPENED TO THE JUSTICE LEAGUES? REGULAR, "OF AMERICA," OR "DARK"?
YOU APPEARED IN A FLASH OF LIGHT A MILE AWAY.
IT WAS ZATANNA. I WAS RIGHT NEXT TO DIANA...
"...AND THOSE WEIRD DOPPELGANGERS SHOWED UP."
--TO GET UP! WHAT DO WE DO, ULTRAMAN?
WHO THE HELL IS THAT?
STAY BACK, STEVE.
I SEE IT.
OUR FUTURES...
ZATANNA, YOU MUST SEND STEVE AWAY RIGHT NOW.
DNES EVETS YAWA!
WHAT? NO--!
SEEK OUT THE TRUTH, COLONEL. YOUR WORLD DEPENDS ON IT.
"I MUST'VE BLACKED OUT..."
...BECAUSE THE NEXT THING I KNOW, I'M ON THAT TABLE WITH A NEEDLE IN MY CHEST.
NOW WHAT HAPPENED HERE, ETTA?
VEET

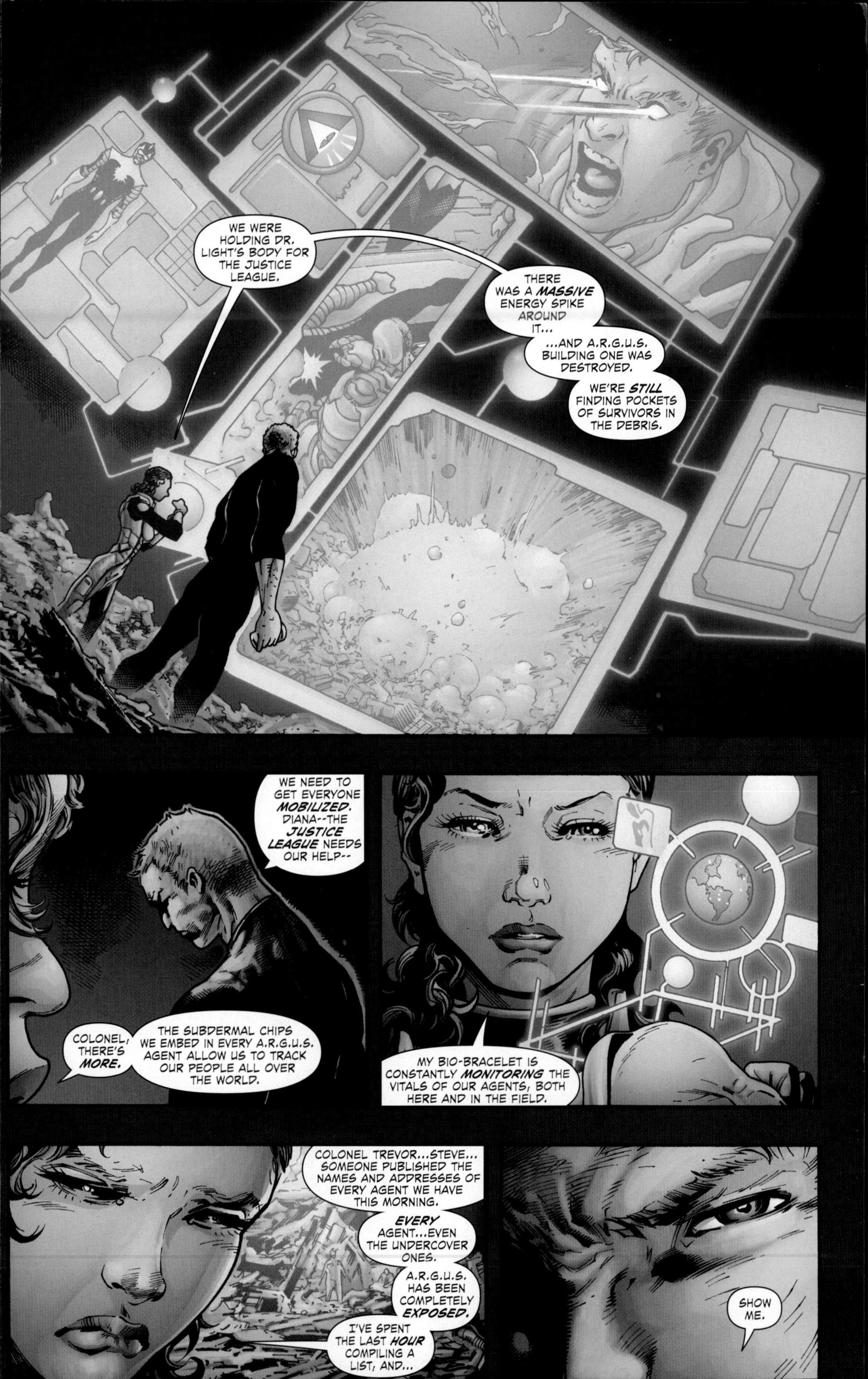
WE WERE HOLDING DR. LIGHT'S BODY FOR THE JUSTICE LEAGUE.
THERE WAS A MASSIVE ENERGY SPIKE AROUND IT...
...AND A.R.G.U.S. BUILDING ONE WAS DESTROYED.
WE'RE STILL FINDING POCKETS OF SURVIVORS IN THE DEBRIS.
WE NEED TO GET EVERYONE MOBILIZED. DIANA--THE JUSTICE LEAGUE NEEDS OUR HELP--
COLONEL, THERE'S MORE.
THE SUBDERMAL CHIPS WE EMBED IN EVERY A.R.G.U.S. AGENT ALLOW US TO TRACK OUR PEOPLE ALL OVER THE WORLD.
MY BIO-BRACELET IS CONSTANTLY MONITORING THE VITALS OF OUR AGENTS, BOTH HERE AND IN THE FIELD.
COLONEL TREVOR...STEVE... SOMEONE PUBLISHED THE NAMES AND ADDRESSES OF EVERY AGENT WE HAVE THIS MORNING.
EVERY AGENT...EVEN THE UNDERCOVER ONES.
A.R.G.U.S. HAS BEEN COMPLETELY EXPOSED.
I'VE SPENT THE LAST HOUR COMPILING A LIST, AND...
SHOW ME.

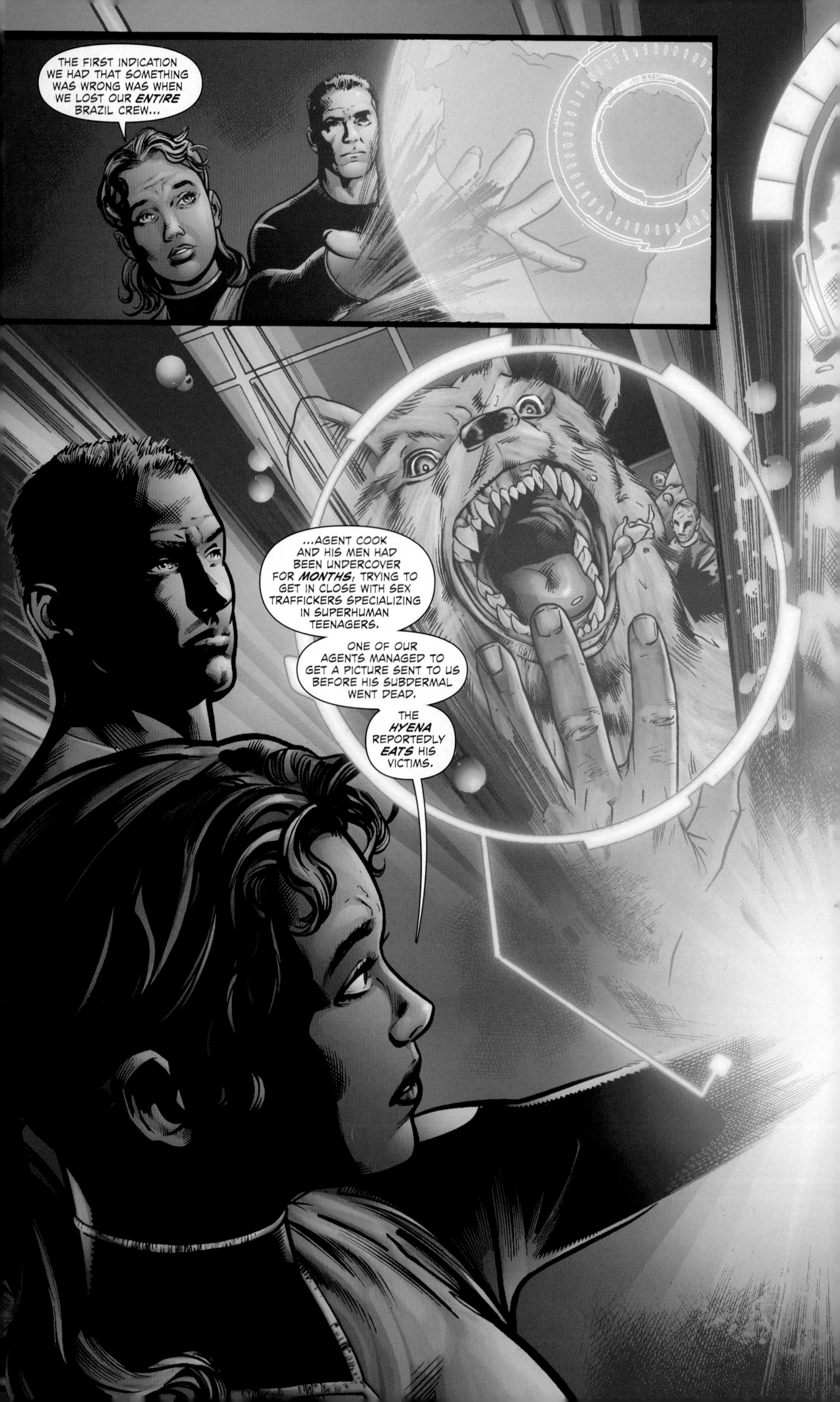
THE FIRST INDICATION WE HAD THAT SOMETHING WAS WRONG WAS WHEN WE LOST OUR ENTIRE BRAZIL CREW...
...AGENT COOK AND HIS MEN HAD BEEN UNDERCOVER FOR MONTHS, TRYING TO GET IN CLOSE WITH SEX TRAFFICKERS SPECIALIZING IN SUPERHUMAN TEENAGERS.
ONE OF OUR AGENTS MANAGED TO GET A PICTURE SENT TO US BEFORE HIS SUBDERMAL WENT DEAD.
THE HYENA REPORTEDLY EATS HIS VICTIMS.

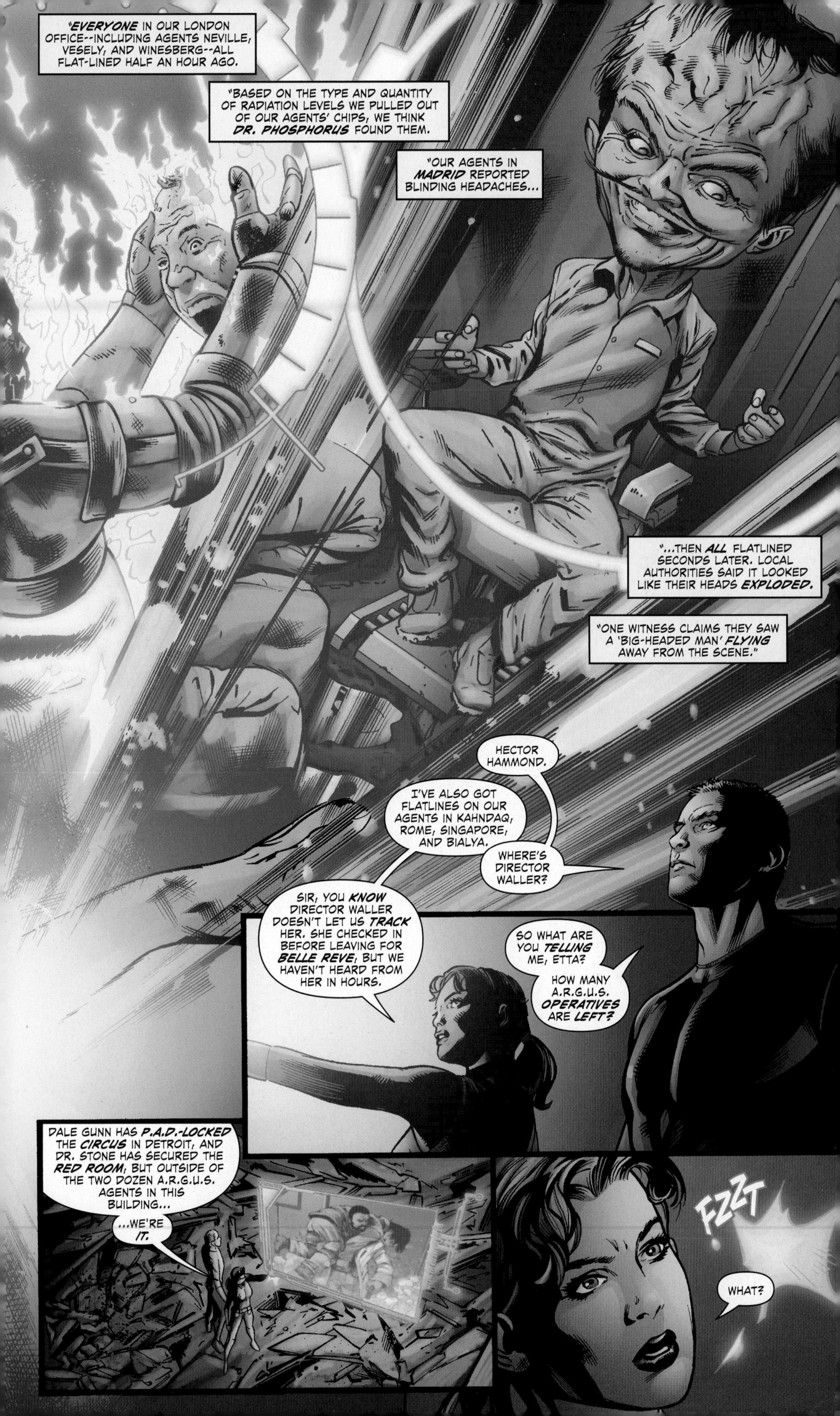
"EVERYONE IN OUR LONDON OFFICE--INCLUDING AGENTS NEVILLE, VESELY, AND WINESBERG--ALL FLAT-LINED HALF AN HOUR AGO.
"BASED ON THE TYPE AND QUANTITY OF RADIATION LEVELS WE PULLED OUT OF OUR AGENTS' CHIPS, WE THINK DR. PHOSPHORUS FOUND THEM.
"OUR AGENTS IN MADRID REPORTED BLINDING HEADACHES...
"...THEN ALL FLATLINED SECONDS LATER. LOCAL AUTHORITIES SAID IT LOOKED LIKE THEIR HEADS EXPLODED.
"ONE WITNESS CLAIMS THEY SAW A 'BIG-HEADED MAN' FLYING AWAY FROM THE SCENE."
HECTOR HAMMOND.
I'VE ALSO GOT FLATLINES ON OUR AGENTS IN KAHNDAQ, ROME, SINGAPORE, AND BIALYA.
WHERE'S DIRECTOR WALLER?
SIR, YOU KNOW DIRECTOR WALLER DOESN'T LET US TRACK HER. SHE CHECKED IN BEFORE LEAVING FOR BELLE REVE, BUT WE HAVEN'T HEARD FROM HER IN HOURS.
SO WHAT ARE YOU TELLING ME, ETTA?
HOW MANY A.R.G.U.S. OPERATIVES ARE LEFT?
DALE GUNN HAS P.A.D.-LOCKED THE CIRCUS IN DETROIT, AND DR. STONE HAS SECURED THE RED ROOM, BUT OUTSIDE OF THE TWO DOZEN A.R.G.U.S. AGENTS IN THIS BUILDING...
...WE'RE IT.
FZZT
WHAT?

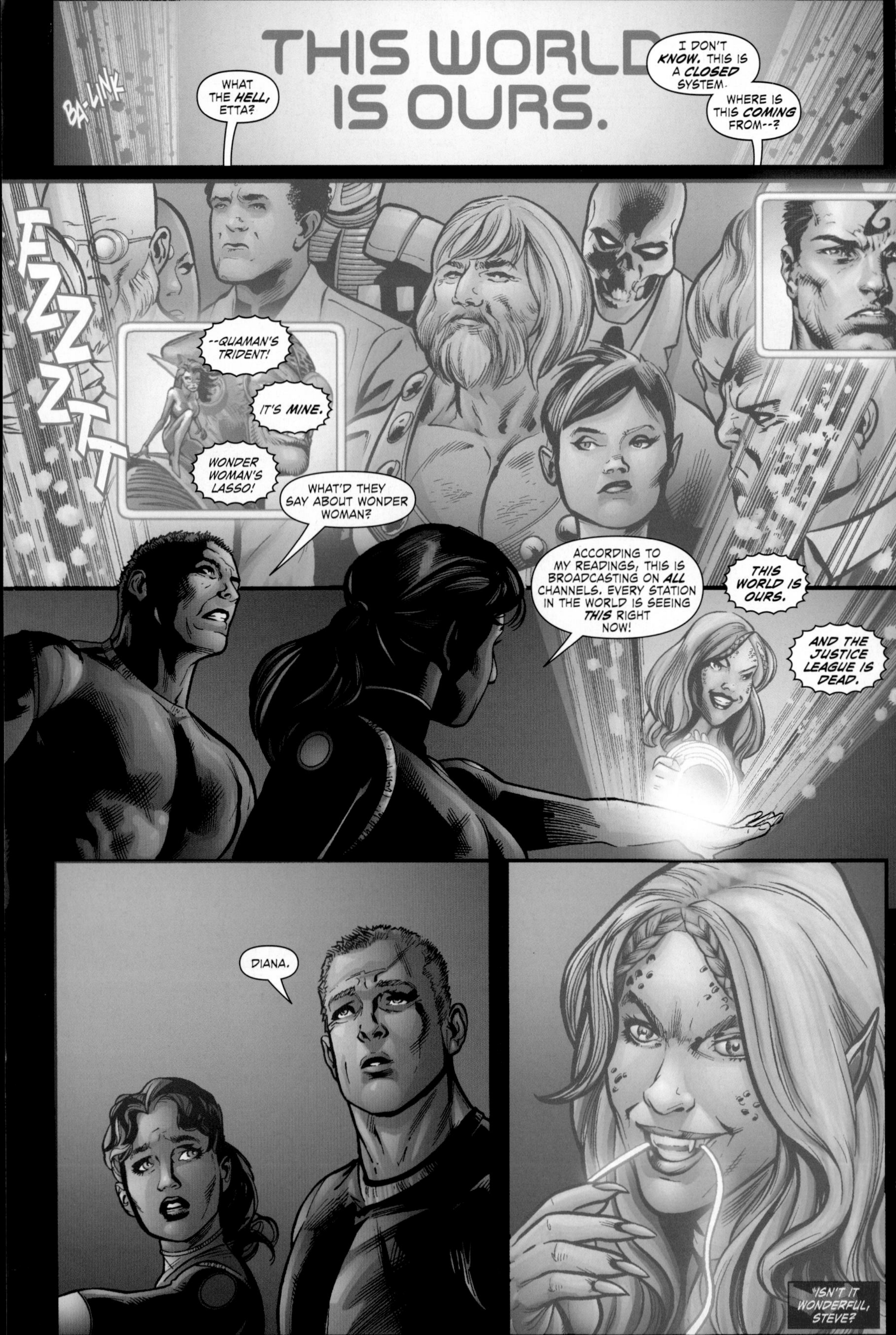
THIS WORLD IS OURS.
BA-LINK
WHAT THE HELL, ETTA?
I DON'T KNOW. THIS IS A CLOSED SYSTEM.
WHERE IS THIS COMING FROM--?
FZZZTTT
--QUAMAN'S TRIDENT!
IT'S MINE.
WONDER WOMAN'S LASSO!
WHAT'D THEY SAY ABOUT WONDER WOMAN?
ACCORDING TO MY READINGS, THIS IS BROADCASTING ON ALL CHANNELS. EVERY STATION IN THE WORLD IS SEEING THIS RIGHT NOW!
THIS WORLD IS OURS.
AND THE JUSTICE LEAGUE IS DEAD.
DIANA.
ISN'T IT WONDERFUL, STEVE?

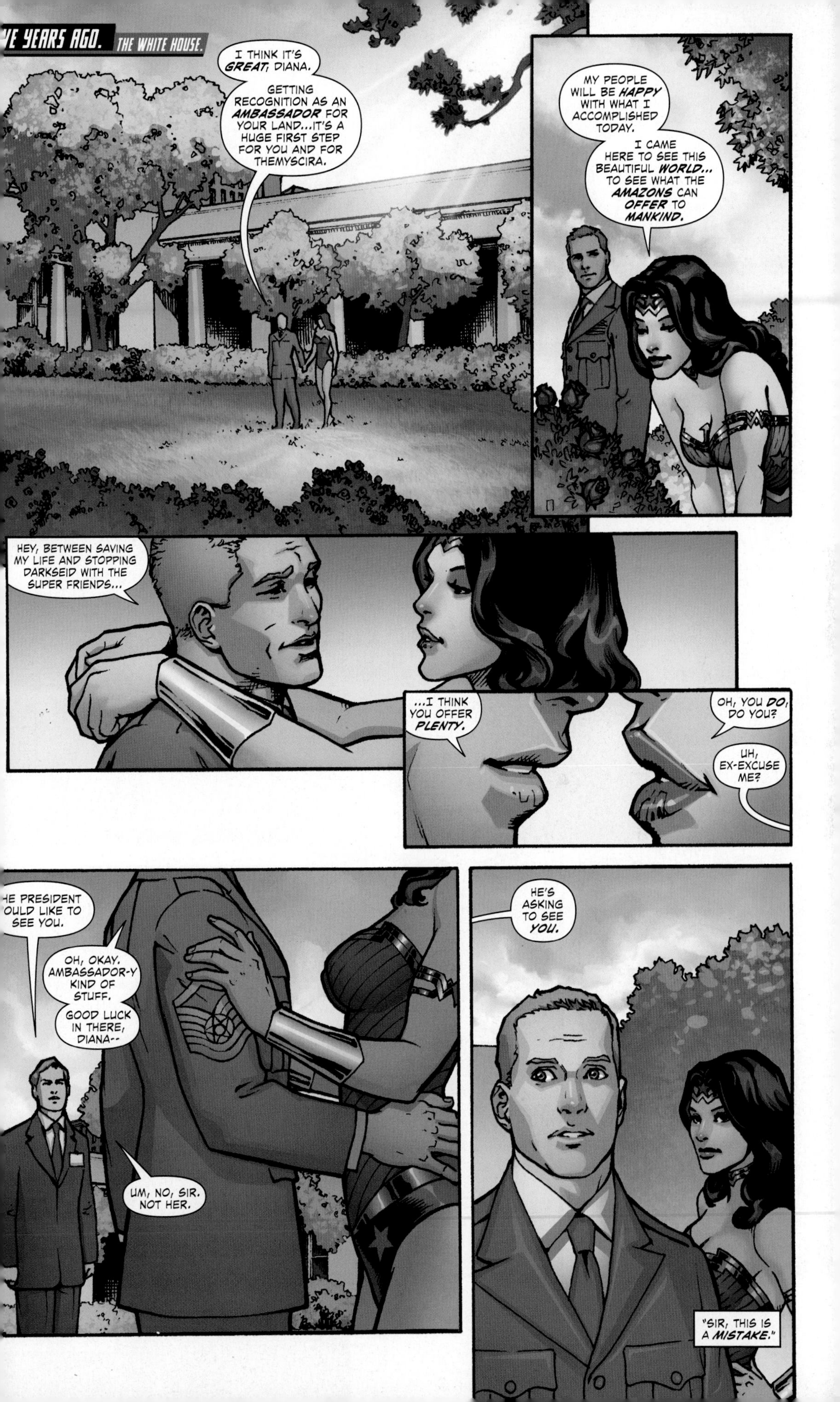

VE YEARS AGO.
THE WHITE HOUSE.
I THINK IT'S GREAT, DIANA.
GETTING RECOGNITION AS AN AMBASSADOR FOR YOUR LAND...IT'S A HUGE FIRST STEP FOR YOU AND FOR THEMYSCIRA.
MY PEOPLE WILL BE HAPPY WITH WHAT I ACCOMPLISHED TODAY.
I CAME HERE TO SEE THIS BEAUTIFUL WORLD... TO SEE WHAT THE AMAZONS CAN OFFER TO MANKIND.
HEY, BETWEEN SAVING MY LIFE AND STOPPING DARKSEID WITH THE SUPER FRIENDS...
...I THINK YOU OFFER PLENTY.
OH, YOU DO, DO YOU?
UH, EX-EXCUSE ME?
HE PRESIDENT OULD LIKE TO SEE YOU.
OH, OKAY. AMBASSADOR-Y KIND OF STUFF.
GOOD LUCK IN THERE, DIANA--
UM, NO, SIR. NOT HER.
HE'S ASKING TO SEE YOU.
"SIR, THIS IS A MISTAKE."

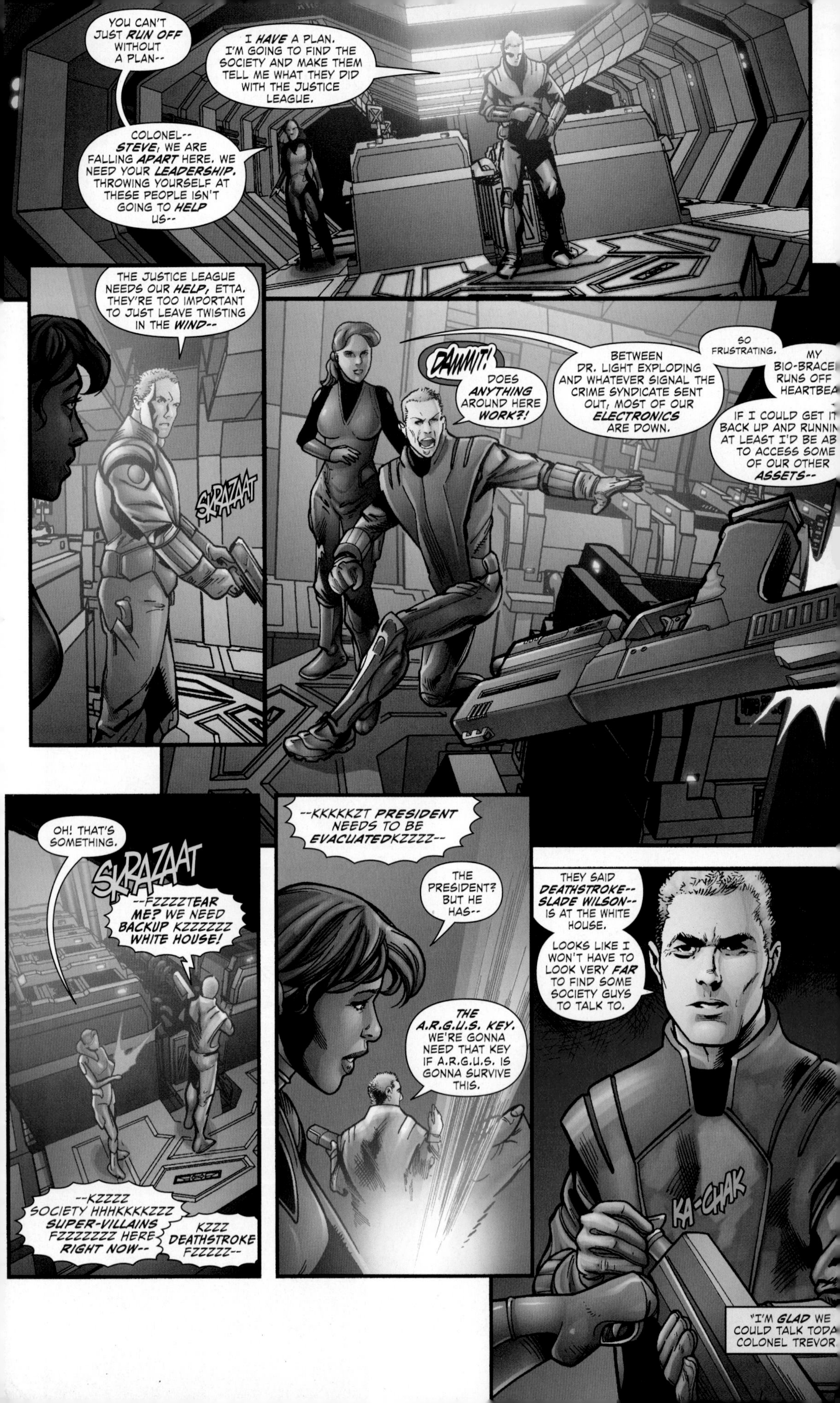
YOU CAN'T JUST RUN OFF WITHOUT A PLAN--
I HAVE A PLAN. I'M GOING TO FIND THE SOCIETY AND MAKE THEM TELL ME WHAT THEY DID WITH THE JUSTICE LEAGUE.
COLONEL-- STEVE, WE ARE FALLING APART HERE. WE NEED YOUR LEADERSHIP. THROWING YOURSELF AT THESE PEOPLE ISN'T GOING TO HELP US--
THE JUSTICE LEAGUE NEEDS OUR HELP, ETTA. THEY'RE TOO IMPORTANT TO JUST LEAVE TWISTING IN THE WIND--
SKRAZAAT
DAMMIT!
DOES ANYTHING AROUND HERE WORK?!
BETWEEN DR. LIGHT EXPLODING AND WHATEVER SIGNAL THE CRIME SYNDICATE SENT OUT, MOST OF OUR ELECTRONICS ARE DOWN.
SO FRUSTRATING.
MY BIO-BRACE RUNS OFF HEARTBEA
IF I COULD GET IT BACK UP AND RUNNIN AT LEAST I'D BE AB TO ACCESS SOME OF OUR OTHER ASSETS--
OH! THAT'S SOMETHING.
SKRAZAAT
--FZZZZZTEAR ME? WE NEED BACKUP KZZZZZZ WHITE HOUSE!
--KZZZZ SOCIETY HHHKKKKZZZ SUPER-VILLAINS FZZZZZZZ HERE RIGHT NOW--
KZZZ DEATHSTROKE FZZZZZ--
--KKKKKZT PRESIDENT NEEDS TO BE EVACUATEDKZZZZ--
THE PRESIDENT? BUT HE HAS--
THE A.R.G.U.S. KEY. WE'RE GONNA NEED THAT KEY IF A.R.G.U.S. IS GONNA SURVIVE THIS.
THEY SAID DEATHSTROKE-- SLADE WILSON-- IS AT THE WHITE HOUSE.
LOOKS LIKE I WON'T HAVE TO LOOK VERY FAR TO FIND SOME SOCIETY GUYS TO TALK TO.
KA-CHAK
"I'M GLAD WE COULD TALK TODA COLONEL TREVOR

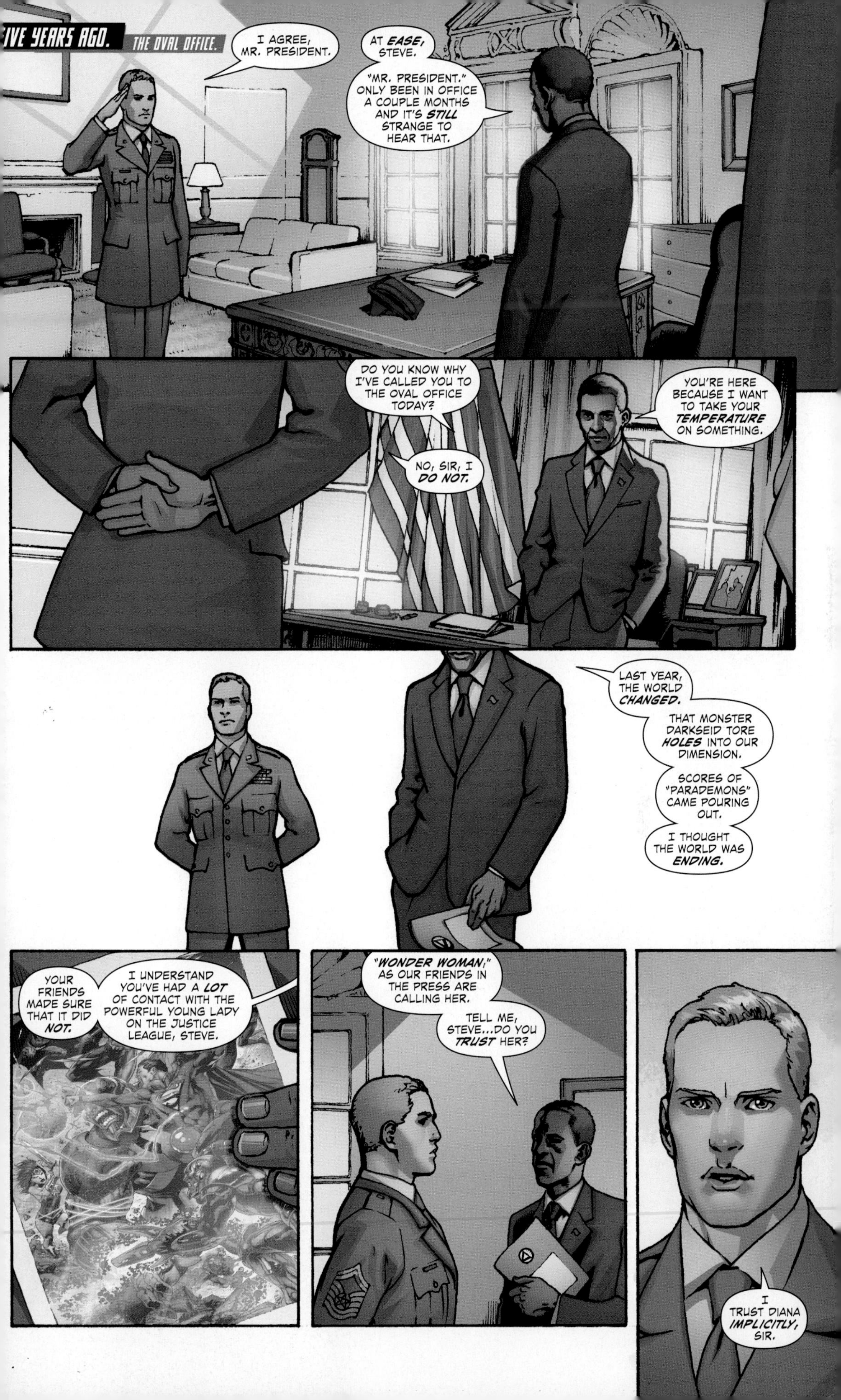
FIVE YEARS AGO.
THE OVAL OFFICE.
I AGREE, MR. PRESIDENT.
AT EASE, STEVE.
"MR. PRESIDENT." ONLY BEEN IN OFFICE A COUPLE MONTHS AND IT'S STILL STRANGE TO HEAR THAT.
DO YOU KNOW WHY I'VE CALLED YOU TO THE OVAL OFFICE TODAY?
NO, SIR, I DO NOT.
YOU'RE HERE BECAUSE I WANT TO TAKE YOUR TEMPERATURE ON SOMETHING.
LAST YEAR, THE WORLD CHANGED.
THAT MONSTER DARKSEID TORE HOLES INTO OUR DIMENSION.
SCORES OF "PARADEMONS" CAME POURING OUT.
I THOUGHT THE WORLD WAS ENDING.
YOUR FRIENDS MADE SURE THAT IT DID NOT.
I UNDERSTAND YOU'VE HAD A LOT OF CONTACT WITH THE POWERFUL YOUNG LADY ON THE JUSTICE LEAGUE, STEVE.
"WONDER WOMAN," AS OUR FRIENDS IN THE PRESS ARE CALLING HER.
TELL ME, STEVE...DO YOU TRUST HER?
I TRUST DIANA IMPLICITLY, SIR.

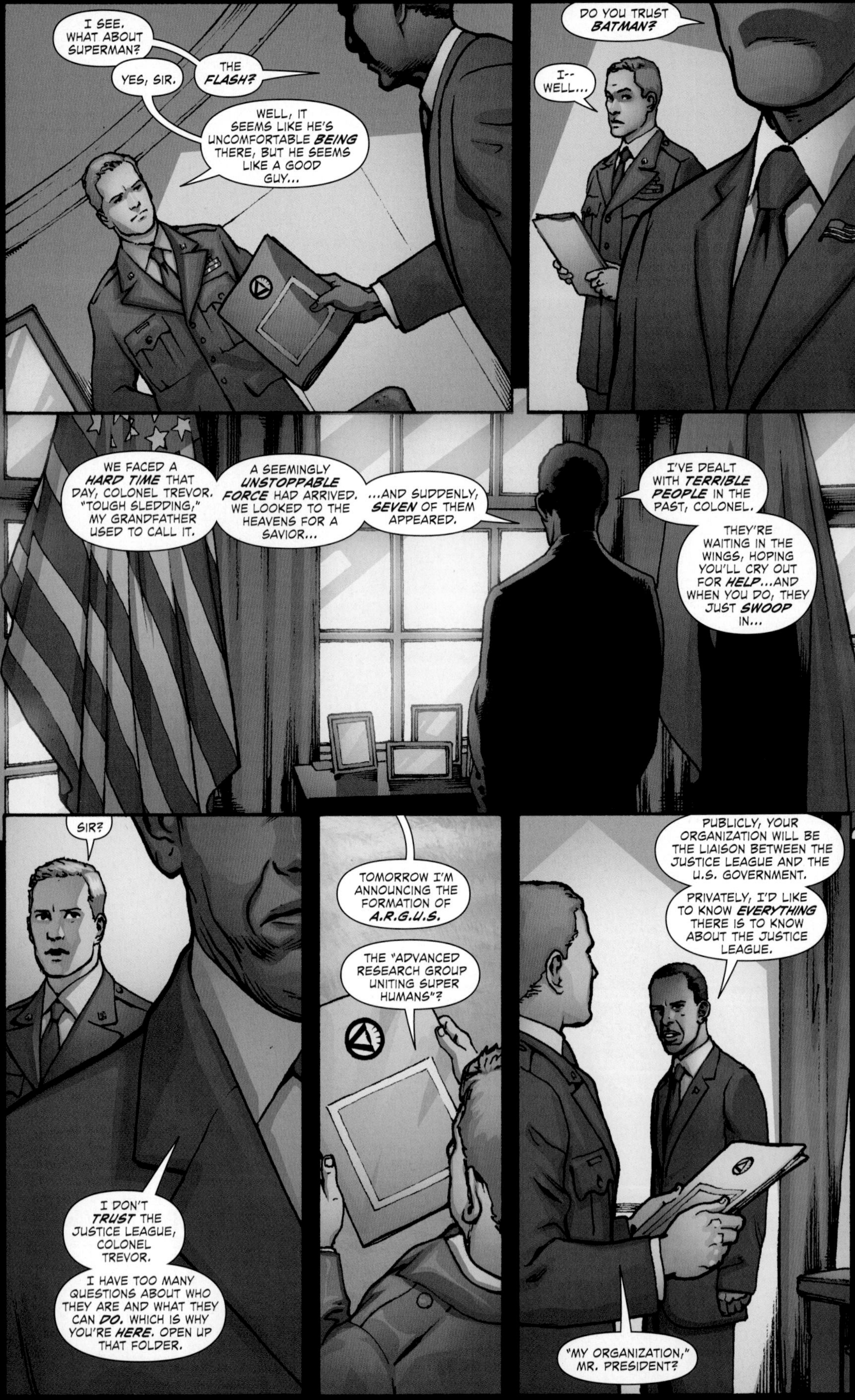

I SEE. WHAT ABOUT SUPERMAN?
YES, SIR.
THE FLASH?
WELL, IT SEEMS LIKE HE'S UNCOMFORTABLE BEING THERE, BUT HE SEEMS LIKE A GOOD GUY...
DO YOU TRUST BATMAN?
I-- WELL...
WE FACED A HARD TIME THAT DAY, COLONEL TREVOR. "TOUGH SLEDDING," MY GRANDFATHER USED TO CALL IT.
A SEEMINGLY UNSTOPPABLE FORCE HAD ARRIVED. WE LOOKED TO THE HEAVENS FOR A SAVIOR...
...AND SUDDENLY, SEVEN OF THEM APPEARED.
I'VE DEALT WITH TERRIBLE PEOPLE IN THE PAST, COLONEL.
THEY'RE WAITING IN THE WINGS, HOPING YOU'LL CRY OUT FOR HELP...AND WHEN YOU DO, THEY JUST SWOOP IN...
SIR?
I DON'T TRUST THE JUSTICE LEAGUE, COLONEL TREVOR.
I HAVE TOO MANY QUESTIONS ABOUT WHO THEY ARE AND WHAT THEY CAN DO. WHICH IS WHY YOU'RE HERE. OPEN UP THAT FOLDER.
TOMORROW I'M ANNOUNCING THE FORMATION OF A.R.G.U.S.
THE "ADVANCED RESEARCH GROUP UNITING SUPER HUMANS"?
PUBLICLY, YOUR ORGANIZATION WILL BE THE LIAISON BETWEEN THE JUSTICE LEAGUE AND THE U.S. GOVERNMENT.
PRIVATELY, I'D LIKE TO KNOW EVERYTHING THERE IS TO KNOW ABOUT THE JUSTICE LEAGUE.
"MY ORGANIZATION," MR. PRESIDENT?

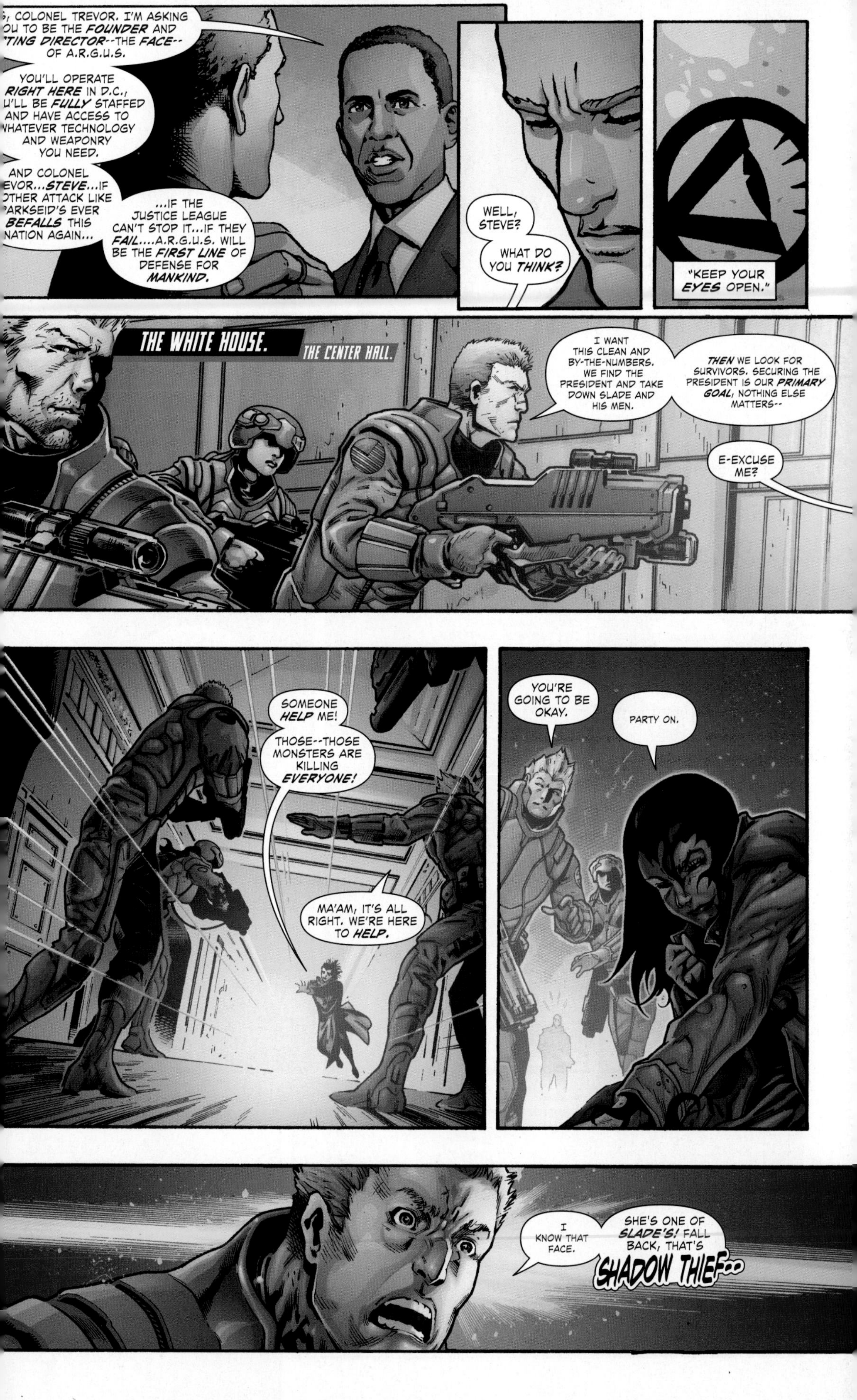

, COLONEL TREVOR. I'M ASKING OU TO BE THE FOUNDER AND TING DIRECTOR--THE FACE-- OF A.R.G.U.S.
YOU'LL OPERATE RIGHT HERE IN D.C., U'LL BE FULLY STAFFED AND HAVE ACCESS TO WHATEVER TECHNOLOGY AND WEAPONRY YOU NEED.
AND COLONEL EVOR...STEVE...IF OTHER ATTACK LIKE ARKSEID'S EVER BEFALLS THIS NATION AGAIN...
...IF THE JUSTICE LEAGUE CAN'T STOP IT...IF THEY FAIL....A.R.G.U.S. WILL BE THE FIRST LINE OF DEFENSE FOR MANKIND.
WELL, STEVE?
WHAT DO YOU THINK?
"KEEP YOUR EYES OPEN."
THE WHITE HOUSE.
THE CENTER HALL.
I WANT THIS CLEAN AND BY-THE-NUMBERS. WE FIND THE PRESIDENT AND TAKE DOWN SLADE AND HIS MEN.
THEN WE LOOK FOR SURVIVORS. SECURING THE PRESIDENT IS OUR PRIMARY GOAL, NOTHING ELSE MATTERS--
E-EXCUSE ME?
SOMEONE HELP ME!
THOSE--THOSE MONSTERS ARE KILLING EVERYONE!
MA'AM, IT'S ALL RIGHT. WE'RE HERE TO HELP.
YOU'RE GOING TO BE OKAY.
PARTY ON.
I KNOW THAT FACE.
SHE'S ONE OF SLADE'S! FALL BACK, THAT'S
SHADOW THIEF--

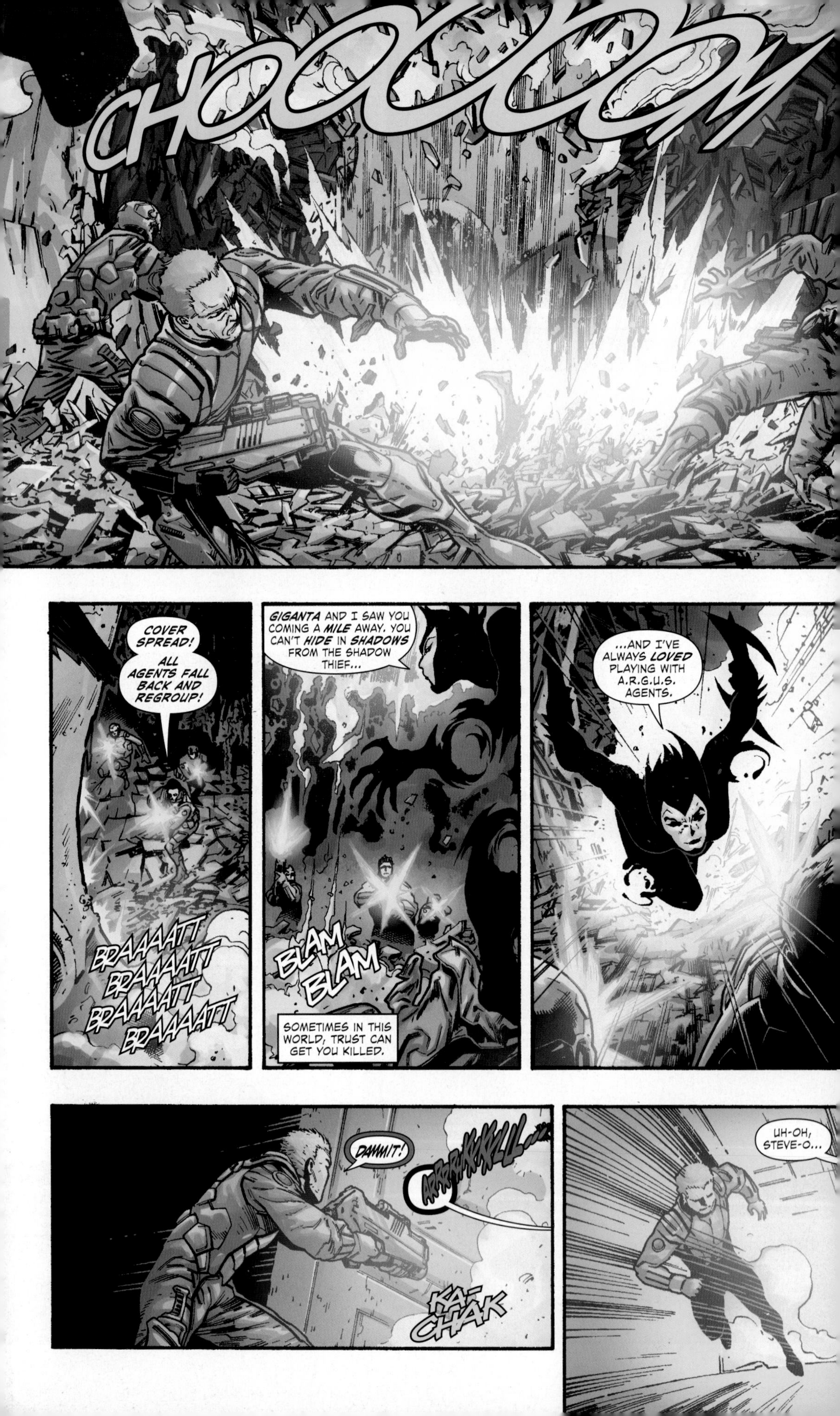
CHOOOOOM
COVER SPREAD! ALL AGENTS FALL BACK AND REGROUP!
BRAAAATT BRAAAATT BRAAAATT BRAAAATT
GIGANTA AND I SAW YOU COMING A MILE AWAY. YOU CAN'T HIDE IN SHADOWS FROM THE SHADOW THIEF...
BLAM BLAM
SOMETIMES IN THIS WORLD, TRUST CAN GET YOU KILLED.
...AND I'VE ALWAYS LOVED PLAYING WITH A.R.G.U.S. AGENTS.
DAMMIT!
ARRRRKKKLLL...
KA-CHAK
UH-OH, STEVE-O...

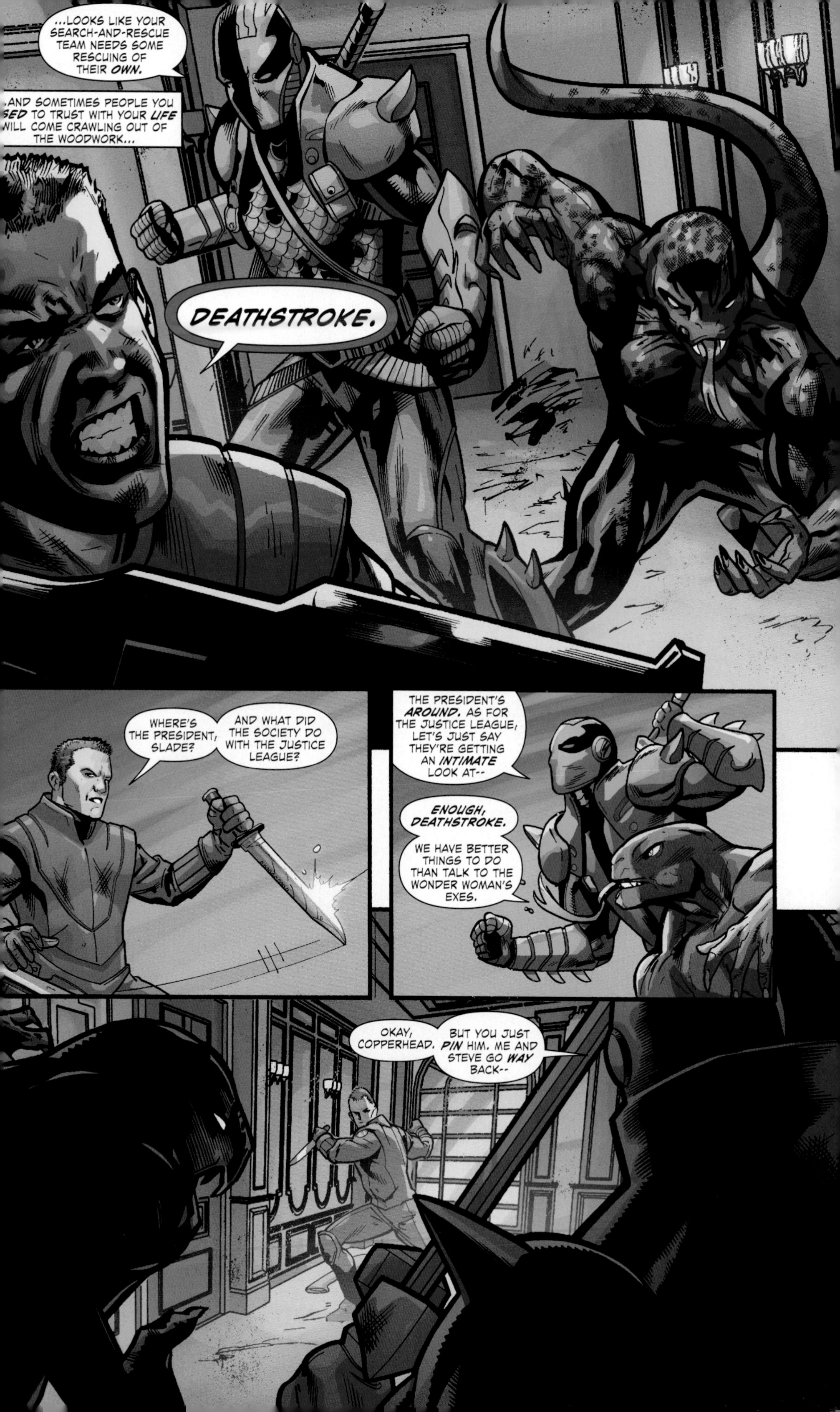
...LOOKS LIKE YOUR SEARCH-AND-RESCUE TEAM NEEDS SOME RESCUING OF THEIR OWN.
...AND SOMETIMES PEOPLE YOU USED TO TRUST WITH YOUR LIFE WILL COME CRAWLING OUT OF THE WOODWORK...
DEATHSTROKE.
WHERE'S THE PRESIDENT, SLADE?
AND WHAT DID THE SOCIETY DO WITH THE JUSTICE LEAGUE?
THE PRESIDENT'S AROUND. AS FOR THE JUSTICE LEAGUE, LET'S JUST SAY THEY'RE GETTING AN INTIMATE LOOK AT--
ENOUGH, DEATHSTROKE.
WE HAVE BETTER THINGS TO DO THAN TALK TO THE WONDER WOMAN'S EXES.
OKAY, COPPERHEAD.
BUT YOU JUST PIN HIM. ME AND STEVE GO WAY BACK--

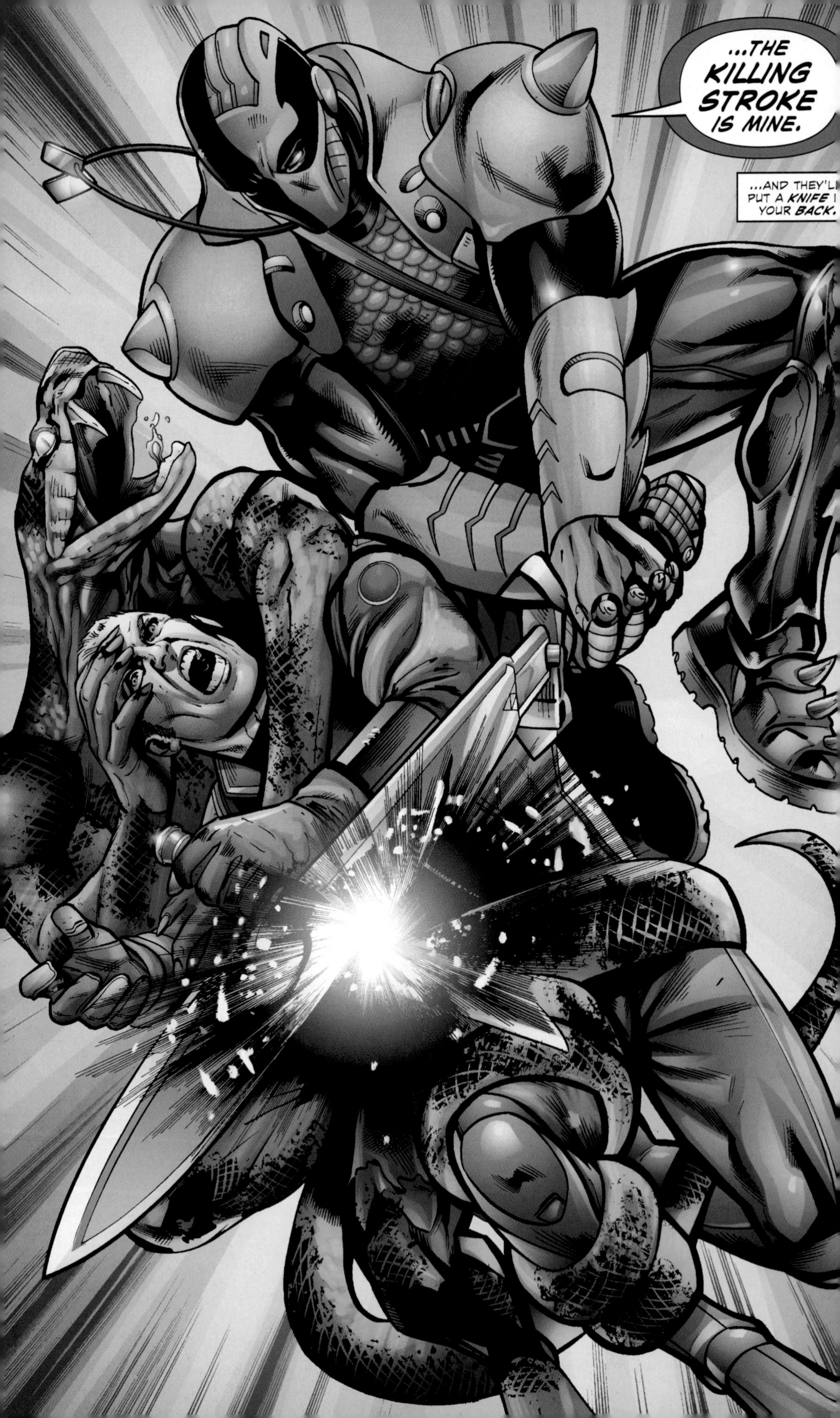
...THE KILLING STROKE IS MINE.
...AND THEY'L PUT A KNIFE I YOUR BACK.

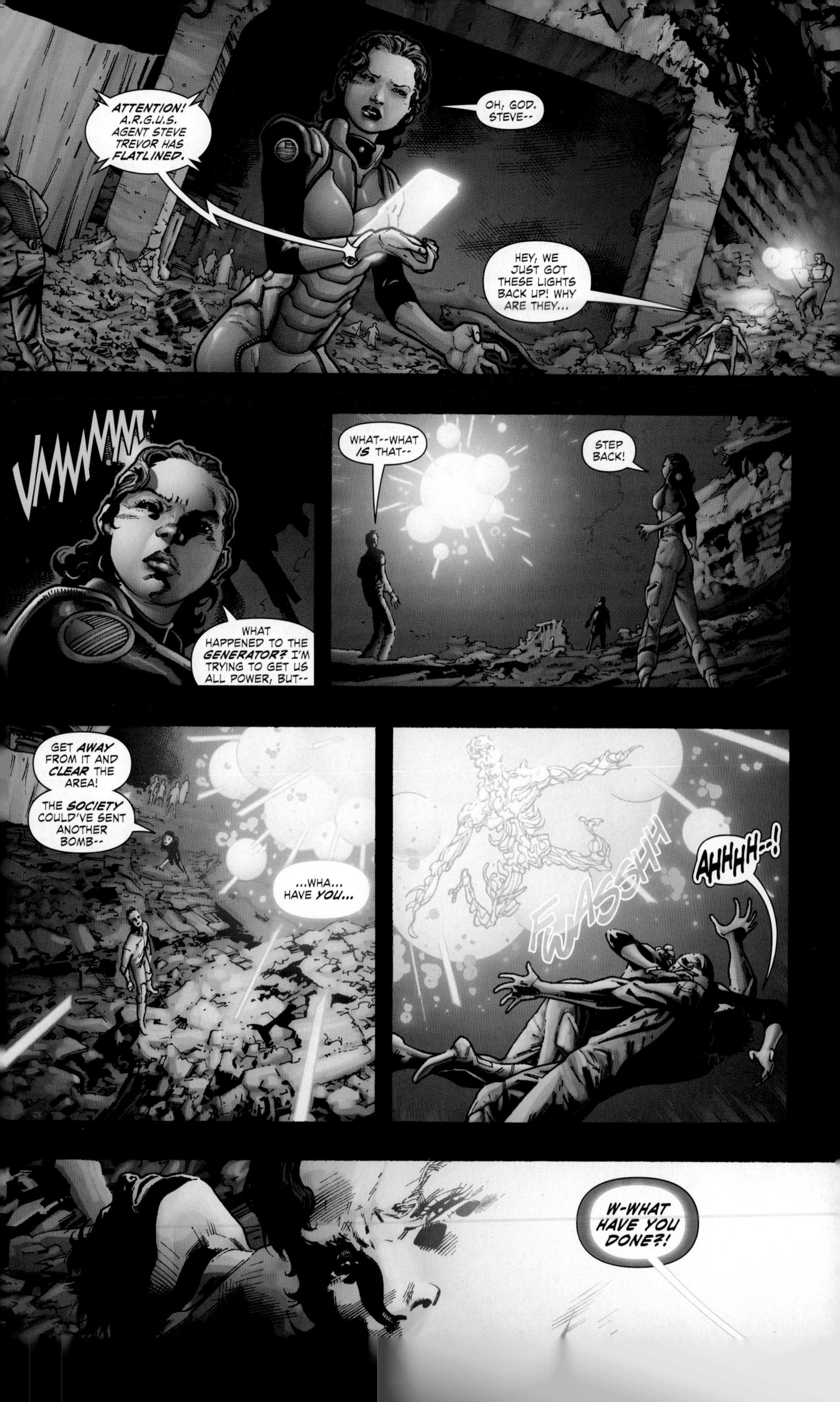

ATTENTION! A.R.G.U.S. AGENT STEVE TREVOR HAS FLATLINED.
OH, GOD. STEVE--
HEY, WE JUST GOT THESE LIGHTS BACK UP! WHY ARE THEY...
WHAT HAPPENED TO THE GENERATOR? I'M TRYING TO GET US ALL POWER, BUT--
WHAT--WHAT IS THAT--
STEP BACK!
GET AWAY FROM IT AND CLEAR THE AREA!
THE SOCIETY COULD'VE SENT ANOTHER BOMB--
...WHA... HAVE YOU...
FWASSHH
AHHHH--!
W-WHAT HAVE YOU DONE?!

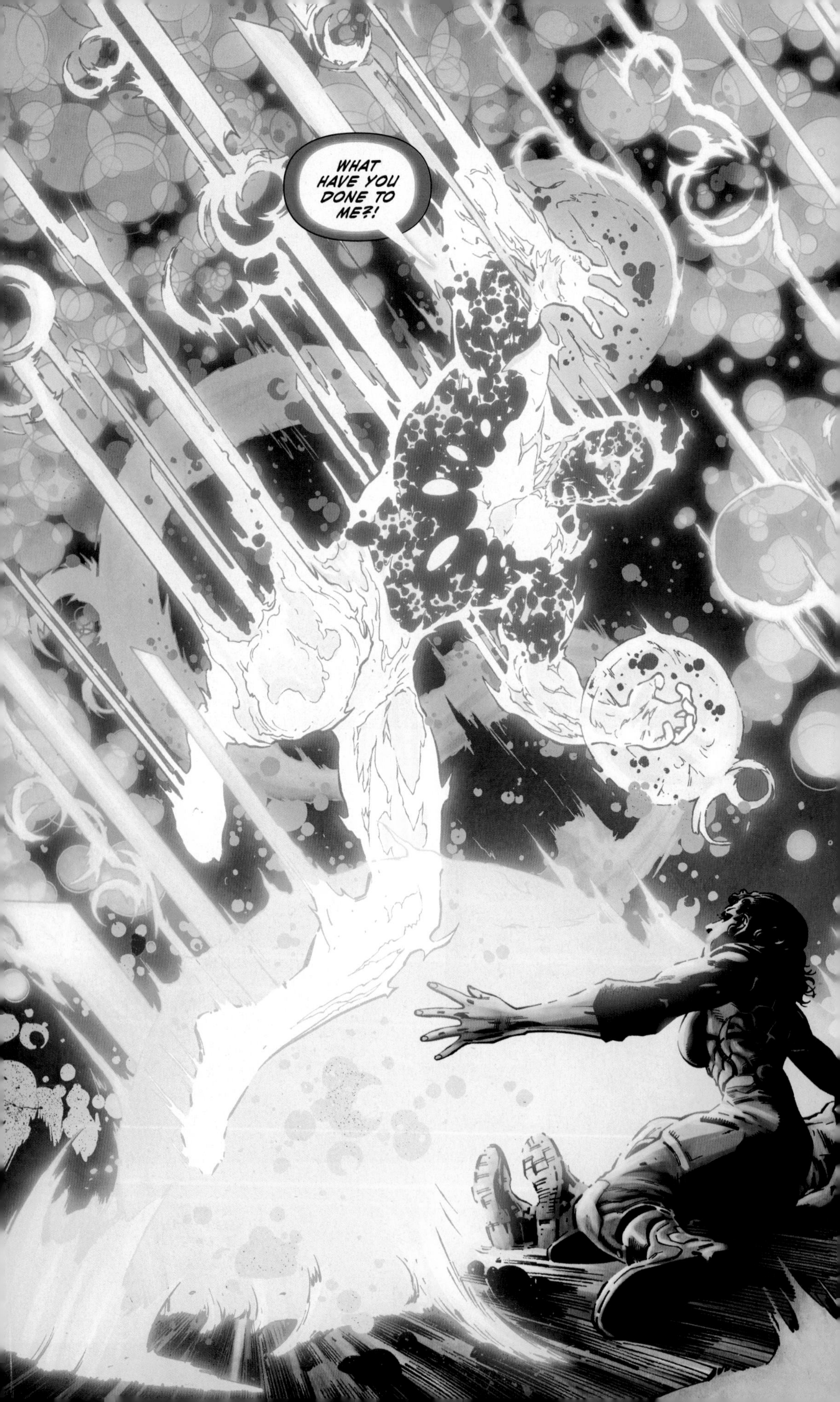
WHAT HAVE YOU DONE TO ME?!

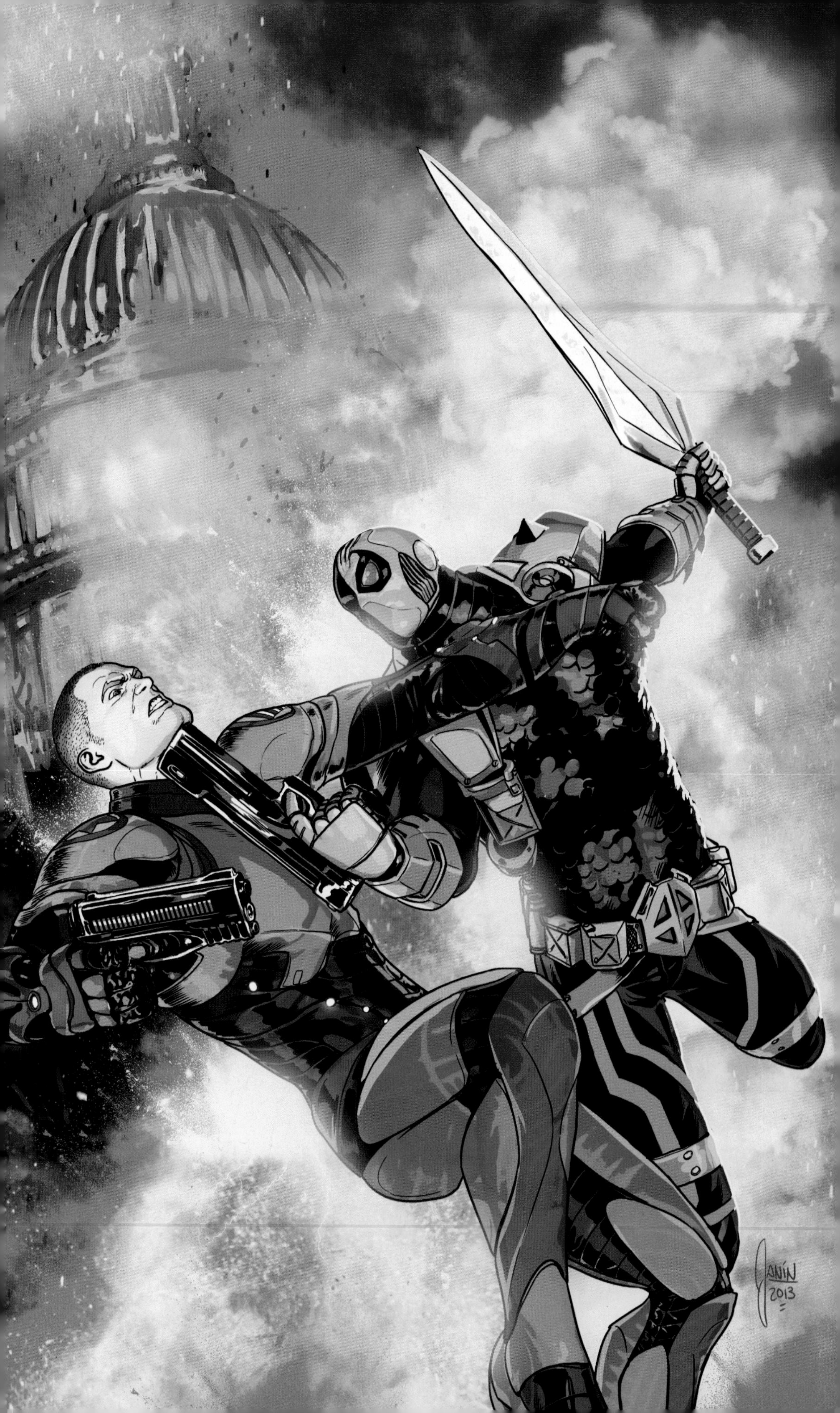

JANÍN
2013

PART TWO: KNOW THYSELF

STERLING GATES Writer **NEIL EDWARDS** Penciller **JASON PAZ JAY LEISTEN** Inkers
NATHAN EYRING Colorist **TAYLOR ESPOSITO** Letterer
Cover Art by **MIKEL JANIN**

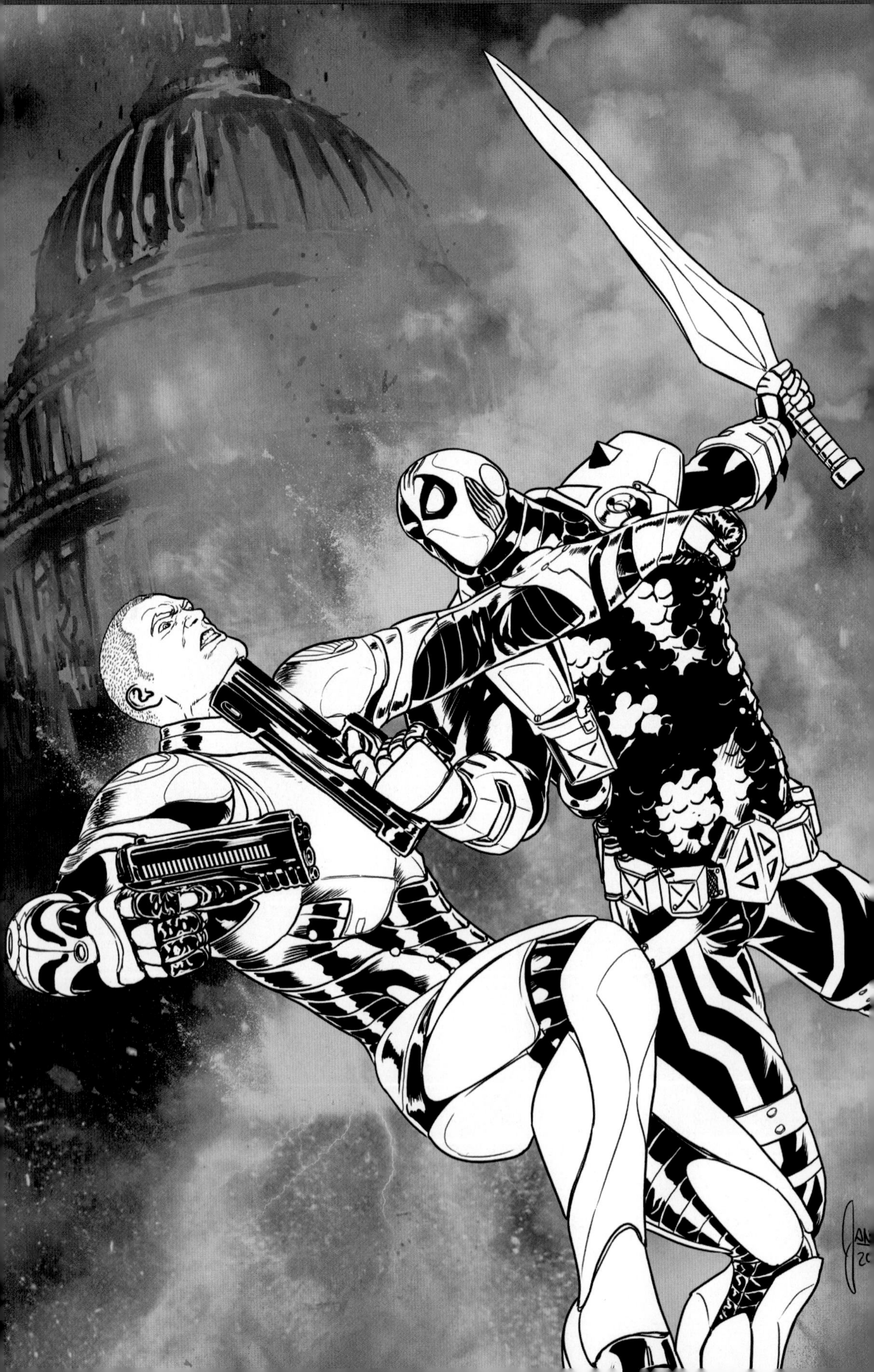

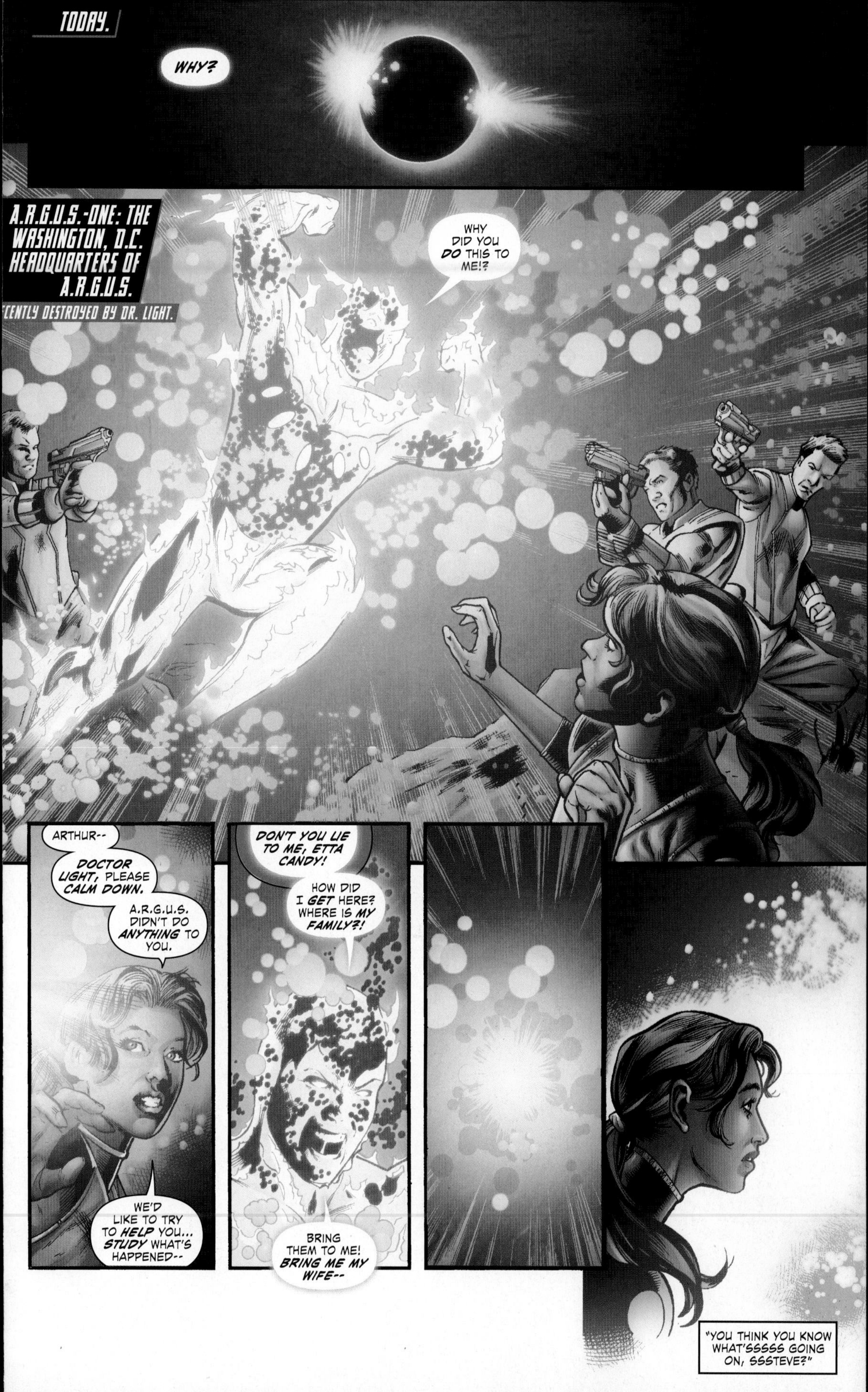
TODAY.
WHY?
A.R.G.U.S.-ONE: THE WASHINGTON, D.C. HEADQUARTERS OF A.R.G.U.S.
...CENTLY DESTROYED BY DR. LIGHT.
WHY DID YOU DO THIS TO ME!?
ARTHUR--
DOCTOR LIGHT, PLEASE CALM DOWN.
A.R.G.U.S. DIDN'T DO ANYTHING TO YOU.
WE'D LIKE TO TRY TO HELP YOU... STUDY WHAT'S HAPPENED--
DON'T YOU LIE TO ME, ETTA CANDY!
HOW DID I GET HERE? WHERE IS MY FAMILY?!
BRING THEM TO ME! BRING ME MY WIFE--
"YOU THINK YOU KNOW WHAT'SSSSS GOING ON, SSSTEVE?"

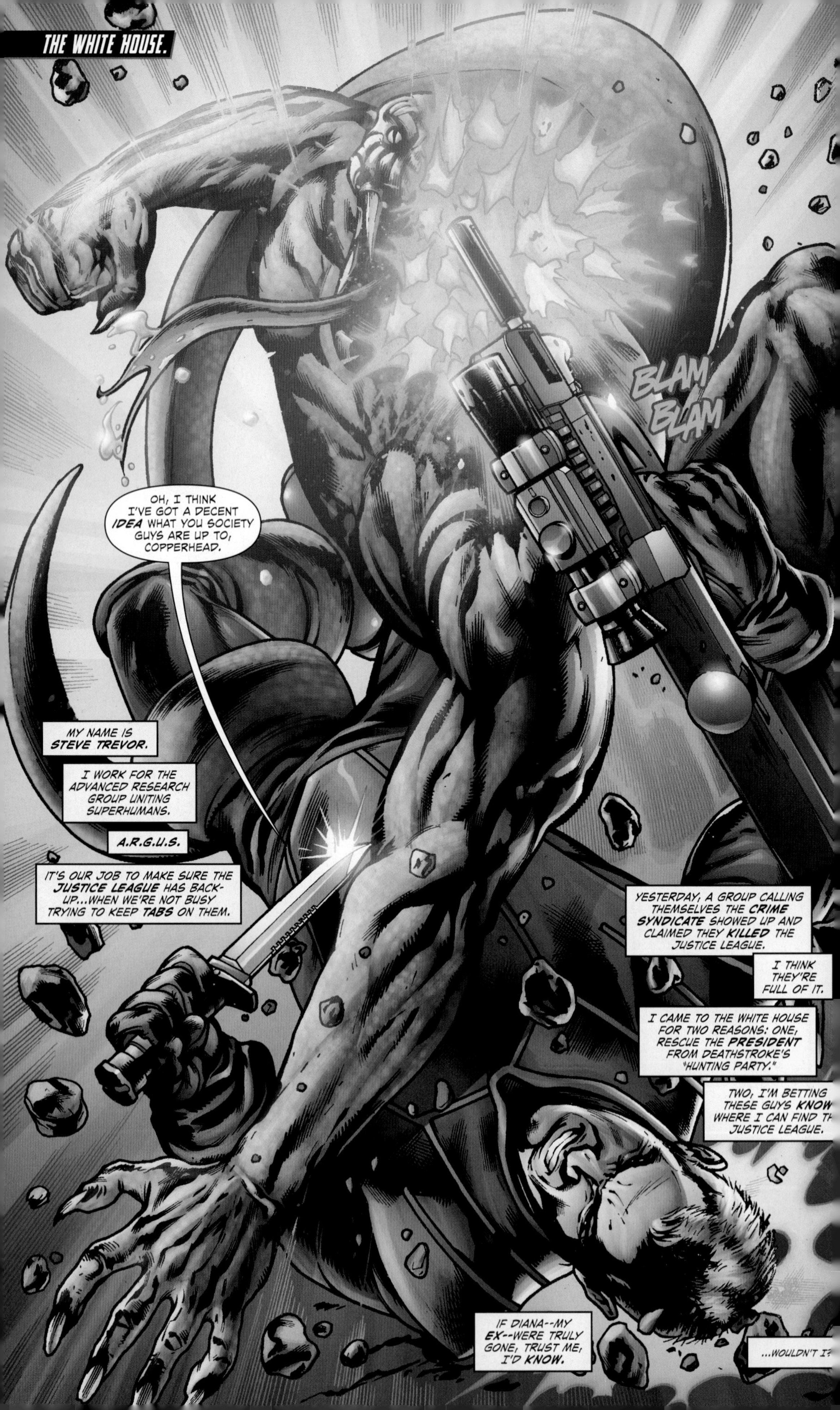
THE WHITE HOUSE.
BLAM BLAM
OH, I THINK I'VE GOT A DECENT IDEA WHAT YOU SOCIETY GUYS ARE UP TO, COPPERHEAD.
MY NAME IS STEVE TREVOR.
I WORK FOR THE ADVANCED RESEARCH GROUP UNITING SUPERHUMANS.
A.R.G.U.S.
IT'S OUR JOB TO MAKE SURE THE JUSTICE LEAGUE HAS BACK-UP...WHEN WE'RE NOT BUSY TRYING TO KEEP TABS ON THEM.
YESTERDAY, A GROUP CALLING THEMSELVES THE CRIME SYNDICATE SHOWED UP AND CLAIMED THEY KILLED THE JUSTICE LEAGUE.
I THINK THEY'RE FULL OF IT.
I CAME TO THE WHITE HOUSE FOR TWO REASONS: ONE, RESCUE THE PRESIDENT FROM DEATHSTROKE'S "HUNTING PARTY."
TWO, I'M BETTING THESE GUYS KNOW WHERE I CAN FIND TH JUSTICE LEAGUE.
IF DIANA--MY EX--WERE TRULY GONE, TRUST ME, I'D KNOW.
...WOULDN'T I?

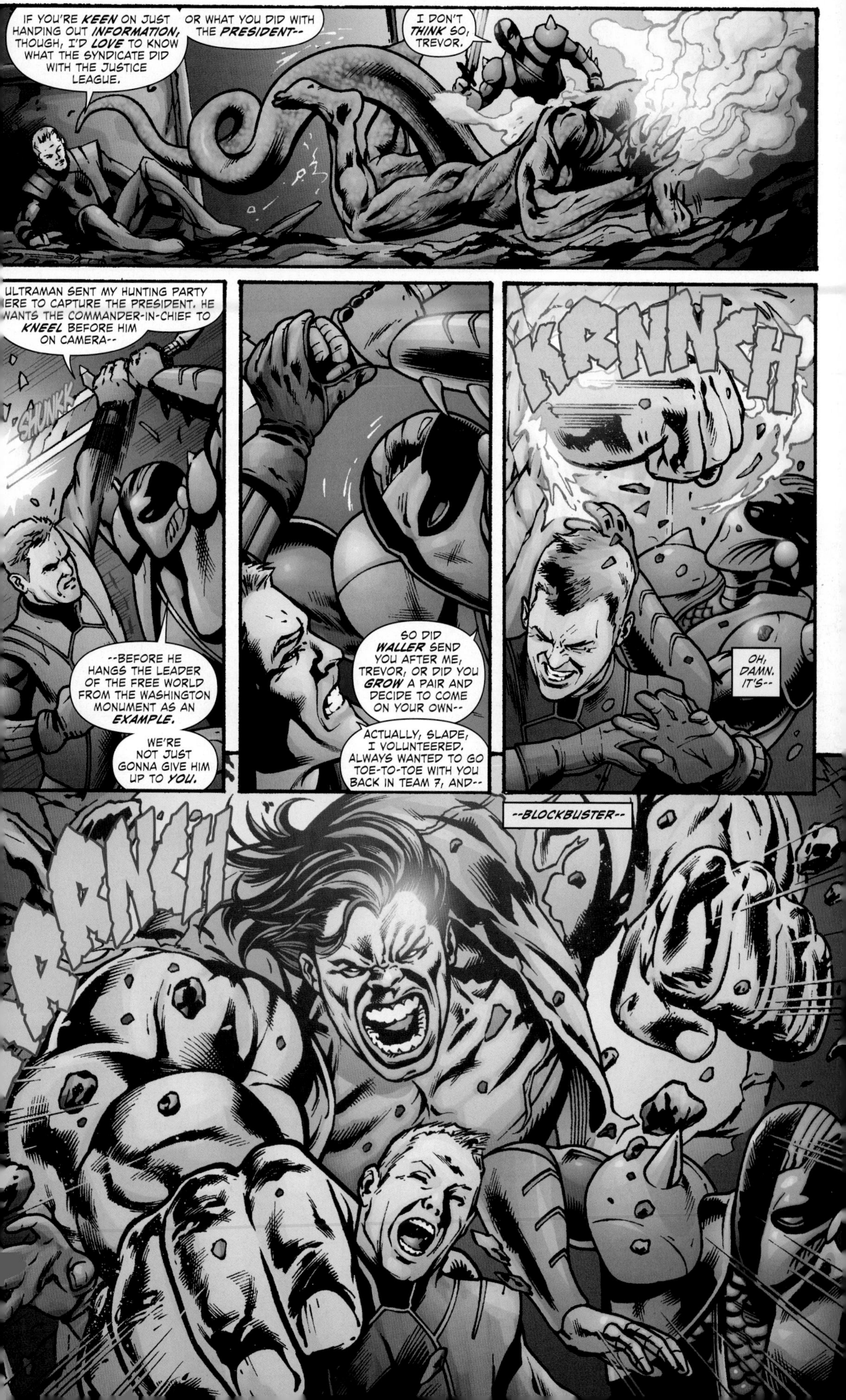

IF YOU'RE KEEN ON JUST HANDING OUT INFORMATION, THOUGH, I'D LOVE TO KNOW WHAT THE SYNDICATE DID WITH THE JUSTICE LEAGUE.
OR WHAT YOU DID WITH THE PRESIDENT--
I DON'T THINK SO, TREVOR.
ULTRAMAN SENT MY HUNTING PARTY HERE TO CAPTURE THE PRESIDENT. HE WANTS THE COMMANDER-IN-CHIEF TO KNEEL BEFORE HIM ON CAMERA--
SHUNKK
--BEFORE HE HANGS THE LEADER OF THE FREE WORLD FROM THE WASHINGTON MONUMENT AS AN EXAMPLE.
WE'RE NOT JUST GONNA GIVE HIM UP TO YOU.
SO DID WALLER SEND YOU AFTER ME, TREVOR, OR DID YOU GROW A PAIR AND DECIDE TO COME ON YOUR OWN--
ACTUALLY, SLADE, I VOLUNTEERED. ALWAYS WANTED TO GO TOE-TO-TOE WITH YOU BACK IN TEAM 7, AND--
KRNNCH
OH, DAMN. IT'S--
--BLOCKBUSTER--

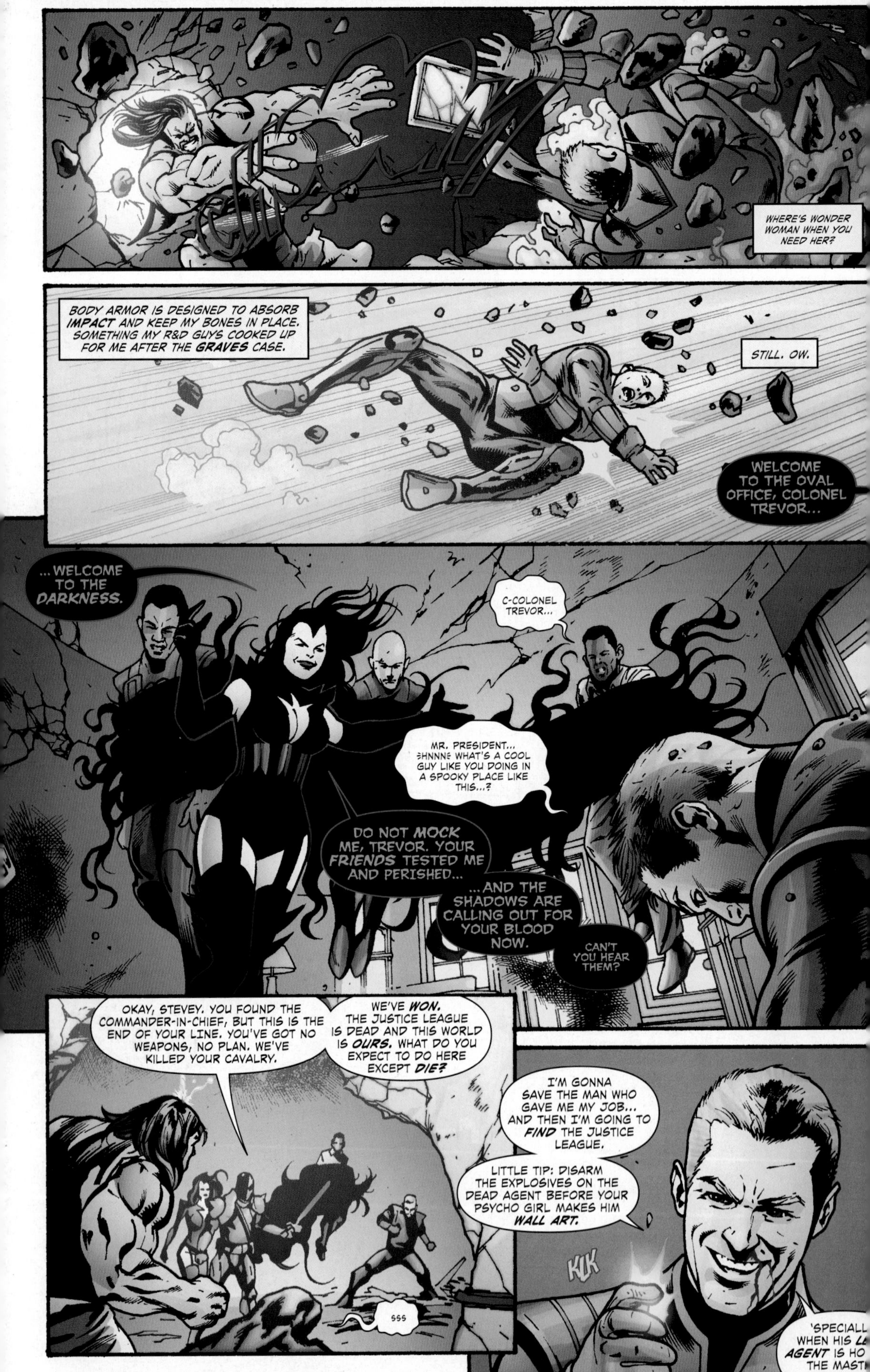
WHERE'S WONDER WOMAN WHEN YOU NEED HER?
BODY ARMOR IS DESIGNED TO ABSORB IMPACT AND KEEP MY BONES IN PLACE. SOMETHING MY R&D GUYS COOKED UP FOR ME AFTER THE GRAVES CASE.
STILL. OW.
WELCOME TO THE OVAL OFFICE, COLONEL TREVOR...
...WELCOME TO THE DARKNESS.
C-COLONEL TREVOR...
MR. PRESIDENT... SHNNN WHAT'S A COOL GUY LIKE YOU DOING IN A SPOOKY PLACE LIKE THIS...?
DO NOT MOCK ME, TREVOR. YOUR FRIENDS TESTED ME AND PERISHED...
...AND THE SHADOWS ARE CALLING OUT FOR YOUR BLOOD NOW.
CAN'T YOU HEAR THEM?
OKAY, STEVEY. YOU FOUND THE COMMANDER-IN-CHIEF, BUT THIS IS THE END OF YOUR LINE. YOU'VE GOT NO WEAPONS, NO PLAN. WE'VE KILLED YOUR CAVALRY.
WE'VE WON. THE JUSTICE LEAGUE IS DEAD AND THIS WORLD IS OURS. WHAT DO YOU EXPECT TO DO HERE EXCEPT DIE?
SSS
I'M GONNA SAVE THE MAN WHO GAVE ME MY JOB... AND THEN I'M GOING TO FIND THE JUSTICE LEAGUE.
LITTLE TIP: DISARM THE EXPLOSIVES ON THE DEAD AGENT BEFORE YOUR PSYCHO GIRL MAKES HIM WALL ART.
KLIK
'SPECIALL WHEN HIS L AGENT IS HO THE MAST DETONATO

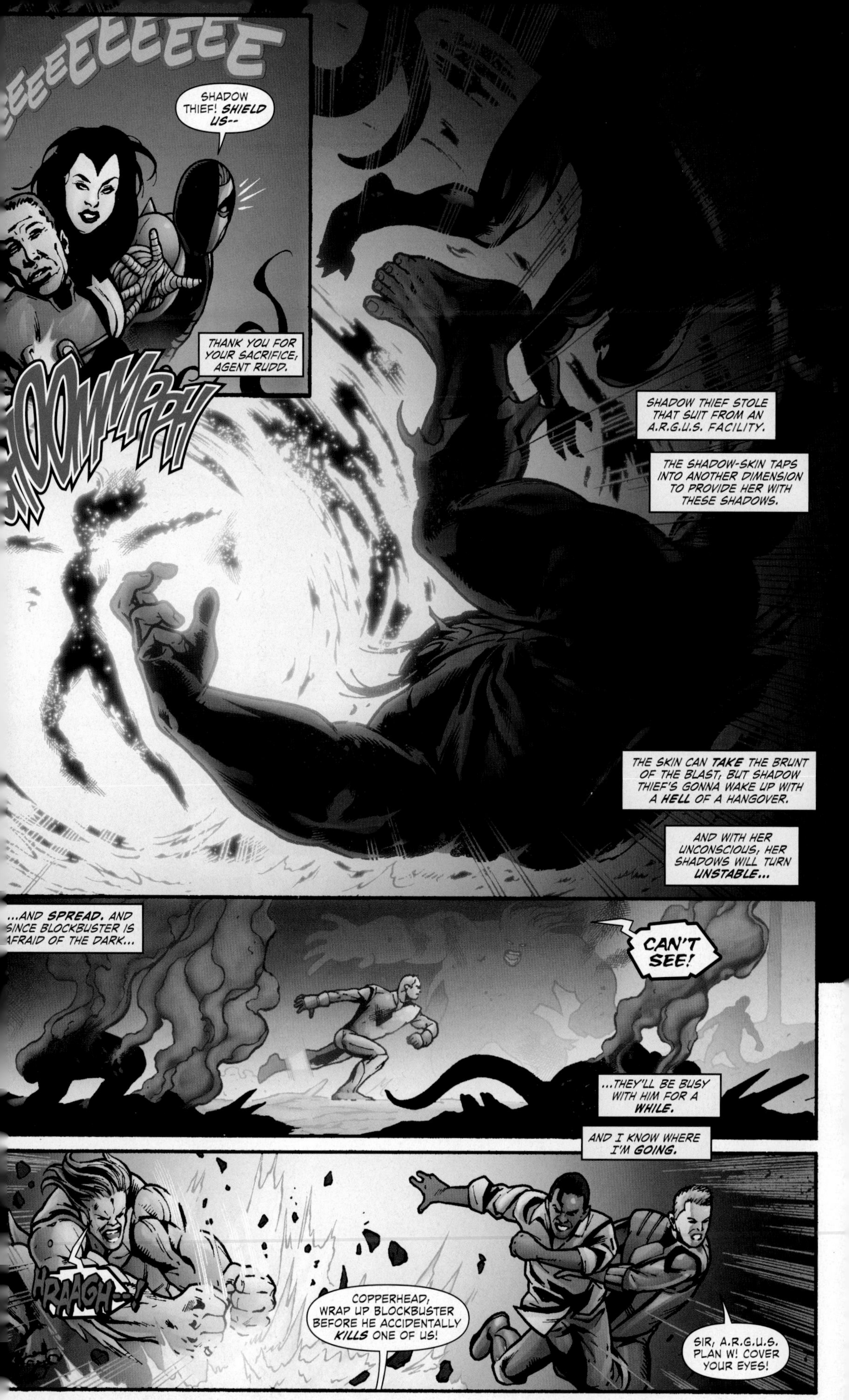
EEEEEEEEEE
SHADOW THIEF! SHIELD US--
THANK YOU FOR YOUR SACRIFICE, AGENT RUDD.
FOOOMMPH
SHADOW THIEF STOLE THAT SUIT FROM AN A.R.G.U.S. FACILITY.
THE SHADOW-SKIN TAPS INTO ANOTHER DIMENSION TO PROVIDE HER WITH THESE SHADOWS.
THE SKIN CAN TAKE THE BRUNT OF THE BLAST, BUT SHADOW THIEF'S GONNA WAKE UP WITH A HELL OF A HANGOVER.
AND WITH HER UNCONSCIOUS, HER SHADOWS WILL TURN UNSTABLE...
...AND SPREAD. AND SINCE BLOCKBUSTER IS AFRAID OF THE DARK...
CAN'T SEE!
...THEY'LL BE BUSY WITH HIM FOR A WHILE.
AND I KNOW WHERE I'M GOING.
HRAAGH--!
COPPERHEAD, WRAP UP BLOCKBUSTER BEFORE HE ACCIDENTALLY KILLS ONE OF US!
SIR, A.R.G.U.S. PLAN W! COVER YOUR EYES!

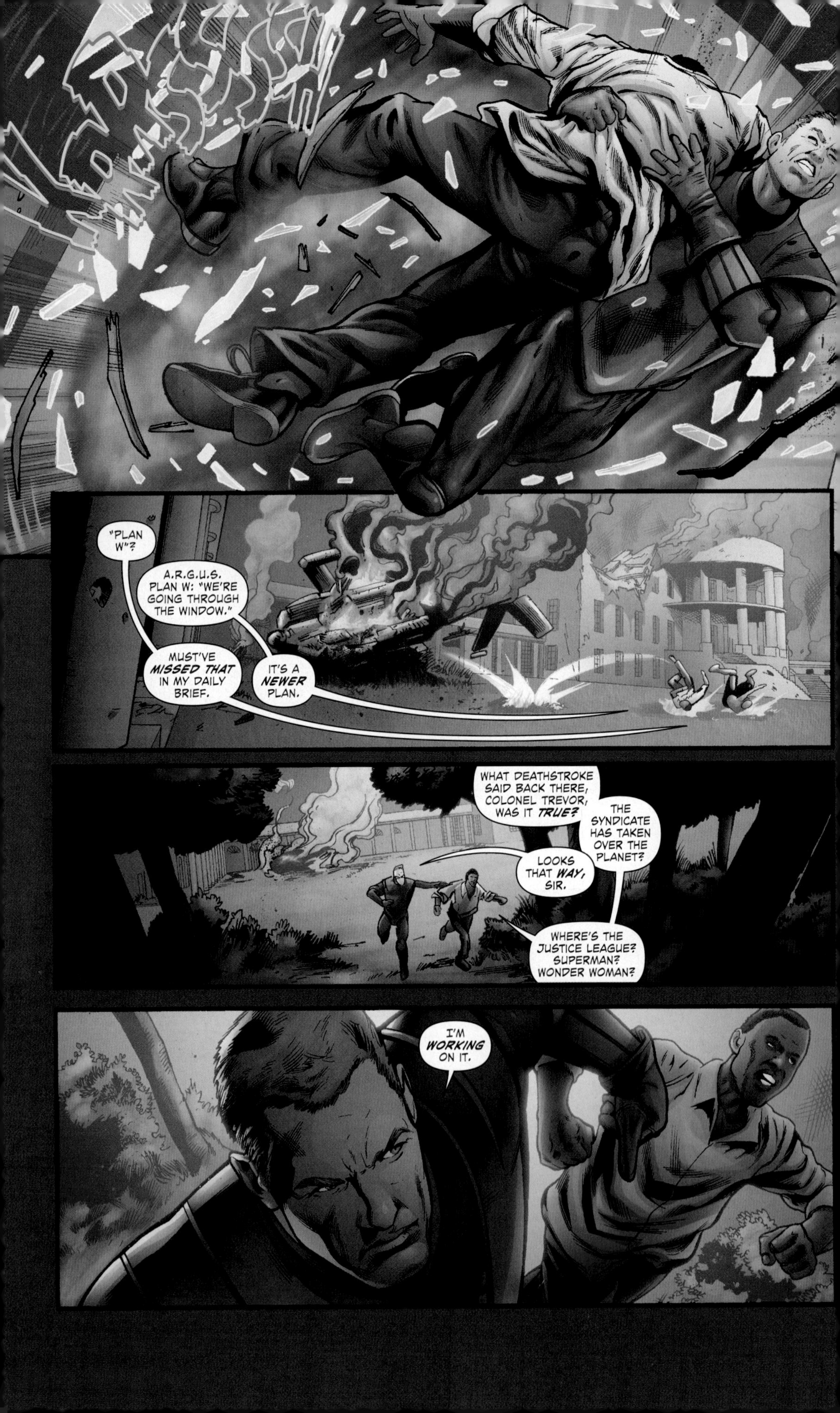
"PLAN W"?
A.R.G.U.S. PLAN W: "WE'RE GOING THROUGH THE WINDOW."
MUST'VE ***MISSED THAT*** IN MY DAILY BRIEF.
IT'S A ***NEWER*** PLAN.
WHAT DEATHSTROKE SAID BACK THERE, COLONEL TREVOR, WAS IT ***TRUE?***
THE SYNDICATE HAS TAKEN OVER THE PLANET?
LOOKS THAT ***WAY,*** SIR.
WHERE'S THE JUSTICE LEAGUE? SUPERMAN? WONDER WOMAN?
I'M ***WORKING*** ON IT.

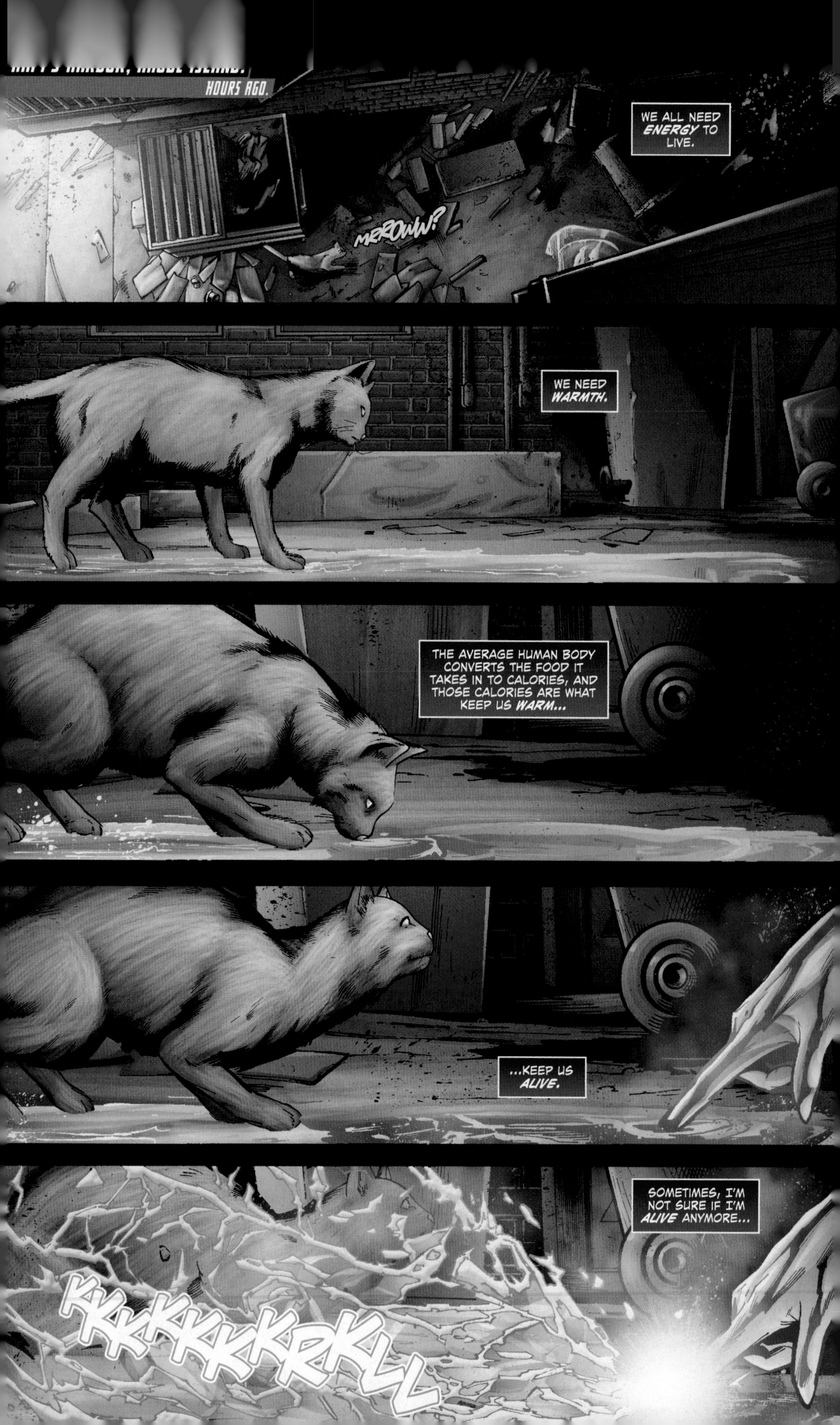
HOURS AGO.
WE ALL NEED ENERGY TO LIVE.
MRROWW?
WE NEED WARMTH.
THE AVERAGE HUMAN BODY CONVERTS THE FOOD IT TAKES IN TO CALORIES, AND THOSE CALORIES ARE WHAT KEEP US WARM...
...KEEP US ALIVE.
SOMETIMES, I'M NOT SURE IF I'M ALIVE ANYMORE...
KKKKKKKRKLL

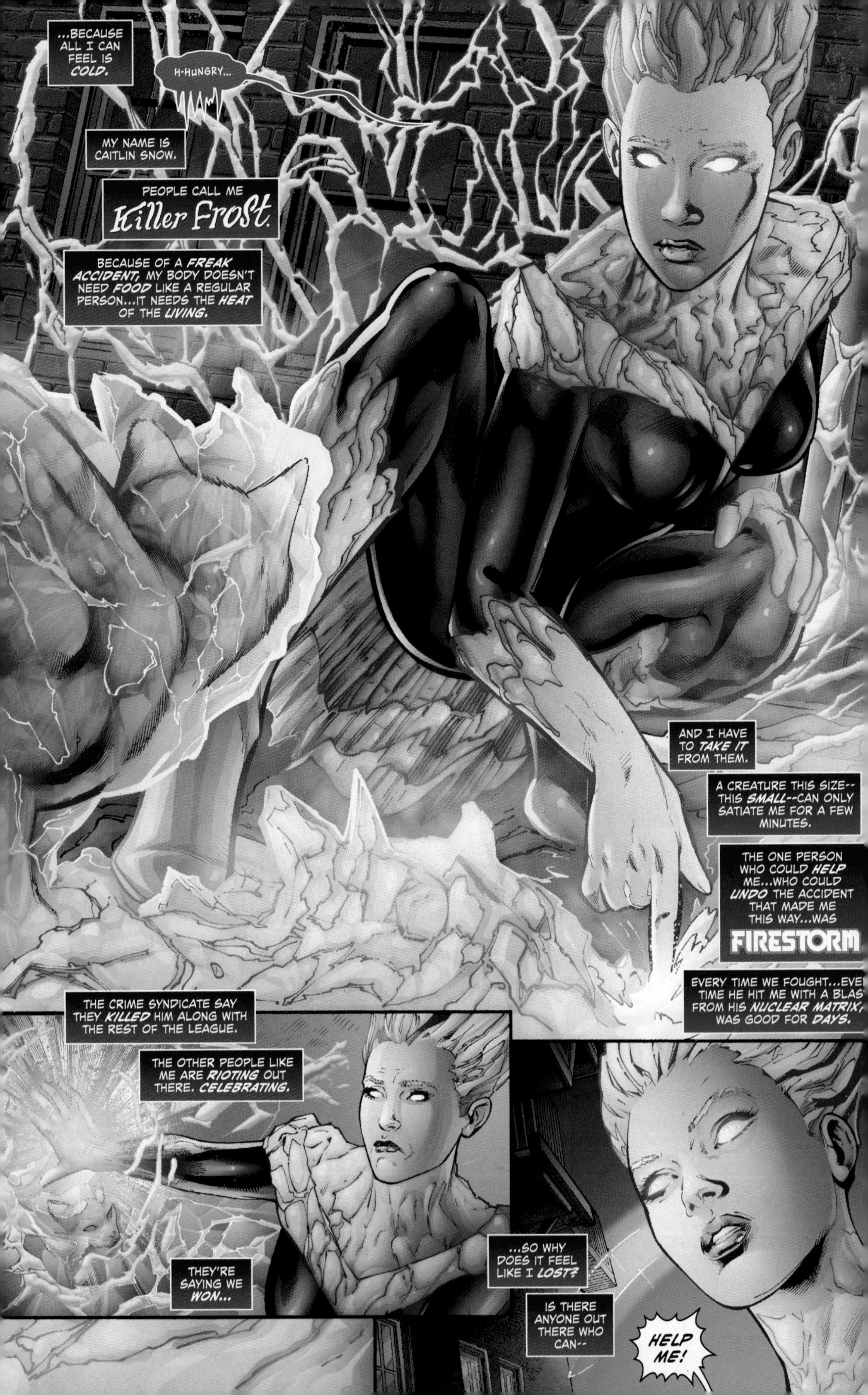
...BECAUSE ALL I CAN FEEL IS COLD.
H-HUNGRY...
MY NAME IS CAITLIN SNOW.
PEOPLE CALL ME
Killer Frost.
BECAUSE OF A FREAK ACCIDENT, MY BODY DOESN'T NEED FOOD LIKE A REGULAR PERSON...IT NEEDS THE HEAT OF THE LIVING.
AND I HAVE TO TAKE IT FROM THEM.
A CREATURE THIS SIZE-- THIS SMALL--CAN ONLY SATIATE ME FOR A FEW MINUTES.
THE ONE PERSON WHO COULD HELP ME...WHO COULD UNDO THE ACCIDENT THAT MADE ME THIS WAY...WAS
FIRESTORM
EVERY TIME WE FOUGHT...EVE TIME HE HIT ME WITH A BLAS FROM HIS NUCLEAR MATRIX, WAS GOOD FOR DAYS.
THE CRIME SYNDICATE SAY THEY KILLED HIM ALONG WITH THE REST OF THE LEAGUE.
THE OTHER PEOPLE LIKE ME ARE RIOTING OUT THERE. CELEBRATING.
THEY'RE SAYING WE WON...
...SO WHY DOES IT FEEL LIKE I LOST?
IS THERE ANYONE OUT THERE WHO CAN--
HELP ME!

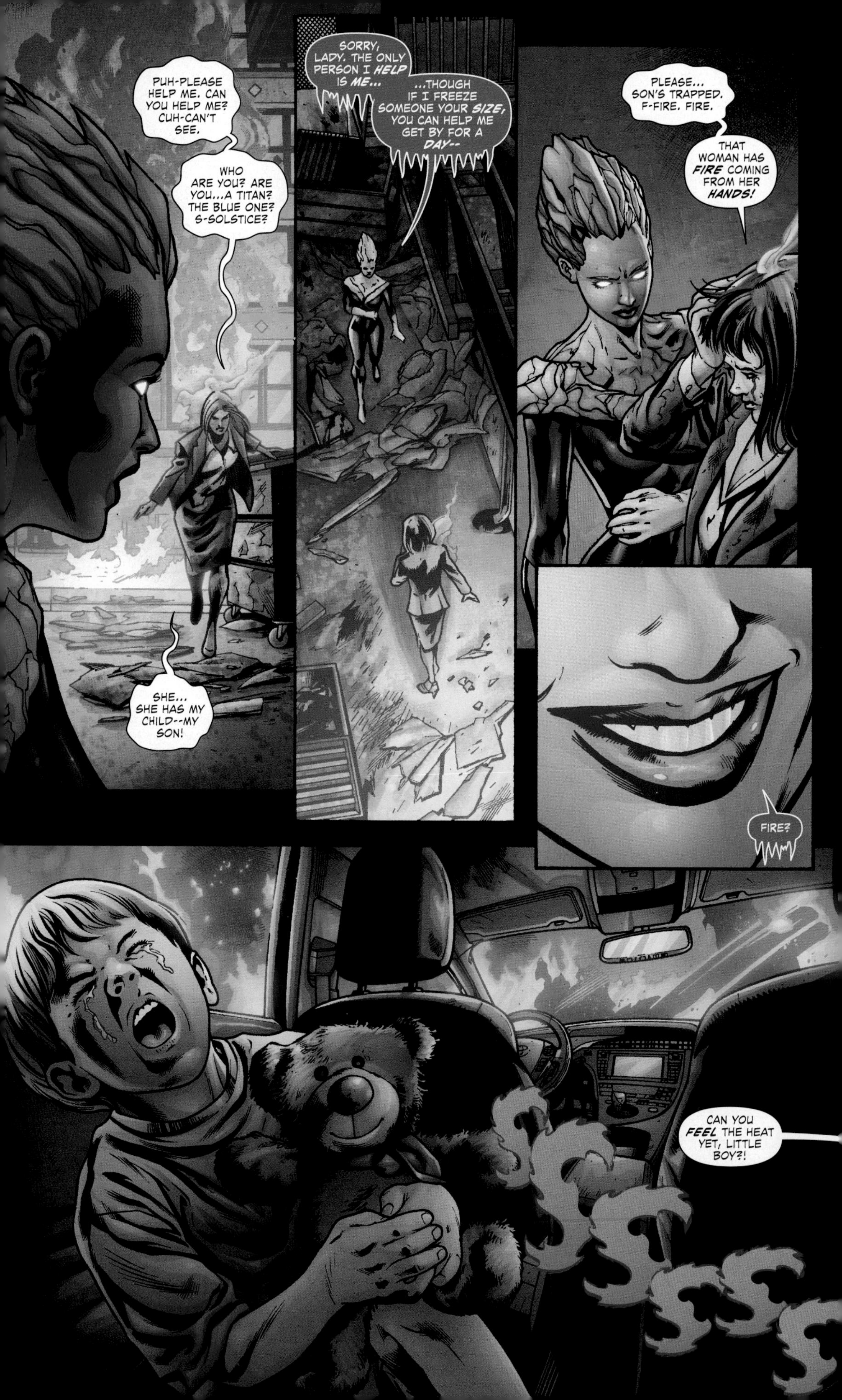

PUH-PLEASE HELP ME. CAN YOU HELP ME? CUH-CAN'T SEE.
WHO ARE YOU? ARE YOU...A TITAN? THE BLUE ONE? S-SOLSTICE?
SHE... SHE HAS MY CHILD--MY SON!
SORRY, LADY. THE ONLY PERSON I HELP IS ME...
...THOUGH IF I FREEZE SOMEONE YOUR SIZE, YOU CAN HELP ME GET BY FOR A DAY--
PLEASE... SON'S TRAPPED. F-FIRE. FIRE.
THAT WOMAN HAS FIRE COMING FROM HER HANDS!
FIRE?
CAN YOU FEEL THE HEAT YET, LITTLE BOY?!

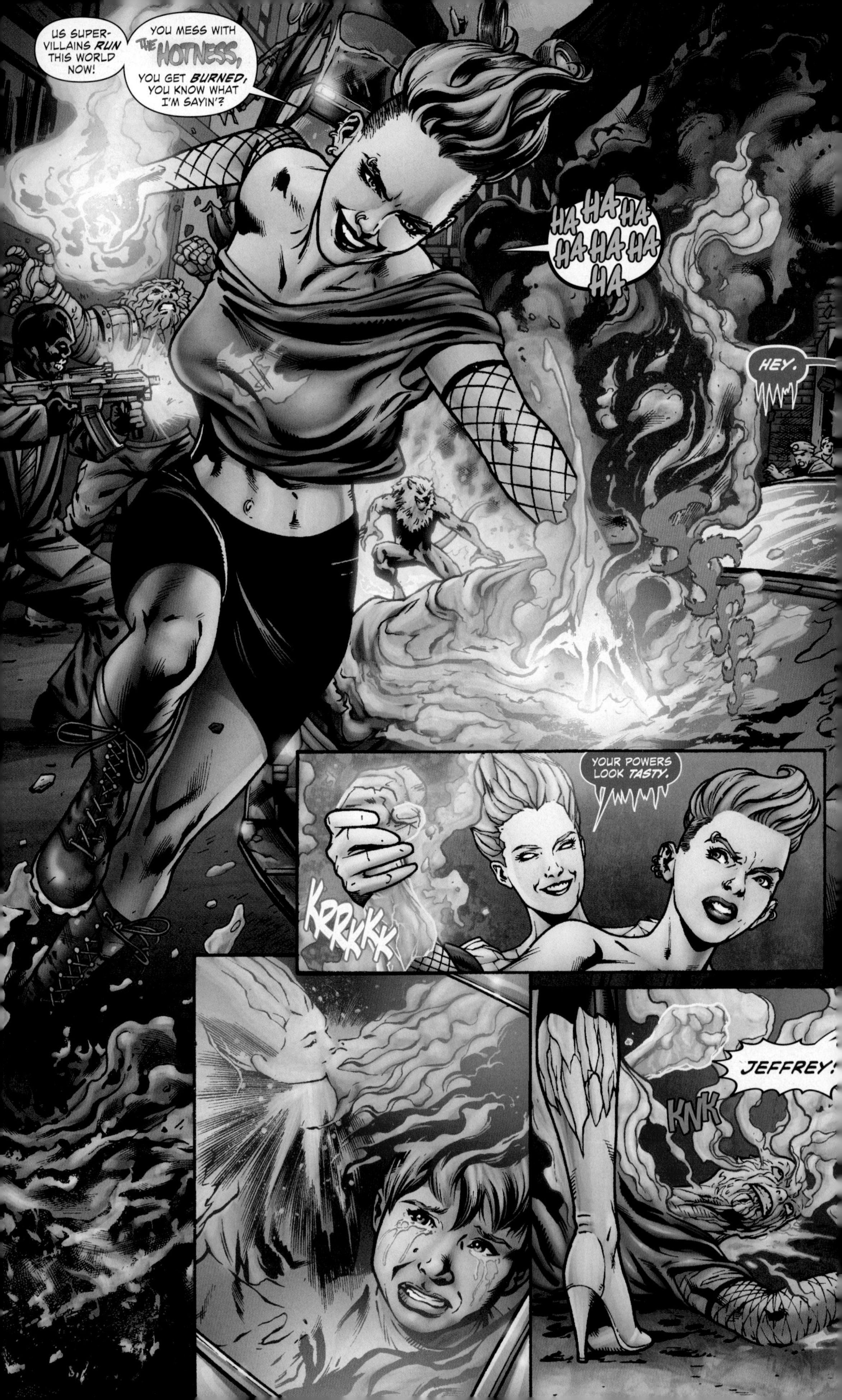

US SUPER-VILLAINS RUN THIS WORLD NOW!
YOU MESS WITH THE HOTNESS, YOU GET BURNED, YOU KNOW WHAT I'M SAYIN'?
HA HA HA HA HA HA HA
HEY.
YOUR POWERS LOOK TASTY.
KRRKKKK
JEFFREY!
KNK

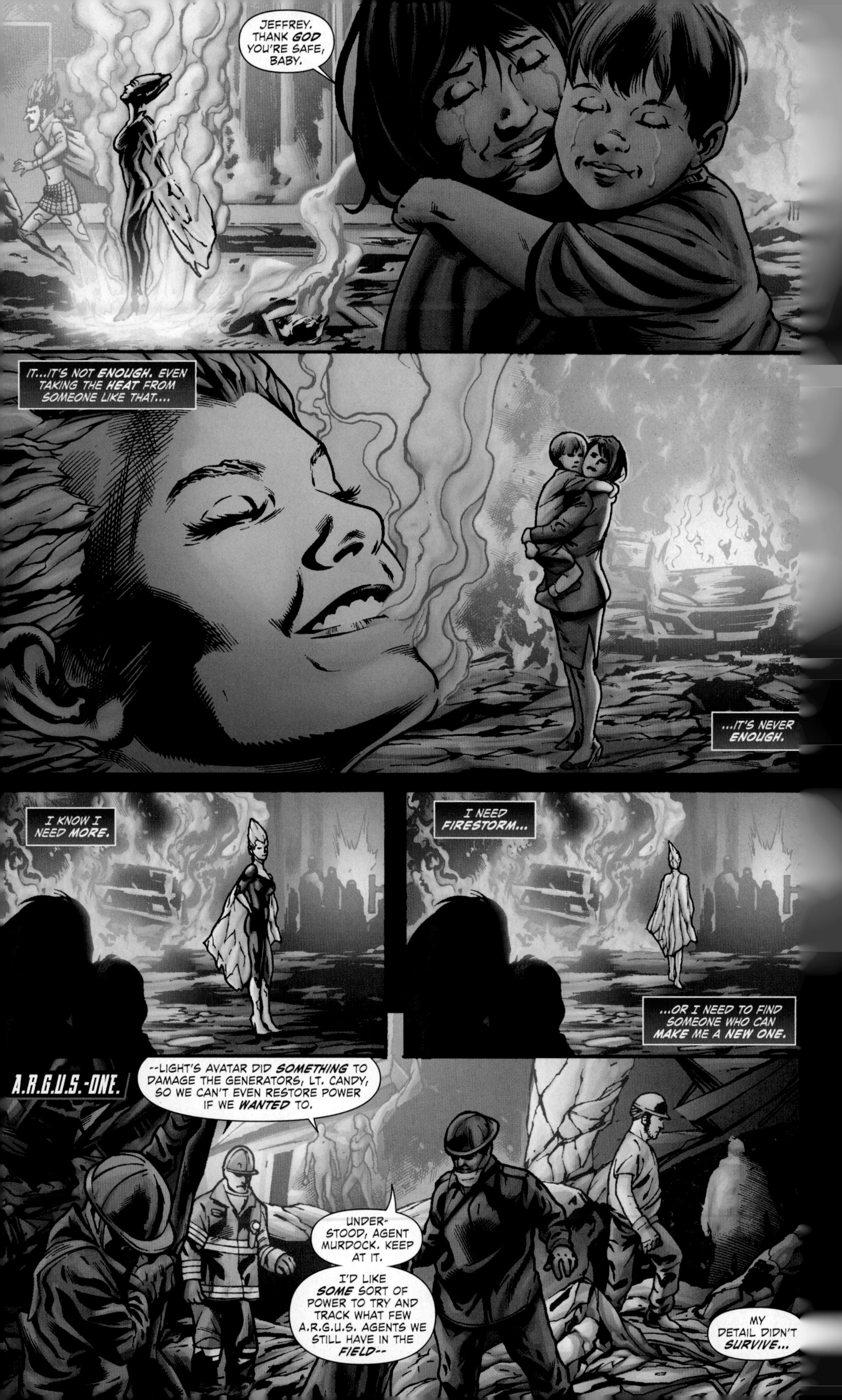
JEFFREY. THANK GOD YOU'RE SAFE, BABY.
IT...IT'S NOT ENOUGH. EVEN TAKING THE HEAT FROM SOMEONE LIKE THAT....
...IT'S NEVER ENOUGH.
I KNOW I NEED MORE.
I NEED FIRESTORM...
...OR I NEED TO FIND SOMEONE WHO CAN MAKE ME A NEW ONE.
A.R.G.U.S.-ONE.
--LIGHT'S AVATAR DID SOMETHING TO DAMAGE THE GENERATORS, LT. CANDY, SO WE CAN'T EVEN RESTORE POWER IF WE WANTED TO.
UNDER-STOOD, AGENT MURDOCK. KEEP AT IT.
I'D LIKE SOME SORT OF POWER TO TRY AND TRACK WHAT FEW A.R.G.U.S. AGENTS WE STILL HAVE IN THE FIELD--
MY DETAIL DIDN'T SURVIVE...

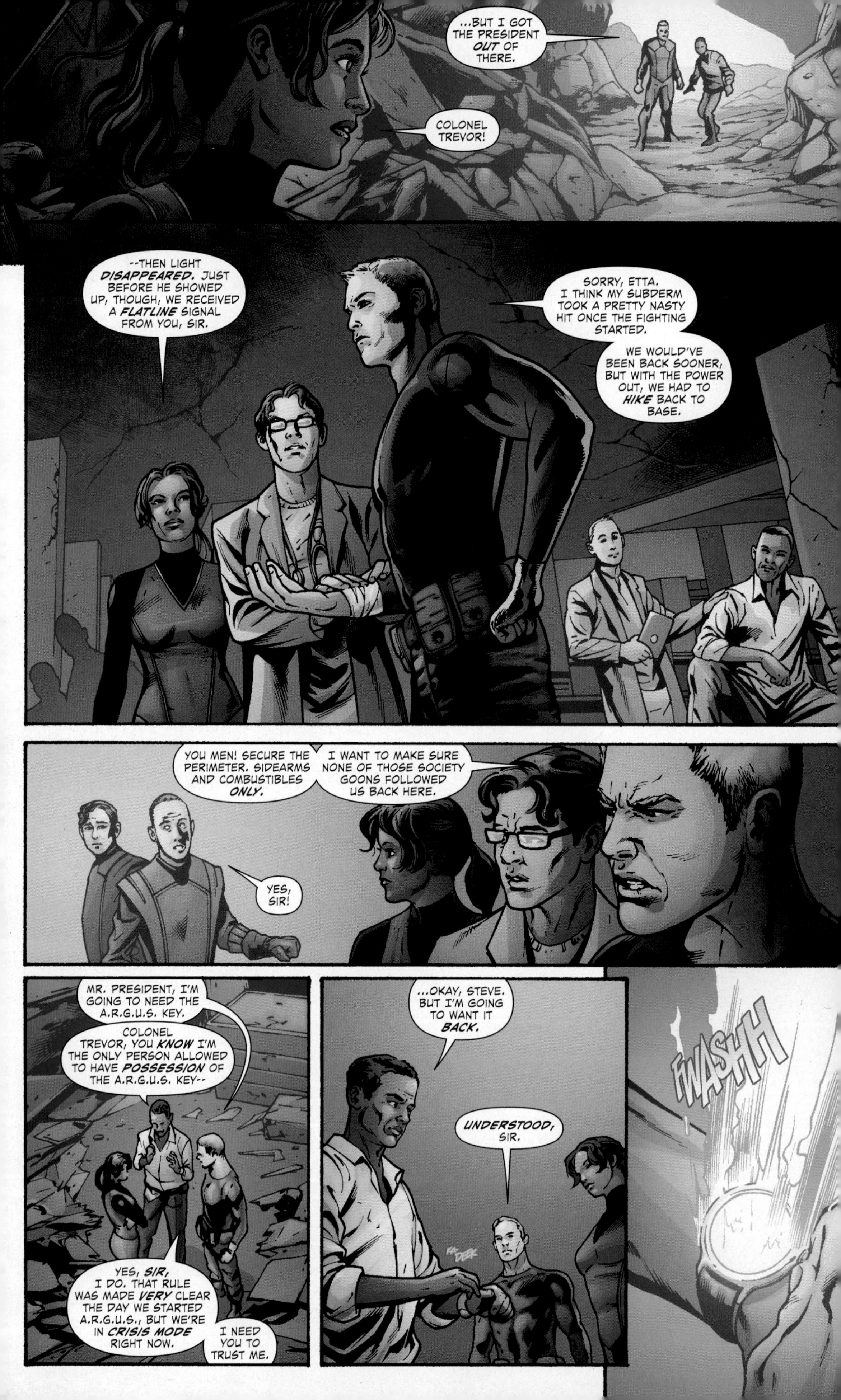

...BUT I GOT THE PRESIDENT OUT OF THERE.
COLONEL TREVOR!
--THEN LIGHT DISAPPEARED. JUST BEFORE HE SHOWED UP, THOUGH, WE RECEIVED A FLATLINE SIGNAL FROM YOU, SIR.
SORRY, ETTA. I THINK MY SUBDERM TOOK A PRETTY NASTY HIT ONCE THE FIGHTING STARTED.
WE WOULD'VE BEEN BACK SOONER, BUT WITH THE POWER OUT, WE HAD TO HIKE BACK TO BASE.
YOU MEN! SECURE THE PERIMETER. SIDEARMS AND COMBUSTIBLES ONLY.
I WANT TO MAKE SURE NONE OF THOSE SOCIETY GOONS FOLLOWED US BACK HERE.
YES, SIR!
MR. PRESIDENT, I'M GOING TO NEED THE A.R.G.U.S. KEY.
COLONEL TREVOR, YOU KNOW I'M THE ONLY PERSON ALLOWED TO HAVE POSSESSION OF THE A.R.G.U.S. KEY--
YES, SIR, I DO. THAT RULE WAS MADE VERY CLEAR THE DAY WE STARTED A.R.G.U.S., BUT WE'RE IN CRISIS MODE RIGHT NOW.
I NEED YOU TO TRUST ME.
...OKAY, STEVE. BUT I'M GOING TO WANT IT BACK.
UNDERSTOOD, SIR.
KA-DEEK
FWASHH

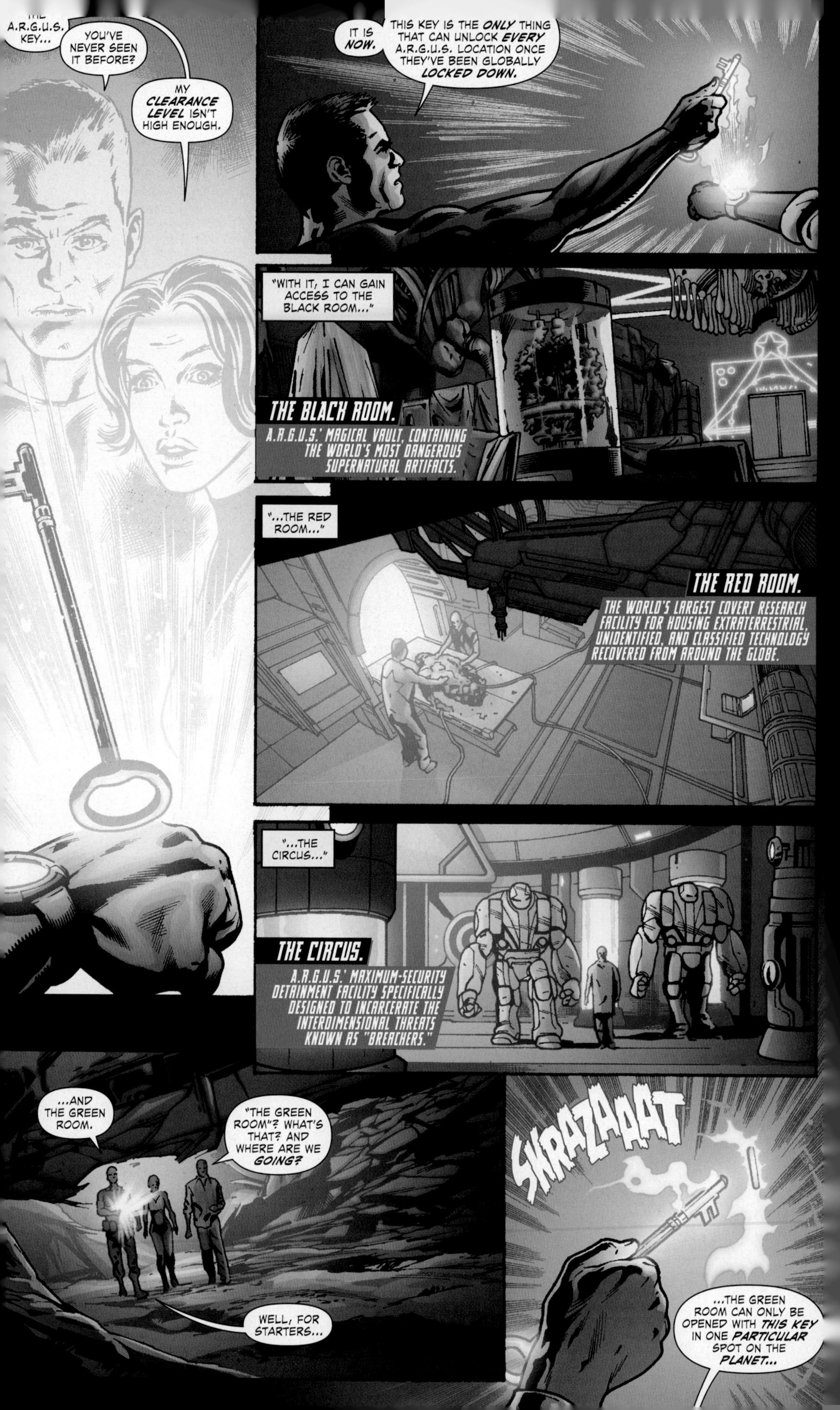
THE A.R.G.U.S. KEY...
YOU'VE NEVER SEEN IT BEFORE?
MY CLEARANCE LEVEL ISN'T HIGH ENOUGH.
IT IS NOW.
THIS KEY IS THE ONLY THING THAT CAN UNLOCK EVERY A.R.G.U.S. LOCATION ONCE THEY'VE BEEN GLOBALLY LOCKED DOWN.
"WITH IT, I CAN GAIN ACCESS TO THE BLACK ROOM..."
THE BLACK ROOM.
A.R.G.U.S.' MAGICAL VAULT, CONTAINING THE WORLD'S MOST DANGEROUS SUPERNATURAL ARTIFACTS.
"...THE RED ROOM..."
THE RED ROOM.
THE WORLD'S LARGEST COVERT RESEARCH FACILITY FOR HOUSING EXTRATERRESTRIAL, UNIDENTIFIED, AND CLASSIFIED TECHNOLOGY RECOVERED FROM AROUND THE GLOBE.
"...THE CIRCUS..."
THE CIRCUS.
A.R.G.U.S.' MAXIMUM-SECURITY DETAINMENT FACILITY SPECIFICALLY DESIGNED TO INCARCERATE THE INTERDIMENSIONAL THREATS KNOWN AS "BREACHERS."
...AND THE GREEN ROOM.
"THE GREEN ROOM"? WHAT'S THAT? AND WHERE ARE WE GOING?
WELL, FOR STARTERS...
SKRAZAAAT
...THE GREEN ROOM CAN ONLY BE OPENED WITH THIS KEY IN ONE PARTICULAR SPOT ON THE PLANET...

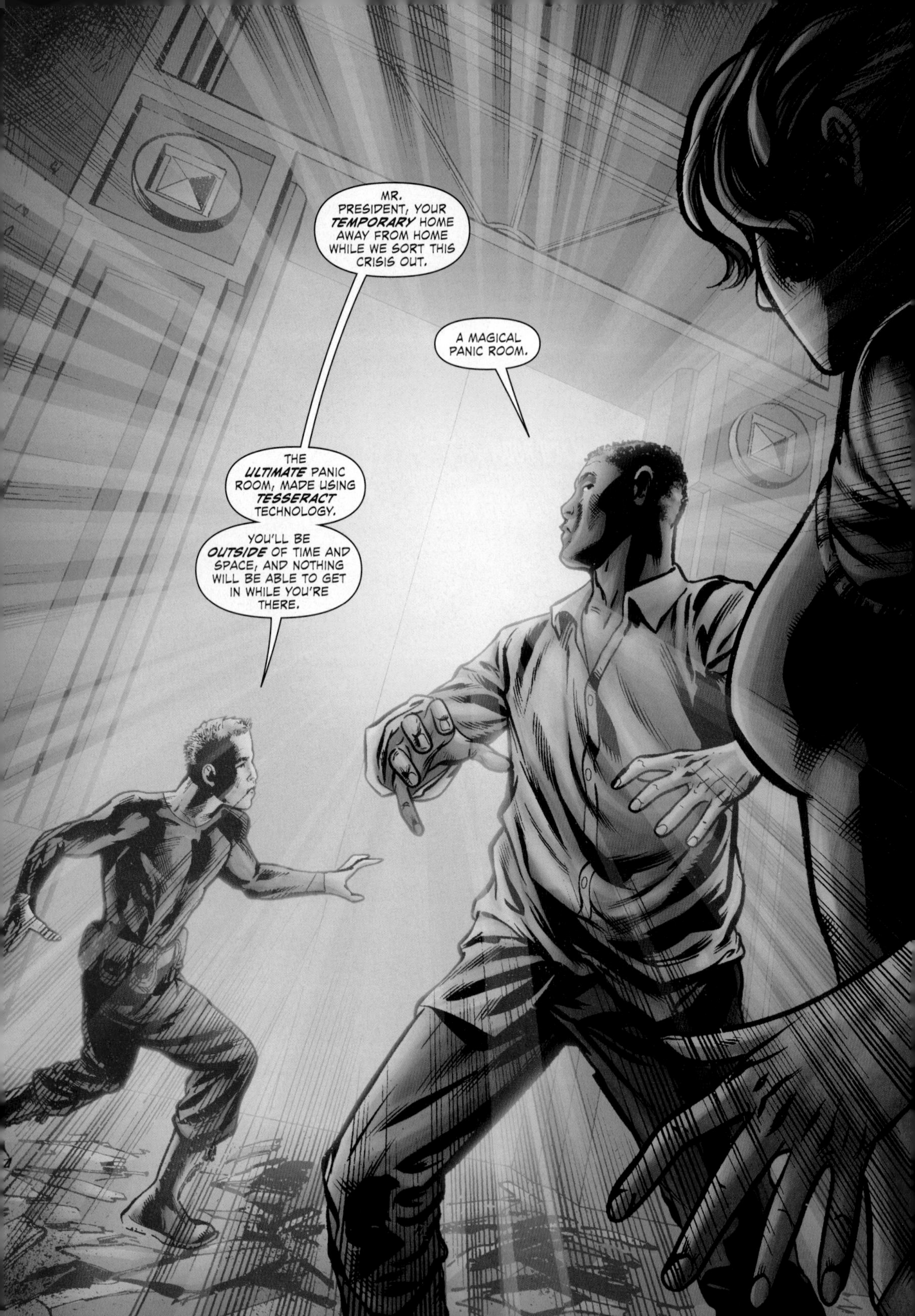

MR. PRESIDENT, YOUR TEMPORARY HOME AWAY FROM HOME WHILE WE SORT THIS CRISIS OUT.
A MAGICAL PANIC ROOM.
THE ULTIMATE PANIC ROOM, MADE USING TESSERACT TECHNOLOGY.
YOU'LL BE OUTSIDE OF TIME AND SPACE, AND NOTHING WILL BE ABLE TO GET IN WHILE YOU'RE THERE.

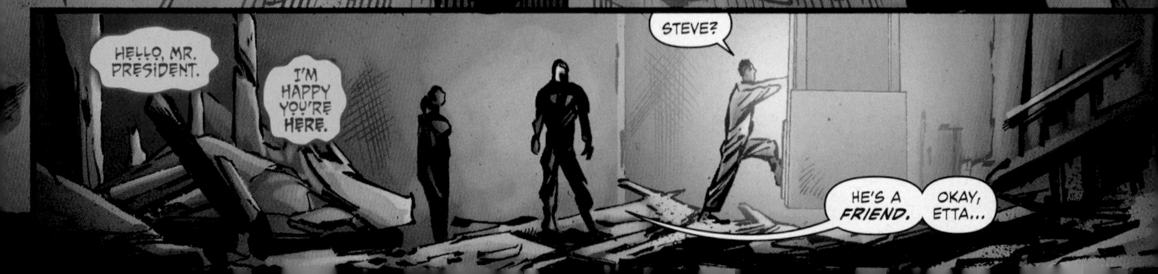

HELLO, MR. PRESIDENT.
I'M HAPPY YOU'RE HERE.
STEVE?
HE'S A FRIEND.
OKAY, ETTA...

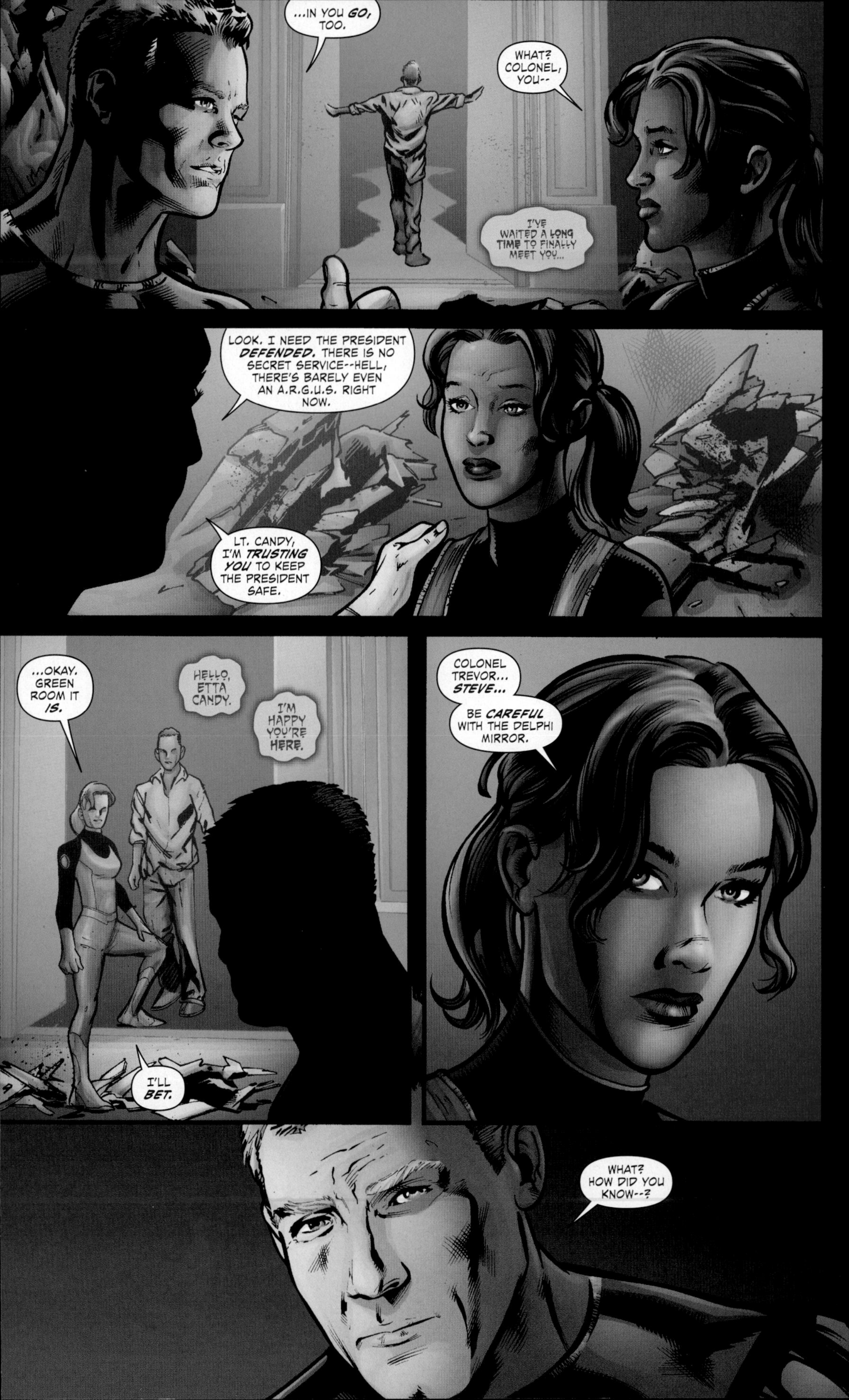
...IN YOU GO, TOO.
WHAT? COLONEL, YOU--
I'VE WAITED A LONG TIME TO FINALLY MEET YOU...
LOOK. I NEED THE PRESIDENT DEFENDED. THERE IS NO SECRET SERVICE--HELL, THERE'S BARELY EVEN AN A.R.G.U.S. RIGHT NOW.
LT. CANDY, I'M TRUSTING YOU TO KEEP THE PRESIDENT SAFE.
...OKAY. GREEN ROOM IT IS.
HELLO, ETTA CANDY.
I'M HAPPY YOU'RE HERE.
I'LL BET.
COLONEL TREVOR... STEVE...
BE CAREFUL WITH THE DELPHI MIRROR.
WHAT? HOW DID YOU KNOW--?

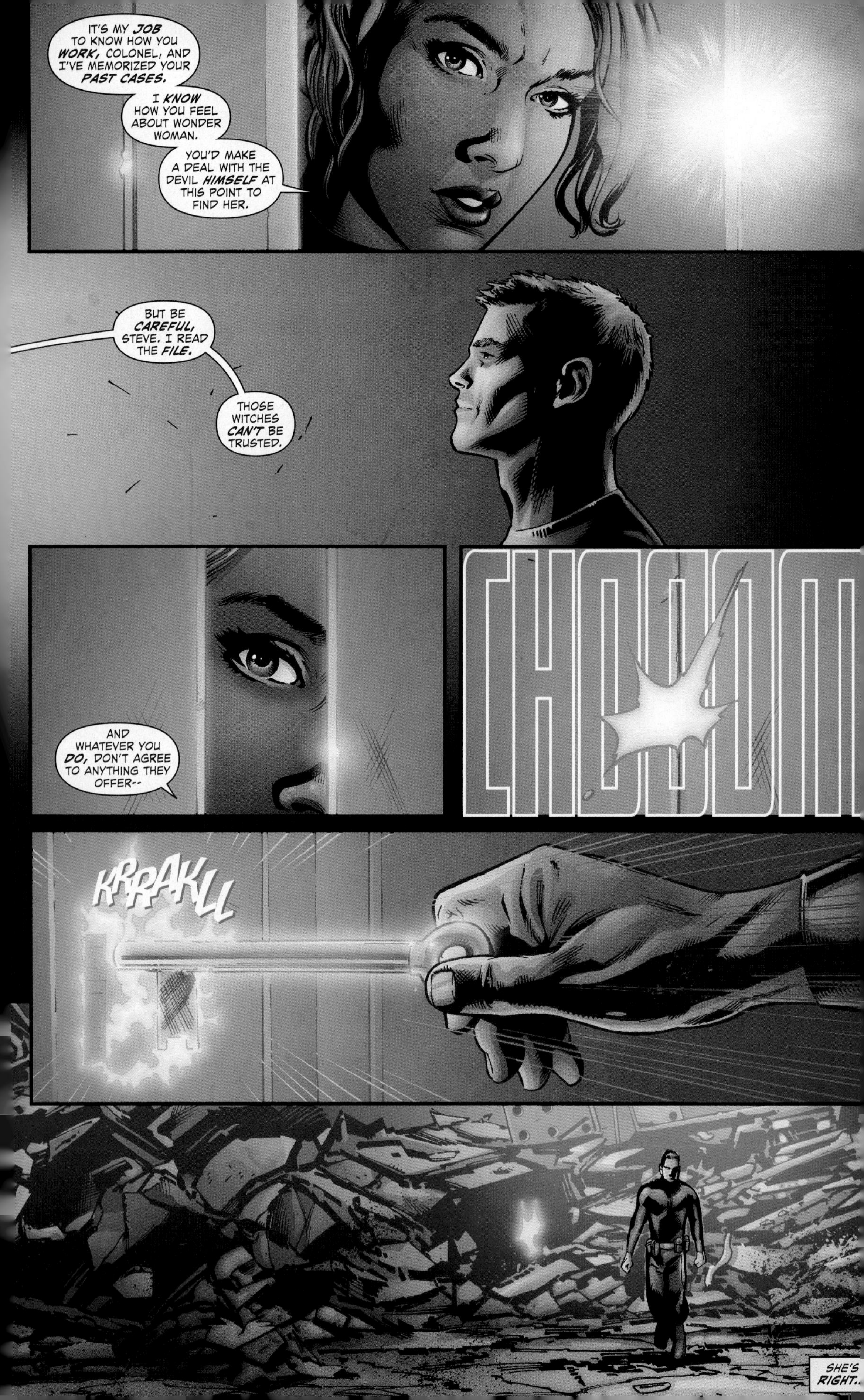
IT'S MY JOB TO KNOW HOW YOU WORK, COLONEL, AND I'VE MEMORIZED YOUR PAST CASES.
I KNOW HOW YOU FEEL ABOUT WONDER WOMAN.
YOU'D MAKE A DEAL WITH THE DEVIL HIMSELF AT THIS POINT TO FIND HER.
BUT BE CAREFUL, STEVE. I READ THE FILE.
THOSE WITCHES CAN'T BE TRUSTED.
AND WHATEVER YOU DO, DON'T AGREE TO ANYTHING THEY OFFER--
CHOOOM
KRRAKLL
SHE'S RIGHT.

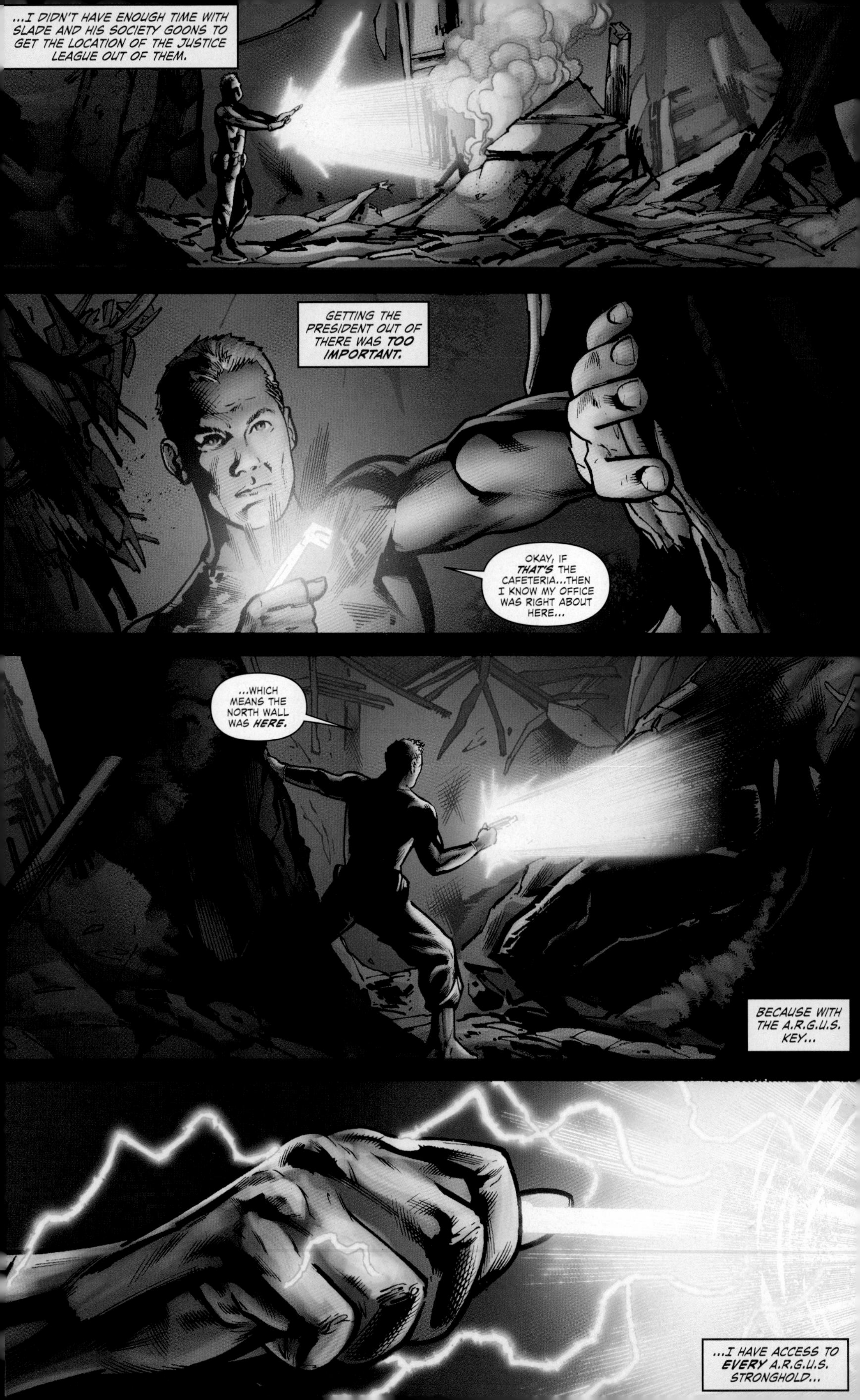
...I DIDN'T HAVE ENOUGH TIME WITH SLADE AND HIS SOCIETY GOONS TO GET THE LOCATION OF THE JUSTICE LEAGUE OUT OF THEM.
GETTING THE PRESIDENT OUT OF THERE WAS TOO IMPORTANT.
OKAY, IF THAT'S THE CAFETERIA...THEN I KNOW MY OFFICE WAS RIGHT ABOUT HERE...
...WHICH MEANS THE NORTH WALL WAS HERE.
BECAUSE WITH THE A.R.G.U.S. KEY...
...I HAVE ACCESS TO EVERY A.R.G.U.S. STRONGHOLD...

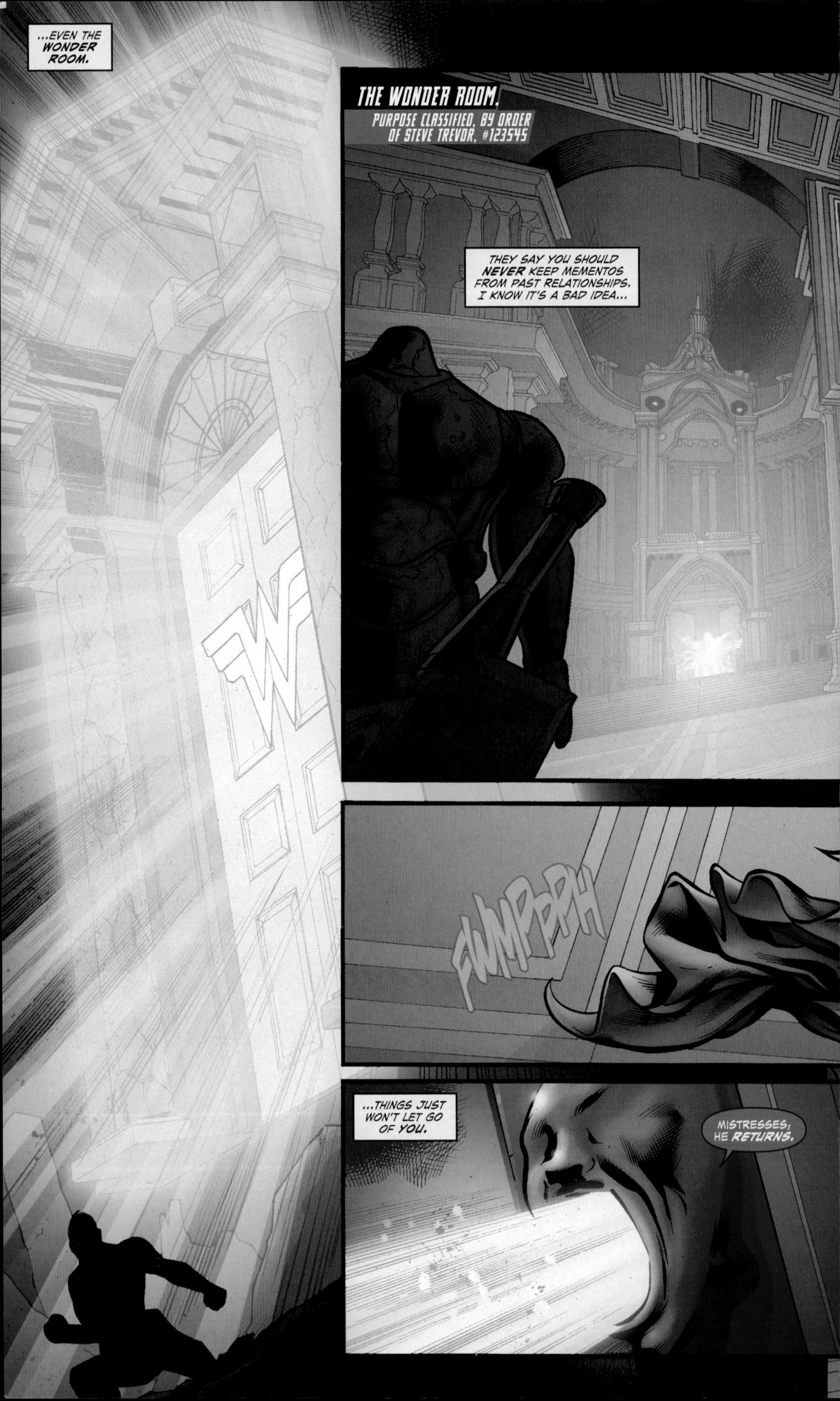
...EVEN THE WONDER ROOM.
THE WONDER ROOM.
PURPOSE CLASSIFIED, BY ORDER OF STEVE TREVOR, #123545
THEY SAY YOU SHOULD NEVER KEEP MEMENTOS FROM PAST RELATIONSHIPS. I KNOW IT'S A BAD IDEA...
FWMPPH
...THINGS JUST WON'T LET GO OF YOU.
MISTRESSES, HE RETURNS.

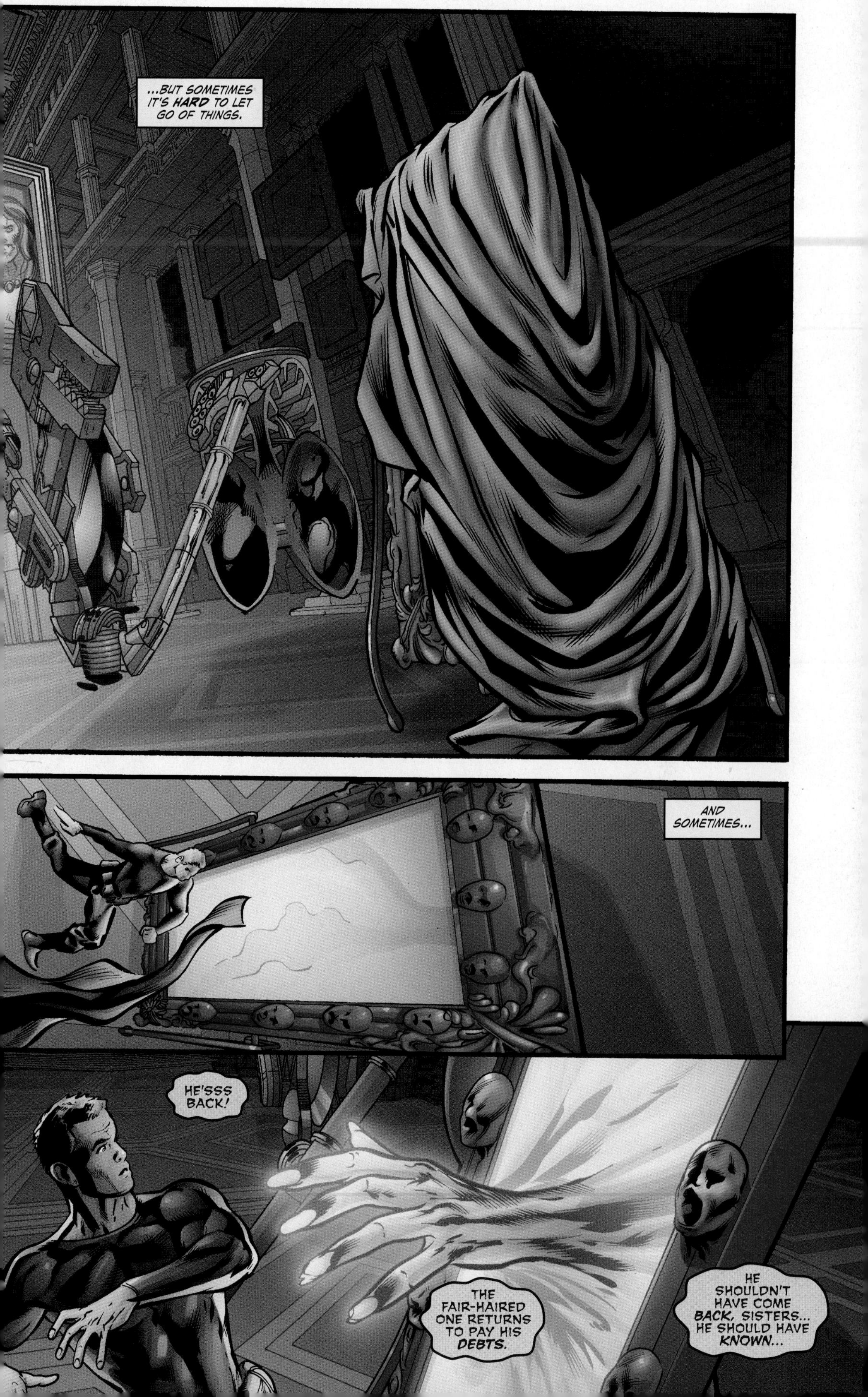
...BUT SOMETIMES IT'S HARD TO LET GO OF THINGS.
AND SOMETIMES...
HE'SSS BACK!
THE FAIR-HAIRED ONE RETURNS TO PAY HIS DEBTS.
HE SHOULDN'T HAVE COME BACK, SISTERS... HE SHOULD HAVE KNOWN...

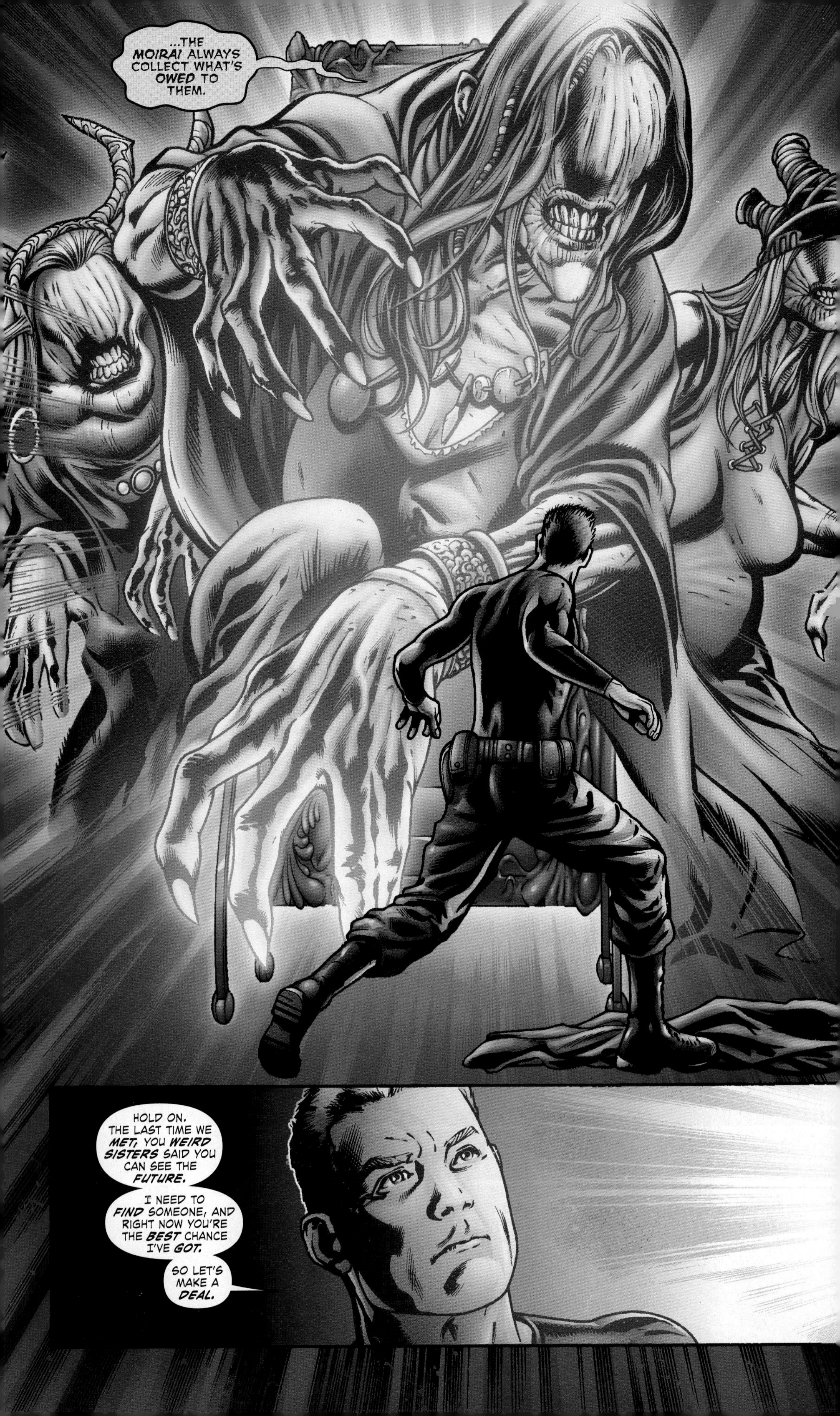
...THE MOIRAI ALWAYS COLLECT WHAT'S OWED TO THEM.
HOLD ON. THE LAST TIME WE MET, YOU WEIRD SISTERS SAID YOU CAN SEE THE FUTURE.
I NEED TO FIND SOMEONE, AND RIGHT NOW YOU'RE THE BEST CHANCE I'VE GOT.
SO LET'S MAKE A DEAL.

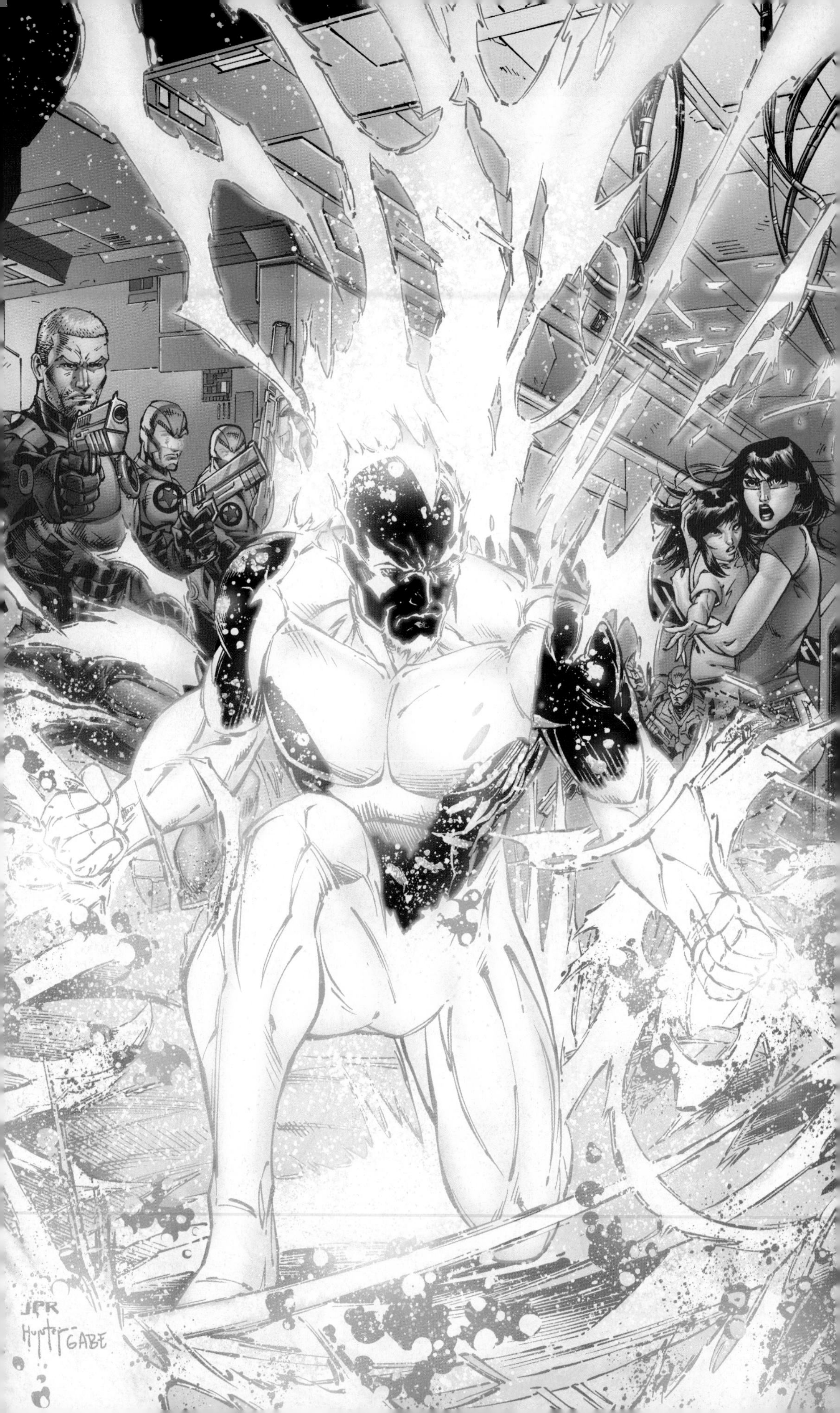
JPR
Hunter GABE

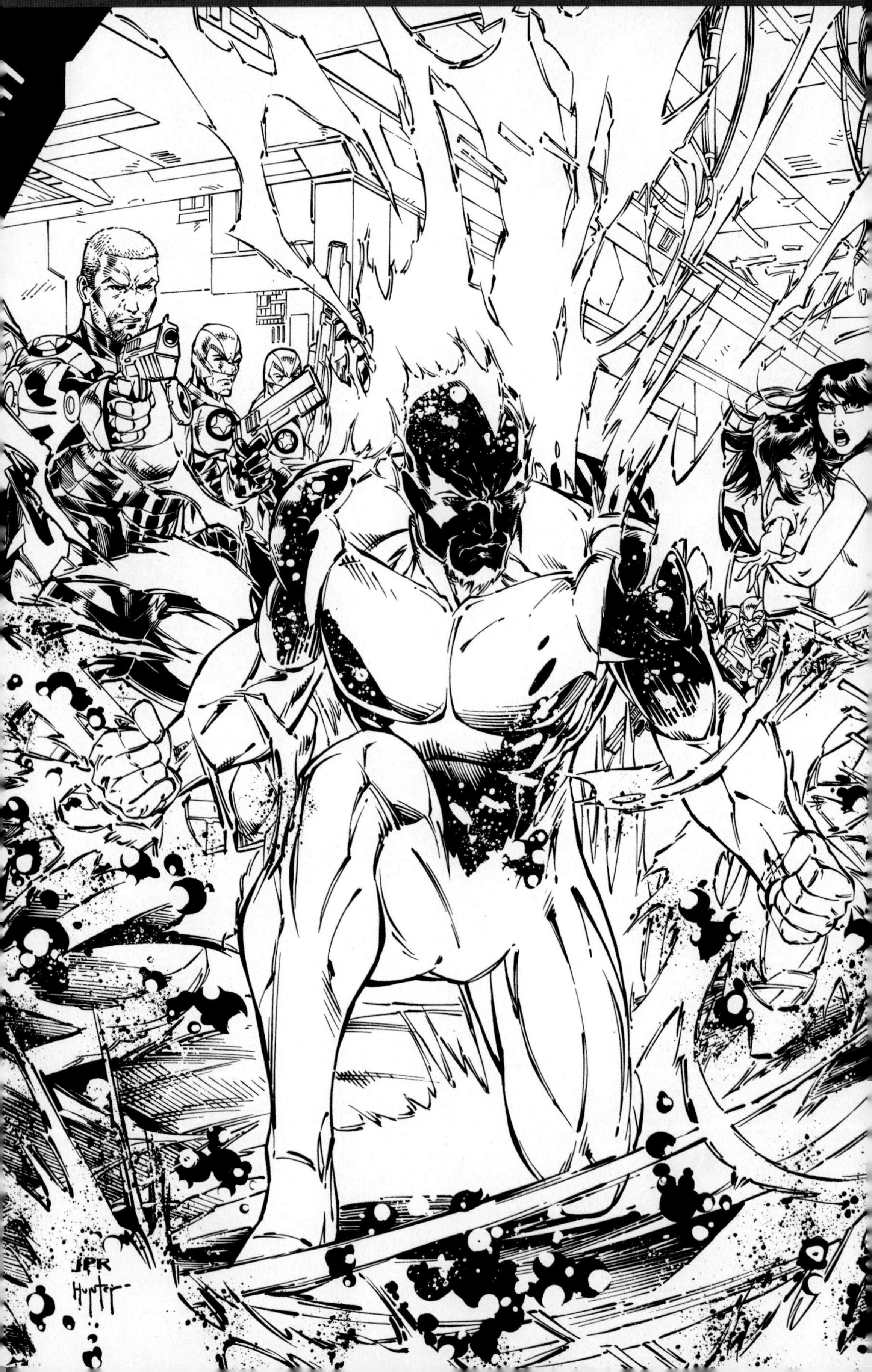
JPR
Hunter

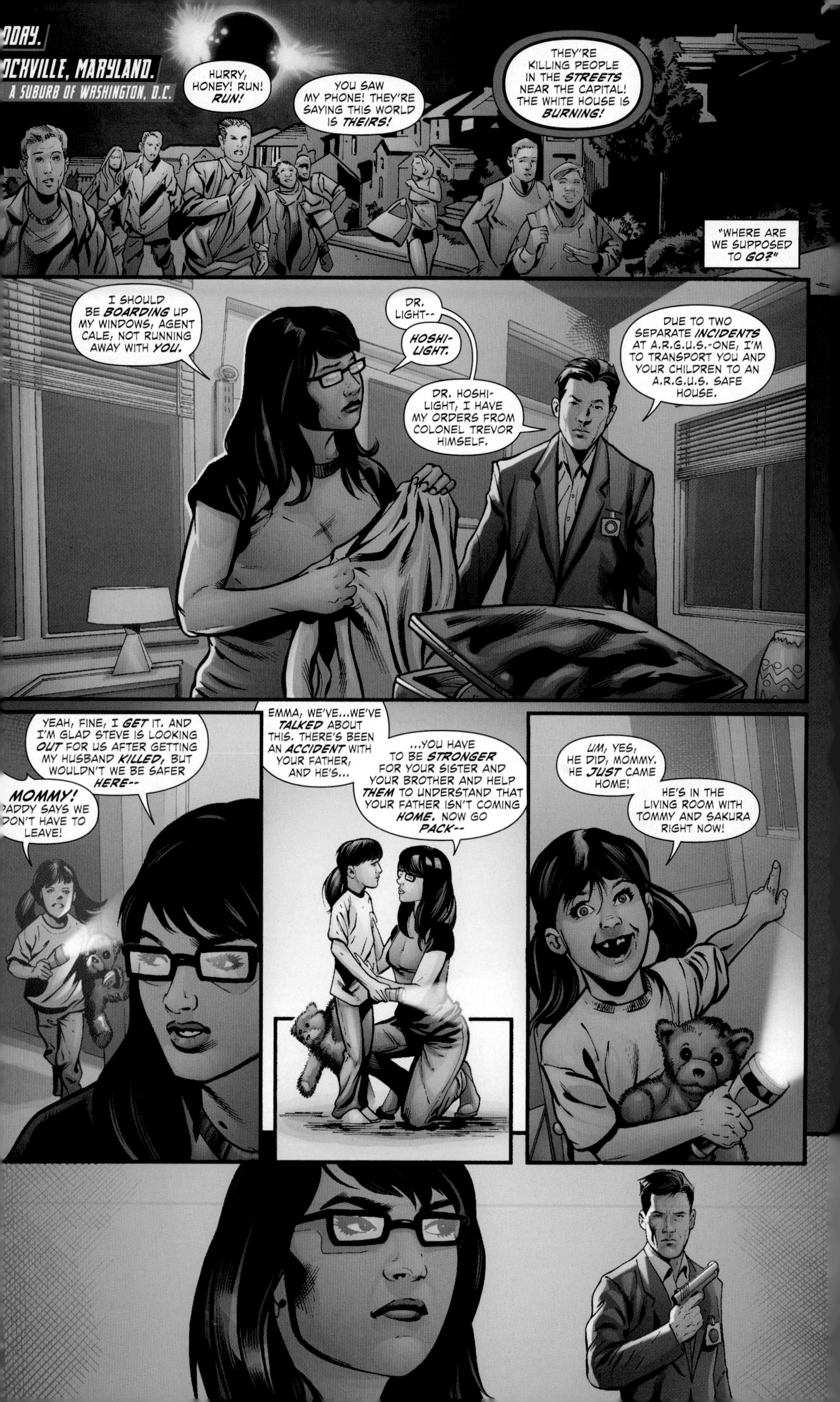

ODAY.
OCKVILLE, MARYLAND.
A SUBURB OF WASHINGTON, D.C.
HURRY, HONEY! RUN! RUN!
YOU SAW MY PHONE! THEY'RE SAYING THIS WORLD IS THEIRS!
THEY'RE KILLING PEOPLE IN THE STREETS NEAR THE CAPITAL! THE WHITE HOUSE IS BURNING!
"WHERE ARE WE SUPPOSED TO GO?"
I SHOULD BE BOARDING UP MY WINDOWS, AGENT CALE, NOT RUNNING AWAY WITH YOU.
DR. LIGHT--
HOSHI-LIGHT.
DR. HOSHI-LIGHT, I HAVE MY ORDERS FROM COLONEL TREVOR HIMSELF.
DUE TO TWO SEPARATE INCIDENTS AT A.R.G.U.S.-ONE, I'M TO TRANSPORT YOU AND YOUR CHILDREN TO AN A.R.G.U.S. SAFE HOUSE.
YEAH, FINE, I GET IT. AND I'M GLAD STEVE IS LOOKING OUT FOR US AFTER GETTING MY HUSBAND KILLED, BUT WOULDN'T WE BE SAFER HERE--
MOMMY! DADDY SAYS WE DON'T HAVE TO LEAVE!
EMMA, WE'VE...WE'VE TALKED ABOUT THIS. THERE'S BEEN AN ACCIDENT WITH YOUR FATHER, AND HE'S...
...YOU HAVE TO BE STRONGER FOR YOUR SISTER AND YOUR BROTHER AND HELP THEM TO UNDERSTAND THAT YOUR FATHER ISN'T COMING HOME. NOW GO PACK--
UM, YES, HE DID, MOMMY. HE JUST CAME HOME!
HE'S IN THE LIVING ROOM WITH TOMMY AND SAKURA RIGHT NOW!

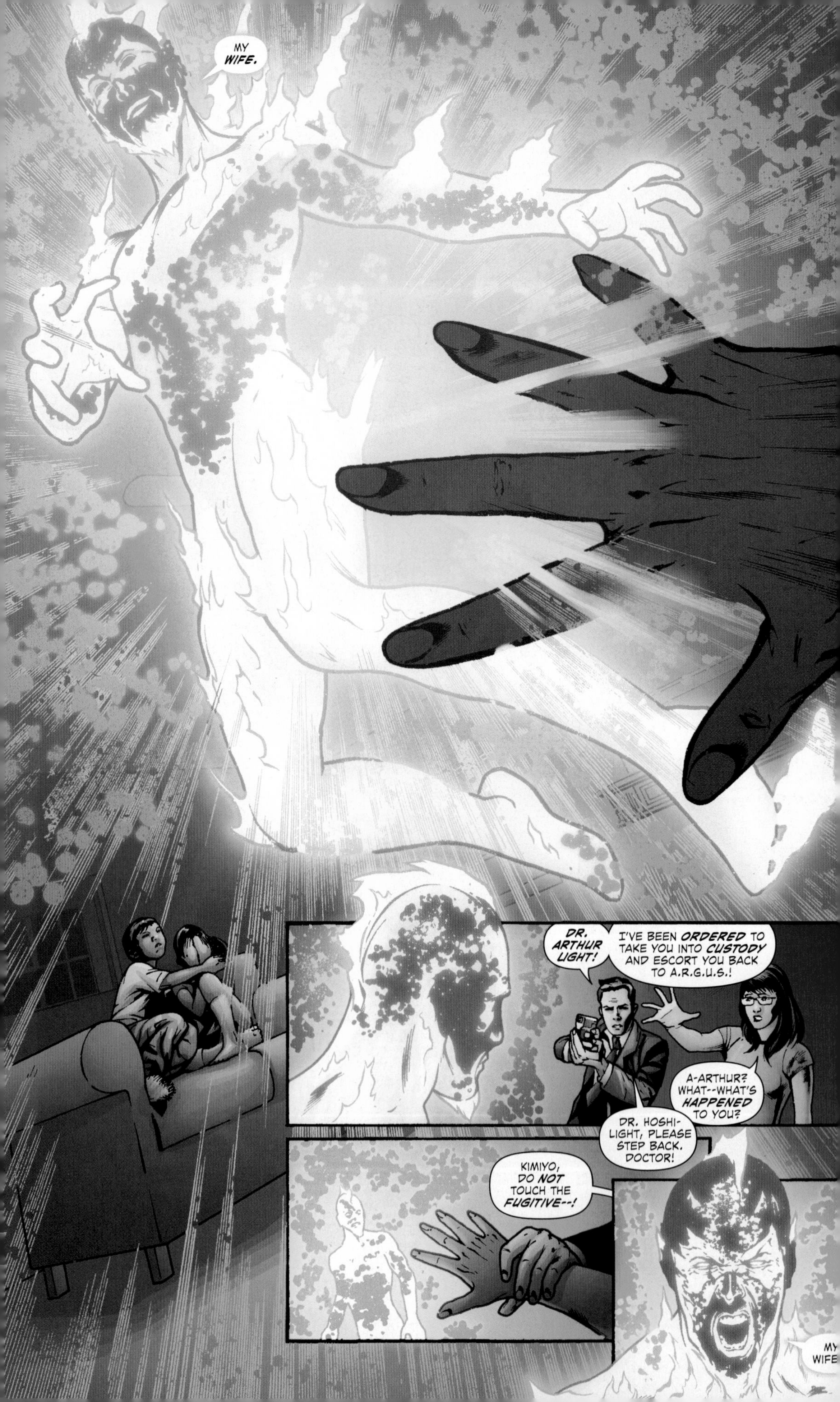
MY WIFE.
DR. ARTHUR LIGHT!
I'VE BEEN ORDERED TO TAKE YOU INTO CUSTODY AND ESCORT YOU BACK TO A.R.G.U.S.!
A-ARTHUR? WHAT--WHAT'S HAPPENED TO YOU?
DR. HOSHI-LIGHT, PLEASE STEP BACK, DOCTOR!
KIMIYO, DO NOT TOUCH THE FUGITIVE--!
MY WIFE

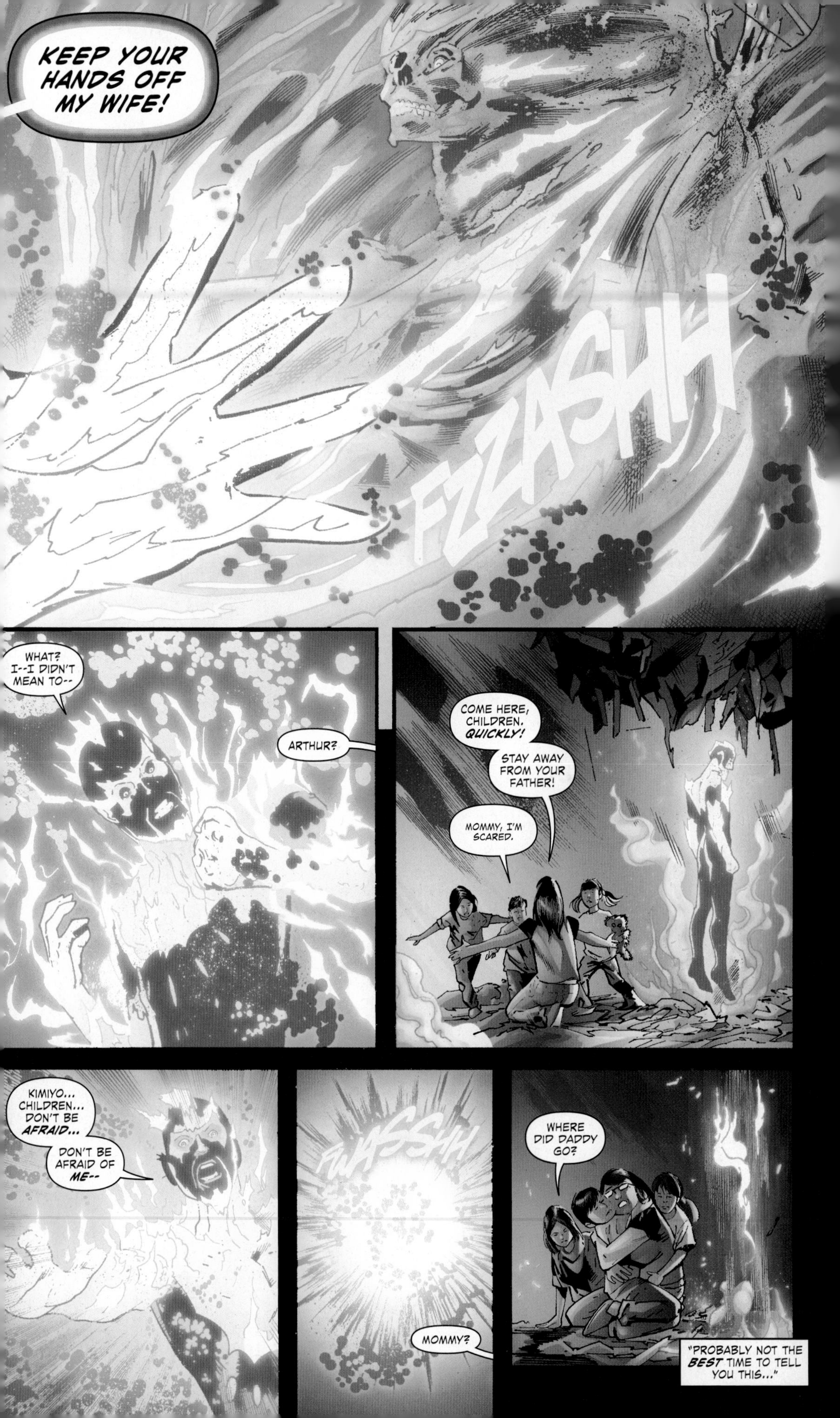
KEEP YOUR HANDS OFF MY WIFE!
FZZASHH
WHAT? I--I DIDN'T MEAN TO--
ARTHUR?
COME HERE, CHILDREN. QUICKLY!
STAY AWAY FROM YOUR FATHER!
MOMMY, I'M SCARED.
KIMIYO... CHILDREN... DON'T BE AFRAID...
DON'T BE AFRAID OF ME--
FWASHH
MOMMY?
WHERE DID DADDY GO?
"PROBABLY NOT THE BEST TIME TO TELL YOU THIS..."

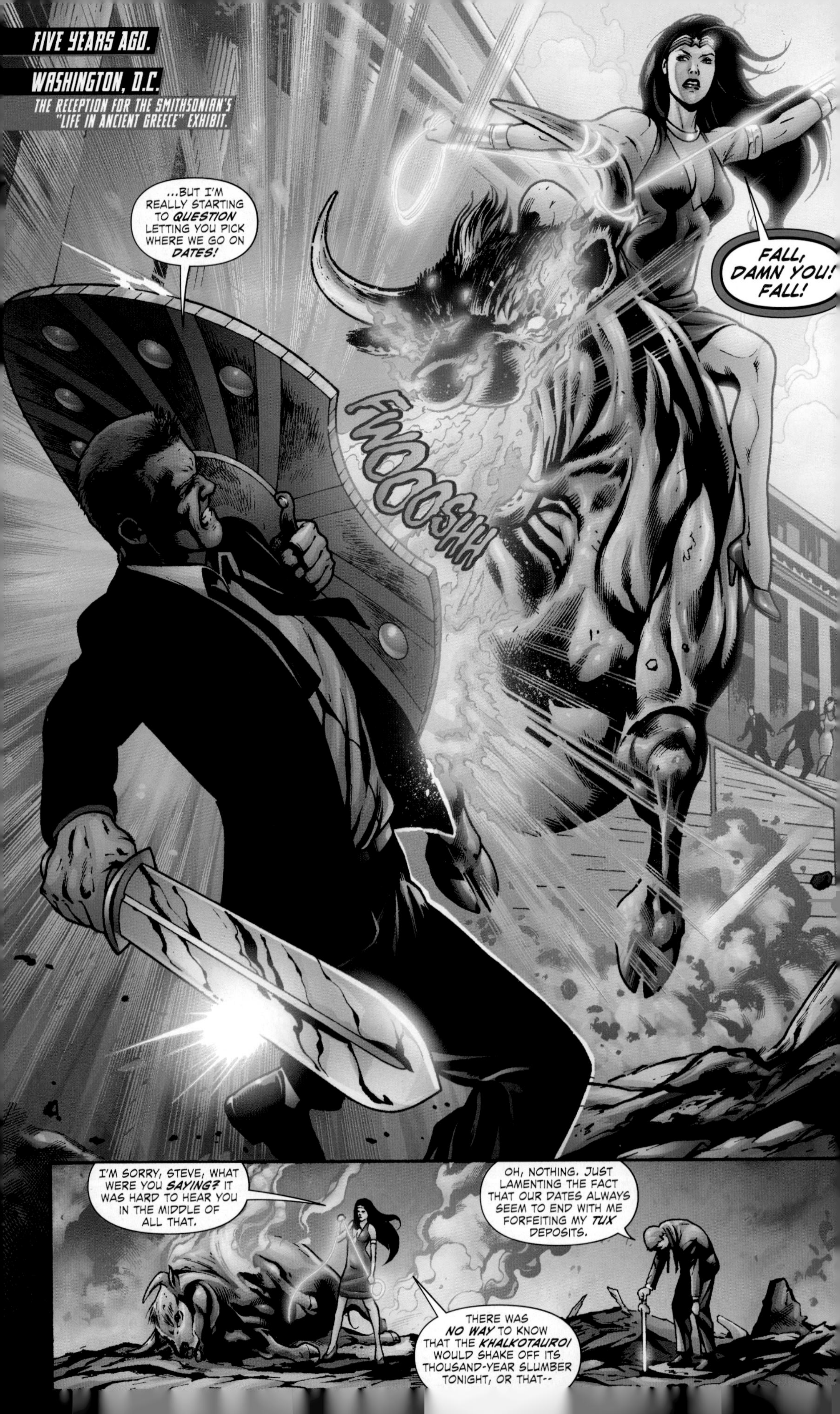
FIVE YEARS AGO.
WASHINGTON, D.C.
THE RECEPTION FOR THE SMITHSONIAN'S "LIFE IN ANCIENT GREECE" EXHIBIT.
...BUT I'M REALLY STARTING TO QUESTION LETTING YOU PICK WHERE WE GO ON DATES!
FALL, DAMN YOU! FALL!
FWOOOSHH
I'M SORRY, STEVE, WHAT WERE YOU SAYING? IT WAS HARD TO HEAR YOU IN THE MIDDLE OF ALL THAT.
OH, NOTHING. JUST LAMENTING THE FACT THAT OUR DATES ALWAYS SEEM TO END WITH ME FORFEITING MY TUX DEPOSITS.
THERE WAS NO WAY TO KNOW THAT THE KHALKOTAUROI WOULD SHAKE OFF ITS THOUSAND-YEAR SLUMBER TONIGHT, OR THAT--

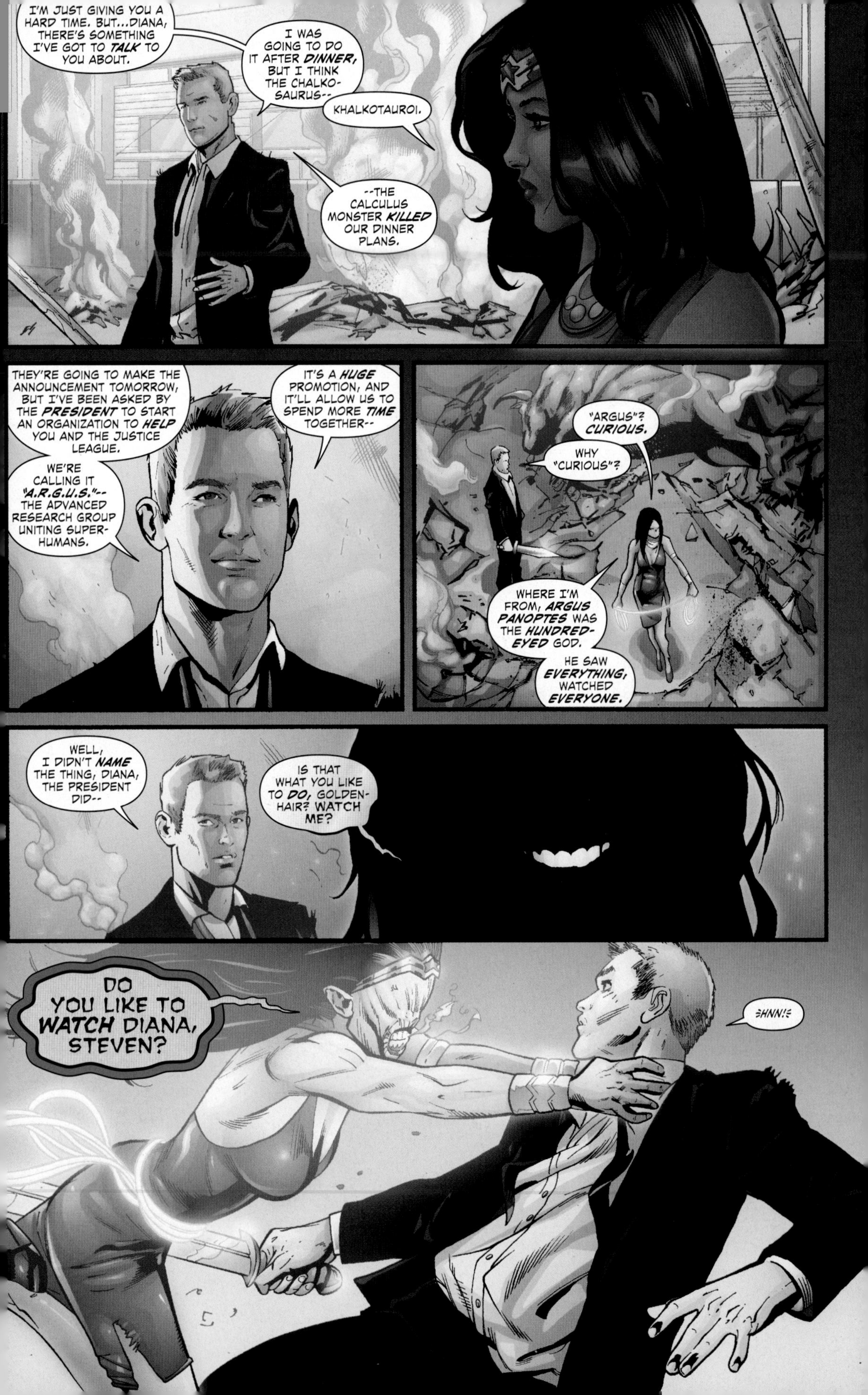
I'M JUST GIVING YOU A HARD TIME. BUT...DIANA, THERE'S SOMETHING I'VE GOT TO TALK TO YOU ABOUT.
I WAS GOING TO DO IT AFTER DINNER, BUT I THINK THE CHALKO-SAURUS--
KHALKOTAUROI.
--THE CALCULUS MONSTER KILLED OUR DINNER PLANS.
THEY'RE GOING TO MAKE THE ANNOUNCEMENT TOMORROW, BUT I'VE BEEN ASKED BY THE PRESIDENT TO START AN ORGANIZATION TO HELP YOU AND THE JUSTICE LEAGUE.
WE'RE CALLING IT "A.R.G.U.S."-- THE ADVANCED RESEARCH GROUP UNITING SUPER-HUMANS.
IT'S A HUGE PROMOTION, AND IT'LL ALLOW US TO SPEND MORE TIME TOGETHER--
"ARGUS"? CURIOUS.
WHY "CURIOUS"?
WHERE I'M FROM, ARGUS PANOPTES WAS THE HUNDRED-EYED GOD.
HE SAW EVERYTHING, WATCHED EVERYONE.
WELL, I DIDN'T NAME THE THING, DIANA, THE PRESIDENT DID--
IS THAT WHAT YOU LIKE TO DO, GOLDEN-HAIR? WATCH ME?
DO YOU LIKE TO WATCH DIANA, STEVEN?
HNN!

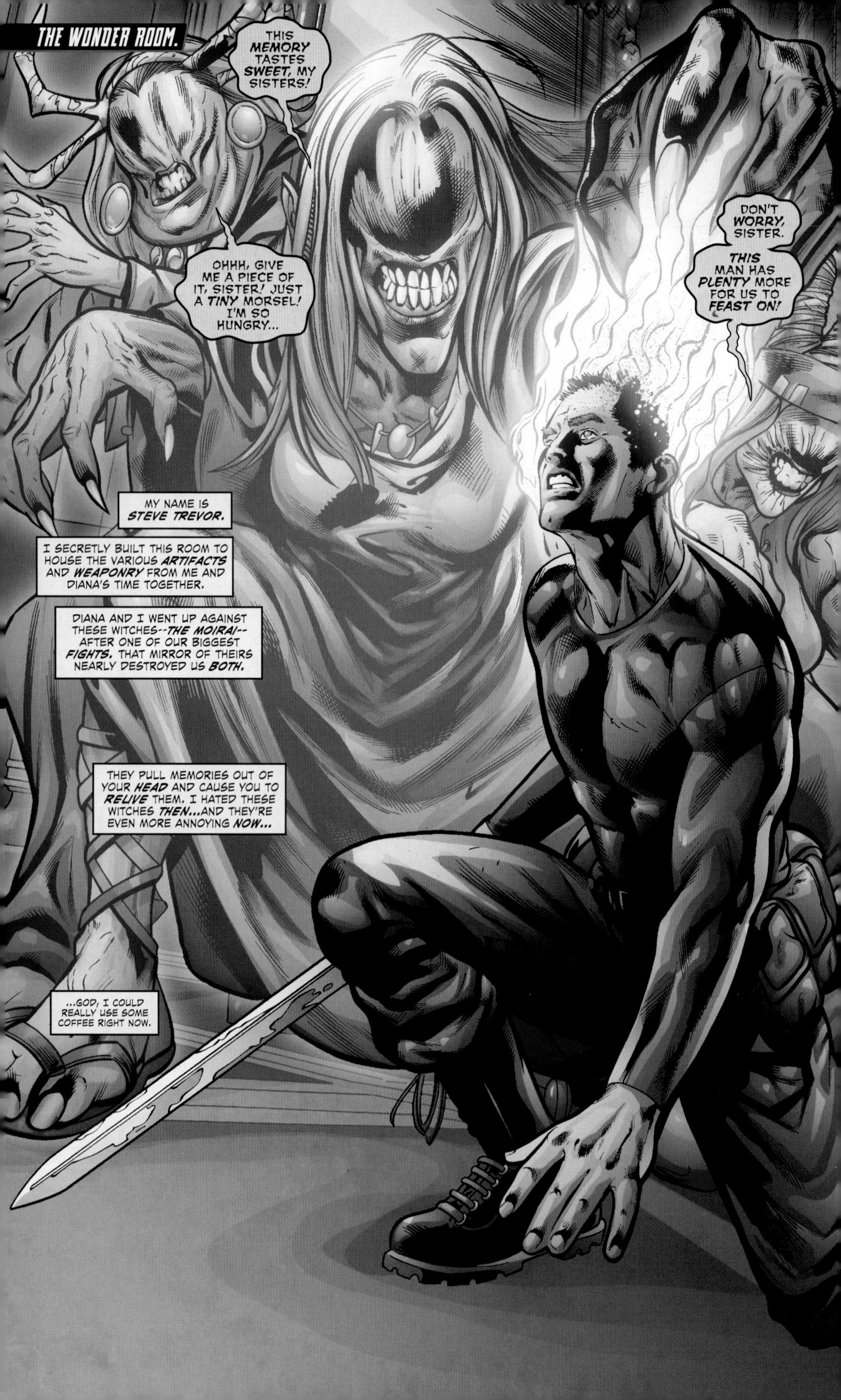
THE WONDER ROOM.
THIS MEMORY TASTES SWEET, MY SISTERS!
OHHH, GIVE ME A PIECE OF IT, SISTER! JUST A TINY MORSEL! I'M SO HUNGRY...
DON'T WORRY, SISTER.
THIS MAN HAS PLENTY MORE FOR US TO FEAST ON!
MY NAME IS STEVE TREVOR.
I SECRETLY BUILT THIS ROOM TO HOUSE THE VARIOUS ARTIFACTS AND WEAPONRY FROM ME AND DIANA'S TIME TOGETHER.
DIANA AND I WENT UP AGAINST THESE WITCHES--THE MOIRAI--AFTER ONE OF OUR BIGGEST FIGHTS. THAT MIRROR OF THEIRS NEARLY DESTROYED US BOTH.
THEY PULL MEMORIES OUT OF YOUR HEAD AND CAUSE YOU TO RELIVE THEM. I HATED THESE WITCHES THEN...AND THEY'RE EVEN MORE ANNOYING NOW...
...GOD, I COULD REALLY USE SOME COFFEE RIGHT NOW.

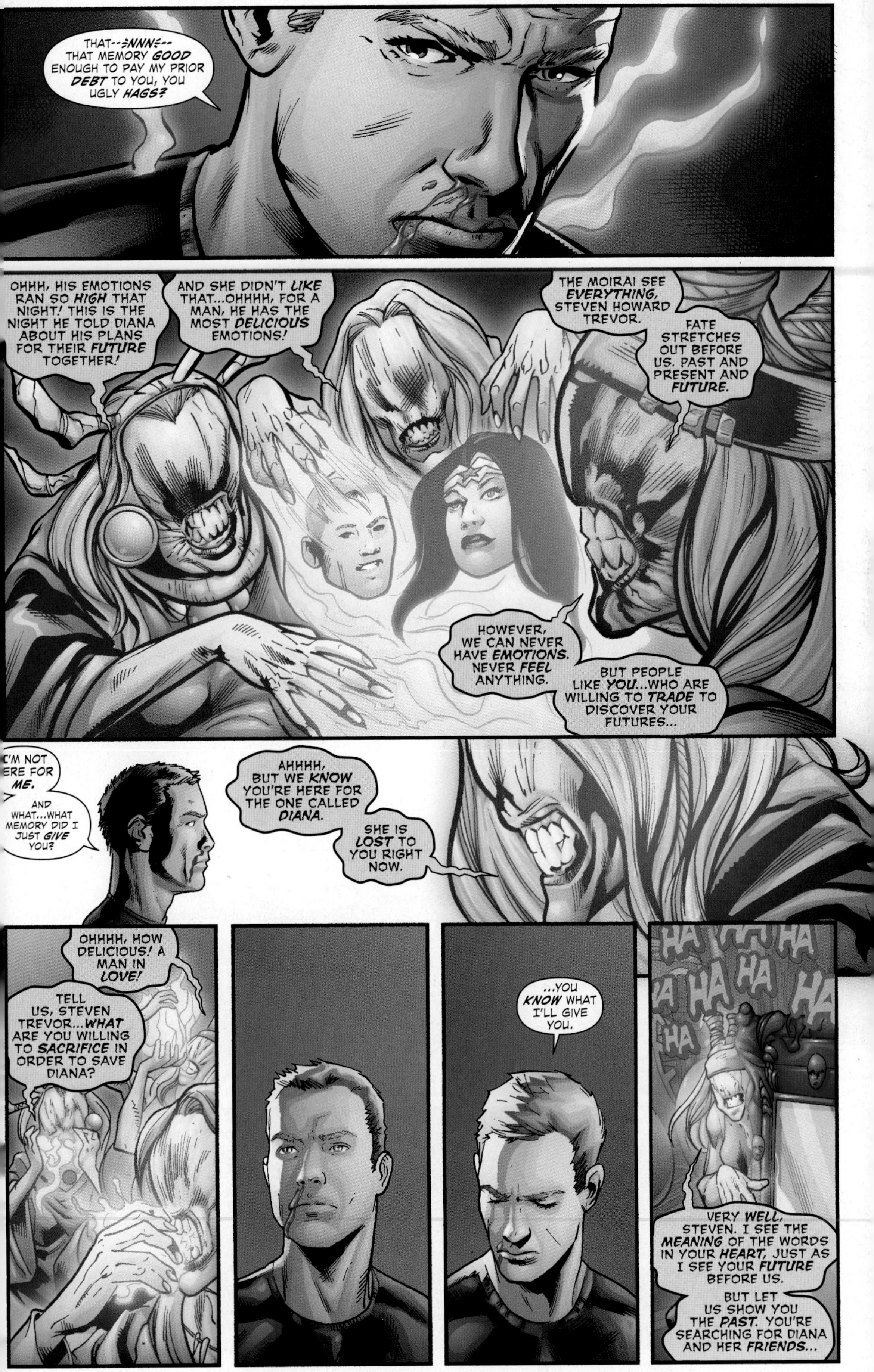

THAT--=NNN=-- THAT MEMORY GOOD ENOUGH TO PAY MY PRIOR DEBT TO YOU, YOU UGLY HAGS?
OHHH, HIS EMOTIONS RAN SO HIGH THAT NIGHT! THIS IS THE NIGHT HE TOLD DIANA ABOUT HIS PLANS FOR THEIR FUTURE TOGETHER!
AND SHE DIDN'T LIKE THAT...OHHHH, FOR A MAN, HE HAS THE MOST DELICIOUS EMOTIONS!
THE MOIRAI SEE EVERYTHING, STEVEN HOWARD TREVOR.
FATE STRETCHES OUT BEFORE US. PAST AND PRESENT AND FUTURE.
HOWEVER, WE CAN NEVER HAVE EMOTIONS. NEVER FEEL ANYTHING.
BUT PEOPLE LIKE YOU...WHO ARE WILLING TO TRADE TO DISCOVER YOUR FUTURES...
I'M NOT HERE FOR ME.
AND WHAT...WHAT MEMORY DID I JUST GIVE YOU?
AHHHH, BUT WE KNOW YOU'RE HERE FOR THE ONE CALLED DIANA.
SHE IS LOST TO YOU RIGHT NOW.
OHHHH, HOW DELICIOUS! A MAN IN LOVE!
TELL US, STEVEN TREVOR...WHAT ARE YOU WILLING TO SACRIFICE IN ORDER TO SAVE DIANA?
...YOU KNOW WHAT I'LL GIVE YOU.
HA HA HA HA HA HA HA HA HA HA
VERY WELL, STEVEN. I SEE THE MEANING OF THE WORDS IN YOUR HEART, JUST AS I SEE YOUR FUTURE BEFORE US.
BUT LET US SHOW YOU THE PAST. YOU'RE SEARCHING FOR DIANA AND HER FRIENDS...

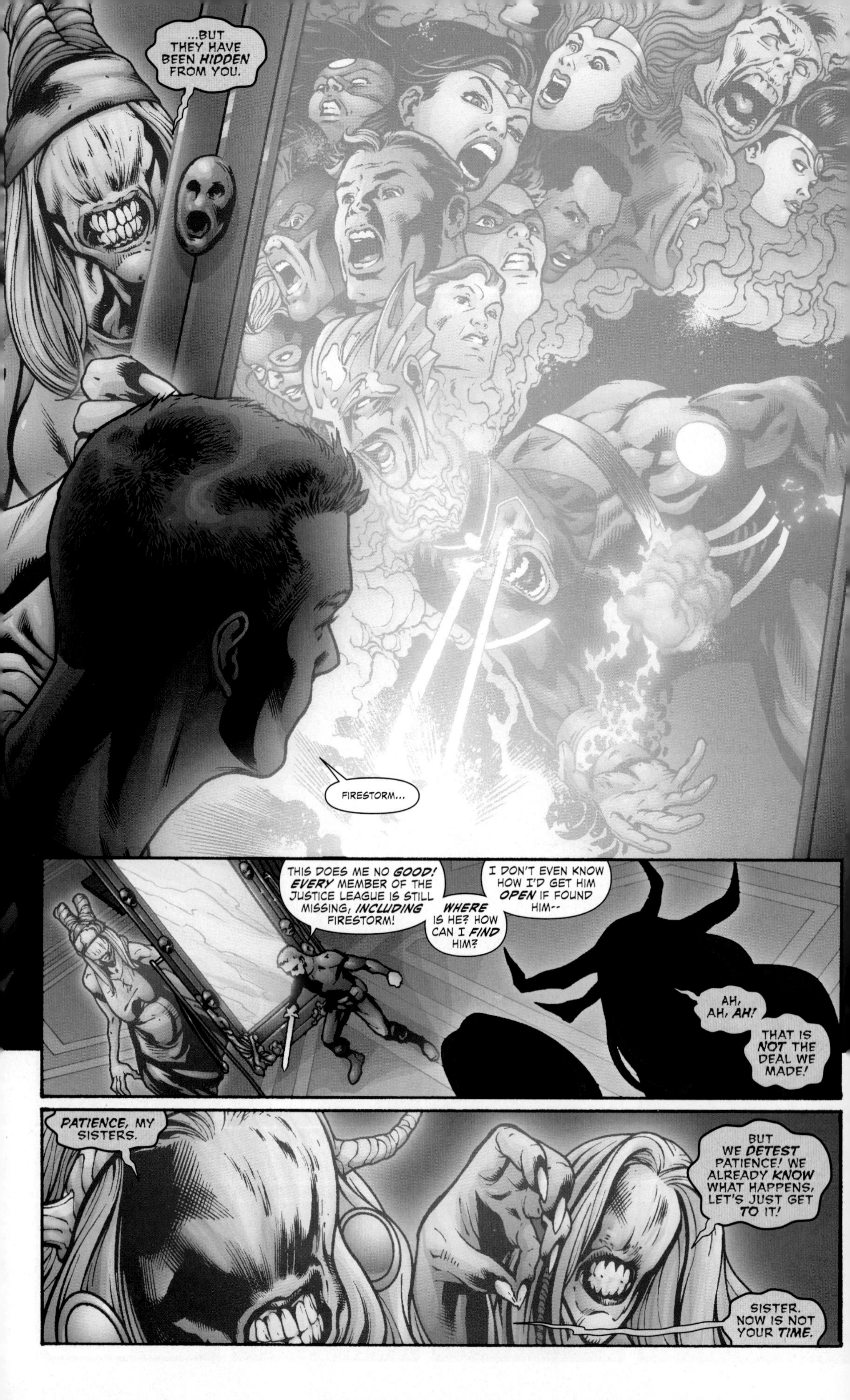
...BUT THEY HAVE BEEN *HIDDEN* FROM YOU.
FIRESTORM...
THIS DOES ME NO *GOOD!* *EVERY* MEMBER OF THE JUSTICE LEAGUE IS STILL MISSING, *INCLUDING* FIRESTORM!
WHERE IS HE? HOW CAN I *FIND* HIM?
I DON'T EVEN KNOW HOW I'D GET HIM *OPEN* IF FOUND HIM--
AH, AH, *AH!*
THAT IS *NOT* THE DEAL WE MADE!
PATIENCE, MY SISTERS.
BUT WE *DETEST* PATIENCE! WE ALREADY *KNOW* WHAT HAPPENS, LET'S JUST GET *TO* IT!
SISTER. NOW IS NOT YOUR *TIME*.

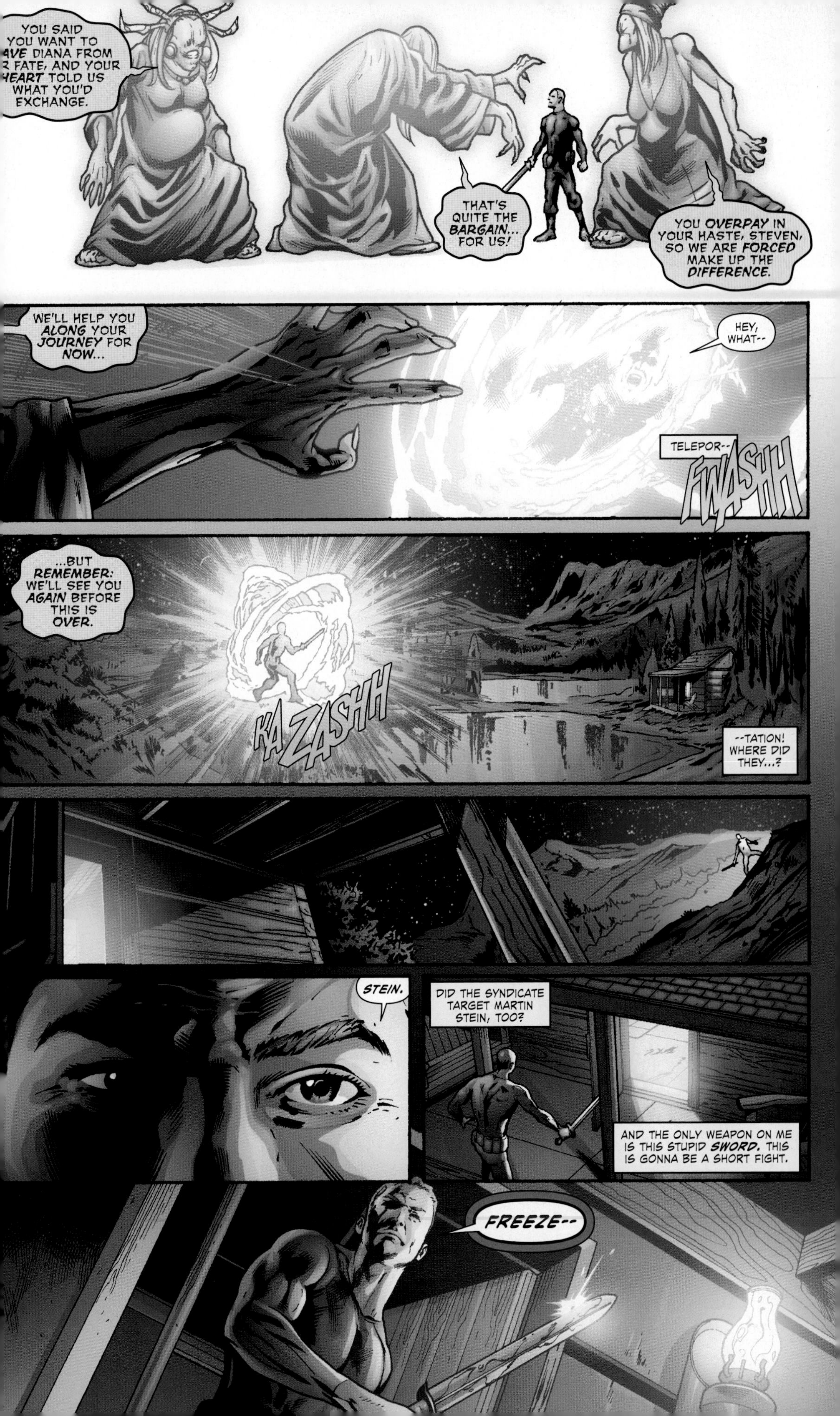
YOU SAID YOU WANT TO AVE DIANA FROM R FATE, AND YOUR HEART TOLD US WHAT YOU'D EXCHANGE.
THAT'S QUITE THE BARGAIN... FOR US!
YOU OVERPAY IN YOUR HASTE, STEVEN, SO WE ARE FORCED MAKE UP THE DIFFERENCE.
WE'LL HELP YOU ALONG YOUR JOURNEY FOR NOW...
HEY, WHAT--
TELEPOR--
FWASHH
...BUT REMEMBER: WE'LL SEE YOU AGAIN BEFORE THIS IS OVER.
KA ZASHH
--TATION! WHERE DID THEY...?
STEIN.
DID THE SYNDICATE TARGET MARTIN STEIN, TOO?
AND THE ONLY WEAPON ON ME IS THIS STUPID SWORD. THIS IS GONNA BE A SHORT FIGHT.
FREEZE--

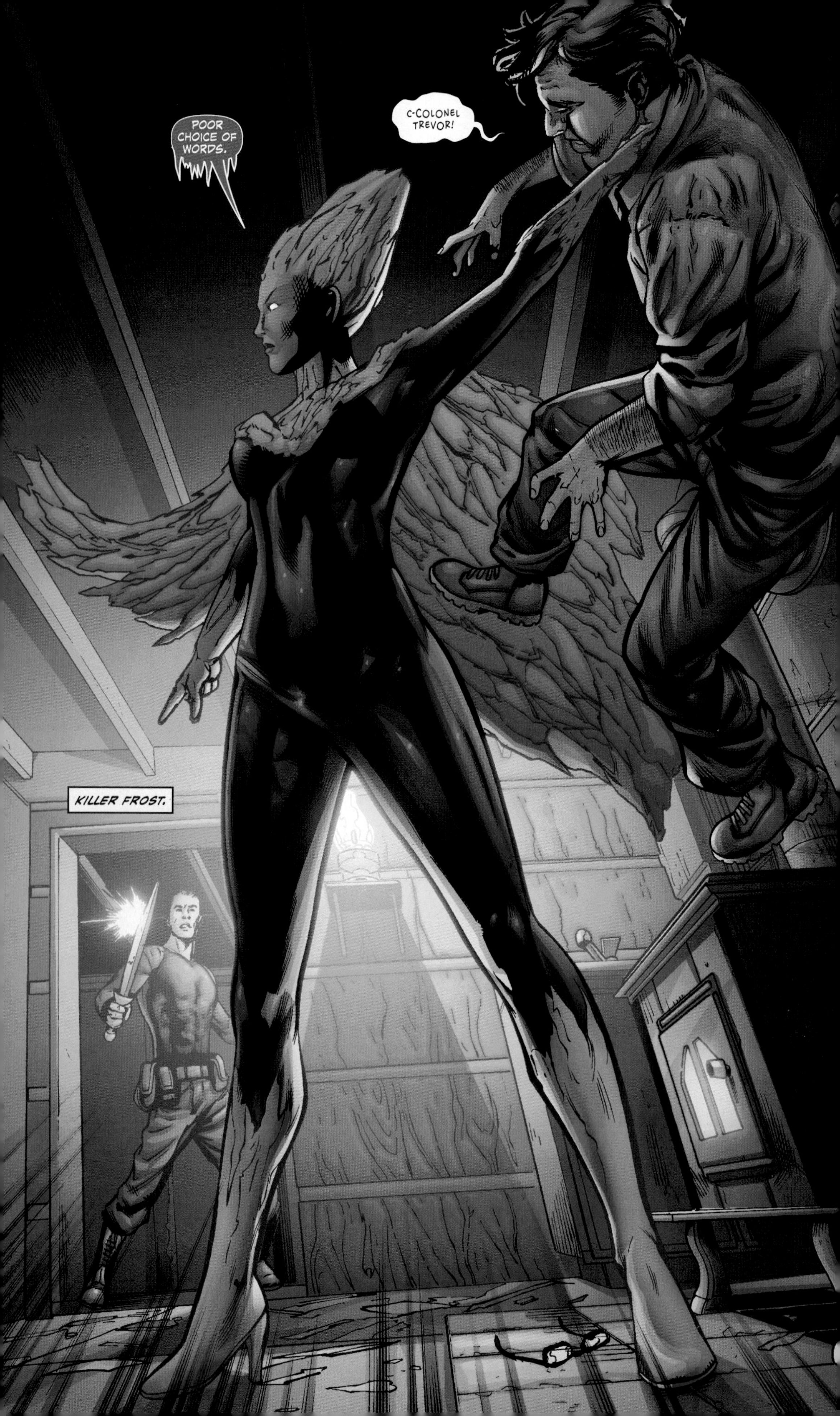
POOR CHOICE OF WORDS.
C-COLONEL TREVOR!
KILLER FROST.

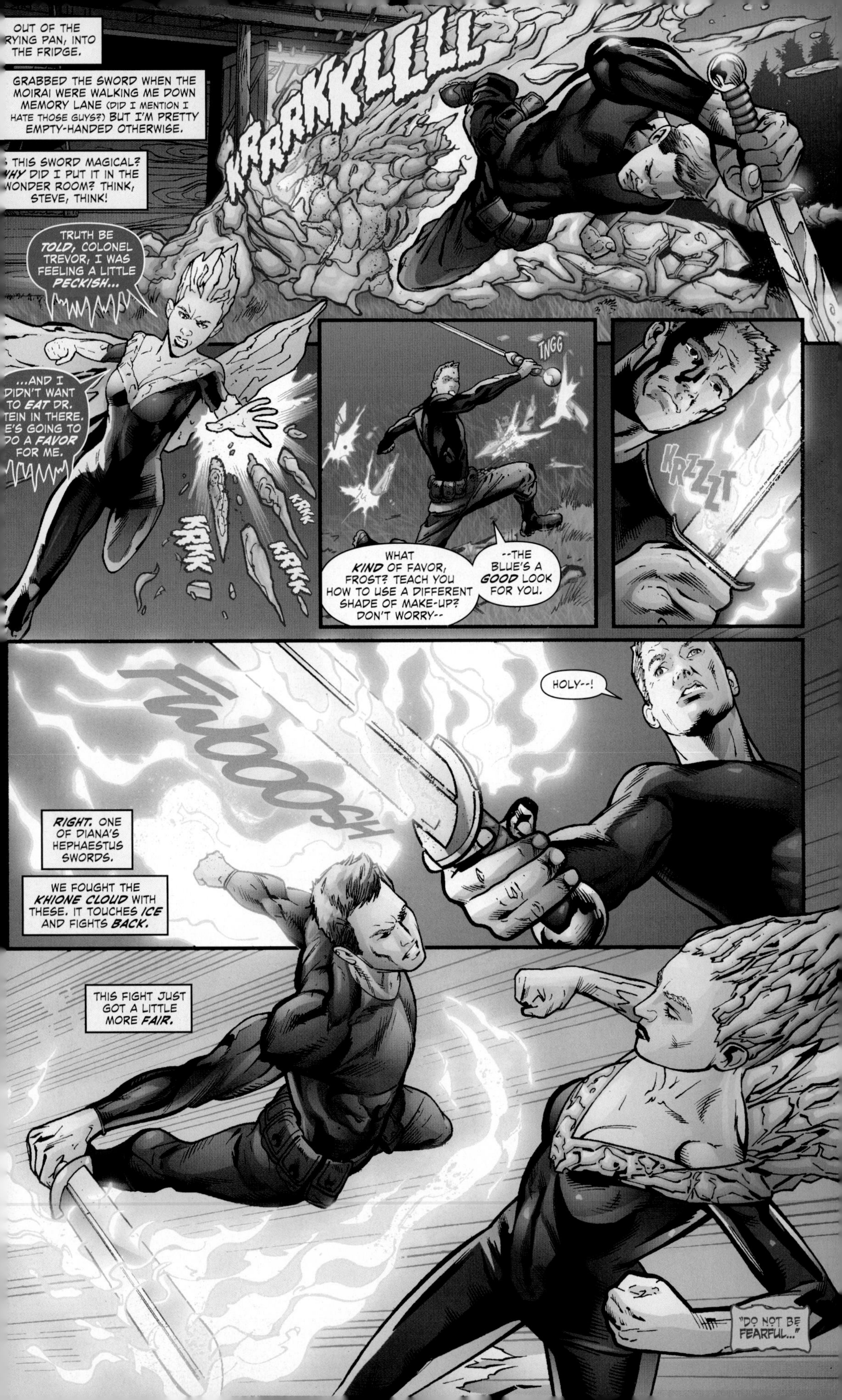

OUT OF THE
RYING PAN, INTO
THE FRIDGE.
GRABBED THE SWORD WHEN THE MOIRAI WERE WALKING ME DOWN MEMORY LANE (DID I MENTION I HATE THOSE GUYS?) BUT I'M PRETTY EMPTY-HANDED OTHERWISE.
S THIS SWORD MAGICAL? WHY DID I PUT IT IN THE WONDER ROOM? THINK, STEVE, THINK!
KRRRKKLLLL
TRUTH BE TOLD, COLONEL TREVOR, I WAS FEELING A LITTLE PECKISH...
...AND I DIDN'T WANT TO EAT DR. TEIN IN THERE. E'S GOING TO DO A FAVOR FOR ME.
KRKK
KRKK
KRKK
TNGG
WHAT KIND OF FAVOR, FROST? TEACH YOU HOW TO USE A DIFFERENT SHADE OF MAKE-UP? DON'T WORRY--
--THE BLUE'S A GOOD LOOK FOR YOU.
KRZZZT
FWOOOSH
HOLY--!
RIGHT. ONE OF DIANA'S HEPHAESTUS SWORDS.
WE FOUGHT THE KHIONE CLOUD WITH THESE. IT TOUCHES ICE AND FIGHTS BACK.
THIS FIGHT JUST GOT A LITTLE MORE FAIR.
"DO NOT BE FEARFUL..."

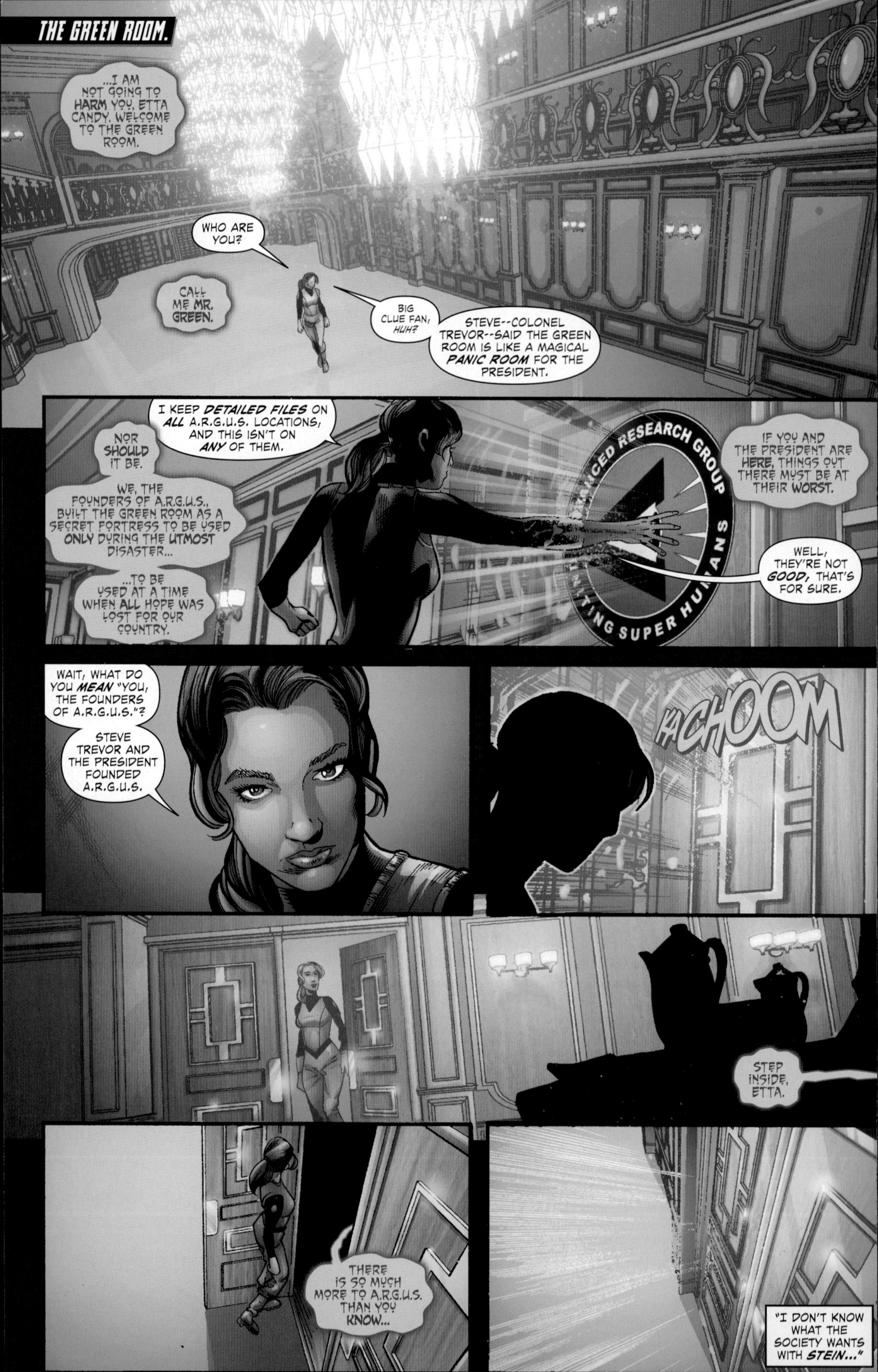
THE GREEN ROOM.
...I AM NOT GOING TO HARM YOU, ETTA CANDY. WELCOME TO THE GREEN ROOM.
WHO ARE YOU?
CALL ME MR. GREEN.
BIG CLUE FAN, HUH?
STEVE--COLONEL TREVOR--SAID THE GREEN ROOM IS LIKE A MAGICAL PANIC ROOM FOR THE PRESIDENT.
I KEEP DETAILED FILES ON ALL A.R.G.U.S. LOCATIONS, AND THIS ISN'T ON ANY OF THEM.
NOR SHOULD IT BE.
WE, THE FOUNDERS OF A.R.G.U.S., BUILT THE GREEN ROOM AS A SECRET FORTRESS TO BE USED ONLY DURING THE UTMOST DISASTER...
...TO BE USED AT A TIME WHEN ALL HOPE WAS LOST FOR OUR COUNTRY.
IF YOU AND THE PRESIDENT ARE HERE, THINGS OUT THERE MUST BE AT THEIR WORST.
WELL, THEY'RE NOT GOOD, THAT'S FOR SURE.
WAIT, WHAT DO YOU MEAN "YOU, THE FOUNDERS OF A.R.G.U.S."?
STEVE TREVOR AND THE PRESIDENT FOUNDED A.R.G.U.S.
KACHOOM
STEP INSIDE, ETTA.
THERE IS SO MUCH MORE TO A.R.G.U.S. THAN YOU KNOW...
"I DON'T KNOW WHAT THE SOCIETY WANTS WITH STEIN..."

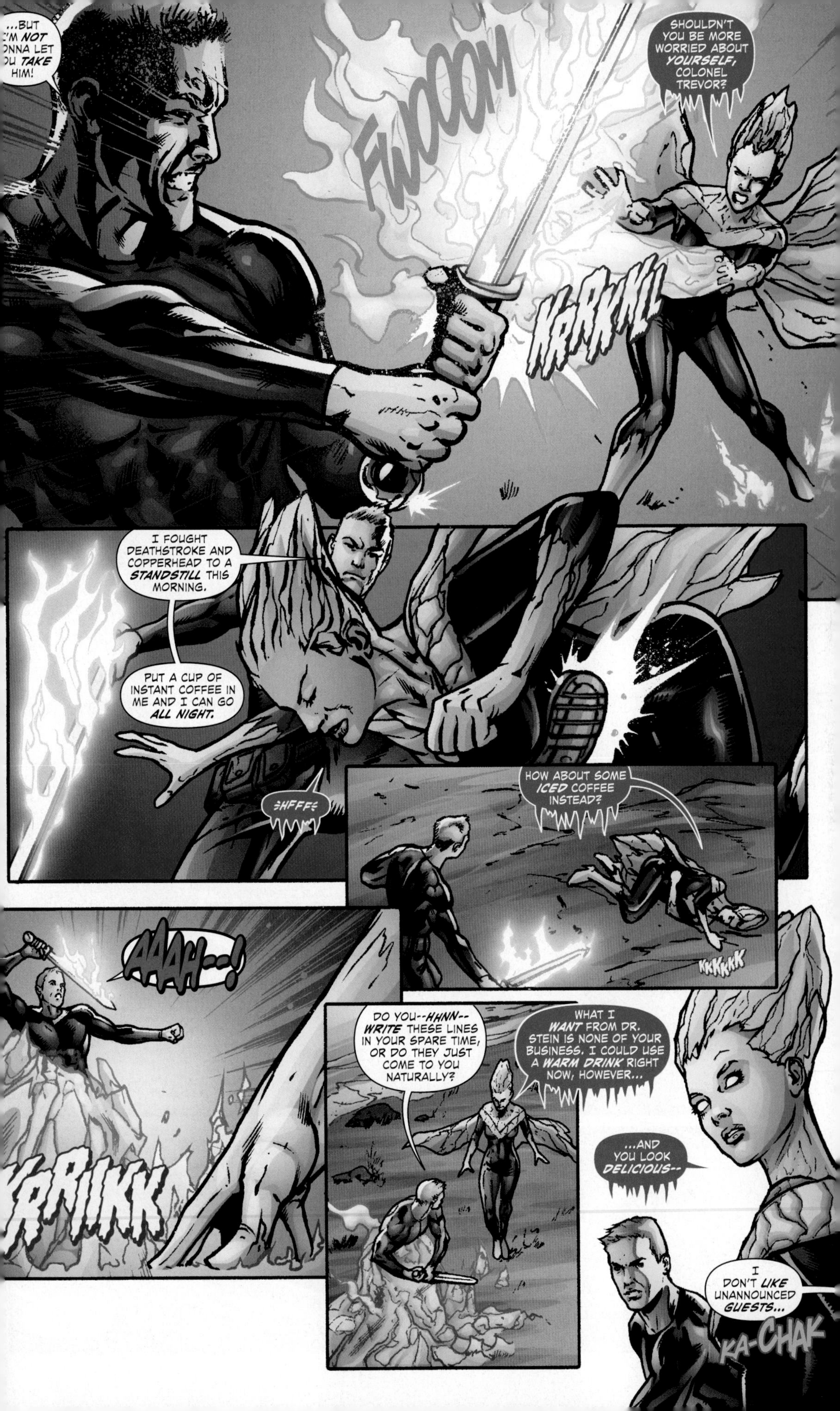

...BUT I'M NOT GONNA LET YOU TAKE HIM!
FWOOOM
SHOULDN'T YOU BE MORE WORRIED ABOUT YOURSELF, COLONEL TREVOR?
KRRKKL
I FOUGHT DEATHSTROKE AND COPPERHEAD TO A STANDSTILL THIS MORNING.
PUT A CUP OF INSTANT COFFEE IN ME AND I CAN GO ALL NIGHT.
HFFF
HOW ABOUT SOME ICED COFFEE INSTEAD?
KKKKKK
AAAH--!
KRRIKK
DO YOU--HHNN--WRITE THESE LINES IN YOUR SPARE TIME, OR DO THEY JUST COME TO YOU NATURALLY?
WHAT I WANT FROM DR. STEIN IS NONE OF YOUR BUSINESS. I COULD USE A WARM DRINK RIGHT NOW, HOWEVER...
...AND YOU LOOK DELICIOUS--
I DON'T LIKE UNANNOUNCED GUESTS...
KA-CHAK

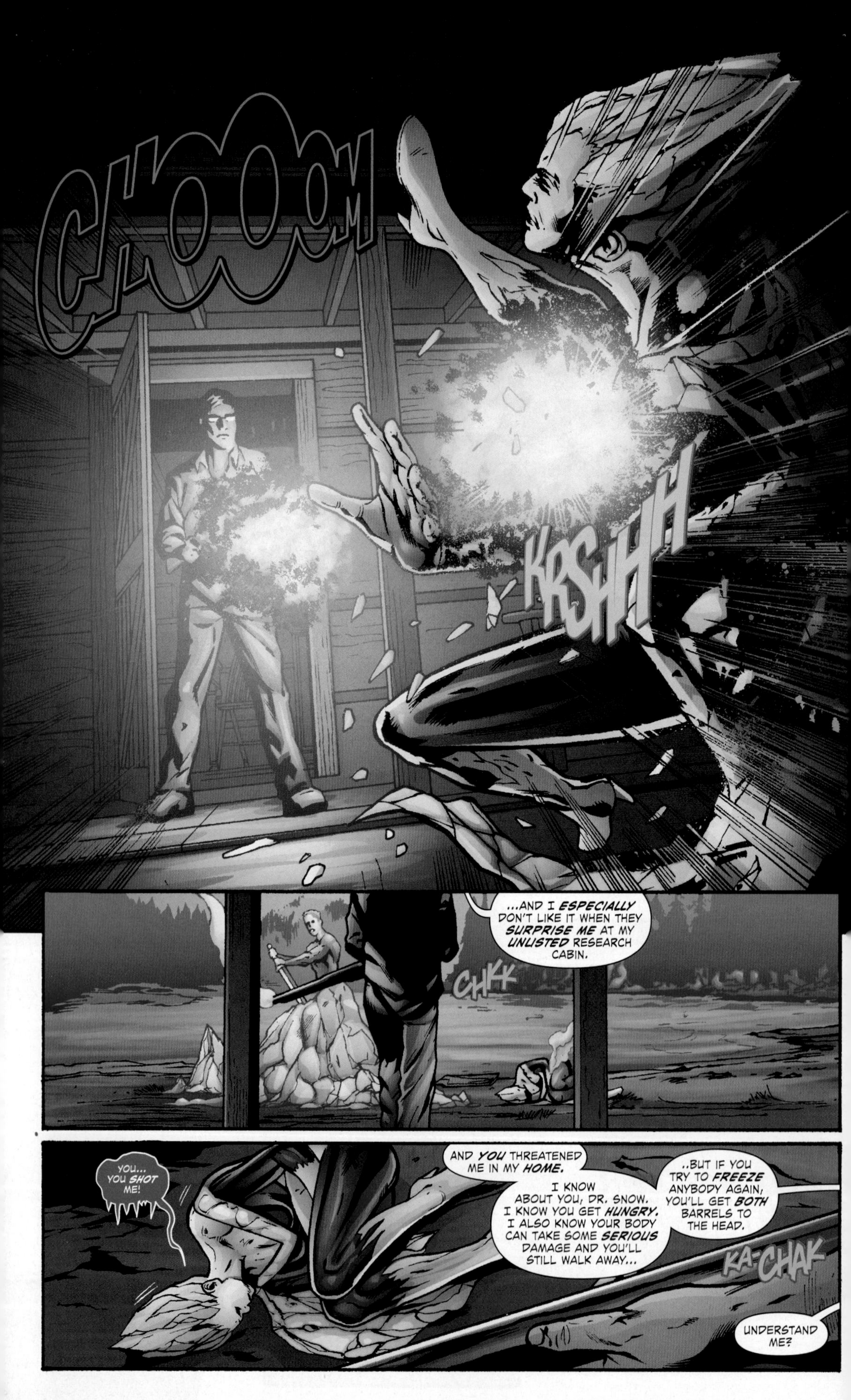

CHOOOOM
KRSHHH
...AND I ESPECIALLY DON'T LIKE IT WHEN THEY SURPRISE ME AT MY UNLISTED RESEARCH CABIN.
CHKK
YOU... YOU SHOT ME!
AND YOU THREATENED ME IN MY HOME.
I KNOW ABOUT YOU, DR. SNOW. I KNOW YOU GET HUNGRY. I ALSO KNOW YOUR BODY CAN TAKE SOME SERIOUS DAMAGE AND YOU'LL STILL WALK AWAY...
..BUT IF YOU TRY TO FREEZE ANYBODY AGAIN, YOU'LL GET BOTH BARRELS TO THE HEAD.
KA-CHAK
UNDERSTAND ME?

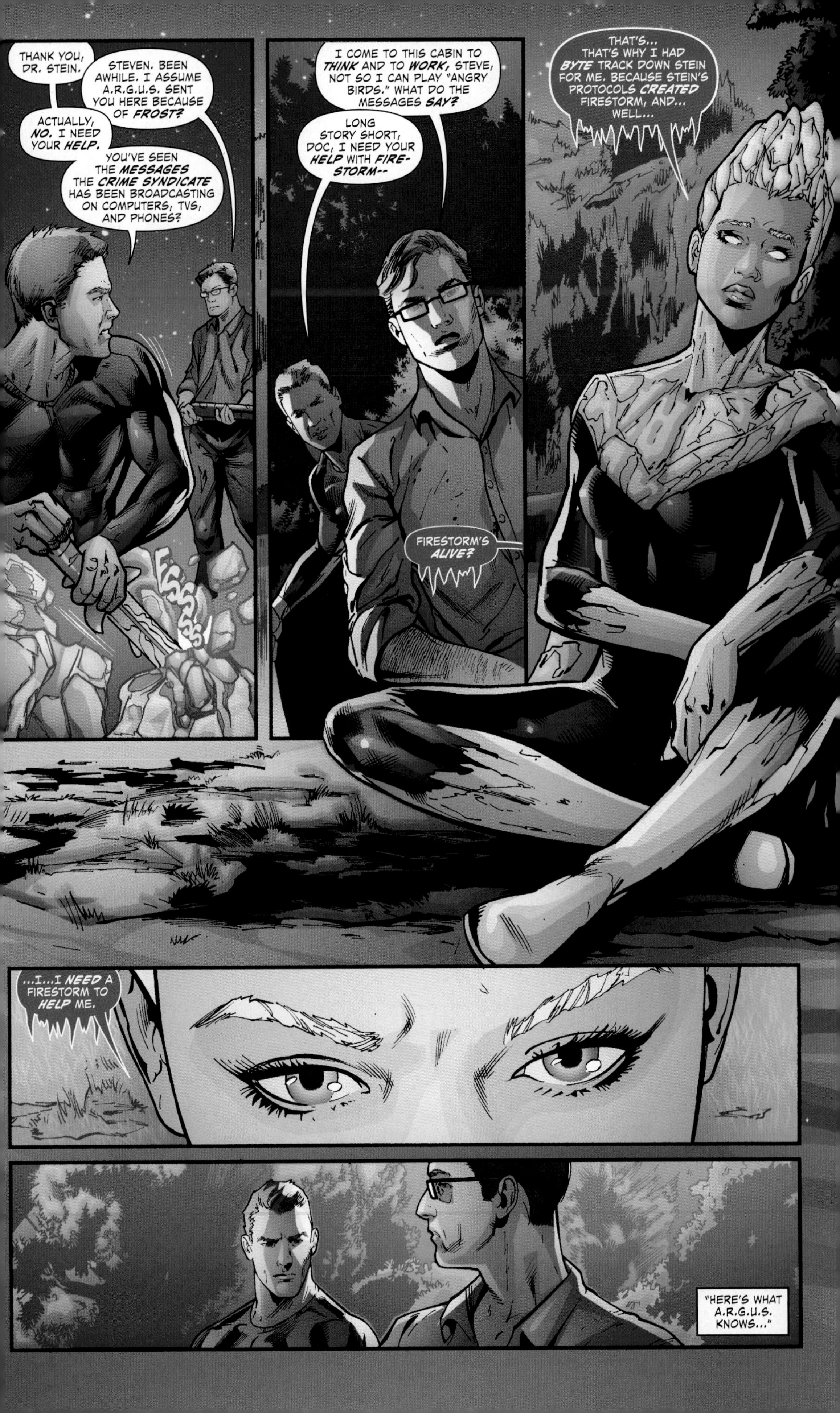
THANK YOU, DR. STEIN.
STEVEN. BEEN AWHILE. I ASSUME A.R.G.U.S. SENT YOU HERE BECAUSE OF FROST?
ACTUALLY, NO. I NEED YOUR HELP.
YOU'VE SEEN THE MESSAGES THE CRIME SYNDICATE HAS BEEN BROADCASTING ON COMPUTERS, TVS, AND PHONES?
I COME TO THIS CABIN TO THINK AND TO WORK, STEVE, NOT SO I CAN PLAY "ANGRY BIRDS." WHAT DO THE MESSAGES SAY?
LONG STORY SHORT, DOC, I NEED YOUR HELP WITH FIRE-STORM--
FIRESTORM'S ALIVE?
THAT'S... THAT'S WHY I HAD BYTE TRACK DOWN STEIN FOR ME. BECAUSE STEIN'S PROTOCOLS CREATED FIRESTORM, AND... WELL...
...I...I NEED A FIRESTORM TO HELP ME.
"HERE'S WHAT A.R.G.U.S. KNOWS..."

...THE SYNDICATE HAS SOMEHOW *TRAPPED* THE JUSTICE LEAGUES--REGULAR, "DARK," AND "OF AMERICA"-- INSIDE FIRESTORM, SO IT'S A *SAFE BET* THEY'RE KEEPING HIM ALIVE.

WE FIND OUT *WHERE* HE IS, WE GET IN, WE GET HIM *OUT,* AND THEN FIGURE OUT A WAY TO OPEN HIM *UP* AND FREE DIANA-- UM, THE JUSTICE LEAGUES.

AND THREE MAGICAL BLIND WITCHES WHO LIVE IN A MAGIC MIRROR IN THE BACK OF A CLOSET TOLD YOU THAT, SO YOU JUST *BELIEVE* THEM?

THE MOIRAI CAN'T LIE ONCE A DEAL HAS BEEN *STRUCK,* FROST, SO, *YES,* I DO.

AND *WATCH* YOUR TONE WITH ME. I TRUST YOU AS FAR AS I TRUST MY LANDLADY AND YOU'VE ALREADY TRIED TO KILL ME *ONCE* TODAY, SO YOU'RE ON THIN IC--

--UGH. NEVER MIND.

SO *HOW DO* WE *FIND* HIM?

I WAS *AT* THE SYNDICATE'S *RALLY.* I SAW THE KIND OF *FIRE-POWER* THEY'RE PACKING. THEY'RE *NOT* MESSING AROUND.

EVEN IF WE *DO* FIND HIM, HOW DO WE OPEN HIM *UP*--

DAMMIT.

DOCTOR?

YOU'RE ALL MISSIN' THE *REALLY IMPORTANT* THING RIGHT IN FRONT OF YOU.

THE *QUANTUM FIELD*--WHAT'S BEEN NICKNAME 'THE FIRESTORM MATRIX"--IS COMPOSED OF *TWO PEOPLE.*

THEIR *FUSION* IS WHAT *FORMS* FIRESTORM.

IT'S THE *CAREFUL* BALANCE BETWEEN TWO PEOPLE WHICH ALLOWS FIRESTORM ACCESS TO THE QUANTUM ENERGIES...THUS ALLOWING HIM TO *ALTER* ATOMIC CHARACTERISTICS.

WHEN THE TWO OF THEM GO OUT OF BALANCE, IT CAN CAUSE PROBLEM' *UNKNOWN*--AND WE G THINGS LIKE THE *FUR* EVENT IN WALTON MILLS LAST YEAR.

$$dV = n \int_{T_i}^{T_f} C_v \, dT = n\bar{C}_v (T_i - T_f) \approx Q_t \left(1 - \frac{T_f}{T_i}\right) = Q - q$$

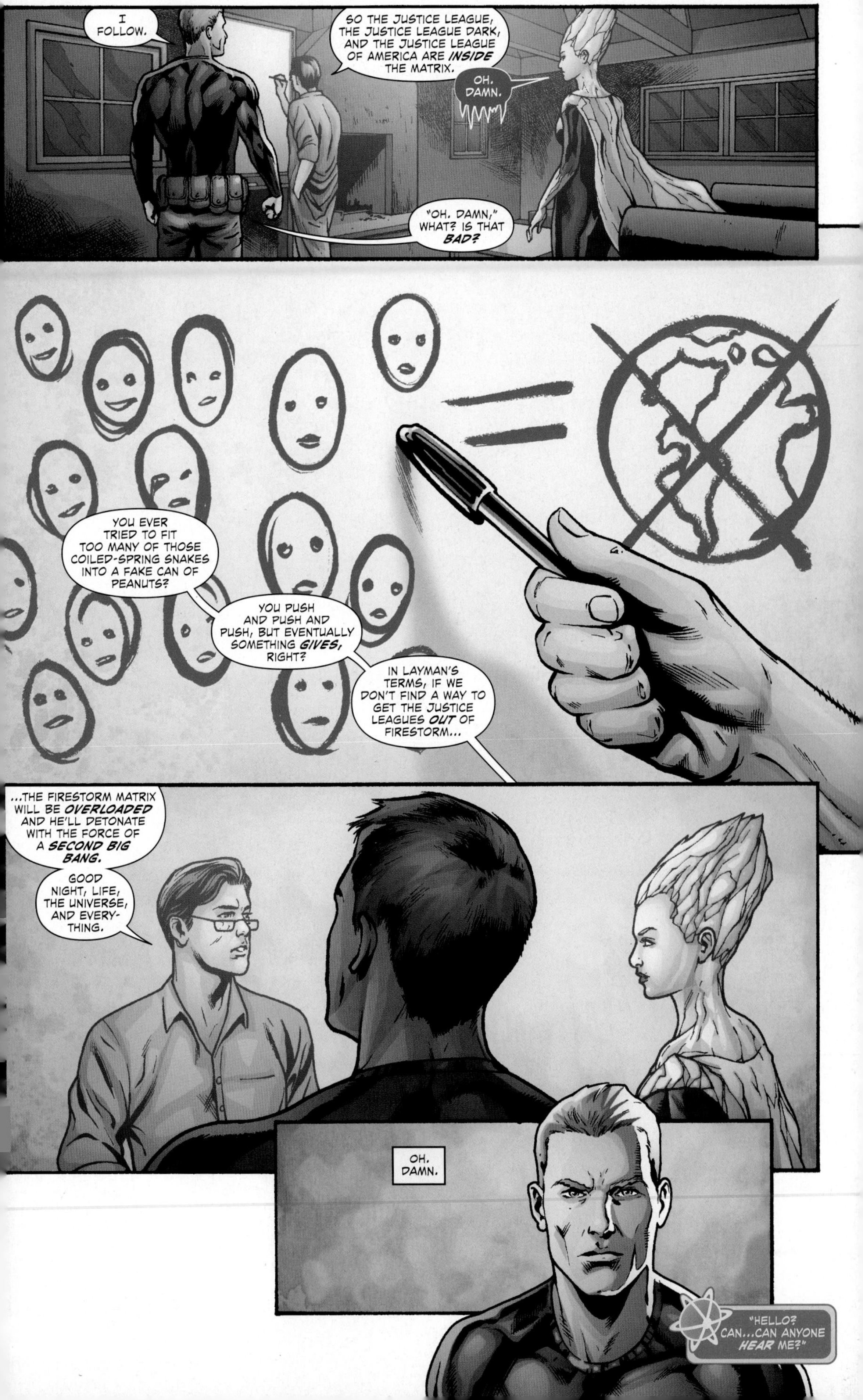
I FOLLOW.
SO THE JUSTICE LEAGUE, THE JUSTICE LEAGUE DARK, AND THE JUSTICE LEAGUE OF AMERICA ARE INSIDE THE MATRIX.
OH. DAMN.
"OH. DAMN," WHAT? IS THAT BAD?
YOU EVER TRIED TO FIT TOO MANY OF THOSE COILED-SPRING SNAKES INTO A FAKE CAN OF PEANUTS?
YOU PUSH AND PUSH AND PUSH, BUT EVENTUALLY SOMETHING GIVES, RIGHT?
IN LAYMAN'S TERMS, IF WE DON'T FIND A WAY TO GET THE JUSTICE LEAGUES OUT OF FIRESTORM...
...THE FIRESTORM MATRIX WILL BE OVERLOADED AND HE'LL DETONATE WITH THE FORCE OF A SECOND BIG BANG.
GOOD NIGHT, LIFE, THE UNIVERSE, AND EVERY-THING.
OH. DAMN.
"HELLO? CAN...CAN ANYONE HEAR ME?"

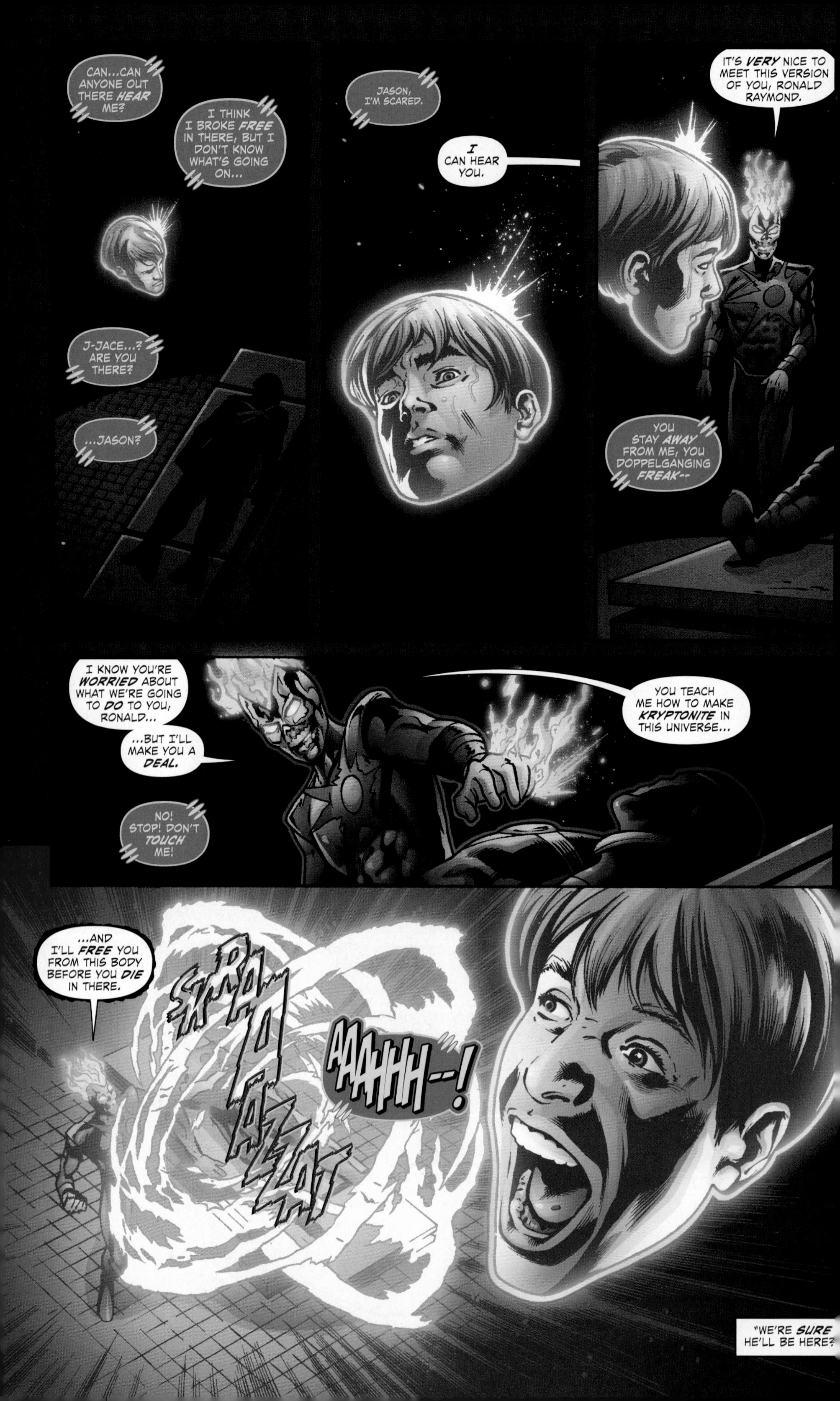
CAN...CAN ANYONE OUT THERE HEAR ME?
I THINK I BROKE FREE IN THERE, BUT I DON'T KNOW WHAT'S GOING ON...
J-JACE...? ARE YOU THERE?
...JASON?
JASON, I'M SCARED.
I CAN HEAR YOU.
IT'S VERY NICE TO MEET THIS VERSION OF YOU, RONALD RAYMOND.
YOU STAY AWAY FROM ME, YOU DOPPELGANGING FREAK--
I KNOW YOU'RE WORRIED ABOUT WHAT WE'RE GOING TO DO TO YOU, RONALD...
...BUT I'LL MAKE YOU A DEAL.
YOU TEACH ME HOW TO MAKE KRYPTONITE IN THIS UNIVERSE...
NO! STOP! DON'T TOUCH ME!
...AND I'LL FREE YOU FROM THIS BODY BEFORE YOU DIE IN THERE.
SKRAZAZZAT
AAAHHH--!
"WE'RE SURE HE'LL BE HERE?

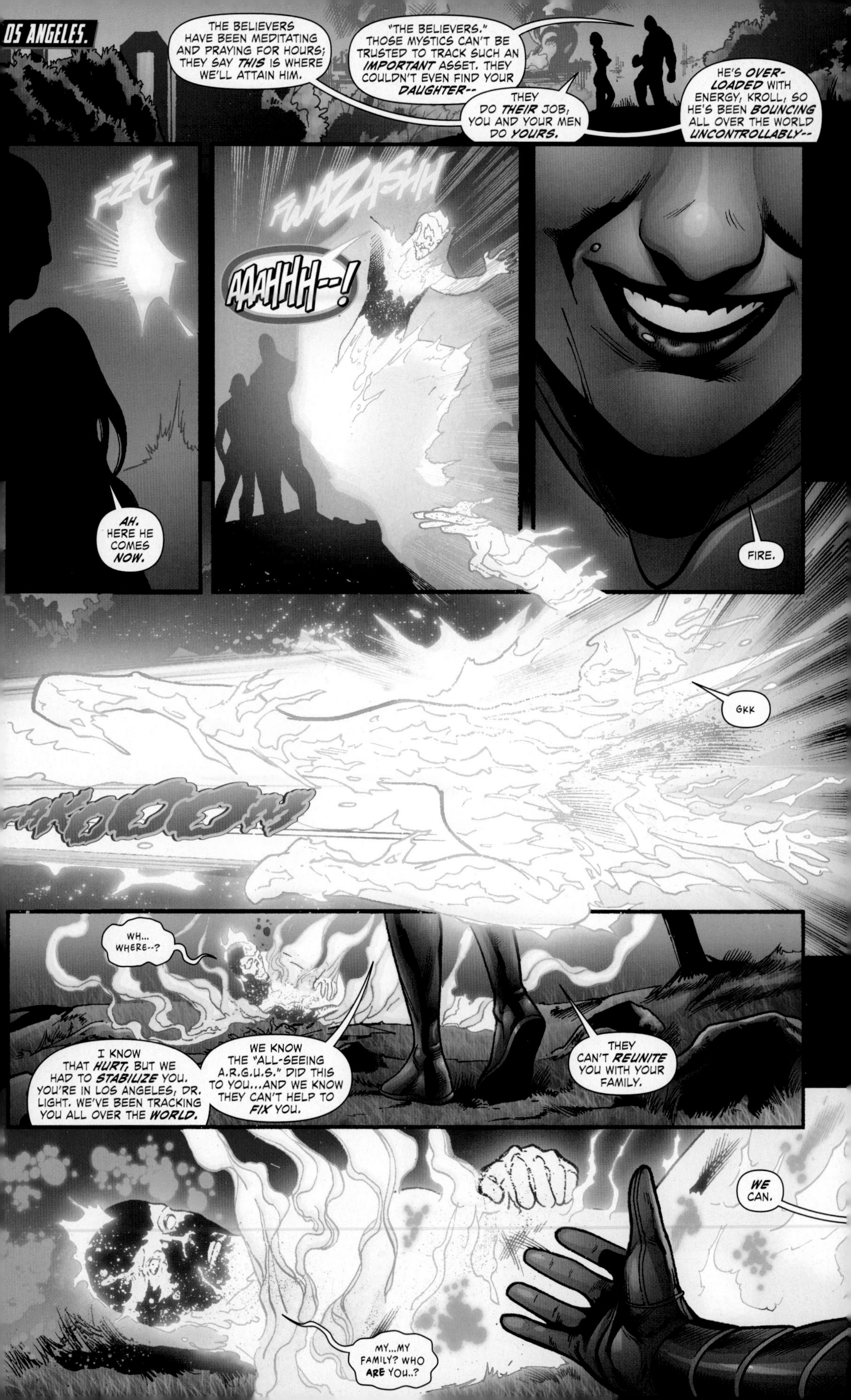
OS ANGELES.
THE BELIEVERS HAVE BEEN MEDITATING AND PRAYING FOR HOURS; THEY SAY THIS IS WHERE WE'LL ATTAIN HIM.
"THE BELIEVERS." THOSE MYSTICS CAN'T BE TRUSTED TO TRACK SUCH AN IMPORTANT ASSET. THEY COULDN'T EVEN FIND YOUR DAUGHTER--
THEY DO THEIR JOB, YOU AND YOUR MEN DO YOURS.
HE'S OVER-LOADED WITH ENERGY, KROLL, SO HE'S BEEN BOUNCING ALL OVER THE WORLD UNCONTROLLABLY--
FZZT
AH. HERE HE COMES NOW.
FWAZASHH
AAAHHH--!
FIRE.
GKK
FAKOOOM
WH... WHERE--?
I KNOW THAT HURT, BUT WE HAD TO STABILIZE YOU. YOU'RE IN LOS ANGELES, DR. LIGHT. WE'VE BEEN TRACKING YOU ALL OVER THE WORLD.
WE KNOW THE "ALL-SEEING A.R.G.U.S." DID THIS TO YOU...AND WE KNOW THEY CAN'T HELP TO FIX YOU.
THEY CAN'T REUNITE YOU WITH YOUR FAMILY.
WE CAN.
MY...MY FAMILY? WHO ARE YOU..?

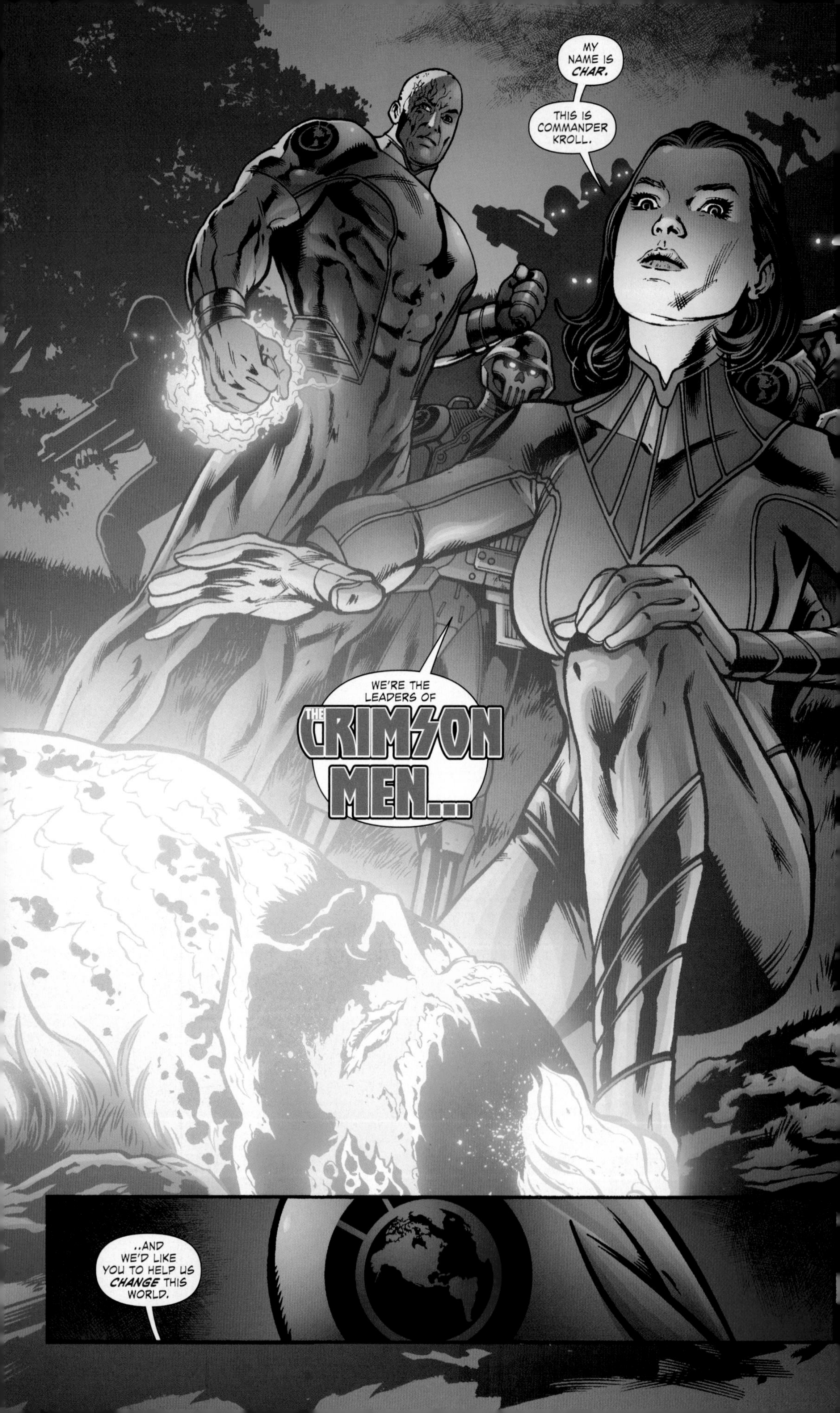
MY NAME IS CHAR.
THIS IS COMMANDER KROLL.
WE'RE THE LEADERS OF THE CRIMSON MEN...
..AND WE'D LIKE YOU TO HELP US CHANGE THIS WORLD.

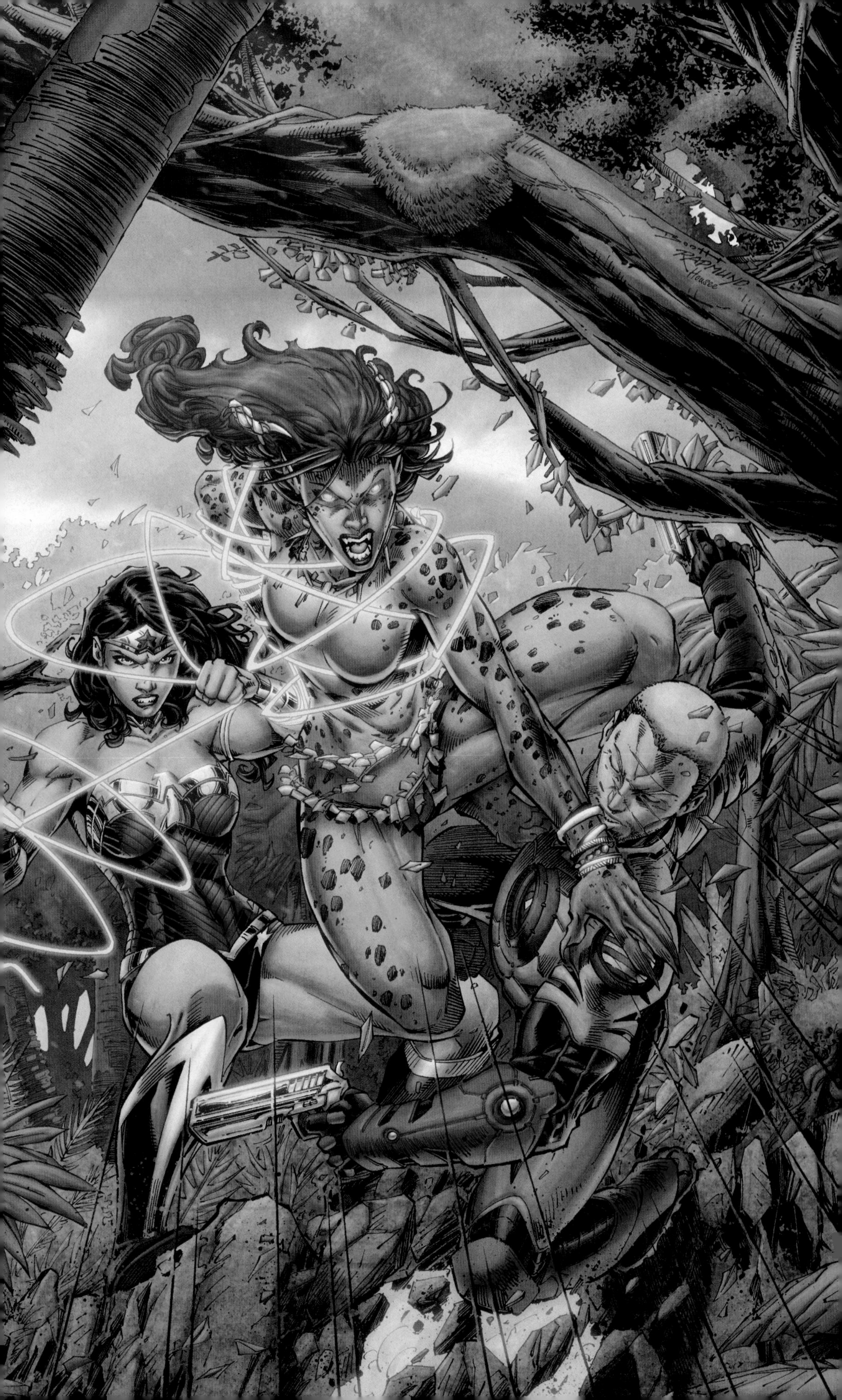

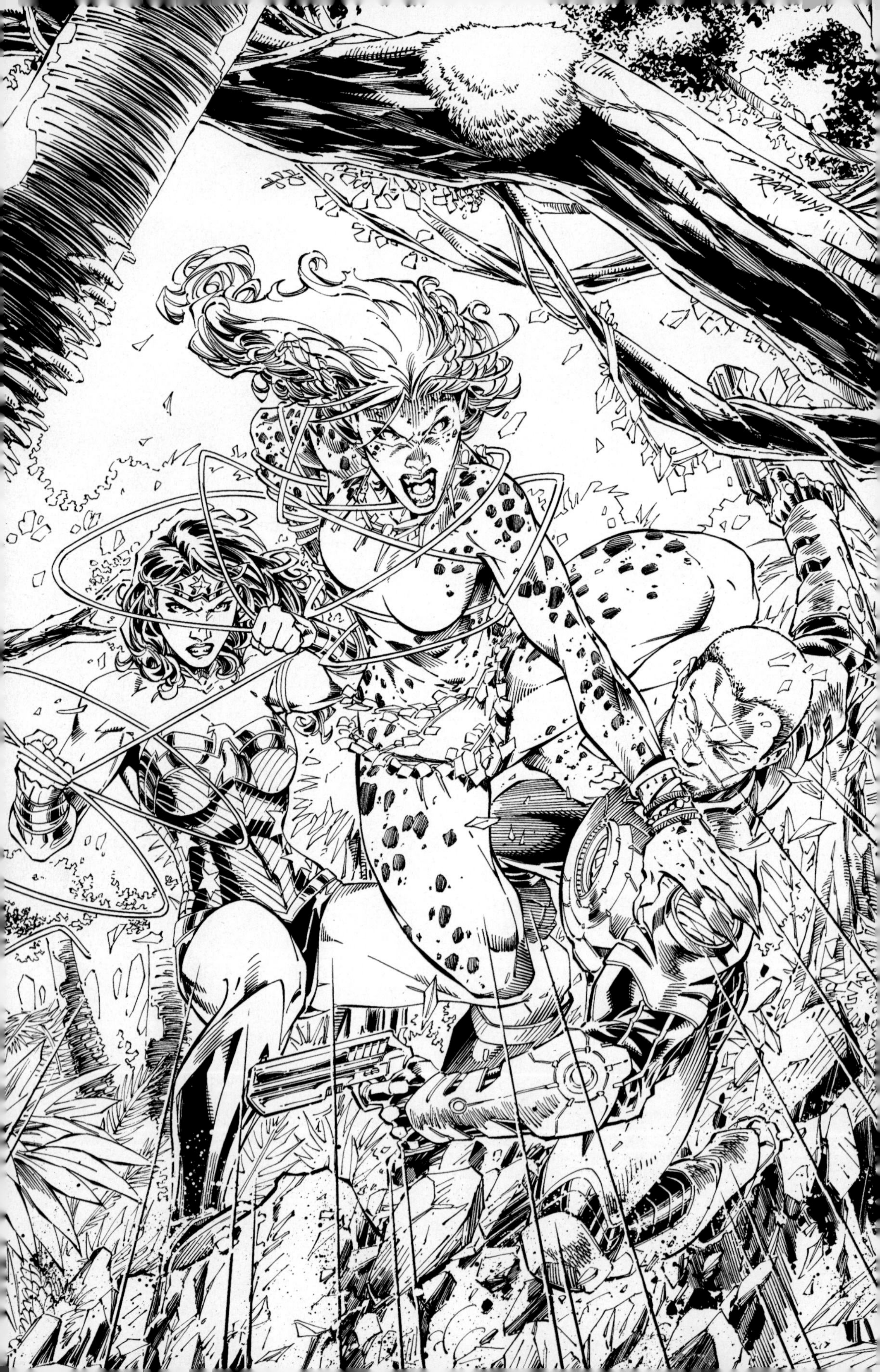

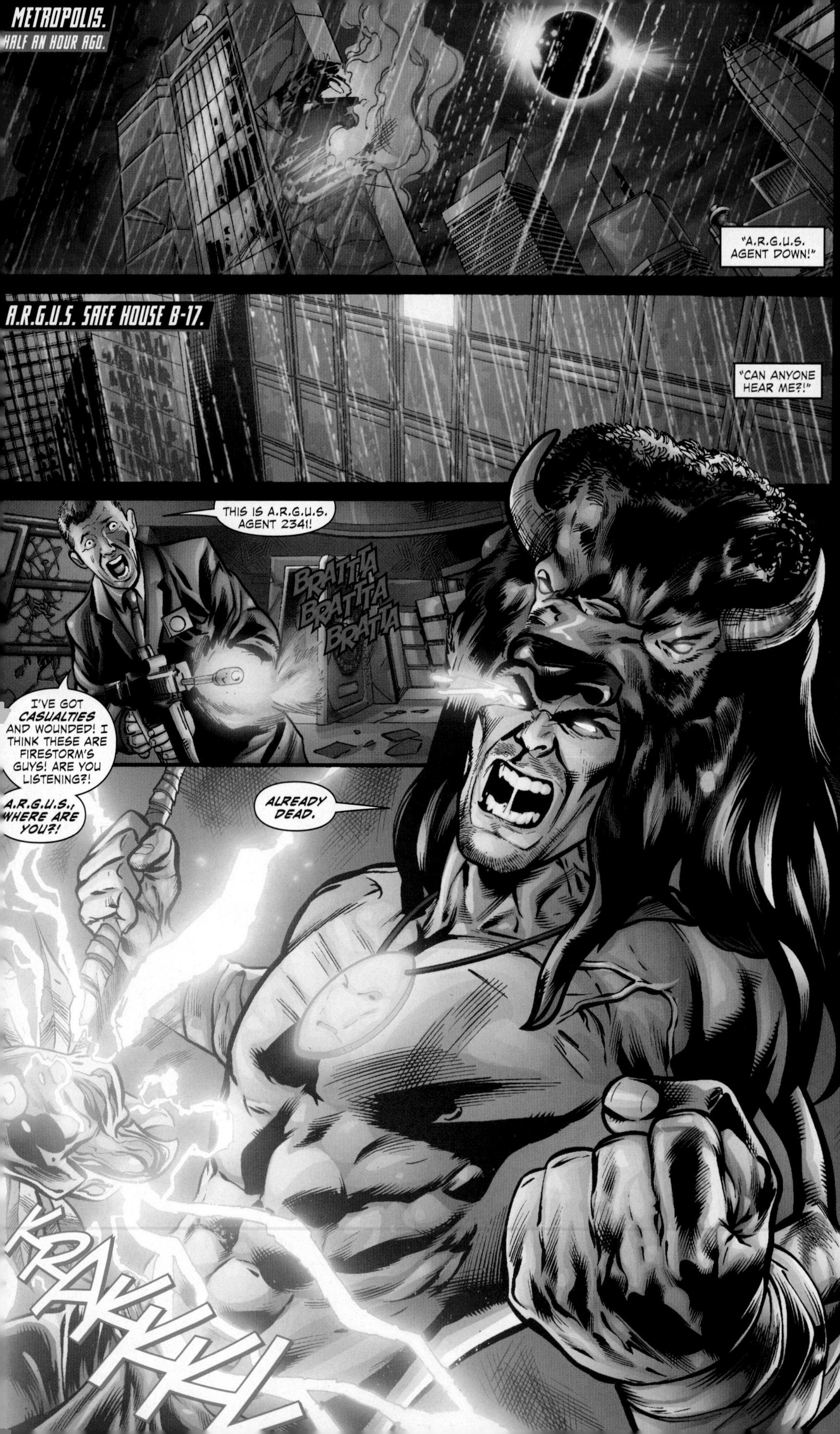
METROPOLIS.
HALF AN HOUR AGO.
"A.R.G.U.S. AGENT DOWN!"
A.R.G.U.S. SAFE HOUSE B-17.
"CAN ANYONE HEAR ME?!"
THIS IS A.R.G.U.S. AGENT 2341!
BRATTTA BRATTTA BRATTTA
I'VE GOT CASUALTIES AND WOUNDED! I THINK THESE ARE FIRESTORM'S GUYS! ARE YOU LISTENING?!
A.R.G.U.S., WHERE ARE YOU?!
ALREADY DEAD.
KRAKKKL

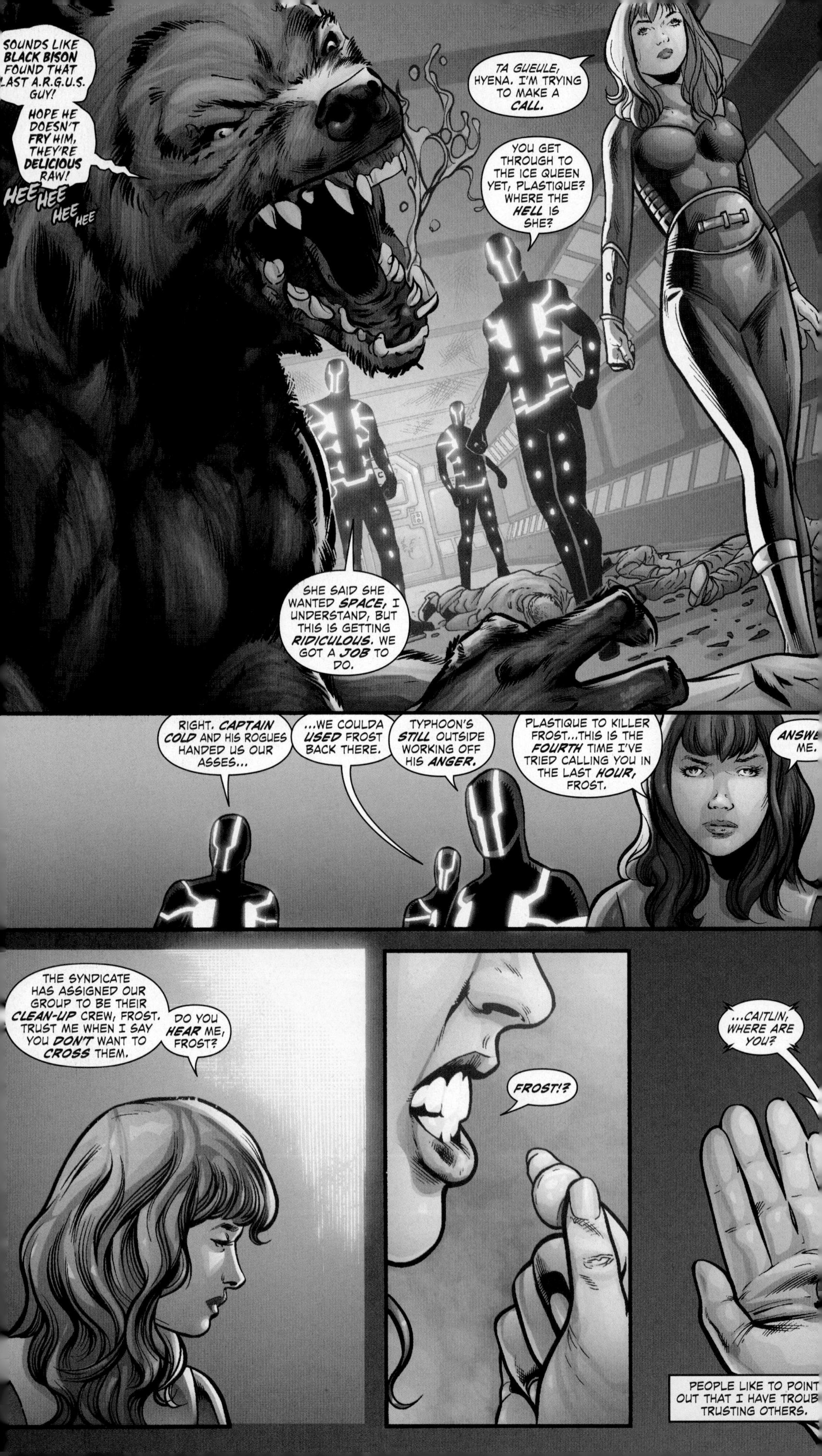

SOUNDS LIKE BLACK BISON FOUND THAT LAST A.R.G.U.S. GUY!
HOPE HE DOESN'T FRY HIM, THEY'RE DELICIOUS RAW!
HEE HEE HEE HEE
TA GUEULE, HYENA. I'M TRYING TO MAKE A CALL.
YOU GET THROUGH TO THE ICE QUEEN YET, PLASTIQUE? WHERE THE HELL IS SHE?
SHE SAID SHE WANTED SPACE, I UNDERSTAND, BUT THIS IS GETTING RIDICULOUS. WE GOT A JOB TO DO.
RIGHT. CAPTAIN COLD AND HIS ROGUES HANDED US OUR ASSES...
...WE COULDA USED FROST BACK THERE.
TYPHOON'S STILL OUTSIDE WORKING OFF HIS ANGER.
PLASTIQUE TO KILLER FROST...THIS IS THE FOURTH TIME I'VE TRIED CALLING YOU IN THE LAST HOUR, FROST.
ANSWE ME.
THE SYNDICATE HAS ASSIGNED OUR GROUP TO BE THEIR CLEAN-UP CREW, FROST. TRUST ME WHEN I SAY YOU DON'T WANT TO CROSS THEM.
DO YOU HEAR ME, FROST?
FROST!?
...CAITLIN, WHERE ARE YOU?
PEOPLE LIKE TO POINT OUT THAT I HAVE TROUB TRUSTING OTHERS.

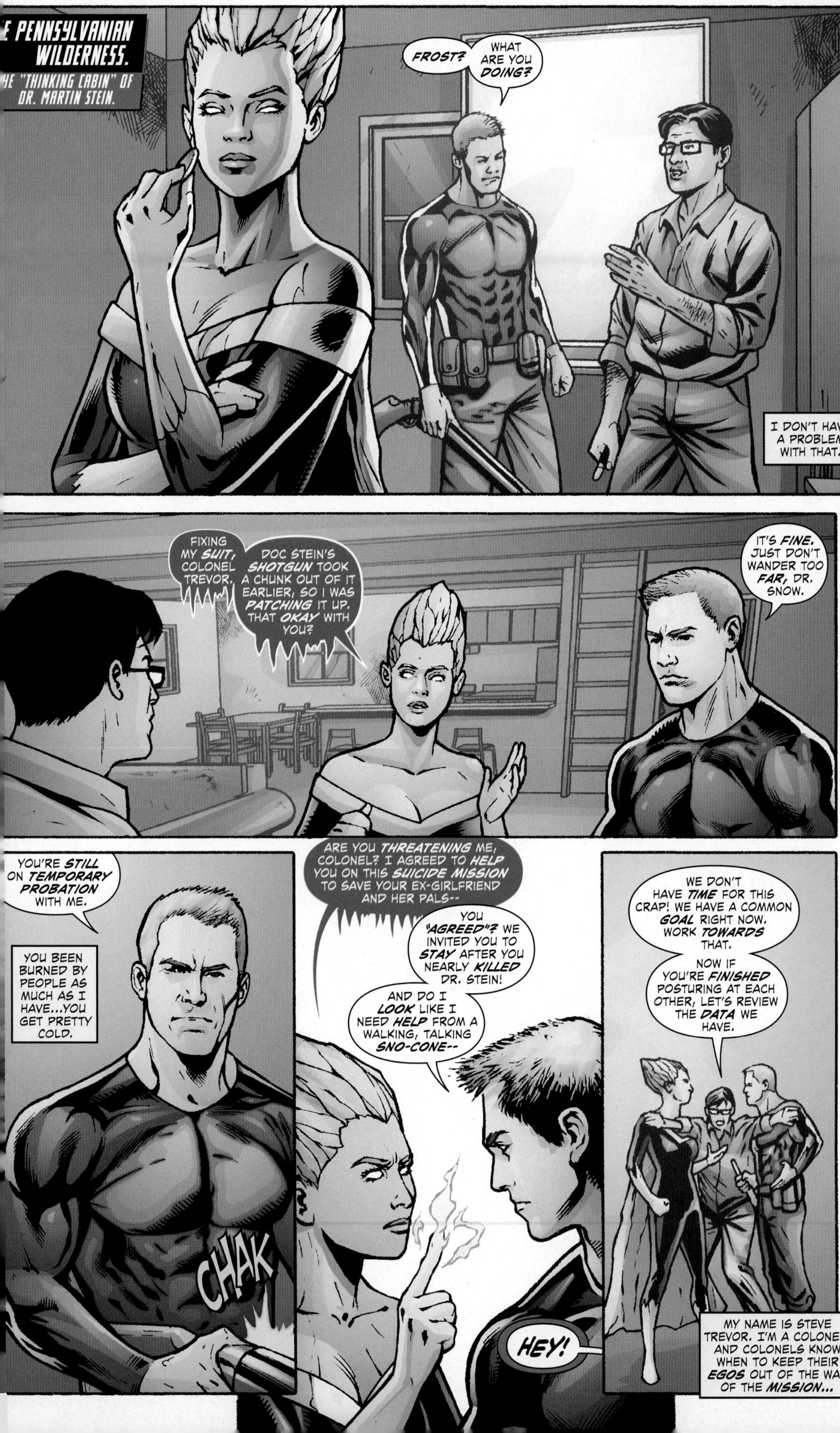
E PENNSYLVANIAN WILDERNESS.
HE "THINKING CABIN" OF DR. MARTIN STEIN.
FROST?
WHAT ARE YOU DOING?
I DON'T HAVE A PROBLEM WITH THAT.
FIXING MY SUIT, COLONEL TREVOR.
DOC STEIN'S SHOTGUN TOOK A CHUNK OUT OF IT EARLIER, SO I WAS PATCHING IT UP. THAT OKAY WITH YOU?
IT'S FINE. JUST DON'T WANDER TOO FAR, DR. SNOW.
YOU'RE STILL ON TEMPORARY PROBATION WITH ME.
YOU BEEN BURNED BY PEOPLE AS MUCH AS I HAVE...YOU GET PRETTY COLD.
CHAK
ARE YOU THREATENING ME, COLONEL? I AGREED TO HELP YOU ON THIS SUICIDE MISSION TO SAVE YOUR EX-GIRLFRIEND AND HER PALS--
YOU "AGREED"? WE INVITED YOU TO STAY AFTER YOU NEARLY KILLED DR. STEIN!
AND DO I LOOK LIKE I NEED HELP FROM A WALKING, TALKING SNO-CONE--
HEY!
WE DON'T HAVE TIME FOR THIS CRAP! WE HAVE A COMMON GOAL RIGHT NOW. WORK TOWARDS THAT.
NOW IF YOU'RE FINISHED POSTURING AT EACH OTHER, LET'S REVIEW THE DATA WE HAVE.
MY NAME IS STEVE TREVOR. I'M A COLONEL. AND COLONELS KNOW WHEN TO KEEP THEIR EGOS OUT OF THE WAY OF THE MISSION...

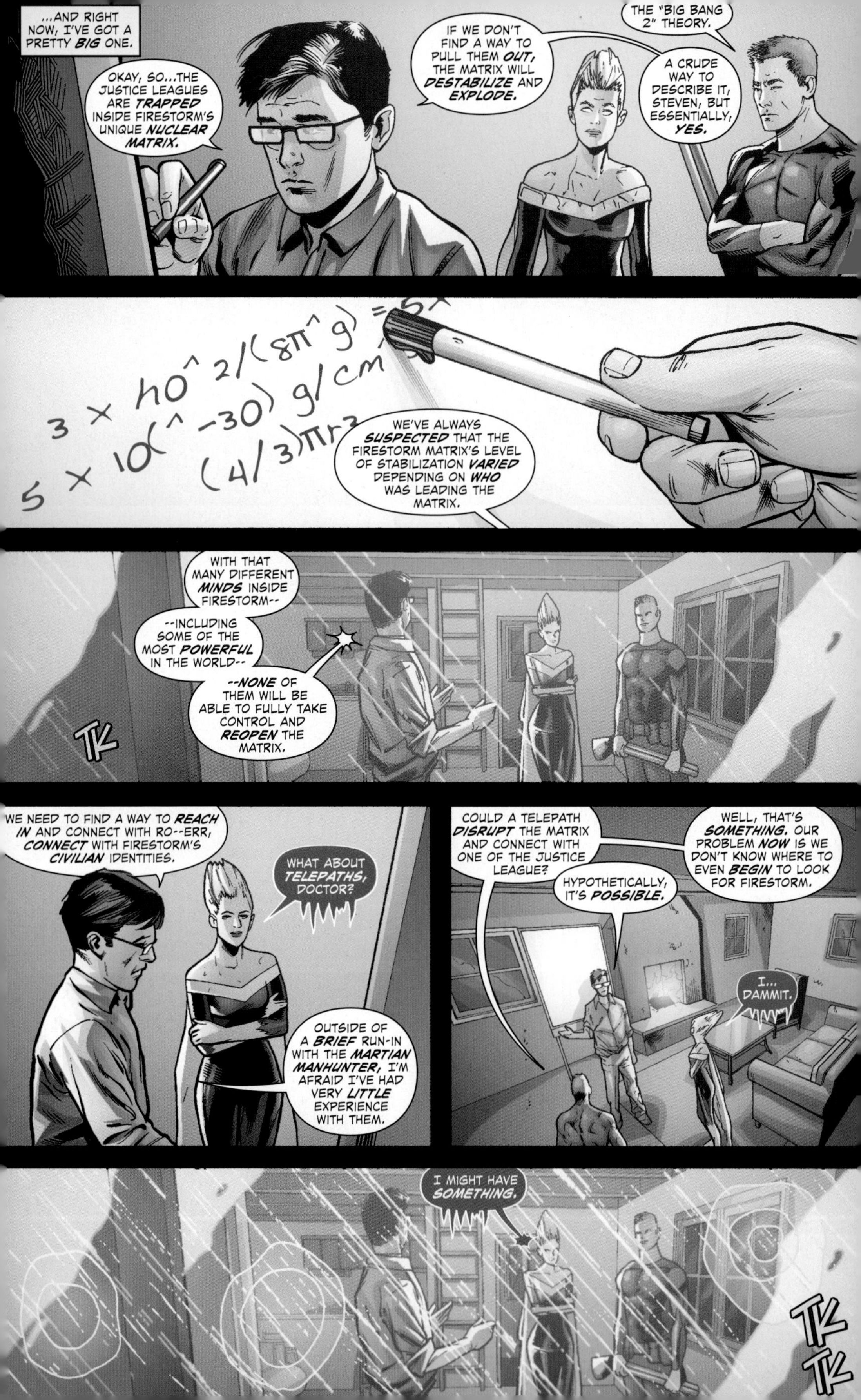
...AND RIGHT NOW, I'VE GOT A PRETTY BIG ONE.
OKAY, SO...THE JUSTICE LEAGUES ARE TRAPPED INSIDE FIRESTORM'S UNIQUE NUCLEAR MATRIX.
IF WE DON'T FIND A WAY TO PULL THEM OUT, THE MATRIX WILL DESTABILIZE AND EXPLODE.
THE "BIG BANG 2" THEORY.
A CRUDE WAY TO DESCRIBE IT, STEVEN, BUT ESSENTIALLY, YES.
3 × 10^2/(8π^g) = 5^
5 × 10(^-30) g/cm
(4/3)πr3
WE'VE ALWAYS SUSPECTED THAT THE FIRESTORM MATRIX'S LEVEL OF STABILIZATION VARIED DEPENDING ON WHO WAS LEADING THE MATRIX.
WITH THAT MANY DIFFERENT MINDS INSIDE FIRESTORM--
--INCLUDING SOME OF THE MOST POWERFUL IN THE WORLD--
--NONE OF THEM WILL BE ABLE TO FULLY TAKE CONTROL AND REOPEN THE MATRIX.
TK
WE NEED TO FIND A WAY TO REACH IN AND CONNECT WITH RO--ERR, CONNECT WITH FIRESTORM'S CIVILIAN IDENTITIES.
WHAT ABOUT TELEPATHS, DOCTOR?
OUTSIDE OF A BRIEF RUN-IN WITH THE MARTIAN MANHUNTER, I'M AFRAID I'VE HAD VERY LITTLE EXPERIENCE WITH THEM.
COULD A TELEPATH DISRUPT THE MATRIX AND CONNECT WITH ONE OF THE JUSTICE LEAGUE?
HYPOTHETICALLY, IT'S POSSIBLE.
WELL, THAT'S SOMETHING. OUR PROBLEM NOW IS WE DON'T KNOW WHERE TO EVEN BEGIN TO LOOK FOR FIRESTORM.
I... DAMMIT.
I MIGHT HAVE SOMETHING.
TK TK

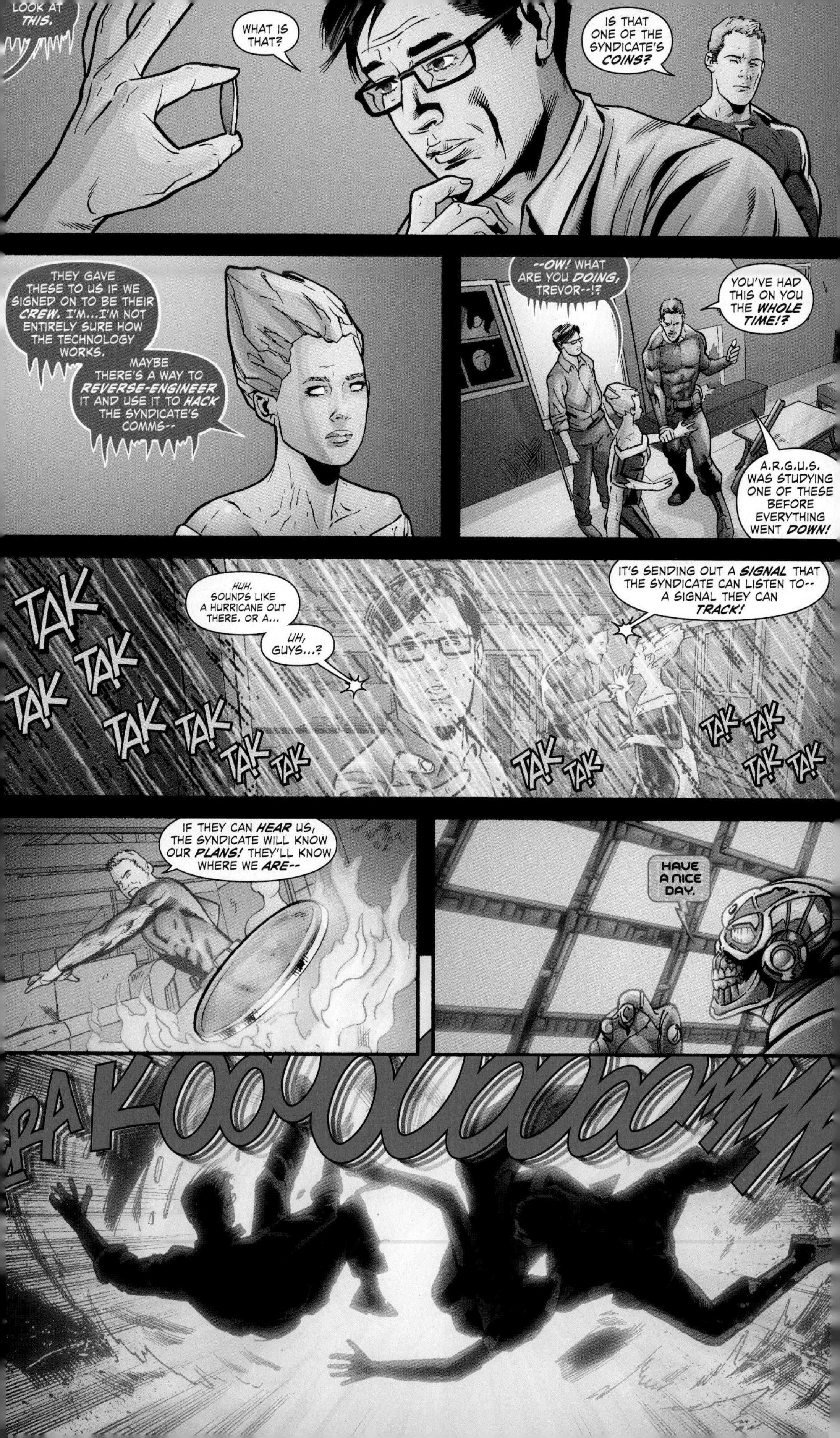

LOOK AT THIS.
WHAT IS THAT?
IS THAT ONE OF THE SYNDICATE'S COINS?
THEY GAVE THESE TO US IF WE SIGNED ON TO BE THEIR CREW. I'M...I'M NOT ENTIRELY SURE HOW THE TECHNOLOGY WORKS.
MAYBE THERE'S A WAY TO REVERSE-ENGINEER IT AND USE IT TO HACK THE SYNDICATE'S COMMS--
--OW! WHAT ARE YOU DOING, TREVOR--!?
YOU'VE HAD THIS ON YOU THE WHOLE TIME!?
A.R.G.U.S. WAS STUDYING ONE OF THESE BEFORE EVERYTHING WENT DOWN!
TAK TAK TAK TAK TAK TAK TAK
HUH. SOUNDS LIKE A HURRICANE OUT THERE. OR A...
UH, GUYS...?
IT'S SENDING OUT A SIGNAL THAT THE SYNDICATE CAN LISTEN TO-- A SIGNAL THEY CAN TRACK!
TAK TAK TAK TAK TAK TAK
IF THEY CAN HEAR US, THE SYNDICATE WILL KNOW OUR PLANS! THEY'LL KNOW WHERE WE ARE--
HAVE A NICE DAY.

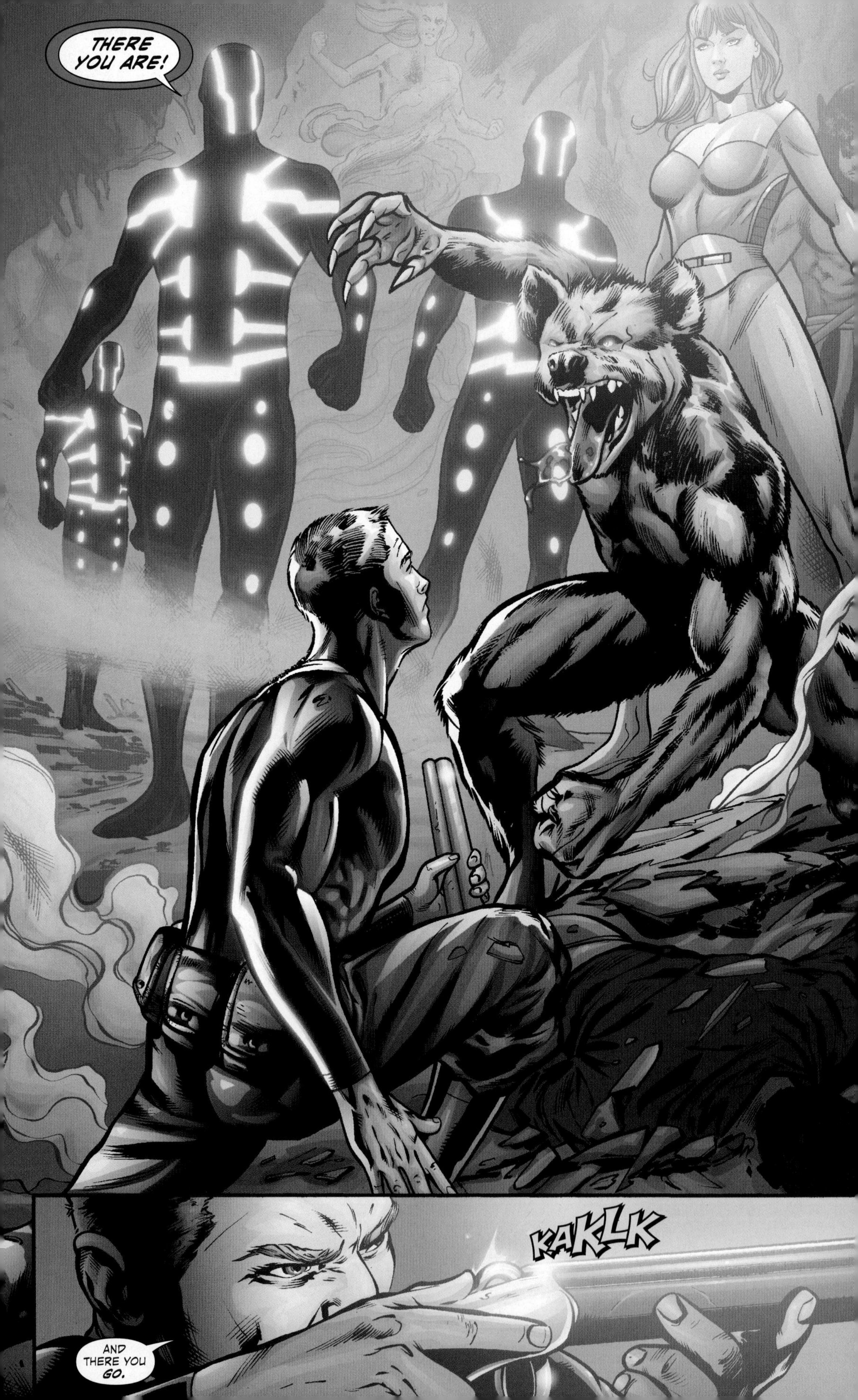
THERE YOU ARE!
KAKLK
AND THERE YOU GO.

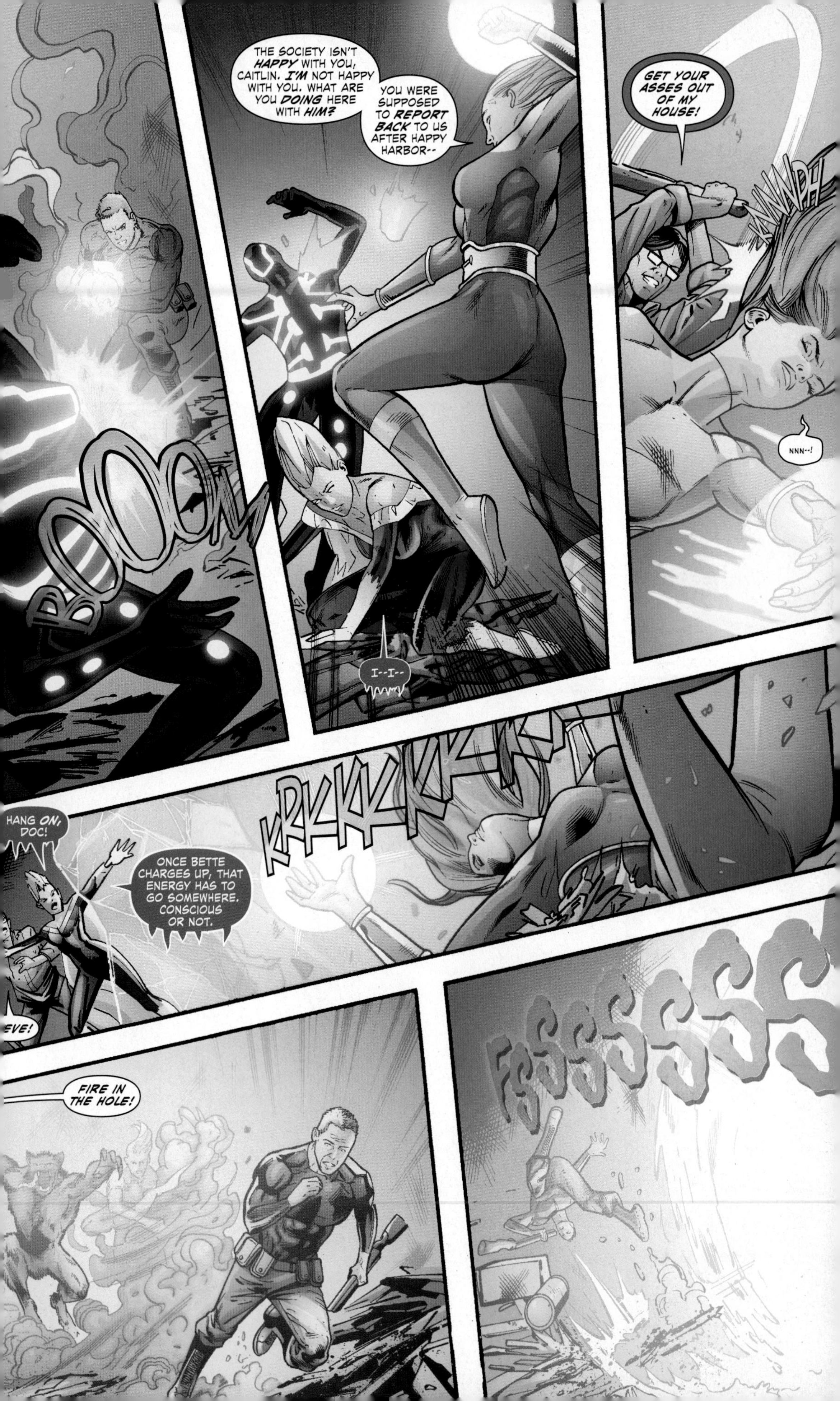

THE SOCIETY ISN'T HAPPY WITH YOU, CAITLIN. I'M NOT HAPPY WITH YOU. WHAT ARE YOU DOING HERE WITH HIM?
YOU WERE SUPPOSED TO REPORT BACK TO US AFTER HAPPY HARBOR--
GET YOUR ASSES OUT OF MY HOUSE!
KRANNNGH
NNN--!
BOOOOM
I--I--
KRKKKKKK
HANG ON, DOC!
ONCE BETTE CHARGES UP, THAT ENERGY HAS TO GO SOMEWHERE. CONSCIOUS OR NOT.
EVE!
FIRE IN THE HOLE!
FSSSSSSSS

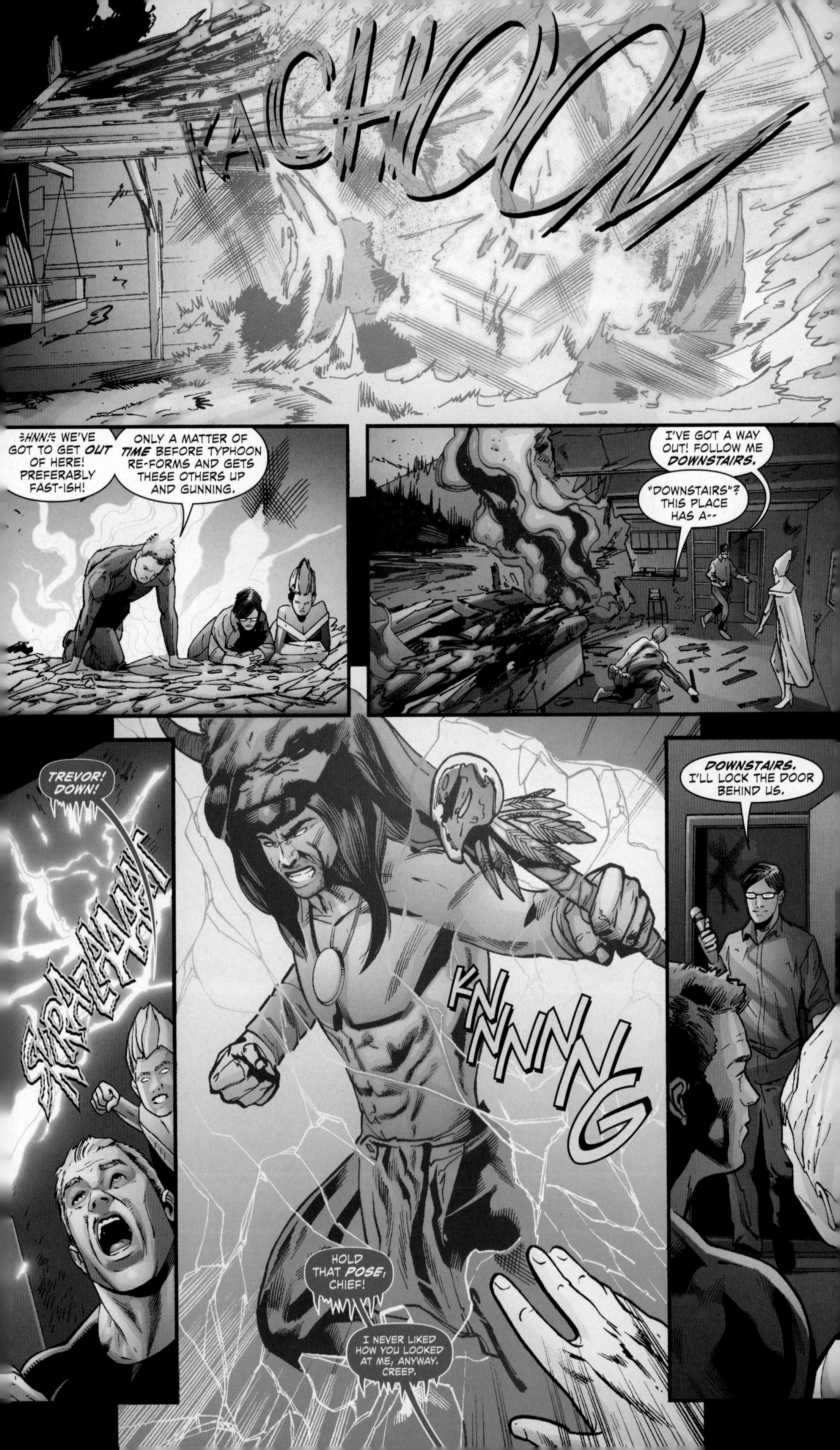
KACHOOM
GHNN! WE'VE GOT TO GET OUT OF HERE! PREFERABLY FAST-ISH!
ONLY A MATTER OF TIME BEFORE TYPHOON RE-FORMS AND GETS THESE OTHERS UP AND GUNNING.
I'VE GOT A WAY OUT! FOLLOW ME DOWNSTAIRS.
"DOWNSTAIRS"? THIS PLACE HAS A--
TREVOR! DOWN!
DOWNSTAIRS. I'LL LOCK THE DOOR BEHIND US.
SKRAKAKAKAKOOM
KNNNNNG
HOLD THAT POSE, CHIEF!
I NEVER LIKED HOW YOU LOOKED AT ME, ANYWAY. CREEP.

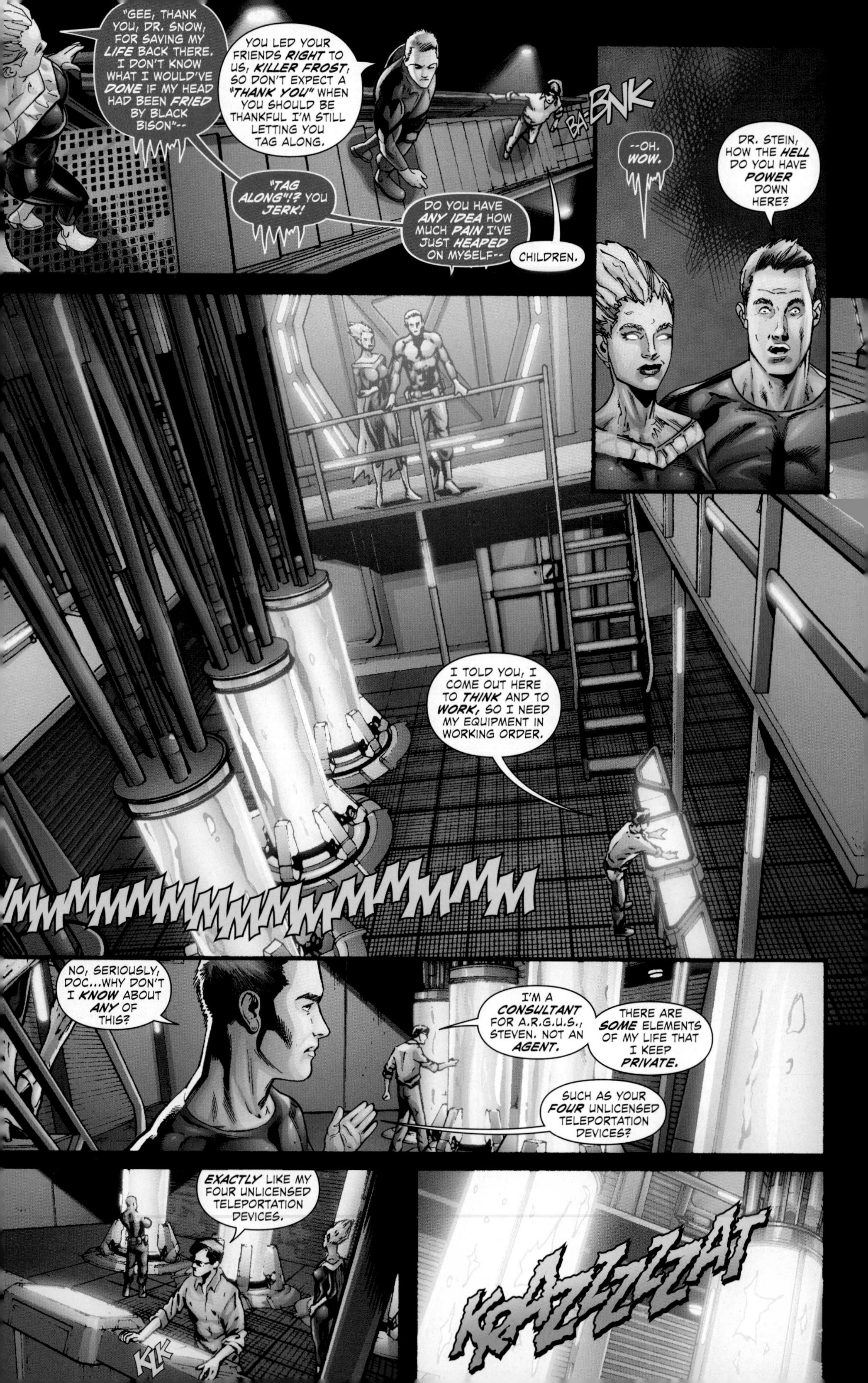
"GEE, THANK YOU, DR. SNOW, FOR SAVING MY LIFE BACK THERE. I DON'T KNOW WHAT I WOULD'VE DONE IF MY HEAD HAD BEEN FRIED BY BLACK BISON"--
YOU LED YOUR FRIENDS RIGHT TO US, KILLER FROST, SO DON'T EXPECT A "THANK YOU" WHEN YOU SHOULD BE THANKFUL I'M STILL LETTING YOU TAG ALONG.
"TAG ALONG"!? YOU JERK!
DO YOU HAVE ANY IDEA HOW MUCH PAIN I'VE JUST HEAPED ON MYSELF--
CHILDREN.
BA-BNK
--OH. WOW.
DR. STEIN, HOW THE HELL DO YOU HAVE POWER DOWN HERE?
I TOLD YOU, I COME OUT HERE TO THINK AND TO WORK, SO I NEED MY EQUIPMENT IN WORKING ORDER.
MMMMMMMMMMMMMMMMMMMM
NO, SERIOUSLY, DOC...WHY DON'T I KNOW ABOUT ANY OF THIS?
I'M A CONSULTANT FOR A.R.G.U.S., STEVEN. NOT AN AGENT.
THERE ARE SOME ELEMENTS OF MY LIFE THAT I KEEP PRIVATE.
SUCH AS YOUR FOUR UNLICENSED TELEPORTATION DEVICES?
EXACTLY LIKE MY FOUR UNLICENSED TELEPORTATION DEVICES.
KLIK
KZAZZZZZAT

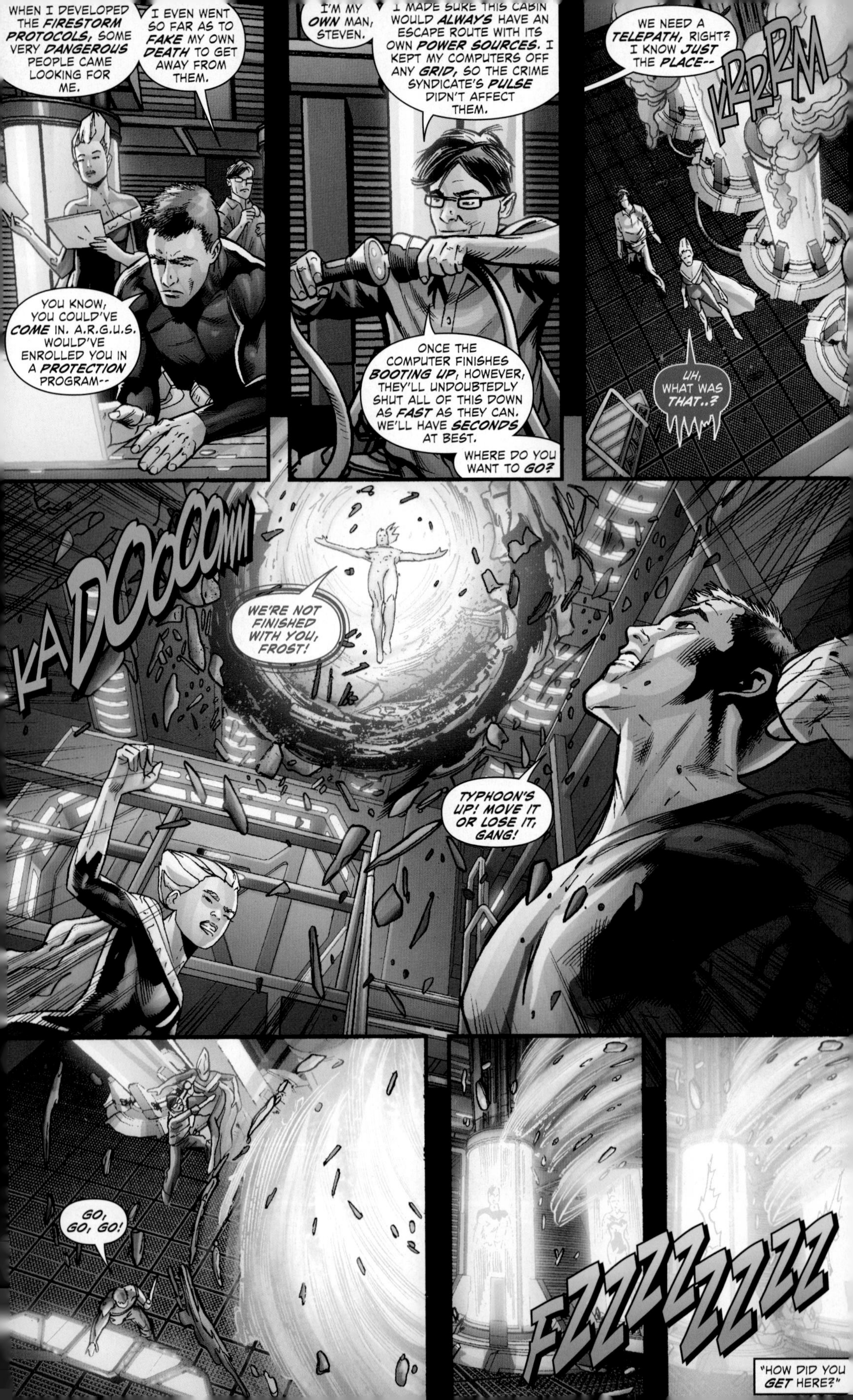
WHEN I DEVELOPED THE FIRESTORM PROTOCOLS, SOME VERY DANGEROUS PEOPLE CAME LOOKING FOR ME.
I EVEN WENT SO FAR AS TO FAKE MY OWN DEATH TO GET AWAY FROM THEM.
YOU KNOW, YOU COULD'VE COME IN. A.R.G.U.S. WOULD'VE ENROLLED YOU IN A PROTECTION PROGRAM--
I'M MY OWN MAN, STEVEN.
I MADE SURE THIS CABIN WOULD ALWAYS HAVE AN ESCAPE ROUTE WITH ITS OWN POWER SOURCES. I KEPT MY COMPUTERS OFF ANY GRID, SO THE CRIME SYNDICATE'S PULSE DIDN'T AFFECT THEM.
ONCE THE COMPUTER FINISHES BOOTING UP, HOWEVER, THEY'LL UNDOUBTEDLY SHUT ALL OF THIS DOWN AS FAST AS THEY CAN. WE'LL HAVE SECONDS AT BEST.
WHERE DO YOU WANT TO GO?
WE NEED A TELEPATH, RIGHT? I KNOW JUST THE PLACE--
KRRRM
UH, WHAT WAS THAT..?
KADOOOOMM
WE'RE NOT FINISHED WITH YOU, FROST!
TYPHOON'S UP! MOVE IT OR LOSE IT, GANG!
GO, GO, GO!
FZZZZZZZZ
"HOW DID YOU GET HERE?"

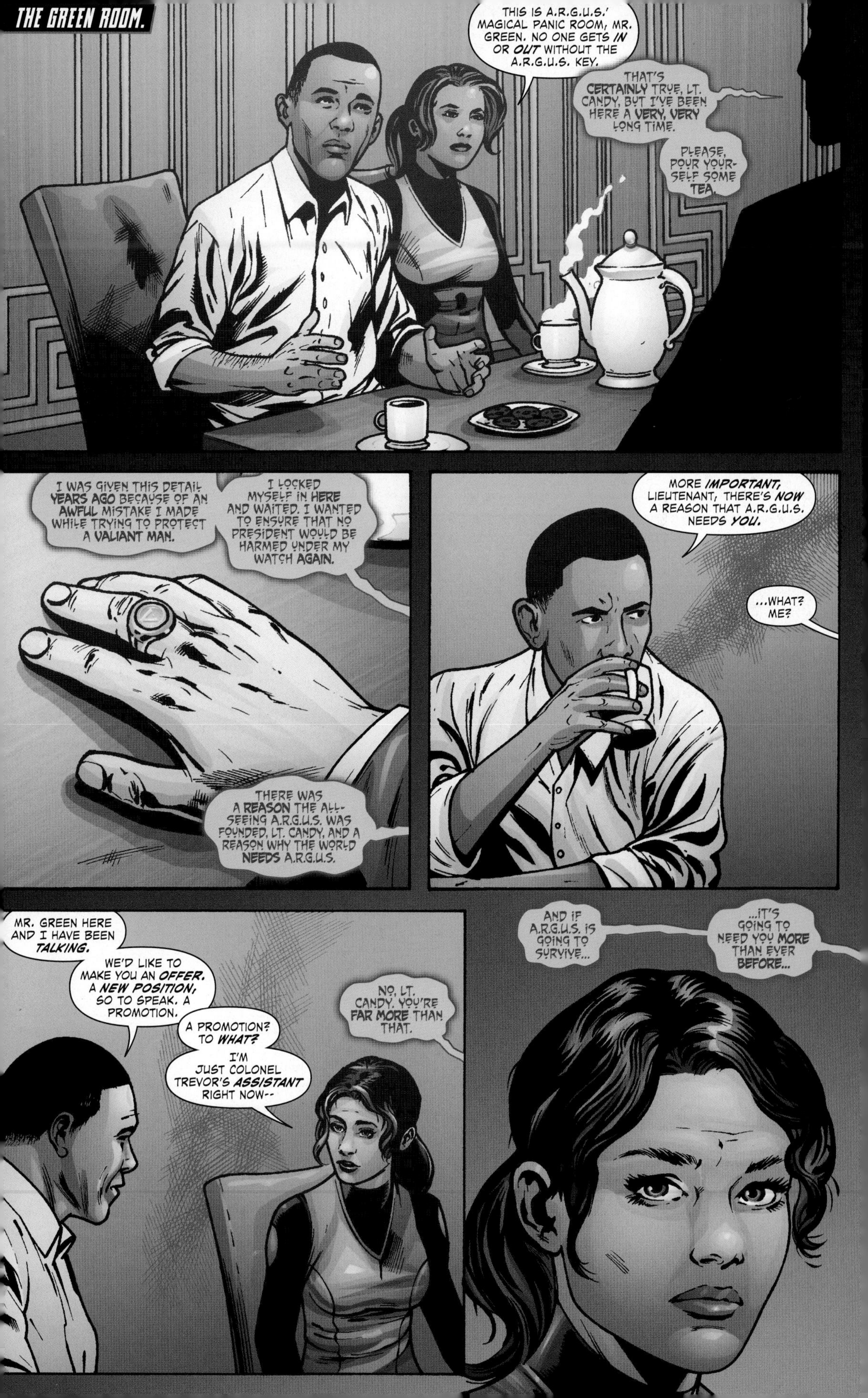
THE GREEN ROOM.
THIS IS A.R.G.U.S.' MAGICAL PANIC ROOM, MR. GREEN. NO ONE GETS IN OR OUT WITHOUT THE A.R.G.U.S. KEY.
THAT'S CERTAINLY TRUE, LT. CANDY, BUT I'VE BEEN HERE A VERY, VERY LONG TIME.
PLEASE, POUR YOURSELF SOME TEA.
I WAS GIVEN THIS DETAIL YEARS AGO BECAUSE OF AN AWFUL MISTAKE I MADE WHILE TRYING TO PROTECT A VALIANT MAN.
I LOCKED MYSELF IN HERE AND WAITED. I WANTED TO ENSURE THAT NO PRESIDENT WOULD BE HARMED UNDER MY WATCH AGAIN.
THERE WAS A REASON THE ALL-SEEING A.R.G.U.S. WAS FOUNDED, LT. CANDY, AND A REASON WHY THE WORLD NEEDS A.R.G.U.S.
MORE IMPORTANT, LIEUTENANT, THERE'S NOW A REASON THAT A.R.G.U.S. NEEDS YOU.
...WHAT? ME?
MR. GREEN HERE AND I HAVE BEEN TALKING.
WE'D LIKE TO MAKE YOU AN OFFER. A NEW POSITION, SO TO SPEAK. A PROMOTION.
A PROMOTION? TO WHAT?
I'M JUST COLONEL TREVOR'S ASSISTANT RIGHT NOW--
NO, LT. CANDY. YOU'RE FAR MORE THAN THAT.
AND IF A.R.G.U.S. IS GOING TO SURVIVE...
...IT'S GOING TO NEED YOU MORE THAN EVER BEFORE...

A.R.G.U.S.' JOB IS...WELL, *COMPLICATED.* WE'RE THE *LAST LINE* OF DEFENSE FOR HUMANITY IF THE JUSTICE LEAGUE FAILS.

WE'RE AN *OFFENSIVE* FORCE, TOO.

TAKE OUR *DETROIT* BASE, FOR EXAMPLE.

WHEN DARKSEID INVADED, HE PUNCHED A *HOLE* INTO OUR REALITY. *WEAKENED* THE SPACES BETWEEN DIMENSIONS.

SKZZZT

AS A RESULT...

FWASHHH

...THIS PLACE GETS A *LOT* OF *BAD TRAFFIC.* UP TO *US* TO PLAY *TRAFFIC COP* AND SHUT IT DOWN.

SO WHERE IS *THIS?*

A.R.G.U.S.' DETROIT STATION. FOLLOW ME.

NNN...

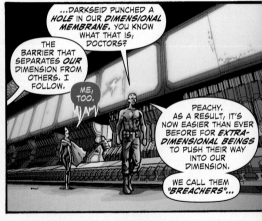

...DARKSEID PUNCHED A *HOLE* IN OUR *DIMENSIONAL MEMBRANE.* YOU KNOW WHAT THAT IS, DOCTORS?

THE BARRIER THAT SEPARATES *OUR* DIMENSION FROM OTHERS. I FOLLOW.

ME, TOO.

PEACHY. AS A RESULT, IT'S NOW EASIER THAN EVER BEFORE FOR *EXTRA-DIMENSIONAL BEINGS* TO PUSH THEIR WAY INTO OUR DIMENSION.

WE CALL THEM *"BREACHERS"*...

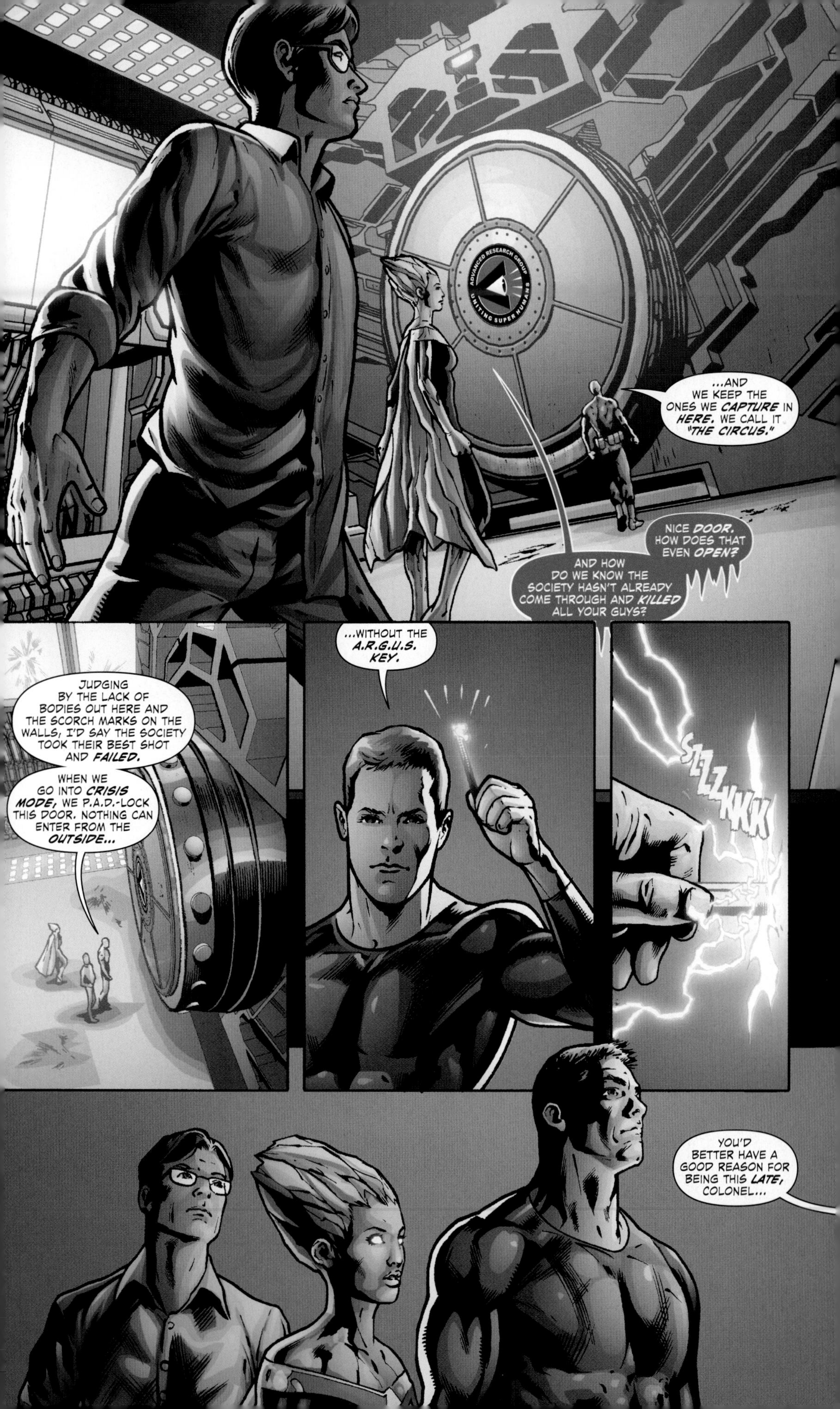
ADVANCED RESEARCH GROUP
UNITING SUPER HUMANS
...AND WE KEEP THE ONES WE CAPTURE IN HERE. WE CALL IT "THE CIRCUS."
NICE DOOR. HOW DOES THAT EVEN OPEN?
AND HOW DO WE KNOW THE SOCIETY HASN'T ALREADY COME THROUGH AND KILLED ALL YOUR GUYS?
JUDGING BY THE LACK OF BODIES OUT HERE AND THE SCORCH MARKS ON THE WALLS, I'D SAY THE SOCIETY TOOK THEIR BEST SHOT AND FAILED.
WHEN WE GO INTO CRISIS MODE, WE P.A.D.-LOCK THIS DOOR. NOTHING CAN ENTER FROM THE OUTSIDE...
...WITHOUT THE A.R.G.U.S. KEY.
SZZZKKK
YOU'D BETTER HAVE A GOOD REASON FOR BEING THIS LATE, COLONEL...

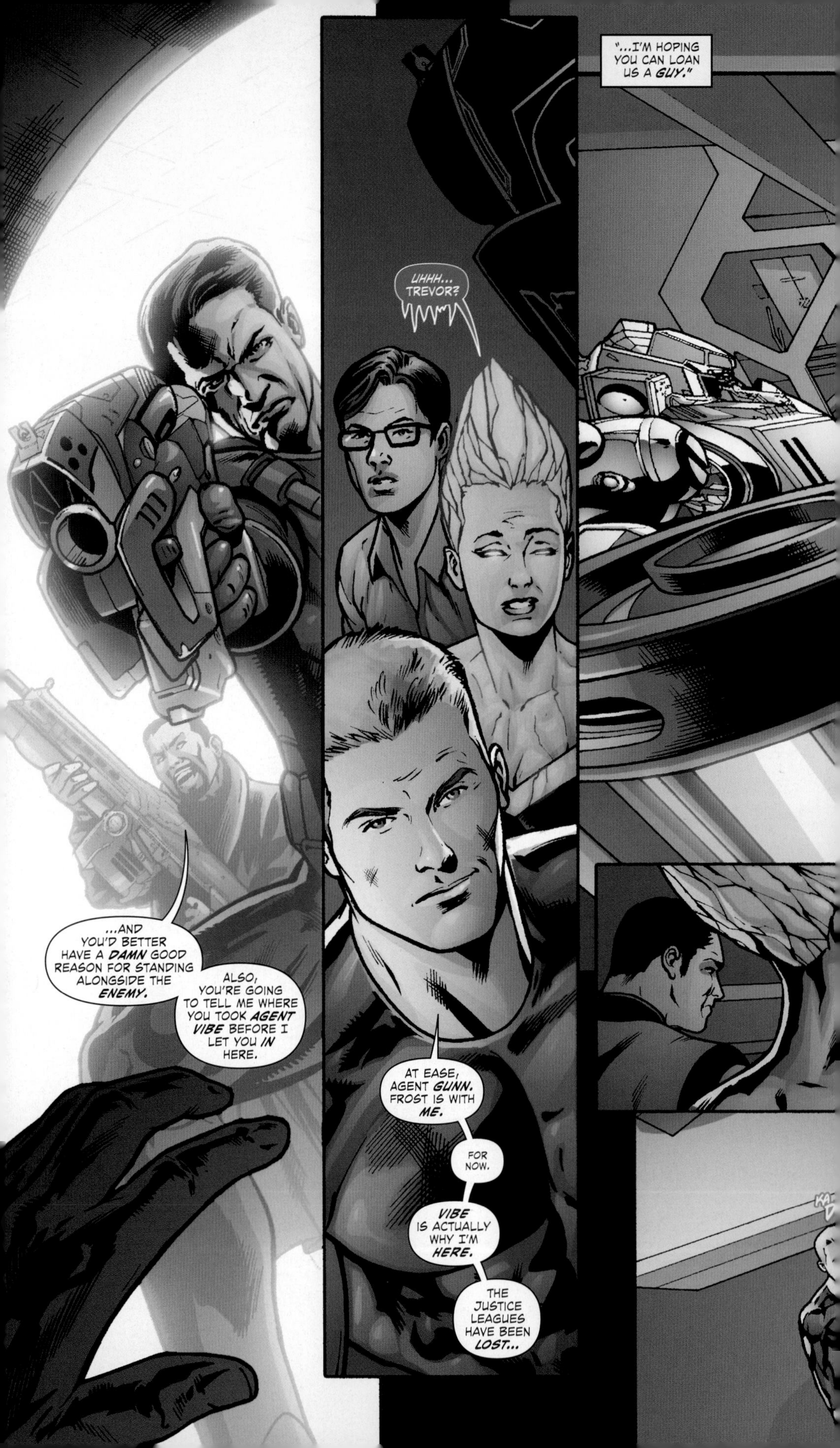
"...I'M HOPING YOU CAN LOAN US A GUY."
UHHH... TREVOR?
...AND YOU'D BETTER HAVE A DAMN GOOD REASON FOR STANDING ALONGSIDE THE ENEMY.
ALSO, YOU'RE GOING TO TELL ME WHERE YOU TOOK AGENT VIBE BEFORE I LET YOU IN HERE.
AT EASE, AGENT GUNN. FROST IS WITH ME.
FOR NOW.
VIBE IS ACTUALLY WHY I'M HERE.
THE JUSTICE LEAGUES HAVE BEEN LOST...

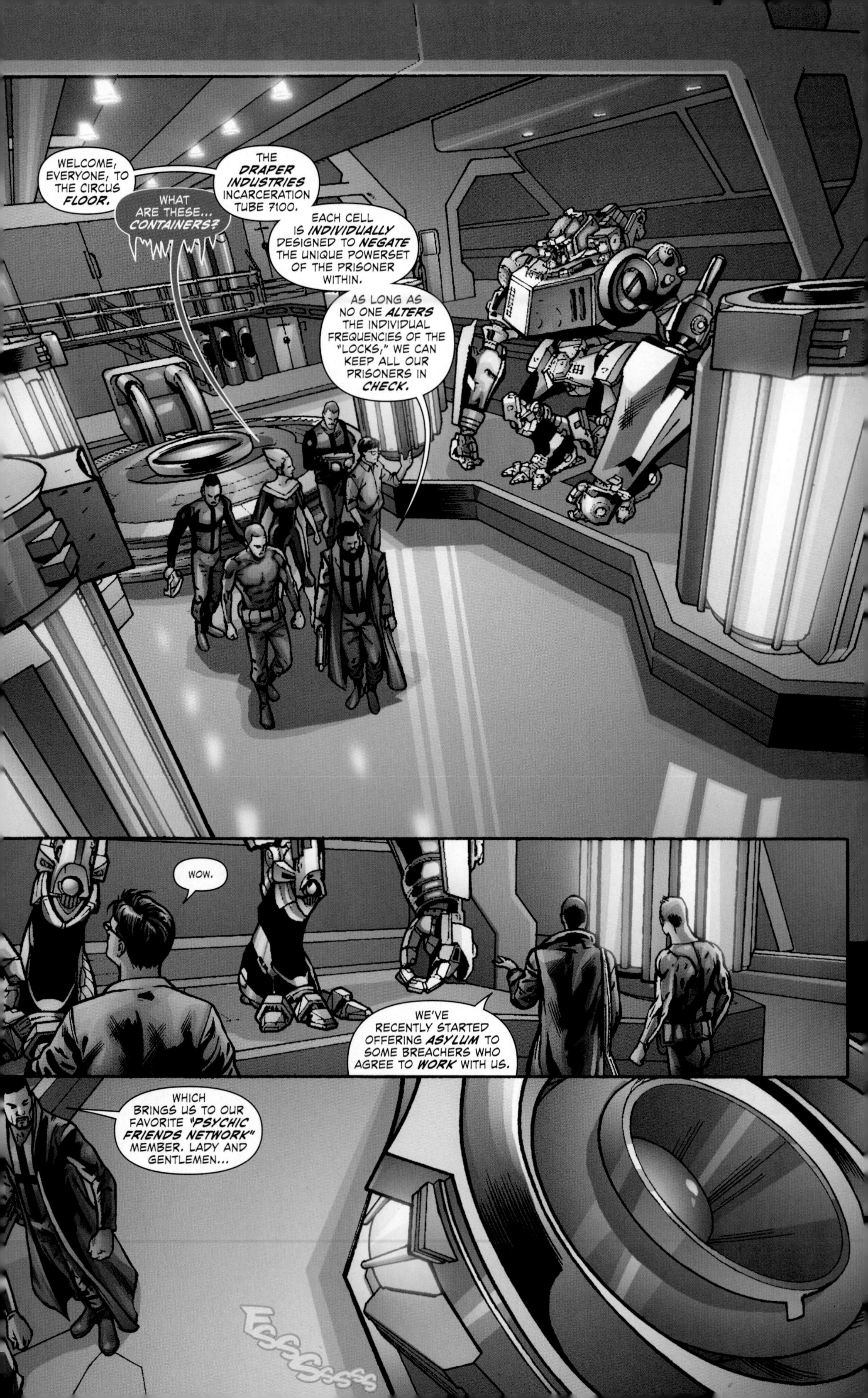
WELCOME, EVERYONE, TO THE CIRCUS FLOOR.
THE DRAPER INDUSTRIES INCARCERATION TUBE 7100.
WHAT ARE THESE... CONTAINERS?
EACH CELL IS INDIVIDUALLY DESIGNED TO NEGATE THE UNIQUE POWERSET OF THE PRISONER WITHIN.
AS LONG AS NO ONE ALTERS THE INDIVIDUAL FREQUENCIES OF THE "LOCKS," WE CAN KEEP ALL OUR PRISONERS IN CHECK.
WOW.
WE'VE RECENTLY STARTED OFFERING ASYLUM TO SOME BREACHERS WHO AGREE TO WORK WITH US.
WHICH BRINGS US TO OUR FAVORITE "PSYCHIC FRIENDS NETWORK" MEMBER. LADY AND GENTLEMEN...
FSSSsssss

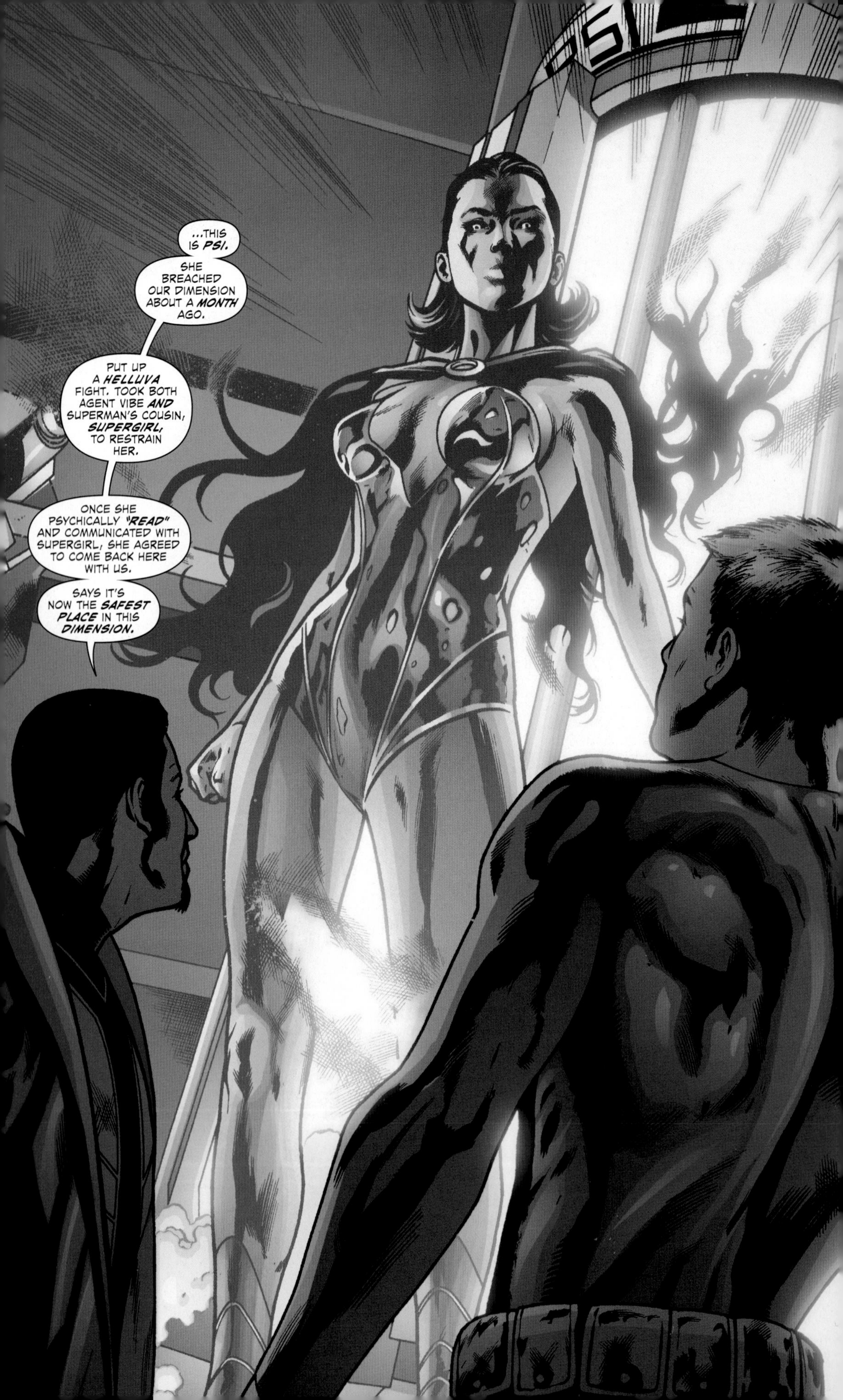

...THIS IS PSI.
SHE BREACHED OUR DIMENSION ABOUT A MONTH AGO.
PUT UP A HELLUVA FIGHT. TOOK BOTH AGENT VIBE AND SUPERMAN'S COUSIN, SUPERGIRL, TO RESTRAIN HER.
ONCE SHE PSYCHICALLY "READ" AND COMMUNICATED WITH SUPERGIRL, SHE AGREED TO COME BACK HERE WITH US.
SAYS IT'S NOW THE SAFEST PLACE IN THIS DIMENSION.

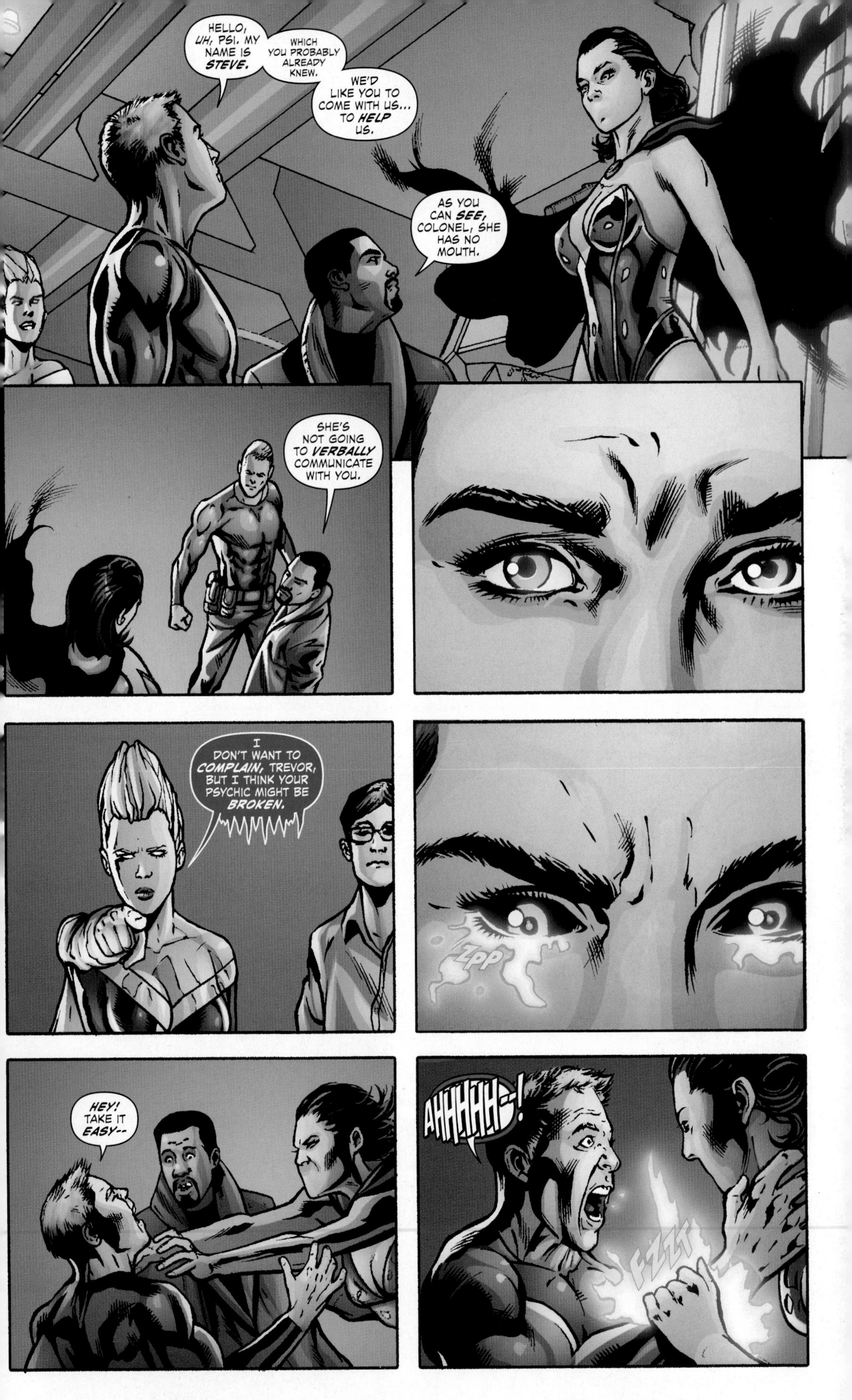
HELLO, *UH*, PSI. MY NAME IS ***STEVE.***
WHICH YOU PROBABLY ALREADY KNEW.
WE'D LIKE YOU TO COME WITH US... TO ***HELP*** US.
AS YOU CAN ***SEE,*** COLONEL, SHE HAS NO MOUTH.
SHE'S NOT GOING TO ***VERBALLY*** COMMUNICATE WITH YOU.
I DON'T WANT TO ***COMPLAIN,*** TREVOR, BUT I THINK YOUR PSYCHIC MIGHT BE ***BROKEN.***
ZPP
HEY! TAKE IT ***EASY--***
AHHHHH--!
FZZT

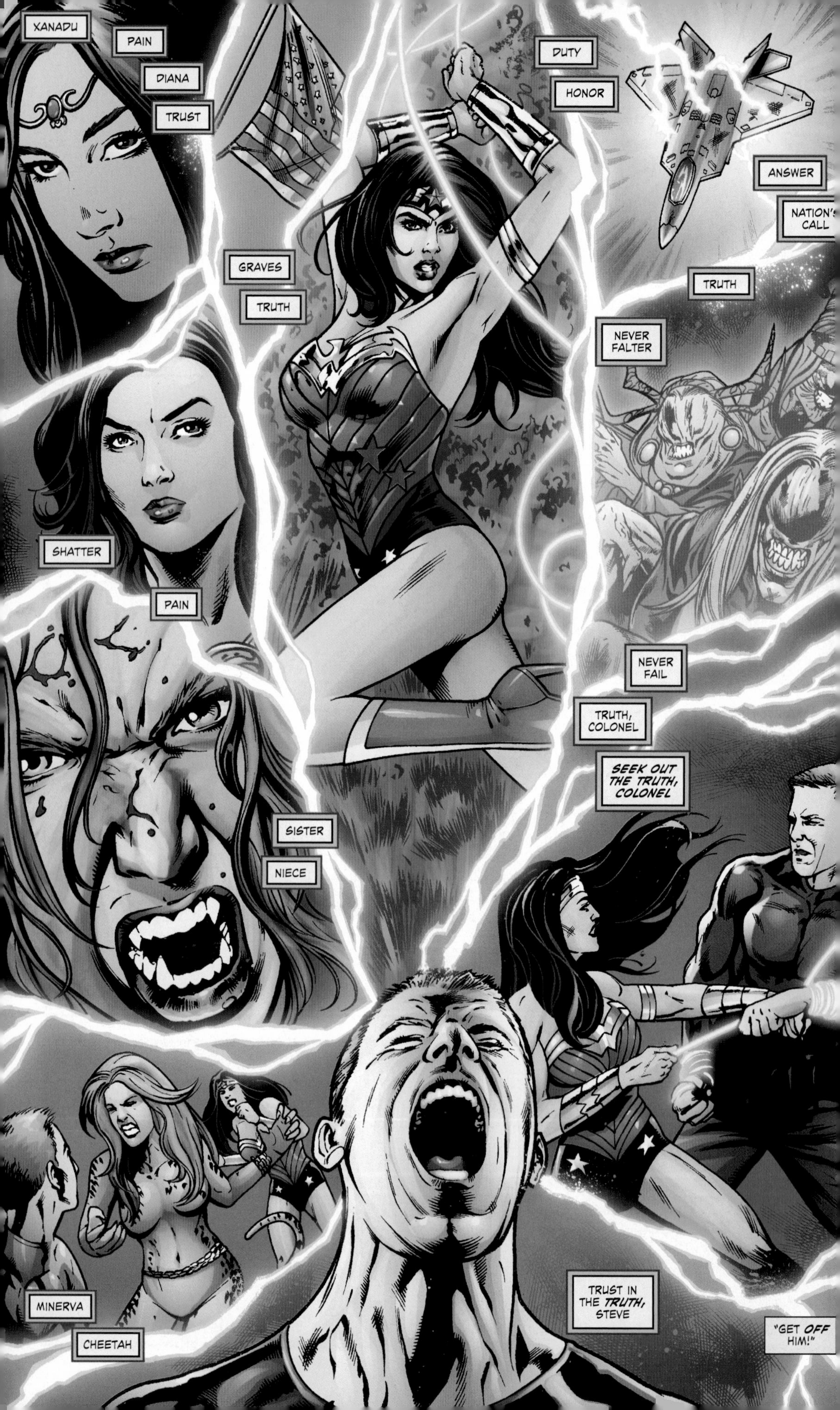
XANADU
PAIN
DIANA
TRUST
DUTY
HONOR
ANSWER
NATION'S CALL
GRAVES
TRUTH
TRUTH
NEVER FALTER
SHATTER
PAIN
NEVER FAIL
TRUTH, COLONEL
SEEK OUT THE TRUTH, COLONEL
SISTER
NIECE
MINERVA
CHEETAH
TRUST IN THE TRUTH, STEVE
"GET OFF HIM!"

LET *GO* OF HIM! GUARDS! **GUARDS!**

HNNNN...

ASYLUM *REVOKED.* LOCK HER *DOWN.*

STEVE, ARE YOU *OKAY*--? WHAT *HAPPENED?*

I-I NEED...

PREP A *GLIDER.* I'M ALSO GONNA NEED A *THERMOS* OF COFFEE AND ACCESS TO THE *ARMORY,* AGENT GUNN.

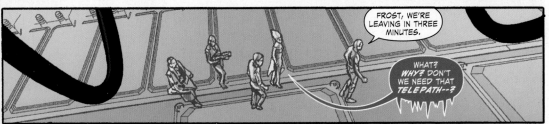

FROST, WE'RE LEAVING IN THREE MINUTES.

WHAT? *WHY?* DON'T WE NEED THAT *TELEPATH*--?

NO. WE DON'T NEED A TELEPATH TO FREE THE JUSTICE LEAGUE.

THE ANSWER WAS STARING ME IN THE FACE ALL ALONG.

XANADU GAVE ME THE *CLUE;* I JUST NEEDED TO CONNECT THE DOTS. THE BRAIN-BLAST *DID* THAT.

IF I'M GOING TO RESCUE WONDER WOMAN--RESCUE *THE JUSTICE LEAGUES*--I NEED THE *LASSO OF TRUTH...*

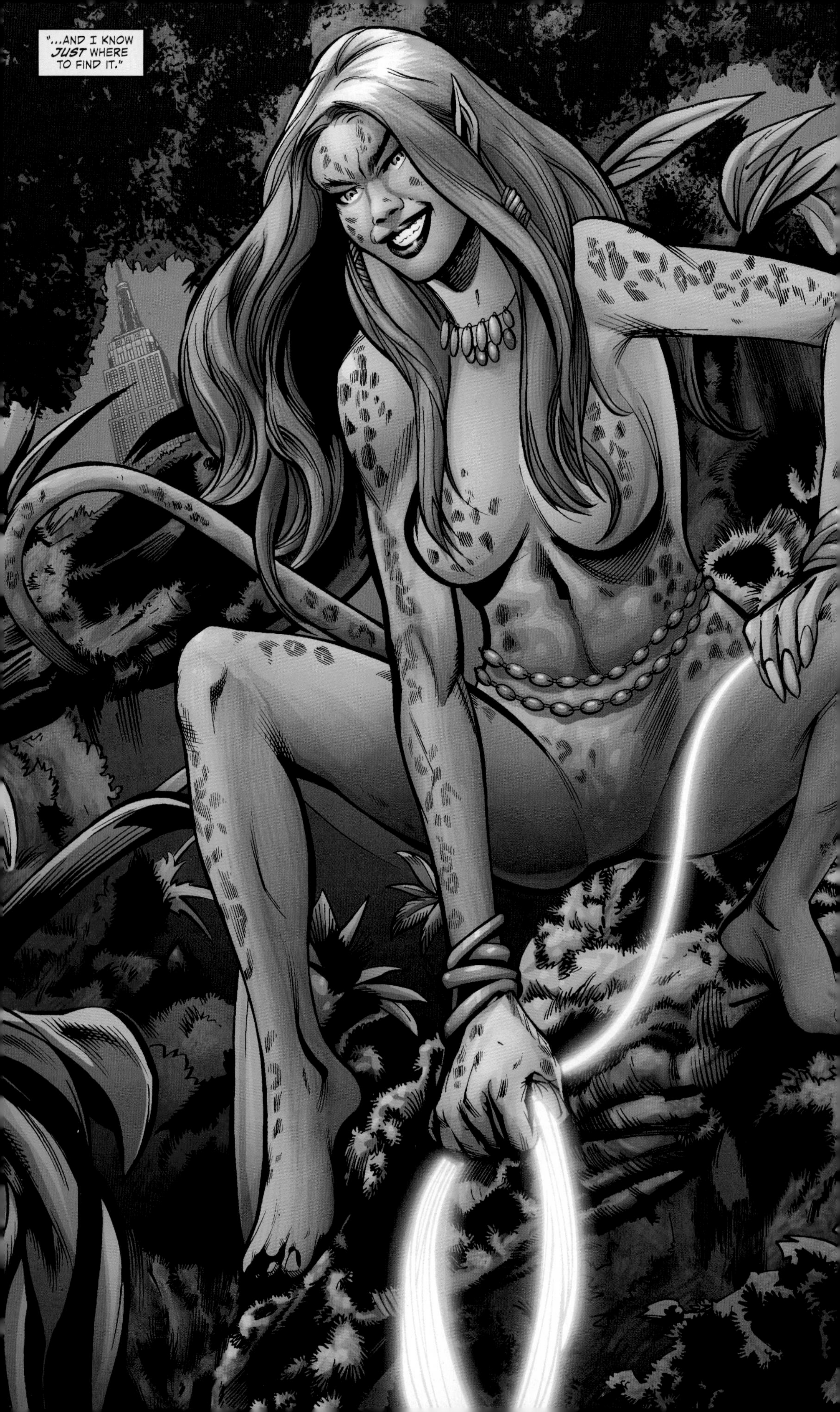
"...AND I KNOW JUST WHERE TO FIND IT."

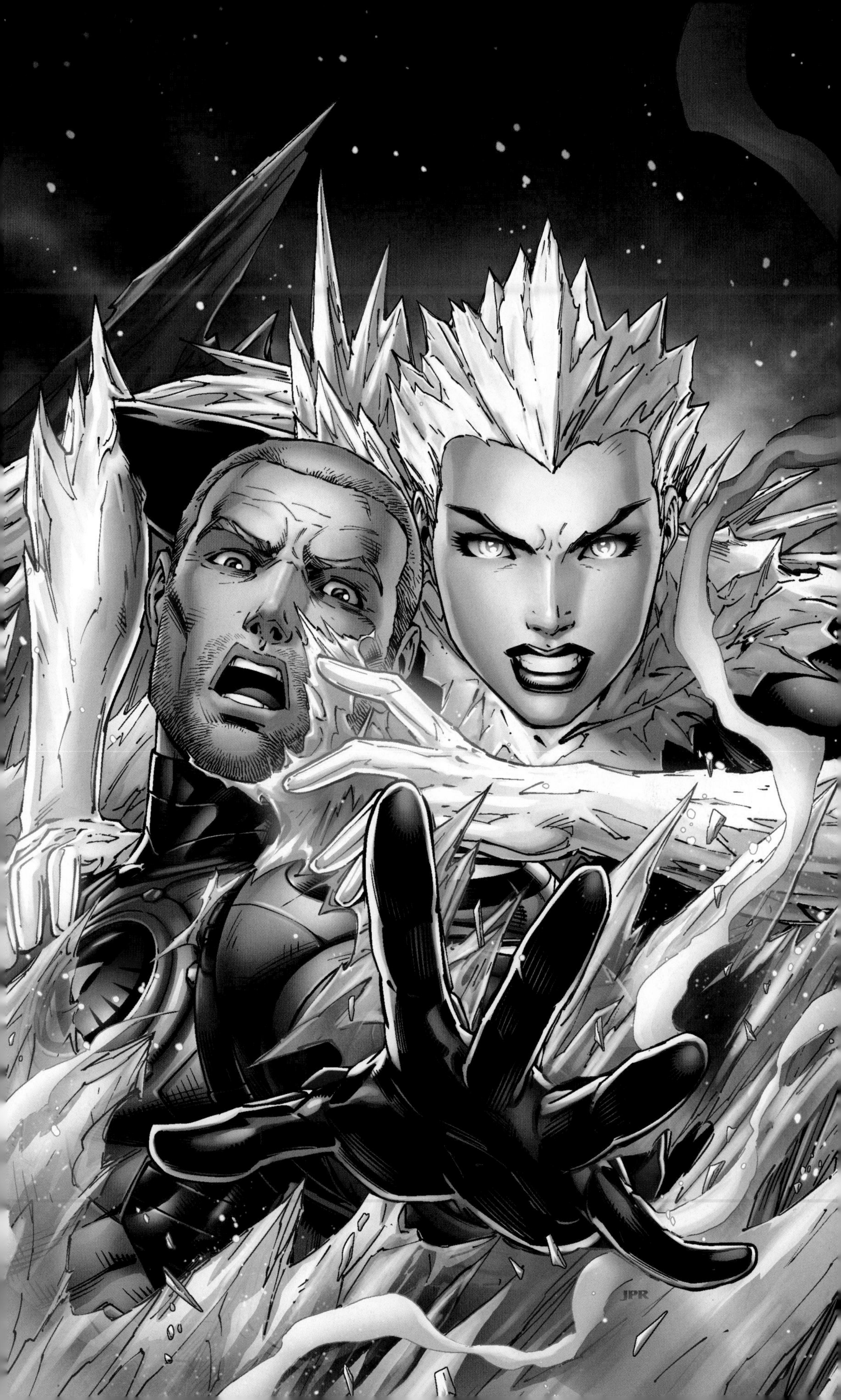

PART FIVE: THE CAGES AND COURAGEOUS

STERLING GATES Writer **NEIL EDWARDS** Penciller **JASON PAZ JAY LEISTEN** Inkers
NATHAN EYRING Colorist **TAYLOR ESPOSITO** Letterer
Cover Art by **JEREMY ROBERTS**

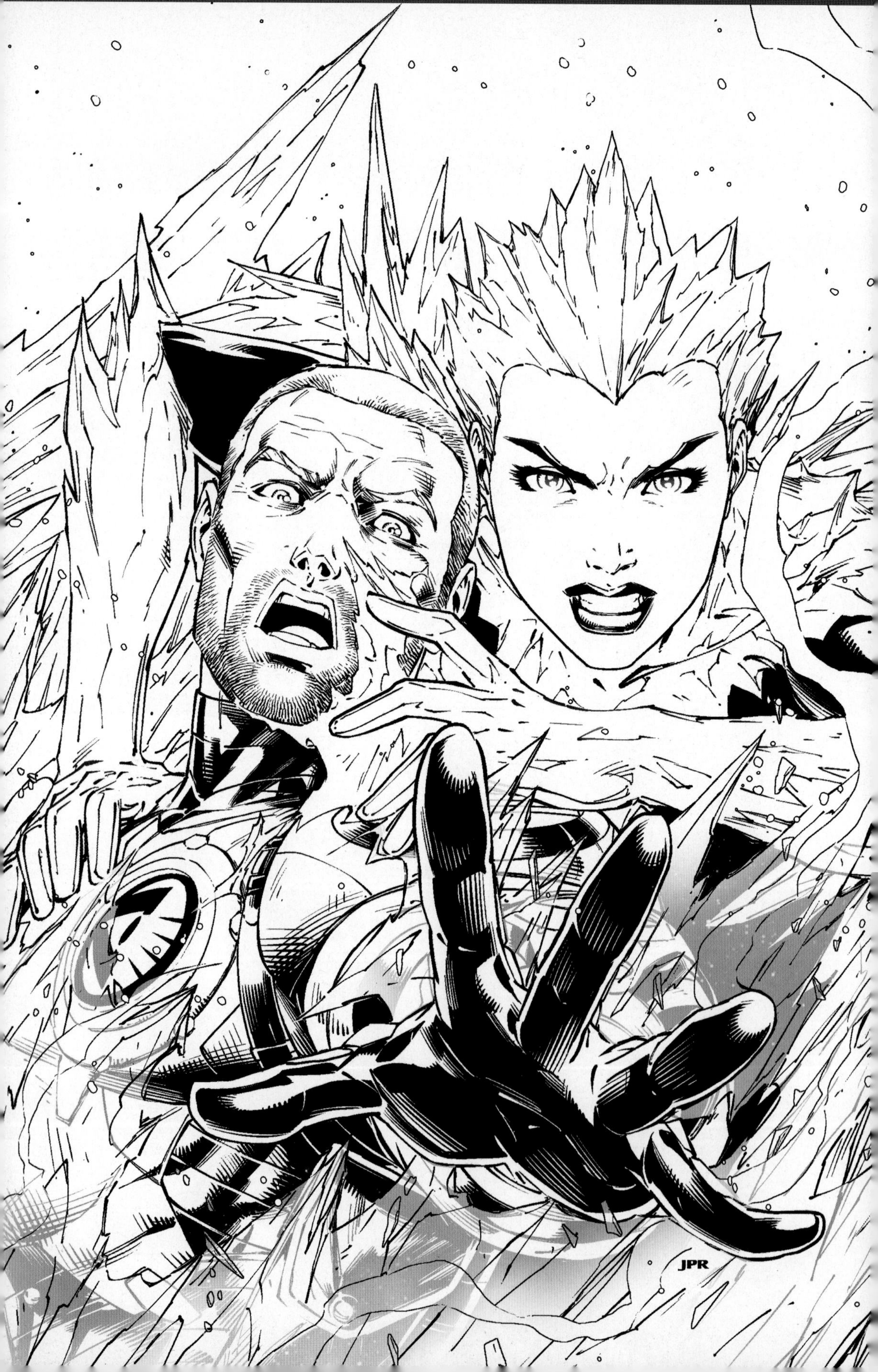
JPR

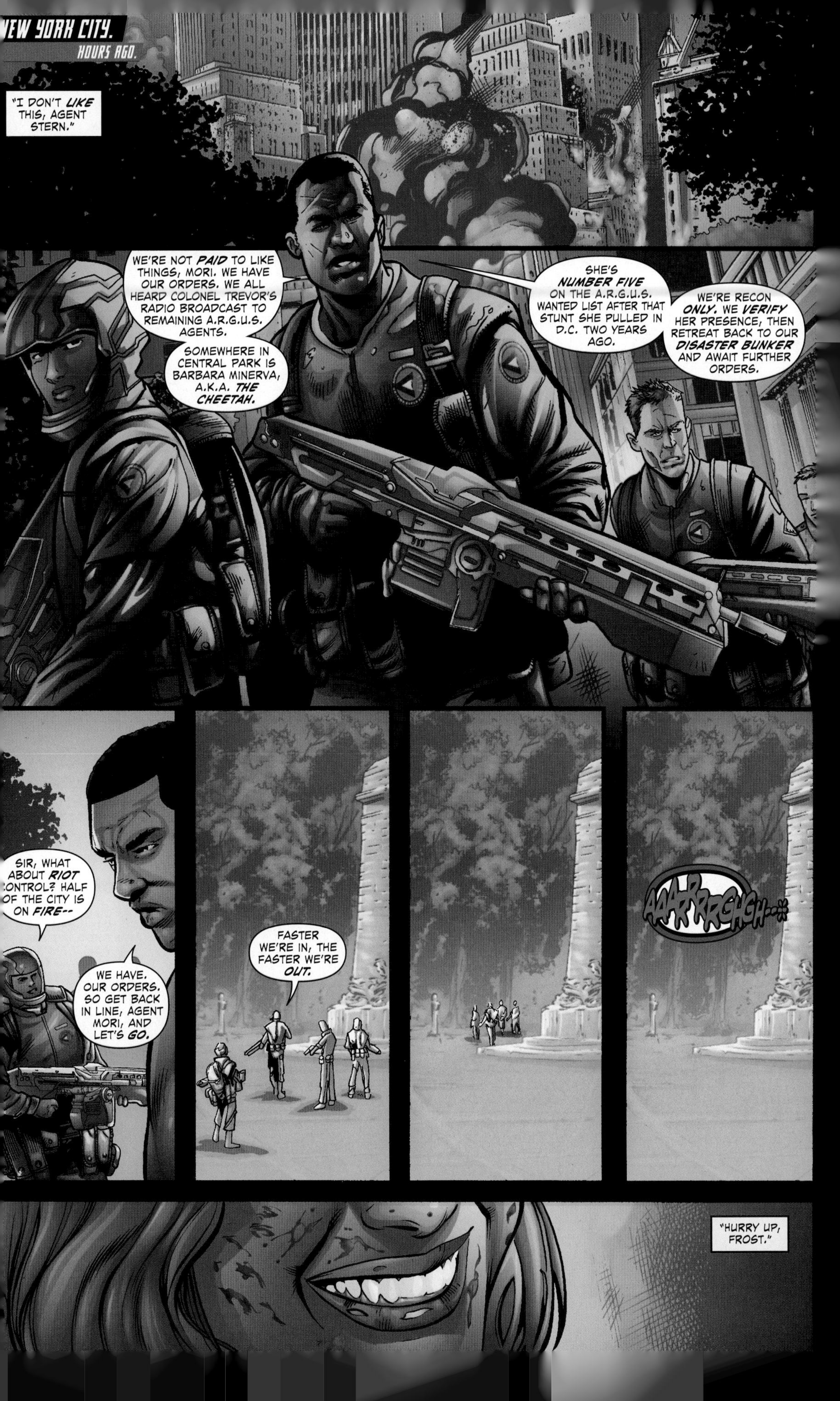
NEW YORK CITY.
HOURS AGO.
"I DON'T LIKE THIS, AGENT STERN."
WE'RE NOT PAID TO LIKE THINGS, MORI. WE HAVE OUR ORDERS. WE ALL HEARD COLONEL TREVOR'S RADIO BROADCAST TO REMAINING A.R.G.U.S. AGENTS.
SOMEWHERE IN CENTRAL PARK IS BARBARA MINERVA, A.K.A. THE CHEETAH.
SHE'S NUMBER FIVE ON THE A.R.G.U.S. WANTED LIST AFTER THAT STUNT SHE PULLED IN D.C. TWO YEARS AGO.
WE'RE RECON ONLY. WE VERIFY HER PRESENCE, THEN RETREAT BACK TO OUR DISASTER BUNKER AND AWAIT FURTHER ORDERS.
SIR, WHAT ABOUT RIOT CONTROL? HALF OF THE CITY IS ON FIRE--
WE HAVE. OUR ORDERS. SO GET BACK IN LINE, AGENT MORI, AND LET'S GO.
FASTER WE'RE IN, THE FASTER WE'RE OUT.
AAARRRRGHGH--!!
"HURRY UP, FROST."

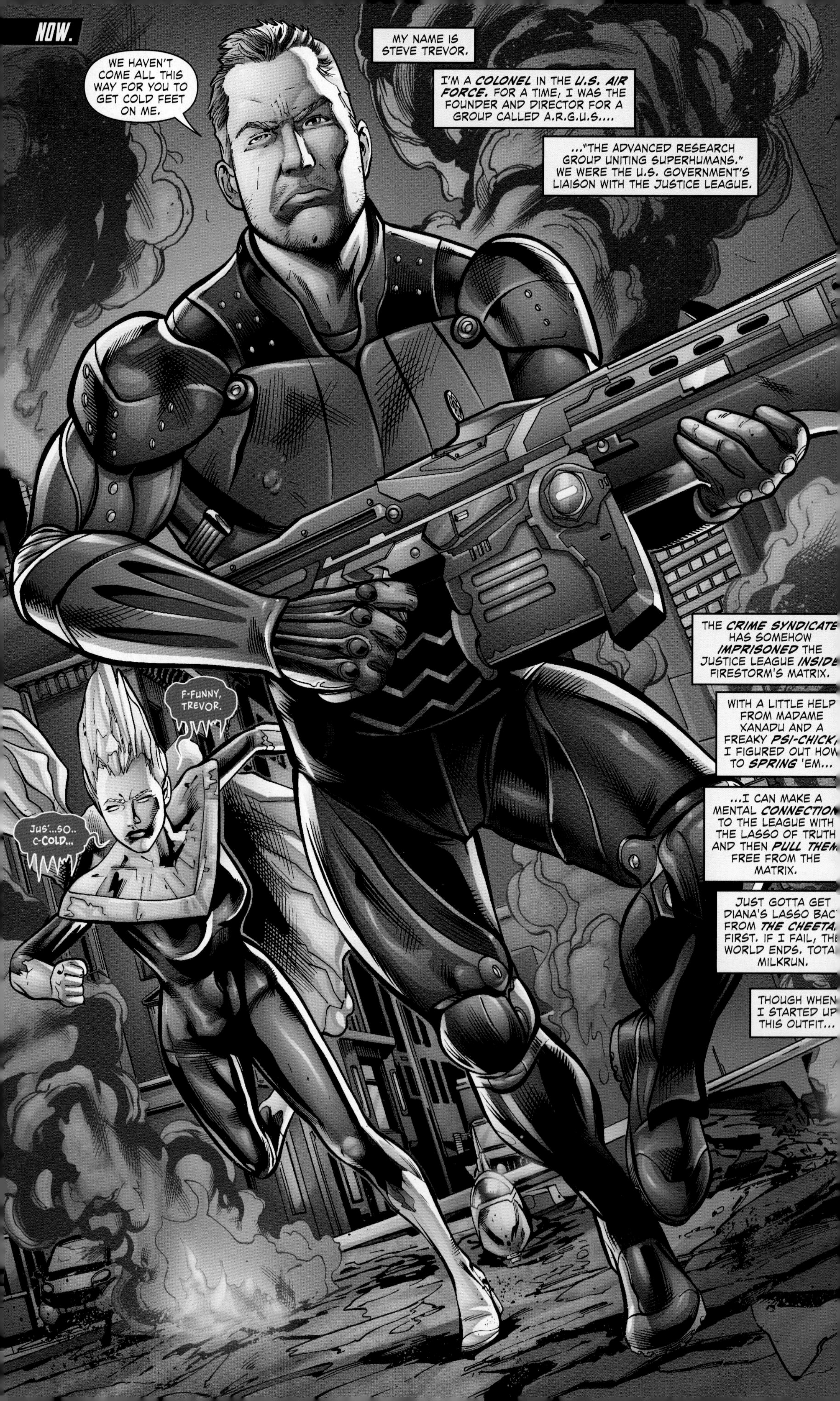
NOW.
MY NAME IS STEVE TREVOR.
WE HAVEN'T COME ALL THIS WAY FOR YOU TO GET COLD FEET ON ME.
I'M A COLONEL IN THE U.S. AIR FORCE. FOR A TIME, I WAS THE FOUNDER AND DIRECTOR FOR A GROUP CALLED A.R.G.U.S....
..."THE ADVANCED RESEARCH GROUP UNITING SUPERHUMANS." WE WERE THE U.S. GOVERNMENT'S LIAISON WITH THE JUSTICE LEAGUE.
THE CRIME SYNDICATE HAS SOMEHOW IMPRISONED THE JUSTICE LEAGUE INSIDE FIRESTORM'S MATRIX.
F-FUNNY, TREVOR.
WITH A LITTLE HELP FROM MADAME XANADU AND A FREAKY PSI-CHICK, I FIGURED OUT HOW TO SPRING 'EM...
JUS'...SO.. C-COLD...
...I CAN MAKE A MENTAL CONNECTION TO THE LEAGUE WITH THE LASSO OF TRUTH AND THEN PULL THEM FREE FROM THE MATRIX.
JUST GOTTA GET DIANA'S LASSO BAC FROM THE CHEETA FIRST. IF I FAIL, TH WORLD ENDS. TOTA MILKRUN.
THOUGH WHEN I STARTED UP THIS OUTFIT...

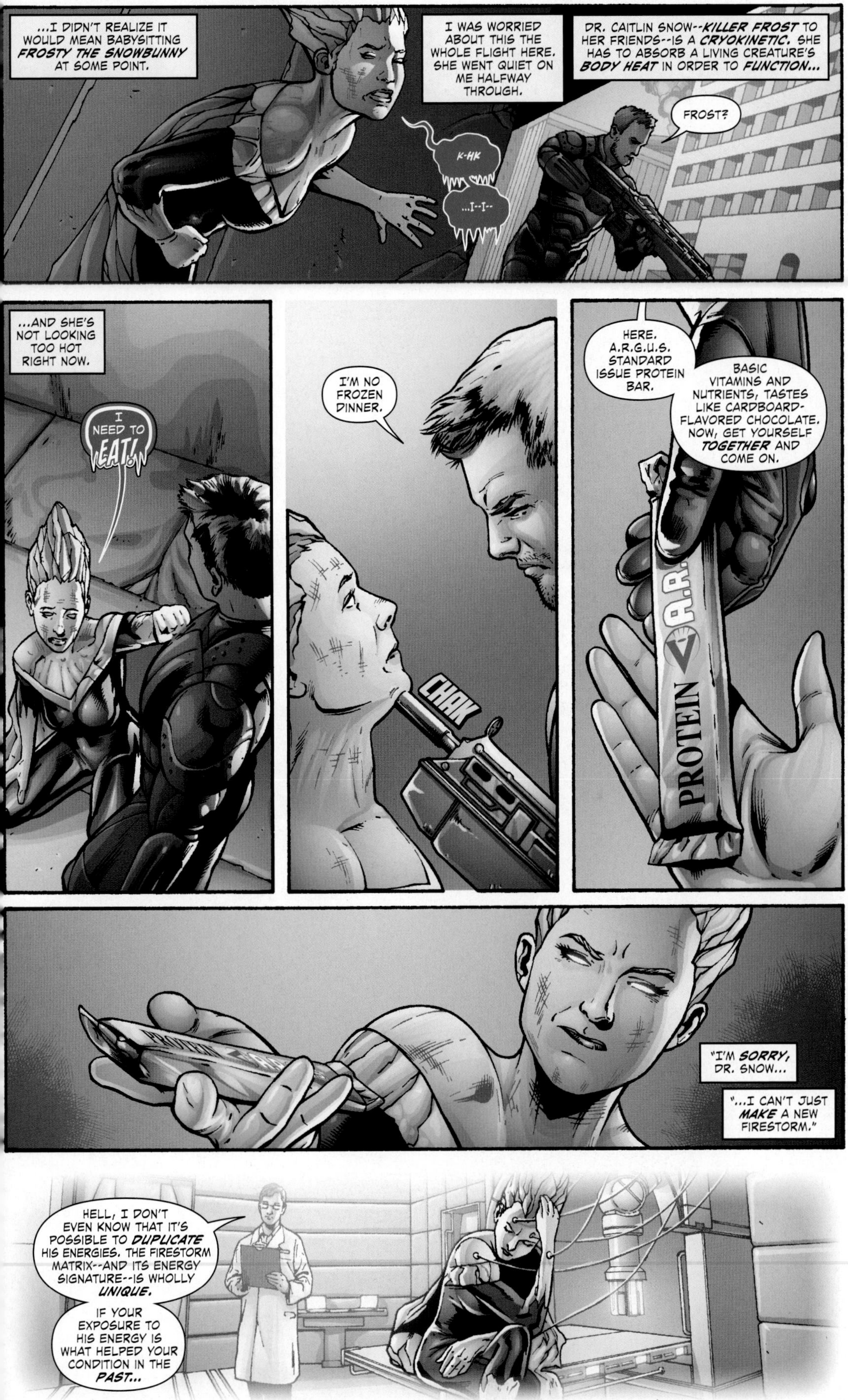
...I DIDN'T REALIZE IT WOULD MEAN BABYSITTING FROSTY THE SNOWBUNNY AT SOME POINT.
I WAS WORRIED ABOUT THIS THE WHOLE FLIGHT HERE. SHE WENT QUIET ON ME HALFWAY THROUGH.
DR. CAITLIN SNOW--KILLER FROST TO HER FRIENDS--IS A CRYOKINETIC. SHE HAS TO ABSORB A LIVING CREATURE'S BODY HEAT IN ORDER TO FUNCTION...
FROST?
K-HK
...I--I--
...AND SHE'S NOT LOOKING TOO HOT RIGHT NOW.
I NEED TO EAT!
I'M NO FROZEN DINNER.
CHAK
HERE. A.R.G.U.S. STANDARD ISSUE PROTEIN BAR.
BASIC VITAMINS AND NUTRIENTS, TASTES LIKE CARDBOARD-FLAVORED CHOCOLATE. NOW, GET YOURSELF TOGETHER AND COME ON.
PROTEIN
A.R.
"I'M SORRY, DR. SNOW...
"...I CAN'T JUST MAKE A NEW FIRESTORM."
HELL, I DON'T EVEN KNOW THAT IT'S POSSIBLE TO DUPLICATE HIS ENERGIES. THE FIRESTORM MATRIX--AND ITS ENERGY SIGNATURE--IS WHOLLY UNIQUE.
IF YOUR EXPOSURE TO HIS ENERGY IS WHAT HELPED YOUR CONDITION IN THE PAST...

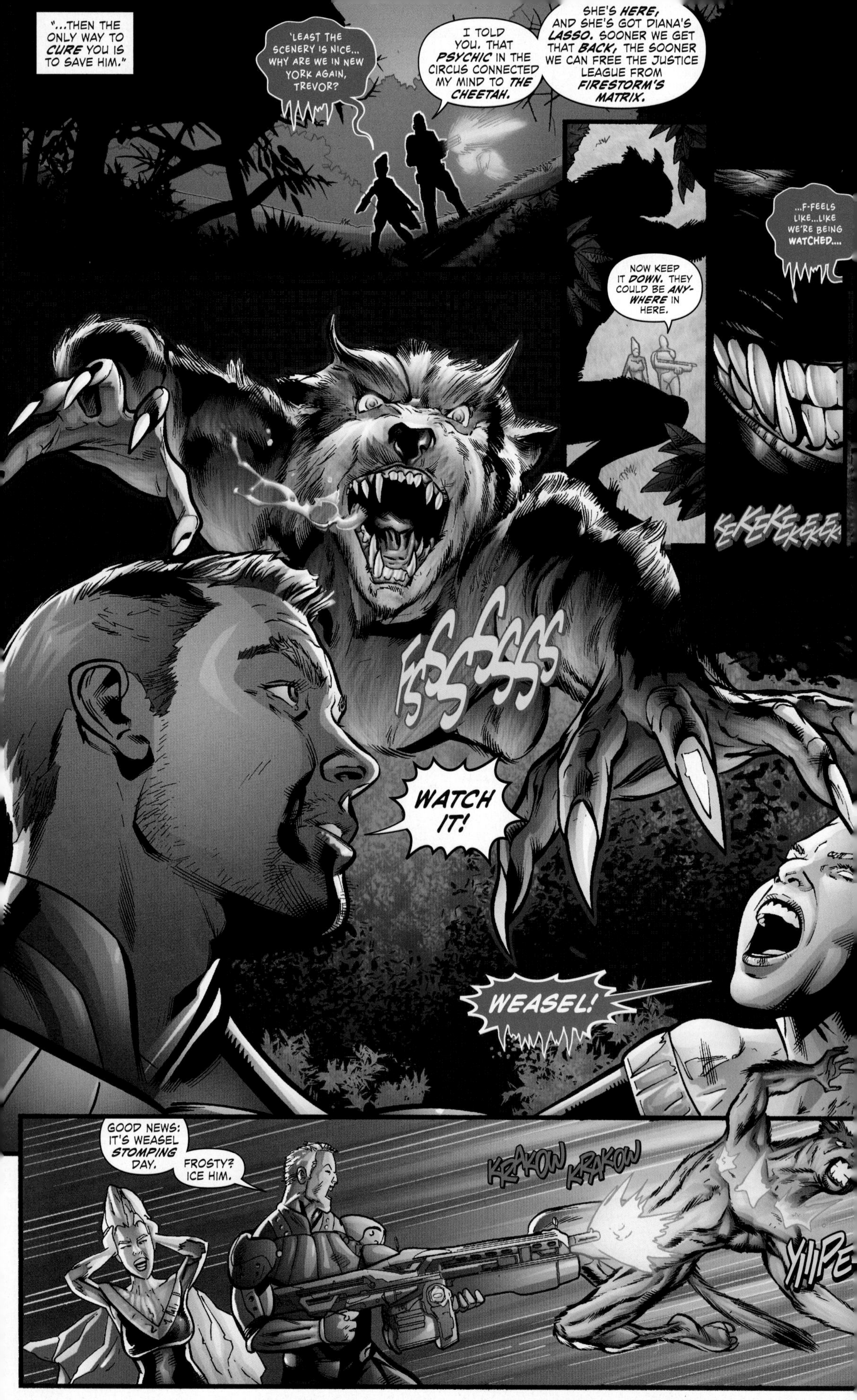
"...THEN THE ONLY WAY TO CURE YOU IS TO SAVE HIM."
'LEAST THE SCENERY IS NICE... WHY ARE WE IN NEW YORK AGAIN, TREVOR?
I TOLD YOU. THAT PSYCHIC IN THE CIRCUS CONNECTED MY MIND TO THE CHEETAH.
SHE'S HERE, AND SHE'S GOT DIANA'S LASSO. SOONER WE GET THAT BACK, THE SOONER WE CAN FREE THE JUSTICE LEAGUE FROM FIRESTORM'S MATRIX.
NOW KEEP IT DOWN. THEY COULD BE ANYWHERE IN HERE.
...F-FEELS LIKE...LIKE WE'RE BEING WATCHED....
KEKEKEKEKEKE
FSSSSSSS
WATCH IT!
WEASEL!
GOOD NEWS: IT'S WEASEL STOMPING DAY.
FROSTY? ICE HIM.
KRAKOW KRAKOW
YIIPE

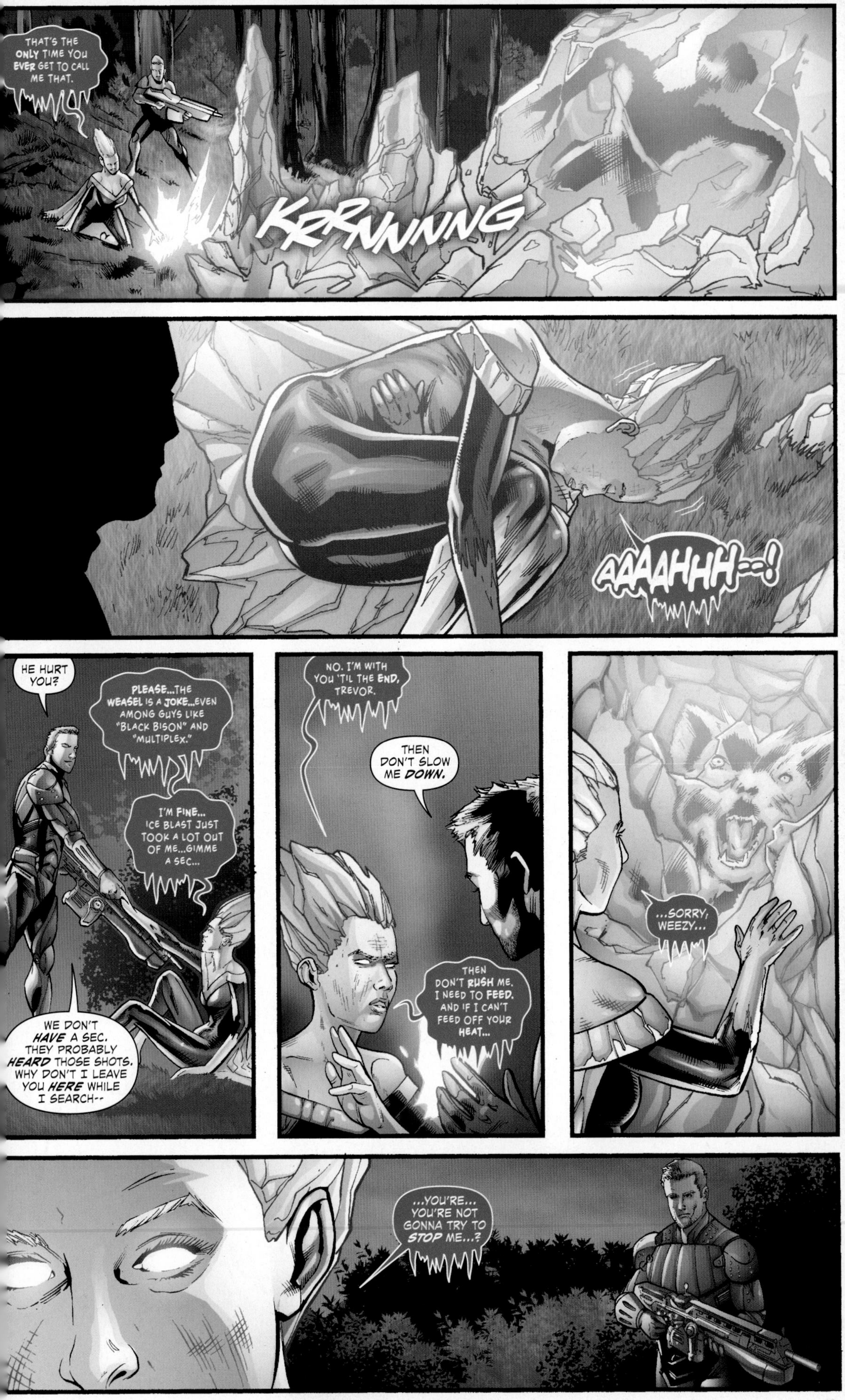
THAT'S THE ONLY TIME YOU EVER GET TO CALL ME THAT.
KRRNNNNG
AAAAHHH--!
HE HURT YOU?
PLEASE...THE WEASEL IS A JOKE...EVEN AMONG GUYS LIKE "BLACK BISON" AND "MULTIPLEX."
I'M FINE... ICE BLAST JUST TOOK A LOT OUT OF ME...GIMME A SEC...
WE DON'T HAVE A SEC. THEY PROBABLY HEARD THOSE SHOTS. WHY DON'T I LEAVE YOU HERE WHILE I SEARCH--
NO. I'M WITH YOU 'TIL THE END, TREVOR.
THEN DON'T SLOW ME DOWN.
THEN DON'T RUSH ME. I NEED TO FEED. AND IF I CAN'T FEED OFF YOUR HEAT...
...SORRY, WEEZY...
...YOU'RE... YOU'RE NOT GONNA TRY TO STOP ME...?

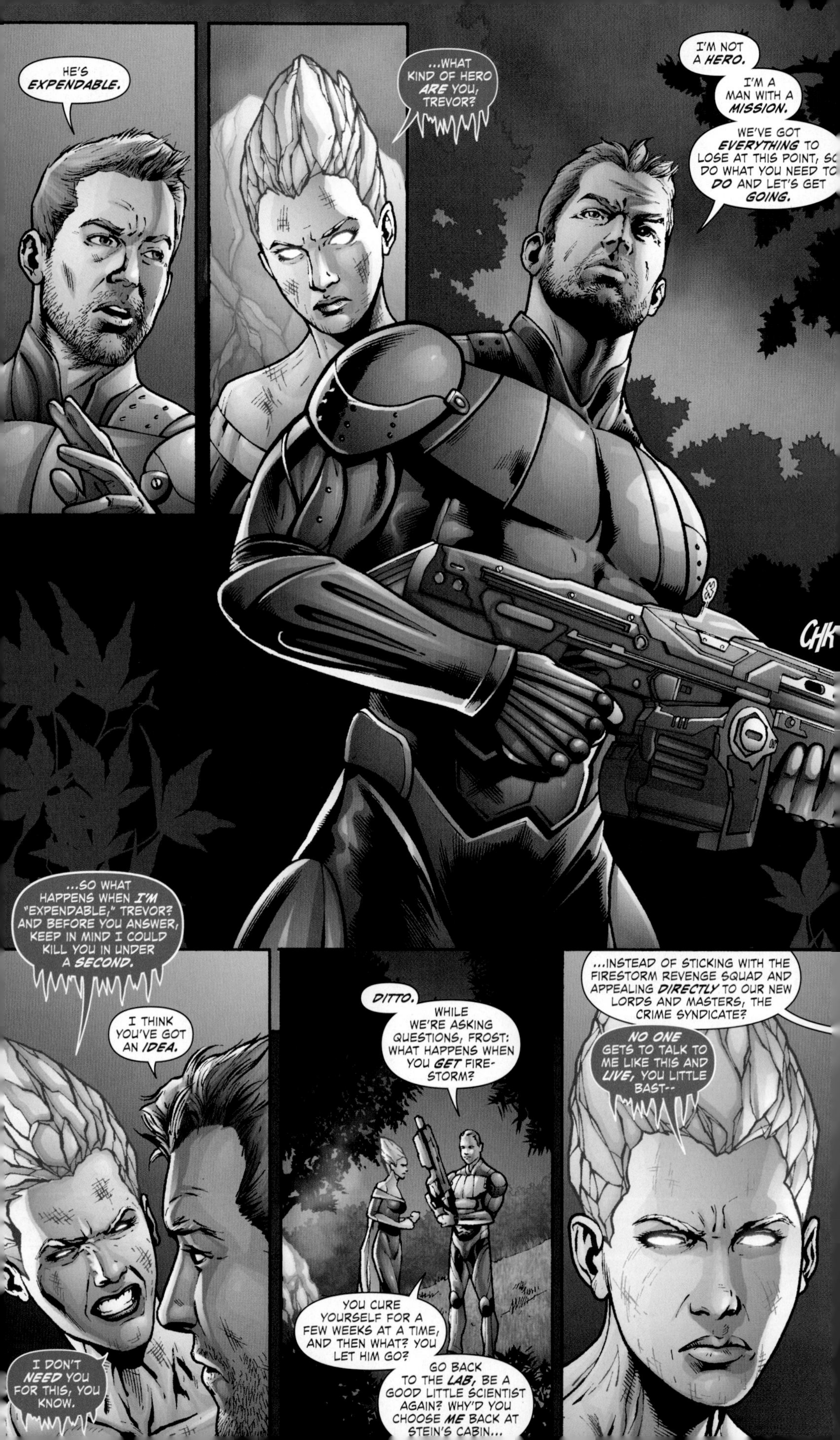
HE'S EXPENDABLE.
...WHAT KIND OF HERO ARE YOU, TREVOR?
I'M NOT A HERO.
I'M A MAN WITH A MISSION.
WE'VE GOT EVERYTHING TO LOSE AT THIS POINT, SO DO WHAT YOU NEED TO DO AND LET'S GET GOING.
CHK
...SO WHAT HAPPENS WHEN I'M "EXPENDABLE," TREVOR? AND BEFORE YOU ANSWER, KEEP IN MIND I COULD KILL YOU IN UNDER A SECOND.
I THINK YOU'VE GOT AN IDEA.
I DON'T NEED YOU FOR THIS, YOU KNOW.
DITTO.
WHILE WE'RE ASKING QUESTIONS, FROST: WHAT HAPPENS WHEN YOU GET FIRE-STORM?
YOU CURE YOURSELF FOR A FEW WEEKS AT A TIME, AND THEN WHAT? YOU LET HIM GO?
GO BACK TO THE LAB, BE A GOOD LITTLE SCIENTIST AGAIN? WHY'D YOU CHOOSE ME BACK AT STEIN'S CABIN...
...INSTEAD OF STICKING WITH THE FIRESTORM REVENGE SQUAD AND APPEALING DIRECTLY TO OUR NEW LORDS AND MASTERS, THE CRIME SYNDICATE?
NO ONE GETS TO TALK TO ME LIKE THIS AND LIVE, YOU LITTLE BAST--

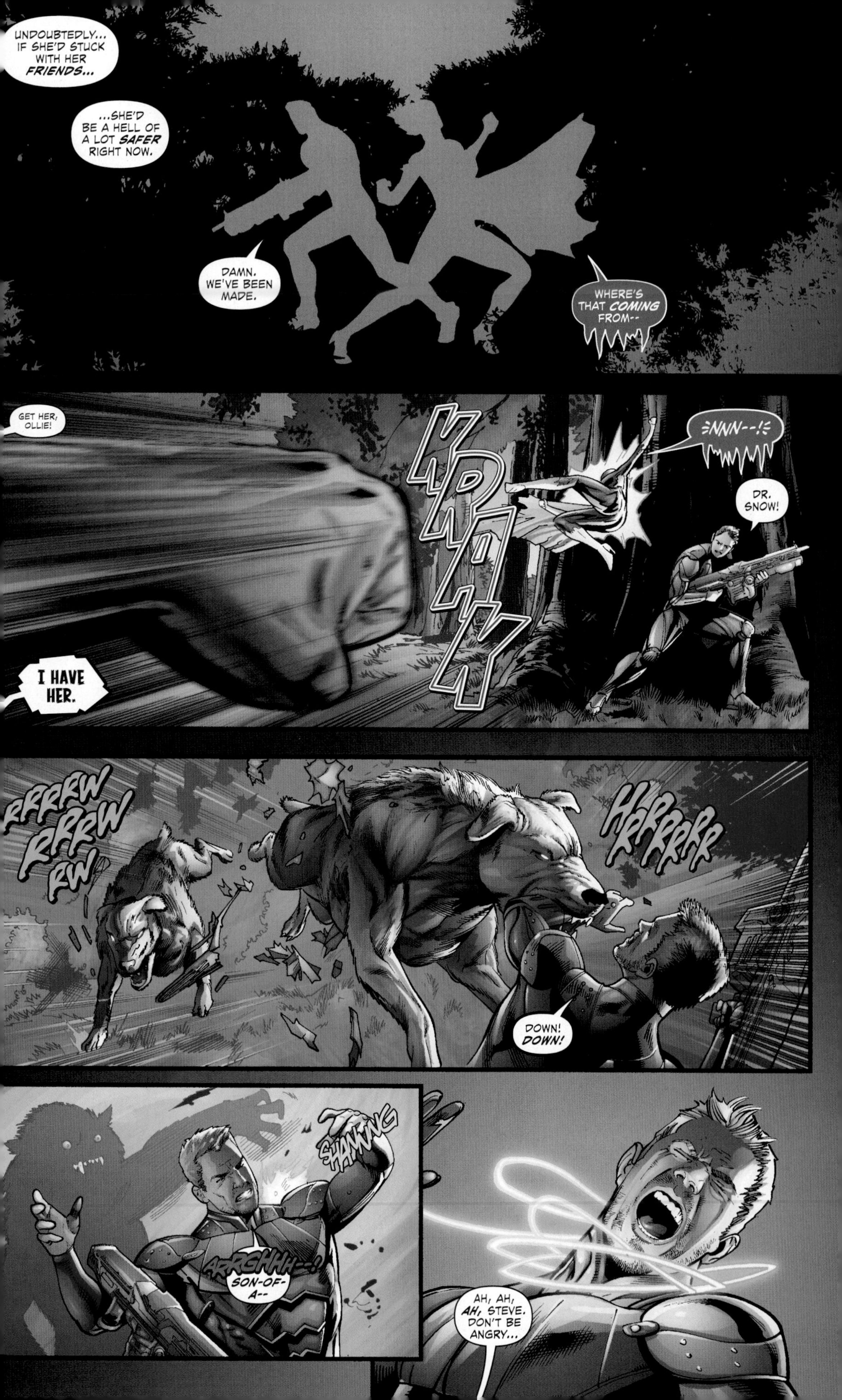
UNDOUBTEDLY... IF SHE'D STUCK WITH HER FRIENDS...
...SHE'D BE A HELL OF A LOT SAFER RIGHT NOW.
DAMN. WE'VE BEEN MADE.
WHERE'S THAT COMING FROM--
GET HER, OLLIE!
KRAKK
NNN--!
DR. SNOW!
I HAVE HER.
RRRRW RRRW RRRRW RW
HRRRRRR
DOWN! DOWN!
SHANNNG
ARRGHHH--! SON-OF-A--
AH, AH, AH, STEVE. DON'T BE ANGRY...

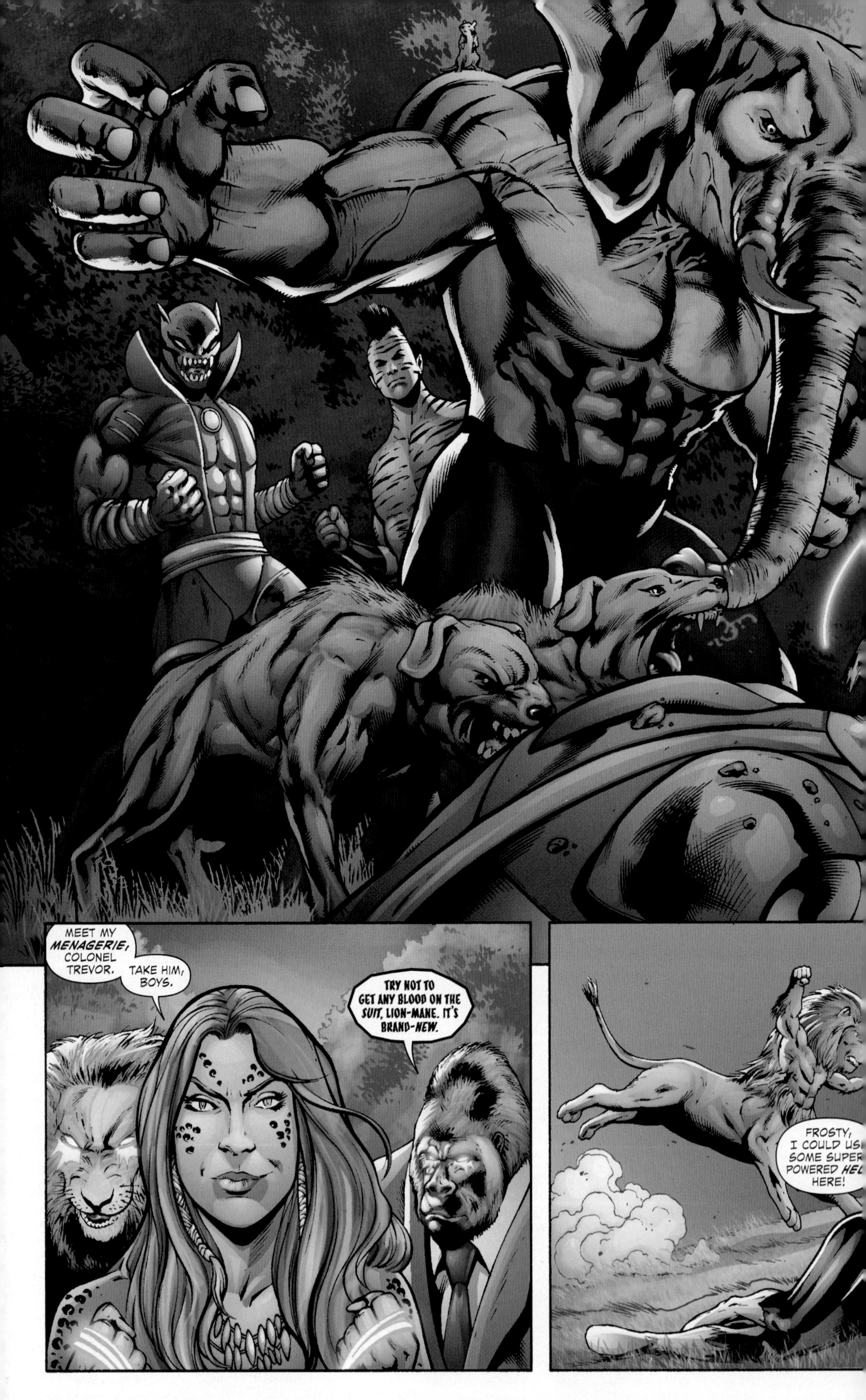
MEET MY *MENAGERIE,* COLONEL TREVOR.
TAKE HIM, BOYS.
TRY NOT TO GET ANY BLOOD ON THE *SUIT,* LION-MANE. IT'S BRAND-*NEW.*
FROSTY, I COULD US SOME SUPER POWERED *HEL* HERE!

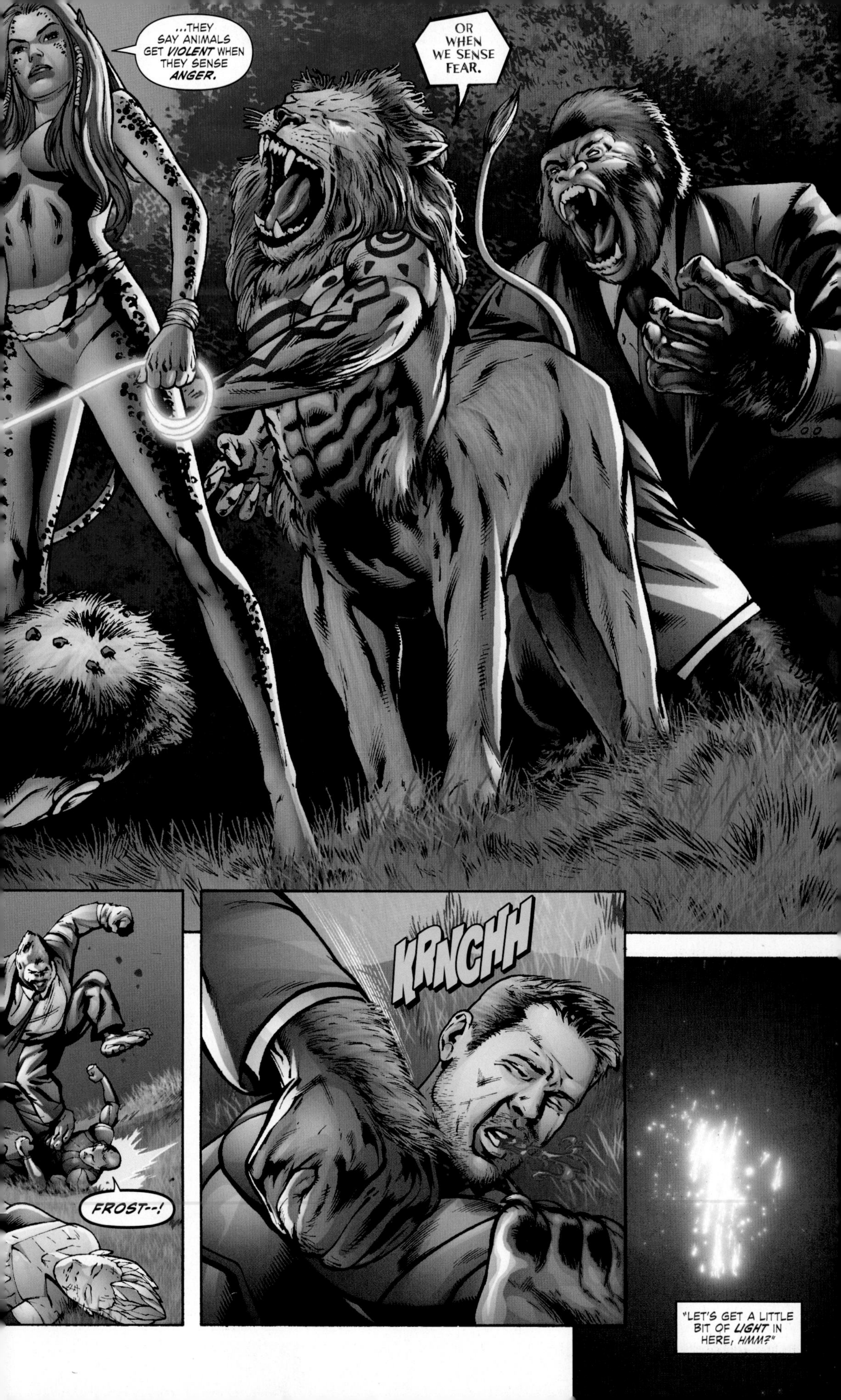
...THEY SAY ANIMALS GET VIOLENT WHEN THEY SENSE ANGER.
OR WHEN WE SENSE FEAR.
FROST--!
KRNCHH
"LET'S GET A LITTLE BIT OF LIGHT IN HERE, HMM?"

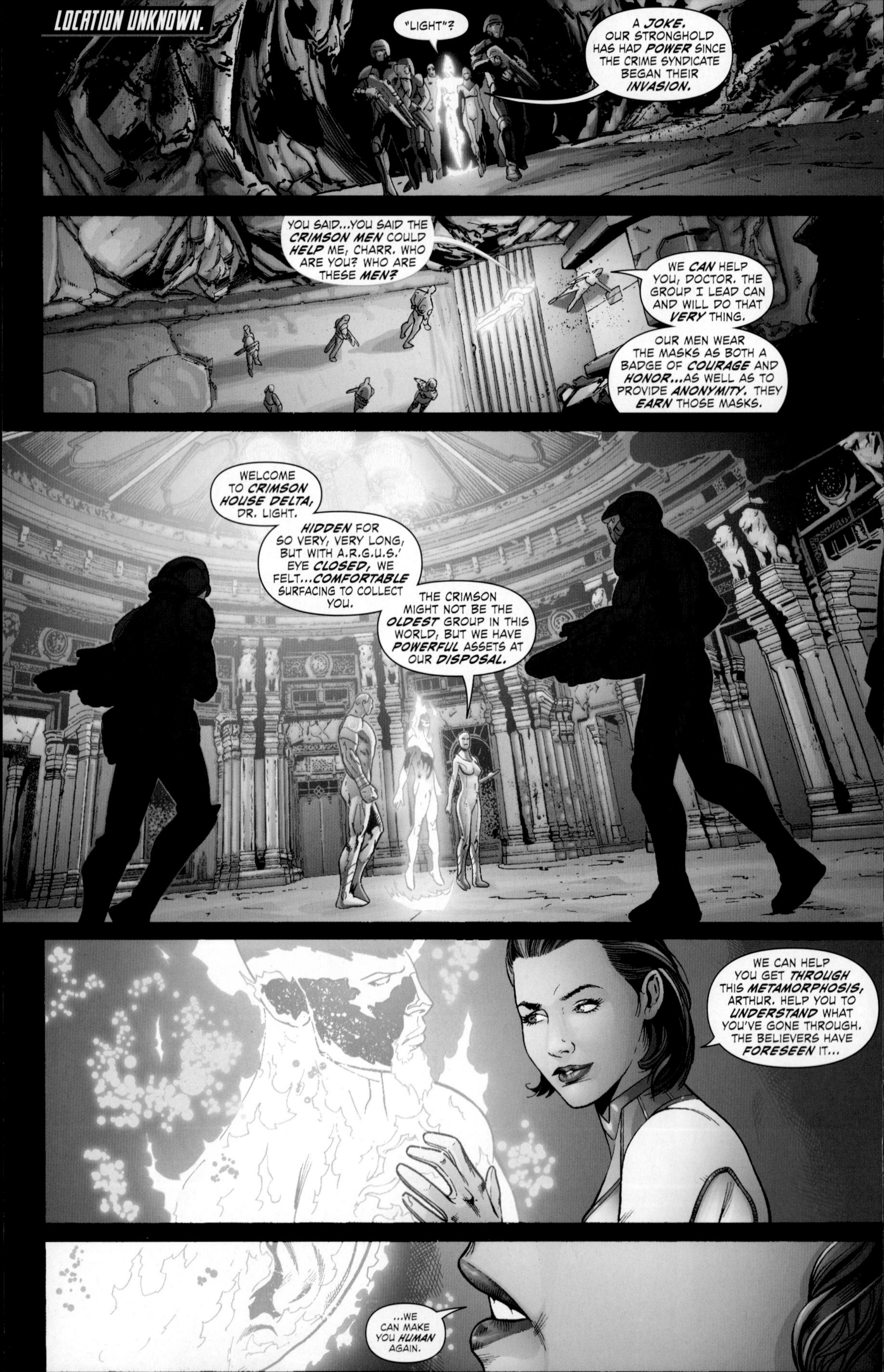
LOCATION UNKNOWN.
"LIGHT"?
A JOKE. OUR STRONGHOLD HAS HAD POWER SINCE THE CRIME SYNDICATE BEGAN THEIR INVASION.
YOU SAID...YOU SAID THE CRIMSON MEN COULD HELP ME, CHARR. WHO ARE YOU? WHO ARE THESE MEN?
WE CAN HELP YOU, DOCTOR. THE GROUP I LEAD CAN AND WILL DO THAT VERY THING.
OUR MEN WEAR THE MASKS AS BOTH A BADGE OF COURAGE AND HONOR...AS WELL AS TO PROVIDE ANONYMITY. THEY EARN THOSE MASKS.
WELCOME TO CRIMSON HOUSE DELTA, DR. LIGHT.
HIDDEN FOR SO VERY, VERY LONG, BUT WITH A.R.G.U.S.' EYE CLOSED, WE FELT...COMFORTABLE SURFACING TO COLLECT YOU.
THE CRIMSON MIGHT NOT BE THE OLDEST GROUP IN THIS WORLD, BUT WE HAVE POWERFUL ASSETS AT OUR DISPOSAL.
WE CAN HELP YOU GET THROUGH THIS METAMORPHOSIS, ARTHUR. HELP YOU TO UNDERSTAND WHAT YOU'VE GONE THROUGH. THE BELIEVERS HAVE FORESEEN IT...
...WE CAN MAKE YOU HUMAN AGAIN.

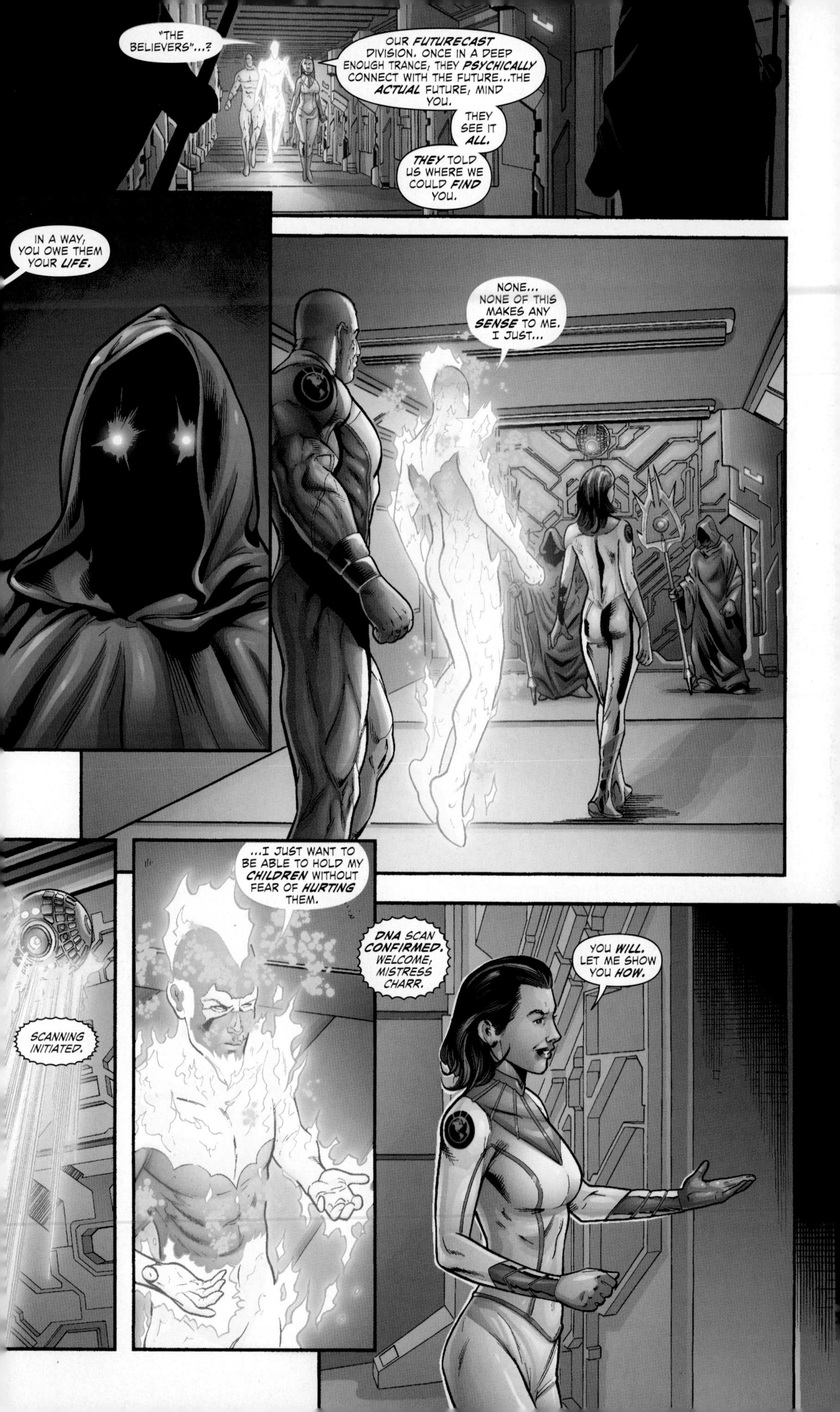
"THE BELIEVERS"...?
OUR FUTURECAST DIVISION. ONCE IN A DEEP ENOUGH TRANCE, THEY PSYCHICALLY CONNECT WITH THE FUTURE...THE ACTUAL FUTURE, MIND YOU.
THEY SEE IT ALL.
THEY TOLD US WHERE WE COULD FIND YOU.
IN A WAY, YOU OWE THEM YOUR LIFE.
NONE... NONE OF THIS MAKES ANY SENSE TO ME. I JUST...
...I JUST WANT TO BE ABLE TO HOLD MY CHILDREN WITHOUT FEAR OF HURTING THEM.
SCANNING INITIATED.
DNA SCAN CONFIRMED. WELCOME, MISTRESS CHARR.
YOU WILL. LET ME SHOW YOU HOW.

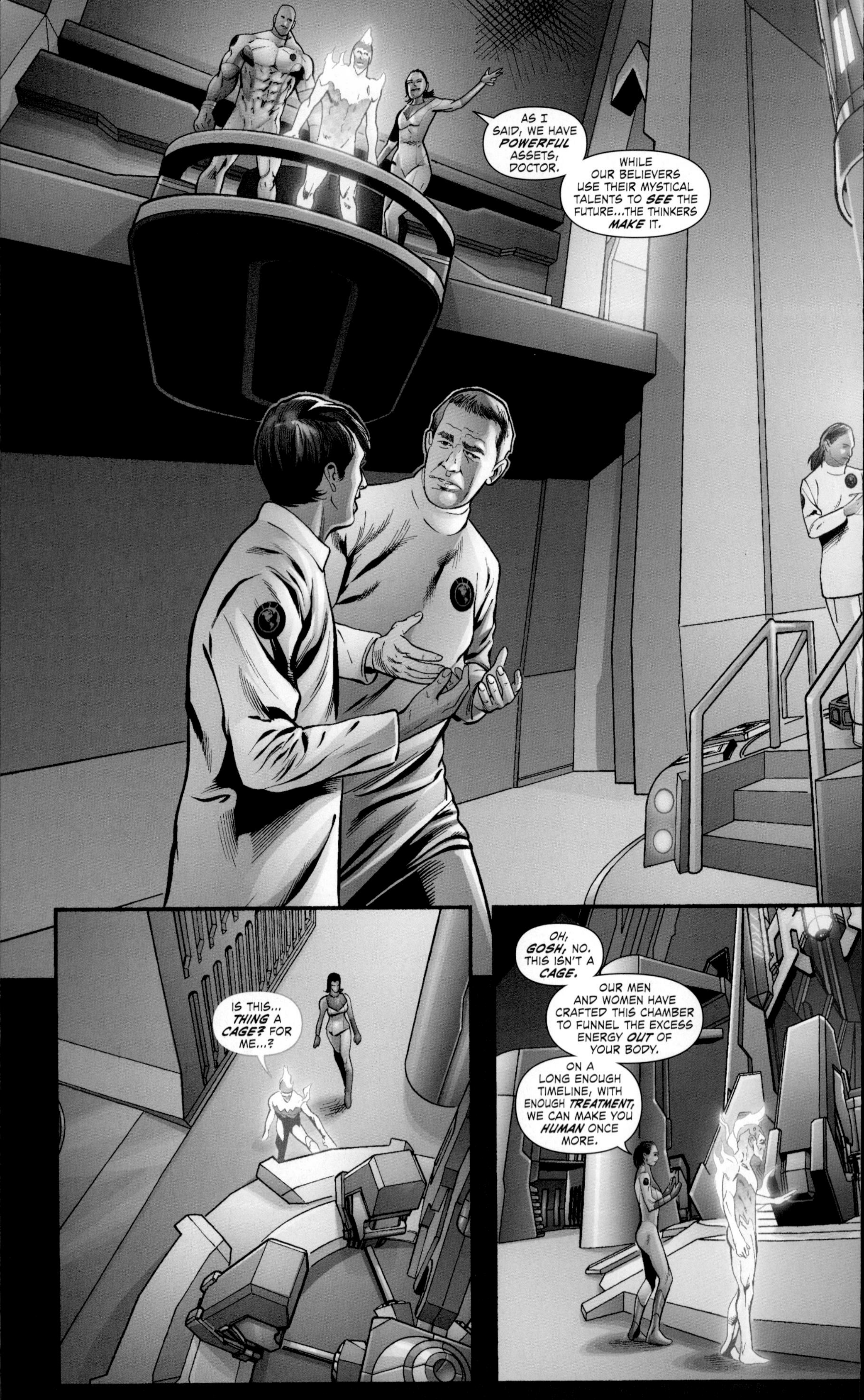
AS I SAID, WE HAVE POWERFUL ASSETS, DOCTOR.
WHILE OUR BELIEVERS USE THEIR MYSTICAL TALENTS TO SEE THE FUTURE...THE THINKERS MAKE IT.
IS THIS... THING A CAGE? FOR ME...?
OH, GOSH, NO. THIS ISN'T A CAGE.
OUR MEN AND WOMEN HAVE CRAFTED THIS CHAMBER TO FUNNEL THE EXCESS ENERGY OUT OF YOUR BODY.
ON A LONG ENOUGH TIMELINE, WITH ENOUGH TREATMENT, WE CAN MAKE YOU HUMAN ONCE MORE.

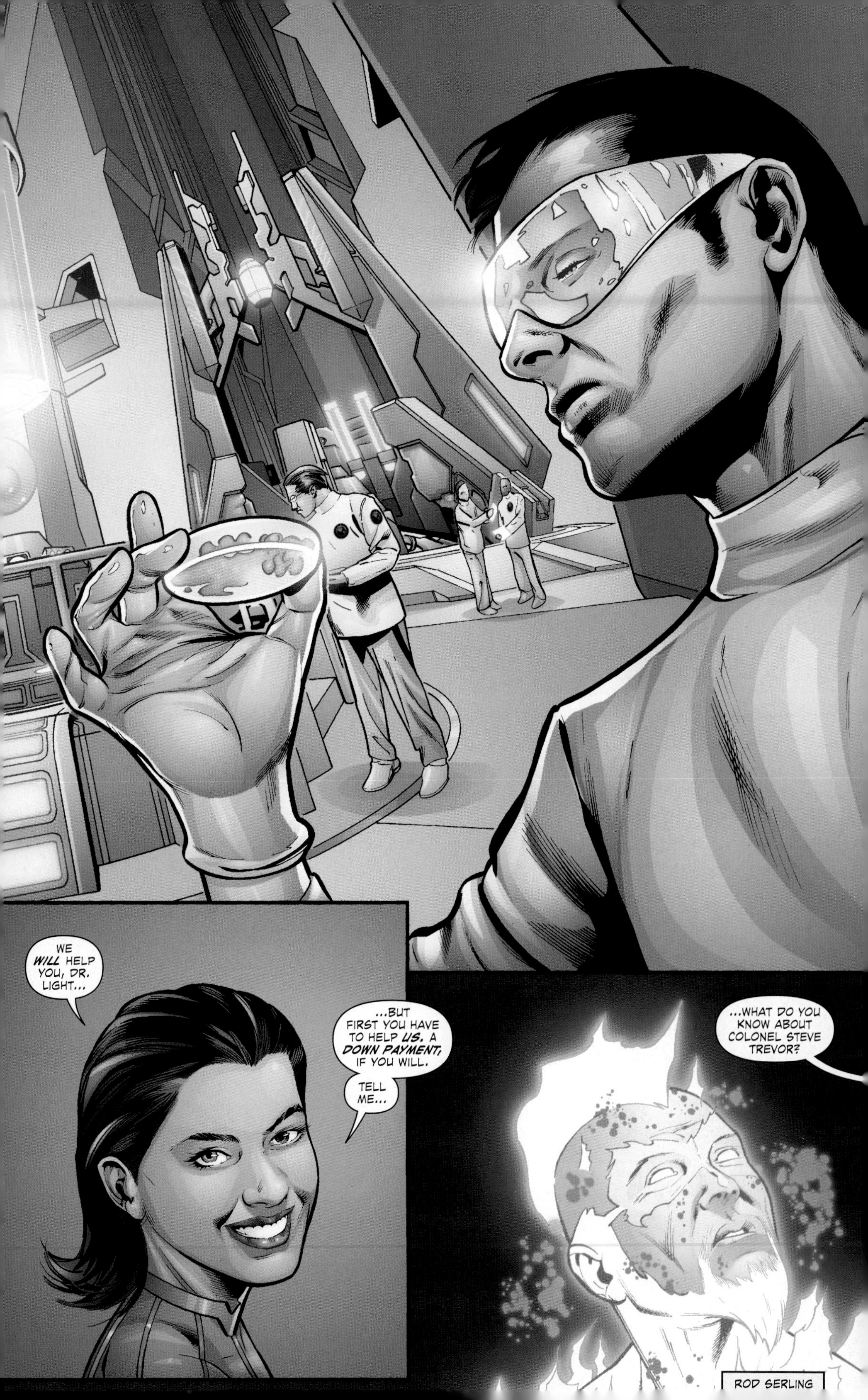
WE *WILL* HELP YOU, DR. LIGHT...
...BUT FIRST YOU HAVE TO HELP *US.* A *DOWN PAYMENT,* IF YOU WILL.
TELL ME...
...WHAT DO YOU KNOW ABOUT COLONEL STEVE TREVOR?
ROD SERLING

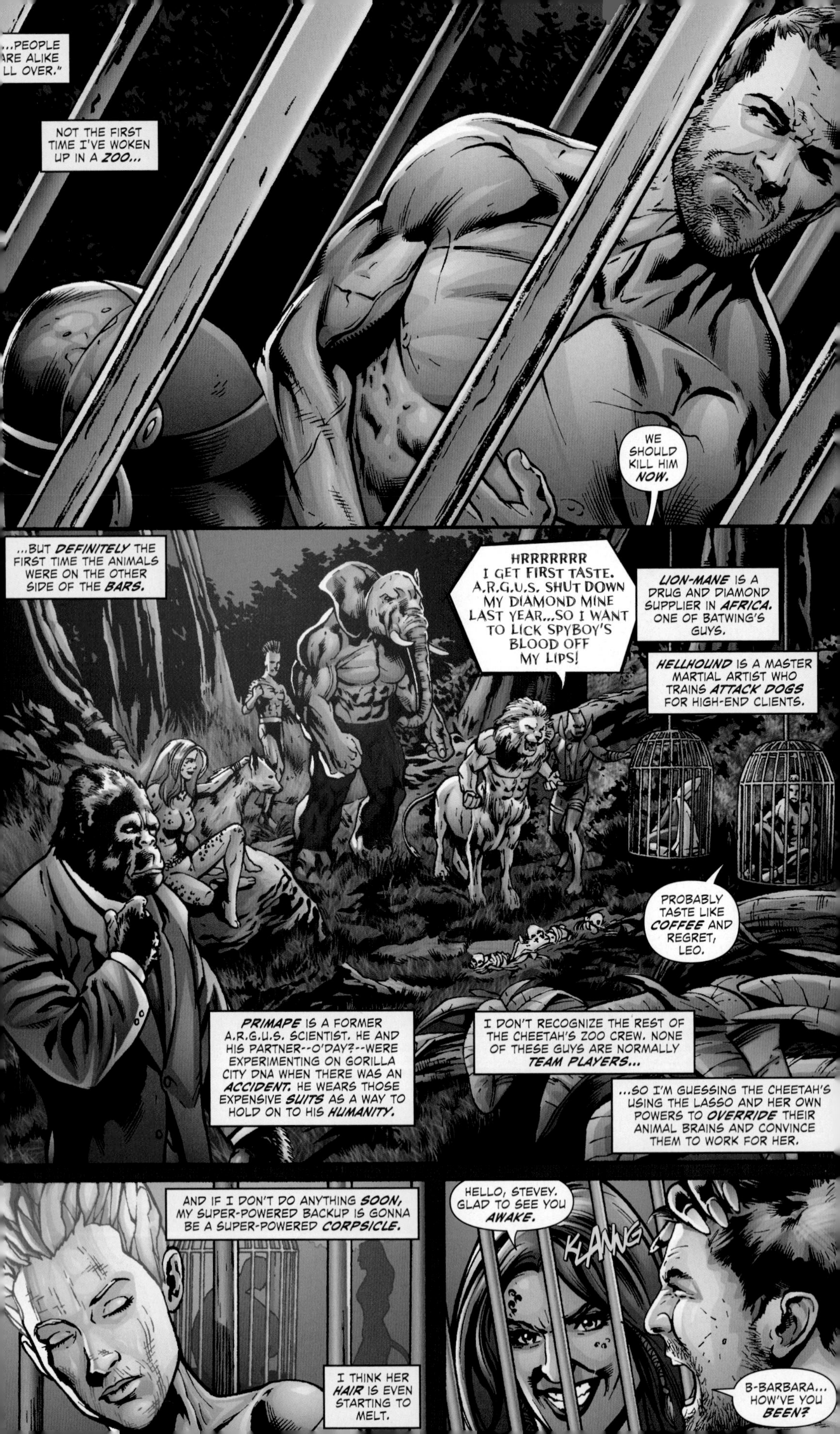
...PEOPLE ARE ALIKE ALL OVER."
NOT THE FIRST TIME I'VE WOKEN UP IN A ZOO...
WE SHOULD KILL HIM NOW.
...BUT DEFINITELY THE FIRST TIME THE ANIMALS WERE ON THE OTHER SIDE OF THE BARS.
HRRRRRRR I GET FIRST TASTE. A.R.G.U.S. SHUT DOWN MY DIAMOND MINE LAST YEAR...SO I WANT TO LICK SPYBOY'S BLOOD OFF MY LIPS!
LION-MANE IS A DRUG AND DIAMOND SUPPLIER IN AFRICA. ONE OF BATWING'S GUYS.
HELLHOUND IS A MASTER MARTIAL ARTIST WHO TRAINS ATTACK DOGS FOR HIGH-END CLIENTS.
PROBABLY TASTE LIKE COFFEE AND REGRET, LEO.
PRIMAPE IS A FORMER A.R.G.U.S. SCIENTIST. HE AND HIS PARTNER--O'DAY?--WERE EXPERIMENTING ON GORILLA CITY DNA WHEN THERE WAS AN ACCIDENT. HE WEARS THOSE EXPENSIVE SUITS AS A WAY TO HOLD ON TO HIS HUMANITY.
I DON'T RECOGNIZE THE REST OF THE CHEETAH'S ZOO CREW. NONE OF THESE GUYS ARE NORMALLY TEAM PLAYERS...
...SO I'M GUESSING THE CHEETAH'S USING THE LASSO AND HER OWN POWERS TO OVERRIDE THEIR ANIMAL BRAINS AND CONVINCE THEM TO WORK FOR HER.
AND IF I DON'T DO ANYTHING SOON, MY SUPER-POWERED BACKUP IS GONNA BE A SUPER-POWERED CORPSICLE.
I THINK HER HAIR IS EVEN STARTING TO MELT.
HELLO, STEVEY. GLAD TO SEE YOU AWAKE.
KLANNG
B-BARBARA... HOW'VE YOU BEEN?

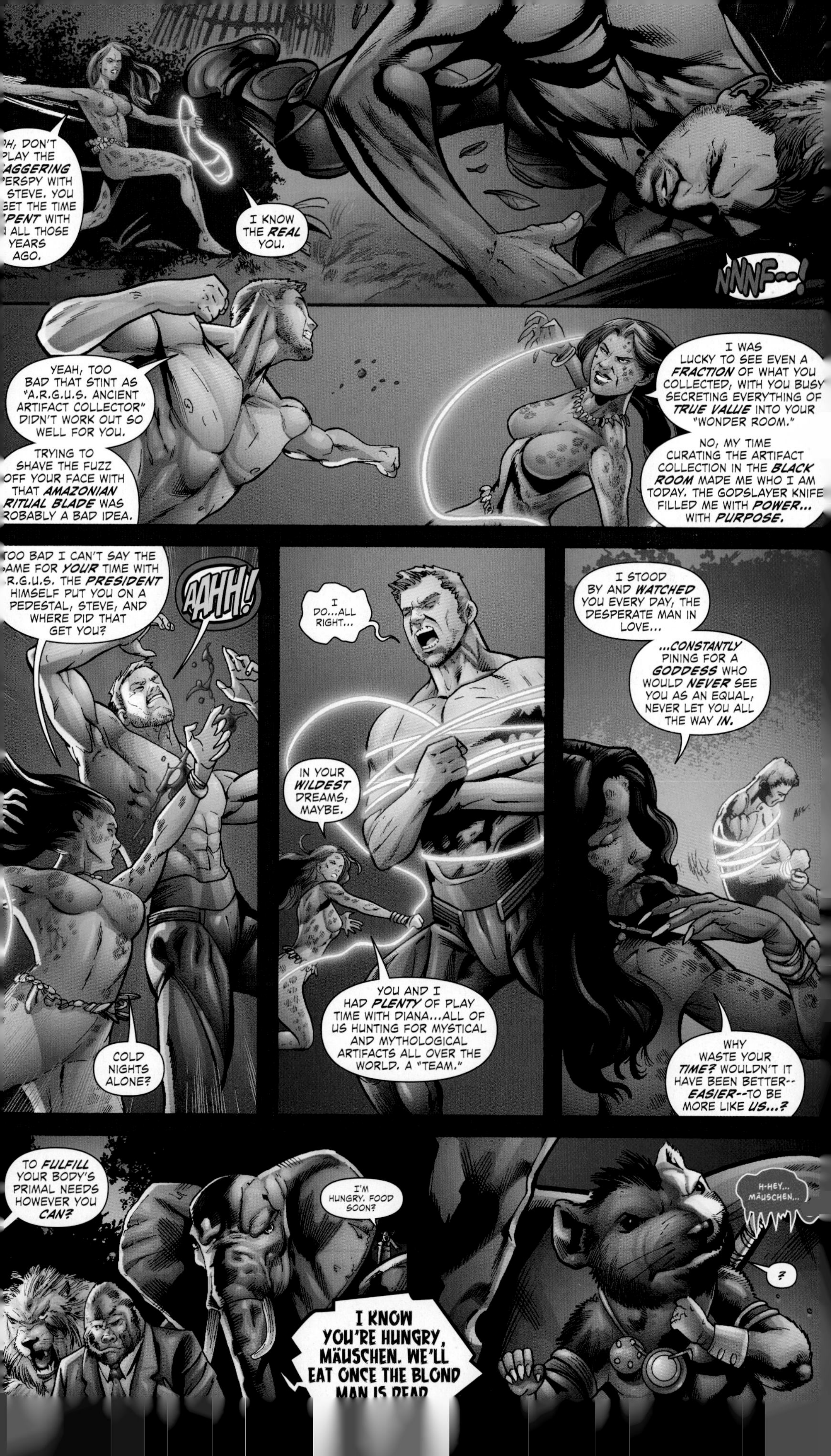
H, DON'T PLAY THE AGGERING PERSPY WITH STEVE. YOU GET THE TIME PENT WITH ALL THOSE YEARS AGO.
I KNOW THE REAL YOU.
NNNF--!
YEAH, TOO BAD THAT STINT AS "A.R.G.U.S. ANCIENT ARTIFACT COLLECTOR" DIDN'T WORK OUT SO WELL FOR YOU.
TRYING TO SHAVE THE FUZZ OFF YOUR FACE WITH THAT AMAZONIAN RITUAL BLADE WAS ROBABLY A BAD IDEA.
I WAS LUCKY TO SEE EVEN A FRACTION OF WHAT YOU COLLECTED, WITH YOU BUSY SECRETING EVERYTHING OF TRUE VALUE INTO YOUR "WONDER ROOM."
NO, MY TIME CURATING THE ARTIFACT COLLECTION IN THE BLACK ROOM MADE ME WHO I AM TODAY. THE GODSLAYER KNIFE FILLED ME WITH POWER... WITH PURPOSE.
TOO BAD I CAN'T SAY THE AME FOR YOUR TIME WITH R.G.U.S. THE PRESIDENT HIMSELF PUT YOU ON A PEDESTAL, STEVE, AND WHERE DID THAT GET YOU?
AAHH!
COLD NIGHTS ALONE?
I DO...ALL RIGHT...
IN YOUR WILDEST DREAMS, MAYBE.
YOU AND I HAD PLENTY OF PLAY TIME WITH DIANA...ALL OF US HUNTING FOR MYSTICAL AND MYTHOLOGICAL ARTIFACTS ALL OVER THE WORLD. A "TEAM."
I STOOD BY AND WATCHED YOU EVERY DAY, THE DESPERATE MAN IN LOVE...
...CONSTANTLY PINING FOR A GODDESS WHO WOULD NEVER SEE YOU AS AN EQUAL, NEVER LET YOU ALL THE WAY IN.
WHY WASTE YOUR TIME? WOULDN'T IT HAVE BEEN BETTER--EASIER--TO BE MORE LIKE US...?
TO FULFILL YOUR BODY'S PRIMAL NEEDS HOWEVER YOU CAN?
I'M HUNGRY. FOOD SOON?
H-HEY... MÄUSCHEN...
?
I KNOW YOU'RE HUNGRY, MÄUSCHEN. WE'LL EAT ONCE THE BLOND MAN IS DEAD

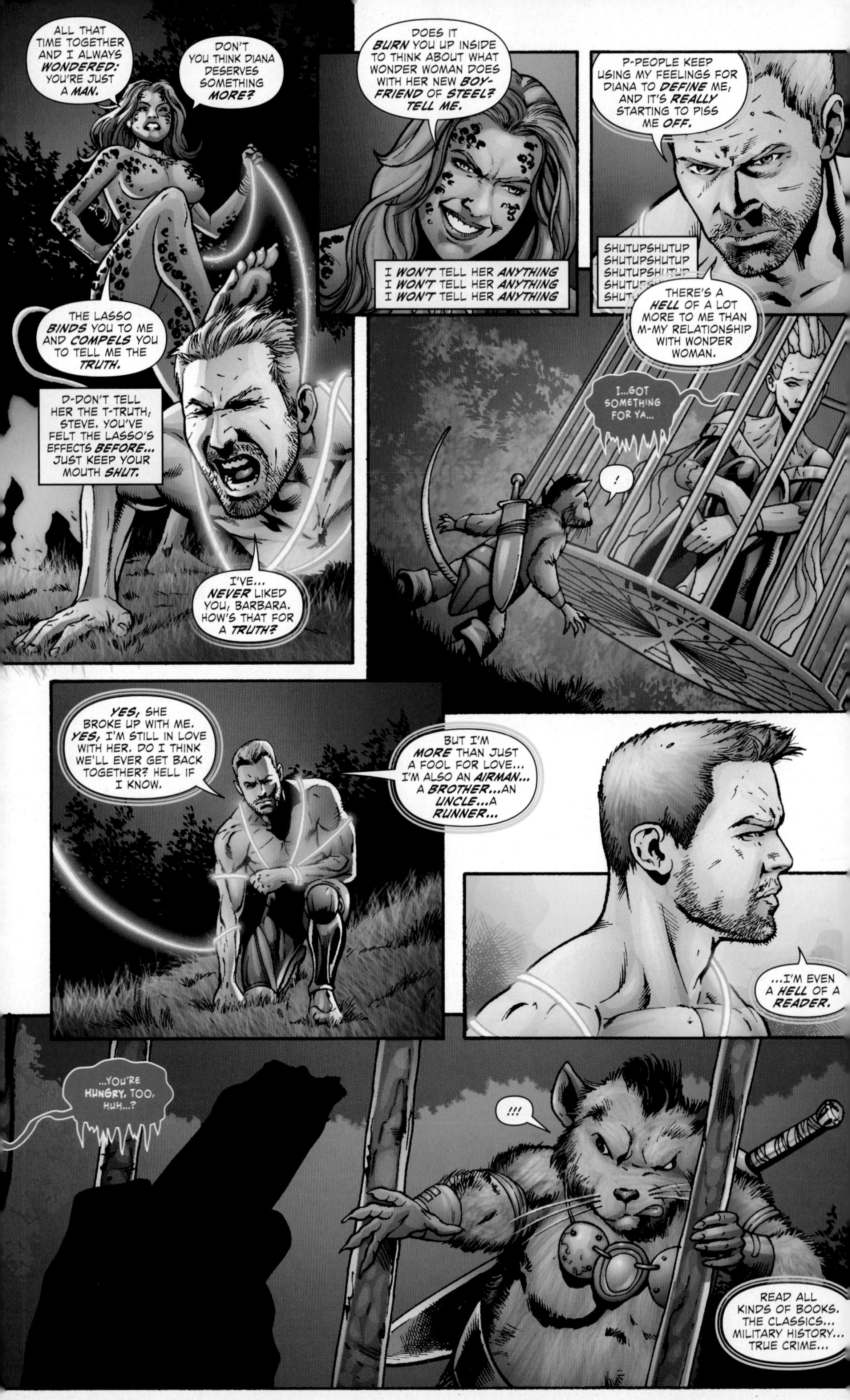
ALL THAT TIME TOGETHER AND I ALWAYS WONDERED: YOU'RE JUST A MAN.
DON'T YOU THINK DIANA DESERVES SOMETHING MORE?
THE LASSO BINDS YOU TO ME AND COMPELS YOU TO TELL ME THE TRUTH.
D-DON'T TELL HER THE T-TRUTH, STEVE. YOU'VE FELT THE LASSO'S EFFECTS BEFORE... JUST KEEP YOUR MOUTH SHUT.
I'VE... NEVER LIKED YOU, BARBARA. HOW'S THAT FOR A TRUTH?
DOES IT BURN YOU UP INSIDE TO THINK ABOUT WHAT WONDER WOMAN DOES WITH HER NEW BOY-FRIEND OF STEEL? TELL ME.
I WON'T TELL HER ANYTHING I WON'T TELL HER ANYTHING I WON'T TELL HER ANYTHING
P-PEOPLE KEEP USING MY FEELINGS FOR DIANA TO DEFINE ME, AND IT'S REALLY STARTING TO PISS ME OFF.
SHUTUPSHUTUP SHUTUPSHUTUP
THERE'S A HELL OF A LOT MORE TO ME THAN M-MY RELATIONSHIP WITH WONDER WOMAN.
I...GOT SOMETHING FOR YA...
!
YES, SHE BROKE UP WITH ME. YES, I'M STILL IN LOVE WITH HER. DO I THINK WE'LL EVER GET BACK TOGETHER? HELL IF I KNOW.
BUT I'M MORE THAN JUST A FOOL FOR LOVE... I'M ALSO AN AIRMAN... A BROTHER...AN UNCLE...A RUNNER...
...I'M EVEN A HELL OF A READER.
...YOU'RE HUNGRY, TOO, HUH...?
!!!
READ ALL KINDS OF BOOKS. THE CLASSICS... MILITARY HISTORY... TRUE CRIME...

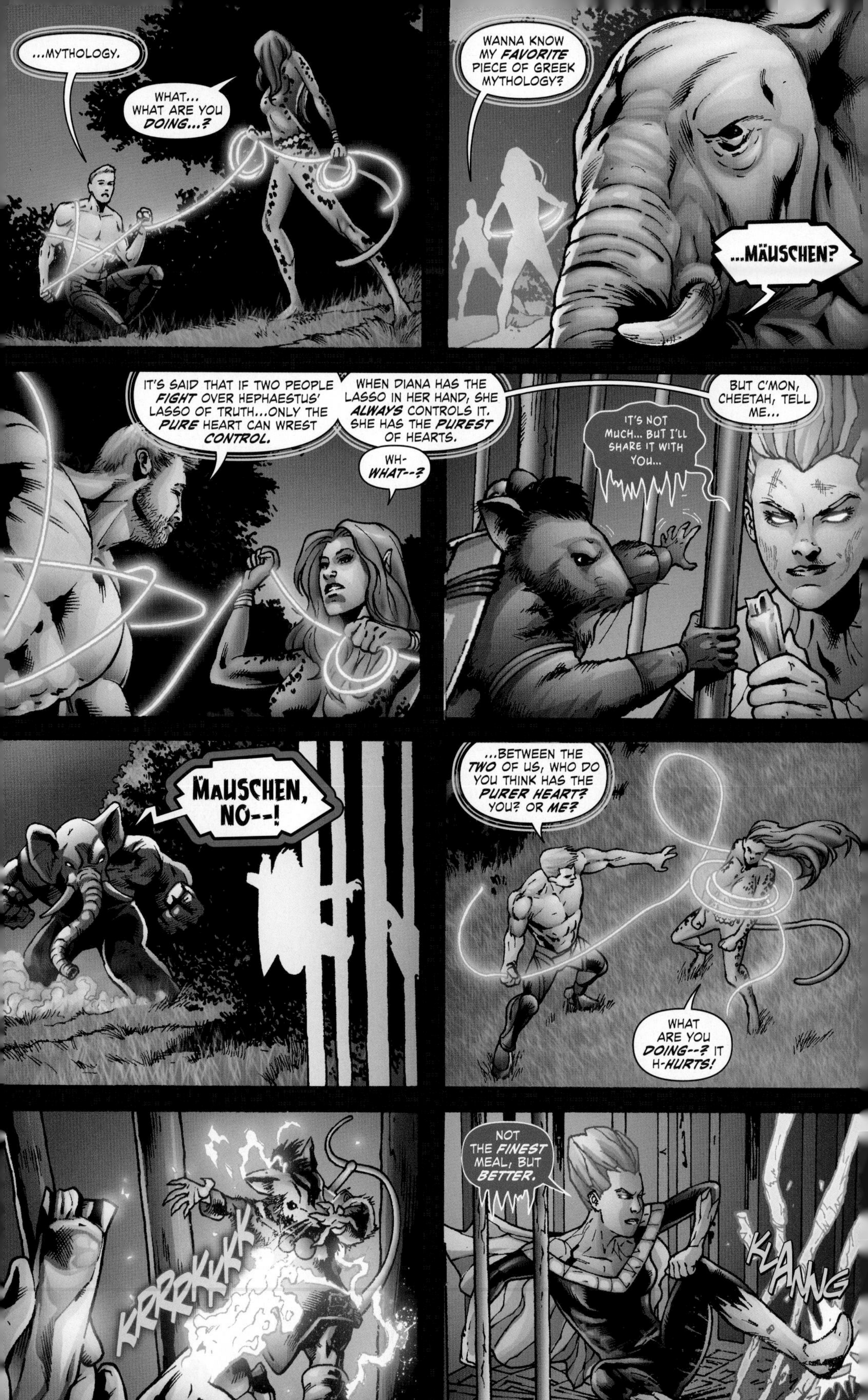
...MYTHOLOGY.
WHAT... WHAT ARE YOU DOING...?
WANNA KNOW MY FAVORITE PIECE OF GREEK MYTHOLOGY?
...MÄUSCHEN?
IT'S SAID THAT IF TWO PEOPLE FIGHT OVER HEPHAESTUS' LASSO OF TRUTH...ONLY THE PURE HEART CAN WREST CONTROL.
WHEN DIANA HAS THE LASSO IN HER HAND, SHE ALWAYS CONTROLS IT. SHE HAS THE PUREST OF HEARTS.
WH- WHAT--?
BUT C'MON, CHEETAH, TELL ME...
IT'S NOT MUCH... BUT I'LL SHARE IT WITH YOU...
MÄUSCHEN, NO--!
...BETWEEN THE TWO OF US, WHO DO YOU THINK HAS THE PURER HEART? YOU? OR ME?
WHAT ARE YOU DOING--? IT H-HURTS!
KRRRKKKK
NOT THE FINEST MEAL, BUT BETTER.
KLANNG

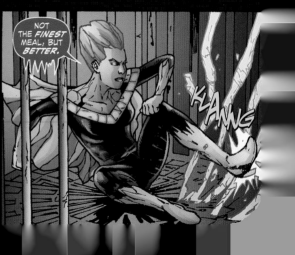

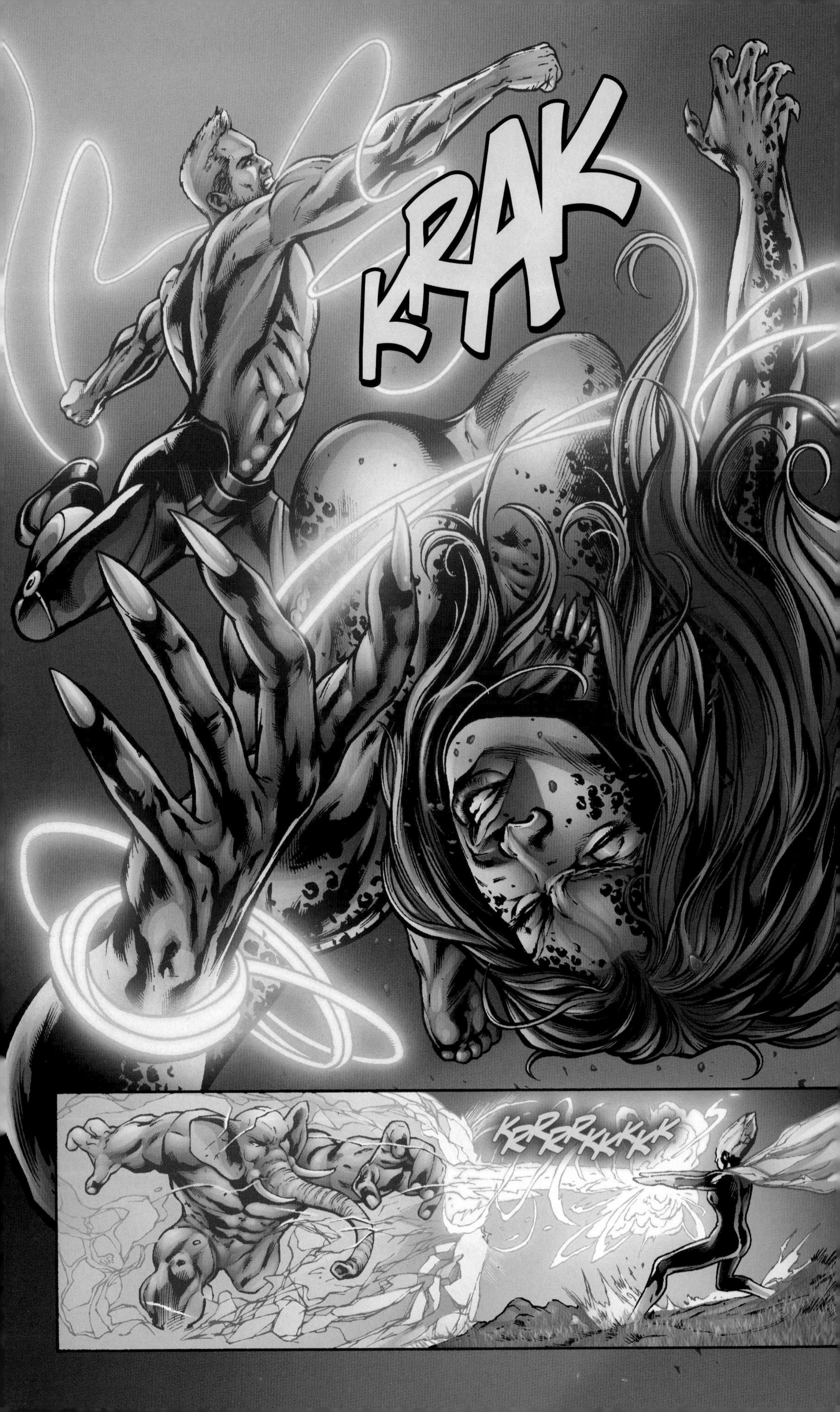
KRAK
KRRRKKKKK

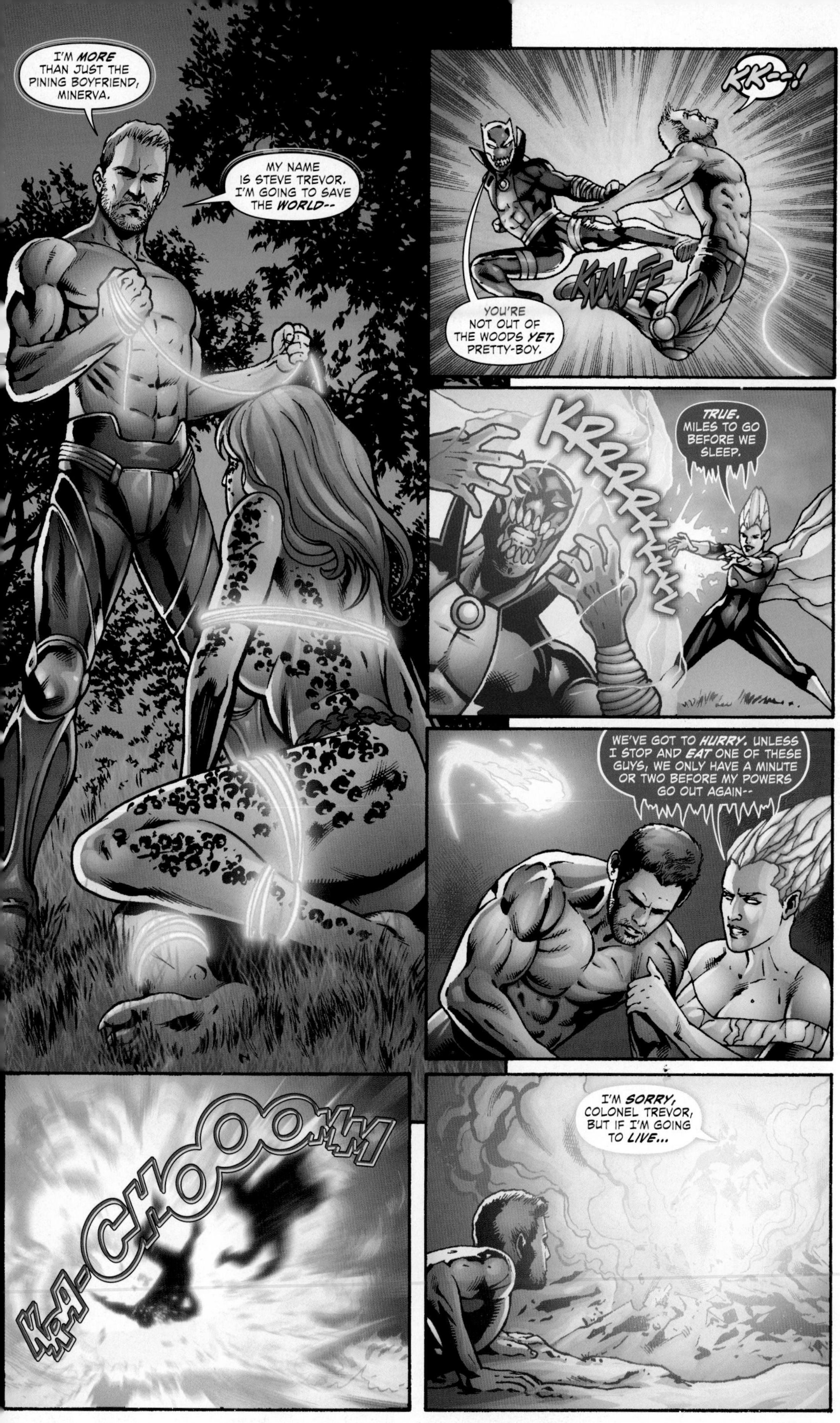
I'M MORE THAN JUST THE PINING BOYFRIEND, MINERVA.
MY NAME IS STEVE TREVOR. I'M GOING TO SAVE THE WORLD--
KK--!
KNNFF
YOU'RE NOT OUT OF THE WOODS YET, PRETTY-BOY.
KRRRRKKKKL
TRUE. MILES TO GO BEFORE WE SLEEP.
WE'VE GOT TO HURRY. UNLESS I STOP AND EAT ONE OF THESE GUYS, WE ONLY HAVE A MINUTE OR TWO BEFORE MY POWERS GO OUT AGAIN--
KA-CHOOOOMM
I'M SORRY, COLONEL TREVOR, BUT IF I'M GOING TO LIVE...

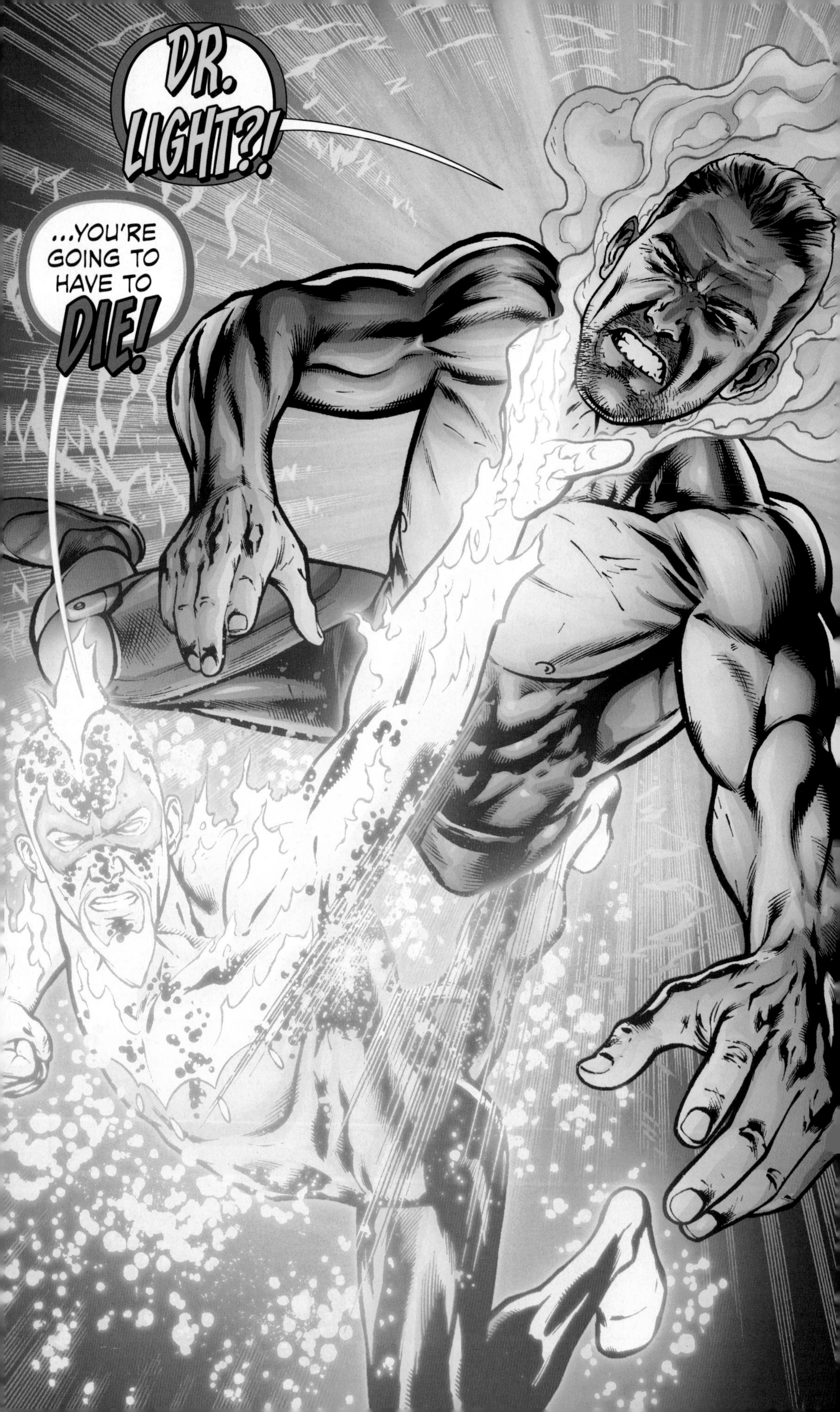
DR. LIGHT?!
...YOU'RE GOING TO HAVE TO DIE!

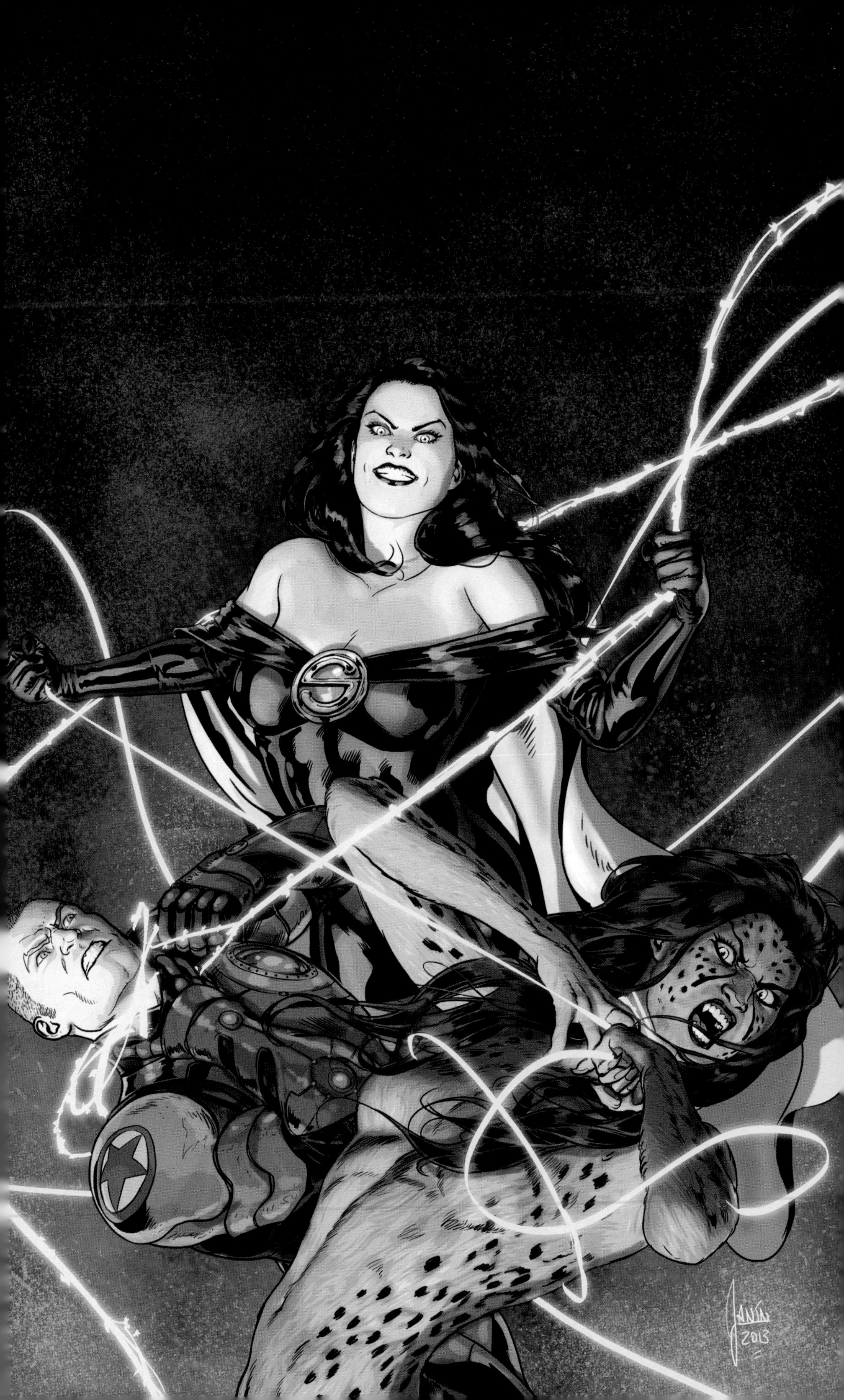

PART SIX: TRUSTFALL

STERLING GATES Writer **NEIL EDWARDS** Penciller **JASON PAZ JAY LEISTEN** Inkers
NATHAN EYRING Colorist **TAYLOR ESPOSITO** Letterer
Cover Art by **MIKEL JANIN**

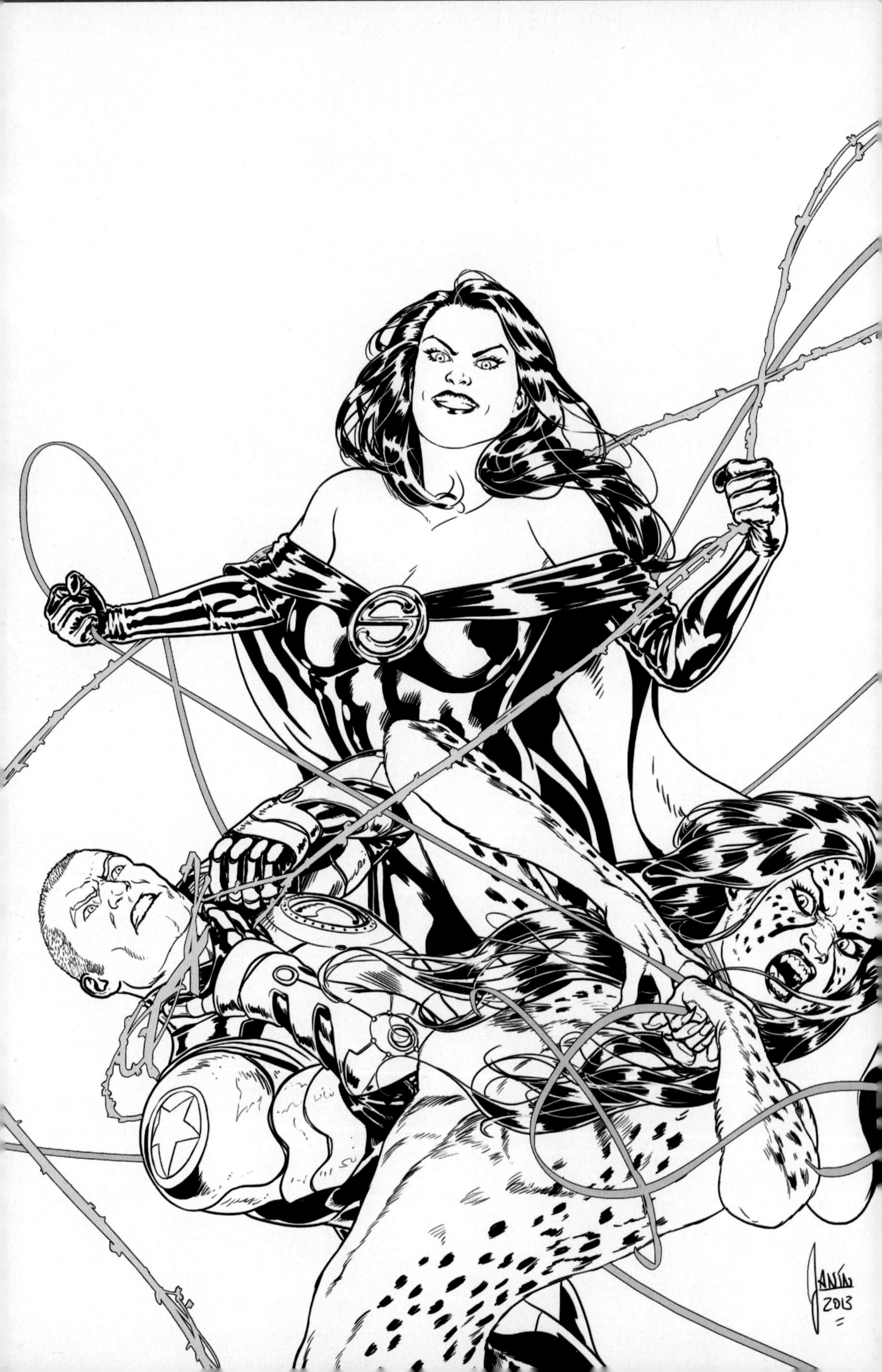

JANIN
2013

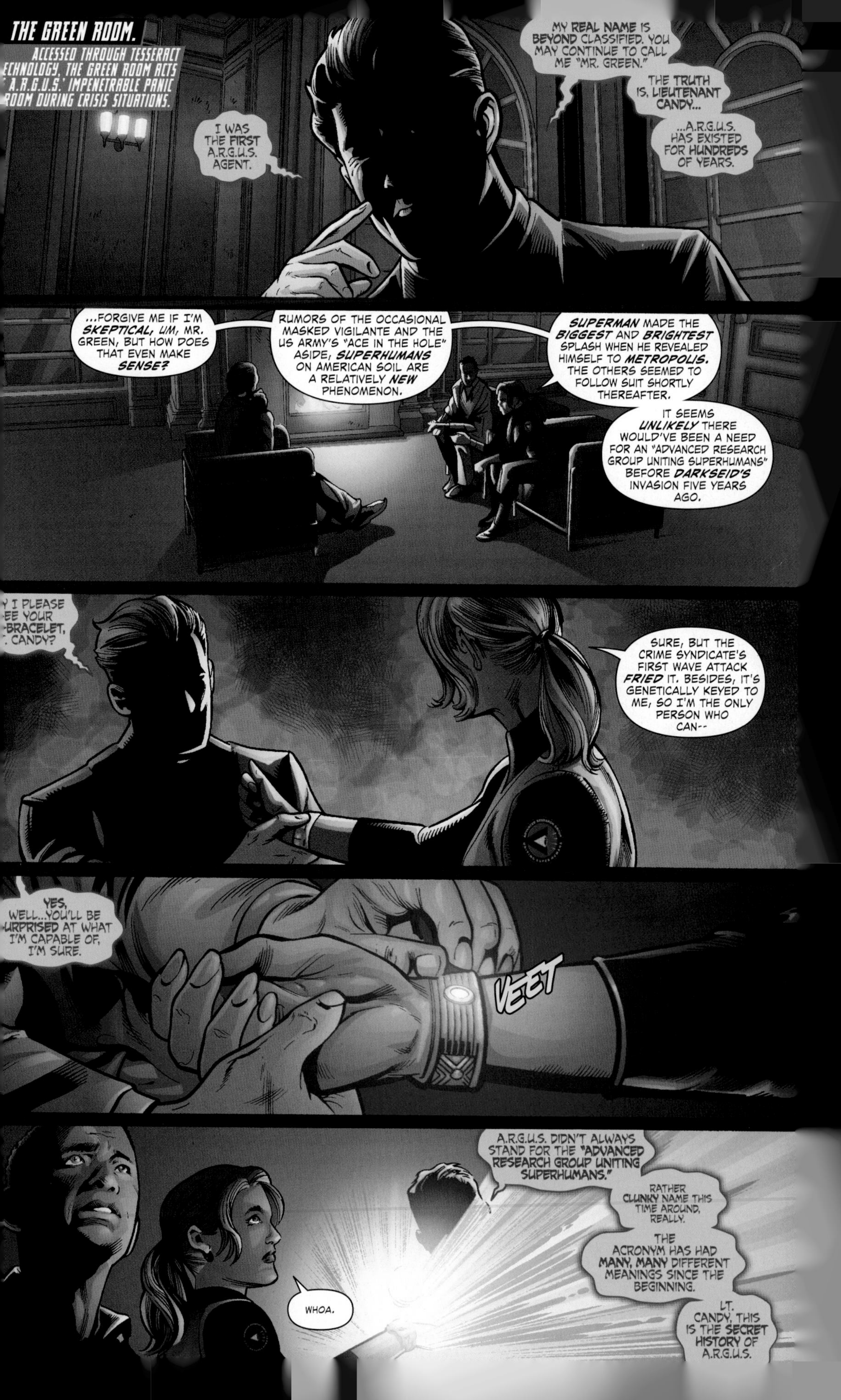

THE GREEN ROOM.
ACCESSED THROUGH TESSERACT ECHNOLOGY, THE GREEN ROOM ACTS A.R.G.U.S.' IMPENETRABLE PANIC ROOM DURING CRISIS SITUATIONS.
I WAS THE FIRST A.R.G.U.S. AGENT.
MY REAL NAME IS BEYOND CLASSIFIED. YOU MAY CONTINUE TO CALL ME "MR. GREEN."
THE TRUTH IS, LIEUTENANT CANDY...
...A.R.G.U.S. HAS EXISTED FOR HUNDREDS OF YEARS.
...FORGIVE ME IF I'M SKEPTICAL, UM, MR. GREEN, BUT HOW DOES THAT EVEN MAKE SENSE?
RUMORS OF THE OCCASIONAL MASKED VIGILANTE AND THE US ARMY'S "ACE IN THE HOLE" ASIDE, SUPERHUMANS ON AMERICAN SOIL ARE A RELATIVELY NEW PHENOMENON.
SUPERMAN MADE THE BIGGEST AND BRIGHTEST SPLASH WHEN HE REVEALED HIMSELF TO METROPOLIS. THE OTHERS SEEMED TO FOLLOW SUIT SHORTLY THEREAFTER.
IT SEEMS UNLIKELY THERE WOULD'VE BEEN A NEED FOR AN "ADVANCED RESEARCH GROUP UNITING SUPERHUMANS" BEFORE DARKSEID'S INVASION FIVE YEARS AGO.
Y I PLEASE EE YOUR BRACELET, . CANDY?
SURE, BUT THE CRIME SYNDICATE'S FIRST WAVE ATTACK FRIED IT. BESIDES, IT'S GENETICALLY KEYED TO ME, SO I'M THE ONLY PERSON WHO CAN--
YES, WELL...YOU'LL BE URPRISED AT WHAT I'M CAPABLE OF, I'M SURE.
VEET
A.R.G.U.S. DIDN'T ALWAYS STAND FOR THE "ADVANCED RESEARCH GROUP UNITING SUPERHUMANS."
RATHER CLUNKY NAME THIS TIME AROUND, REALLY.
THE ACRONYM HAS HAD MANY, MANY DIFFERENT MEANINGS SINCE THE BEGINNING.
WHOA.
LT. CANDY, THIS IS THE SECRET HISTORY OF A.R.G.U.S.

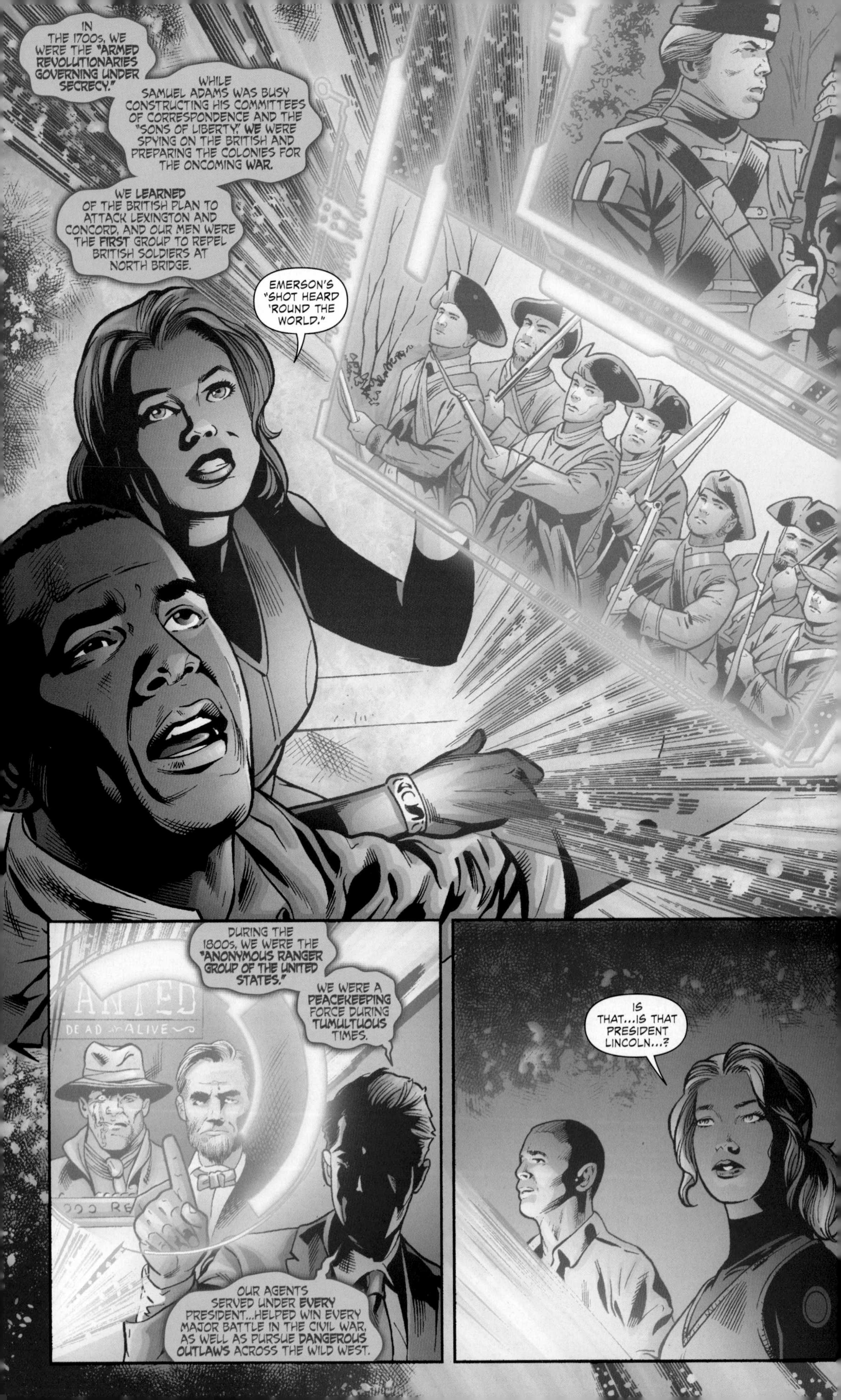

IN THE 1700s, WE WERE THE "ARMED REVOLUTIONARIES GOVERNING UNDER SECRECY."
WHILE SAMUEL ADAMS WAS BUSY CONSTRUCTING HIS COMMITTEES OF CORRESPONDENCE AND THE "SONS OF LIBERTY," WE WERE SPYING ON THE BRITISH AND PREPARING THE COLONIES FOR THE ONCOMING WAR.
WE LEARNED OF THE BRITISH PLAN TO ATTACK LEXINGTON AND CONCORD, AND OUR MEN WERE THE FIRST GROUP TO REPEL BRITISH SOLDIERS AT NORTH BRIDGE.
EMERSON'S "SHOT HEARD 'ROUND THE WORLD."
DURING THE 1800s, WE WERE THE "ANONYMOUS RANGER GROUP OF THE UNITED STATES."
WE WERE A PEACEKEEPING FORCE DURING TUMULTUOUS TIMES.
DEAD ALIVE
OUR AGENTS SERVED UNDER EVERY PRESIDENT...HELPED WIN EVERY MAJOR BATTLE IN THE CIVIL WAR, AS WELL AS PURSUE DANGEROUS OUTLAWS ACROSS THE WILD WEST.
IS THAT...IS THAT PRESIDENT LINCOLN...?

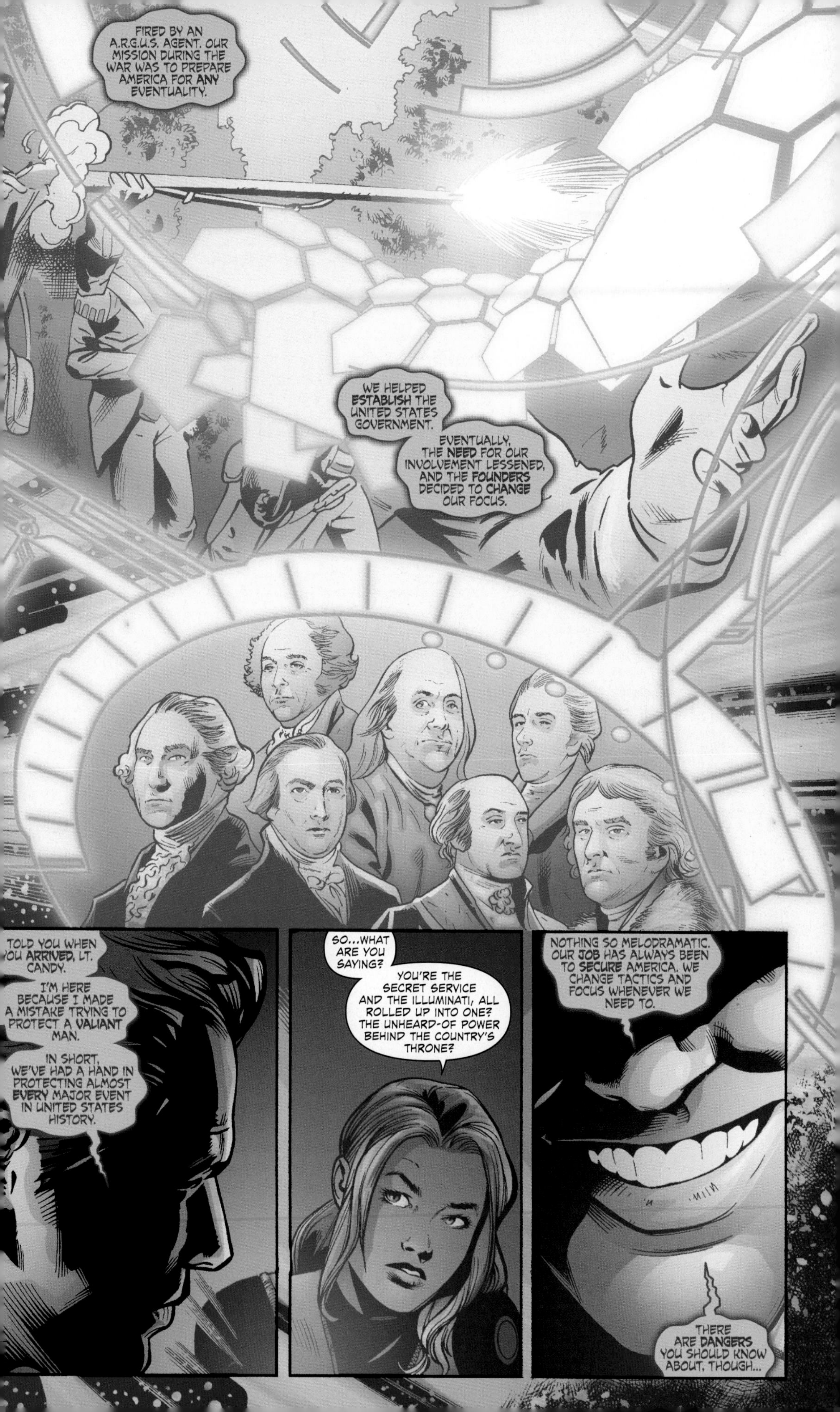

FIRED BY AN A.R.G.U.S. AGENT. OUR MISSION DURING THE WAR WAS TO PREPARE AMERICA FOR ANY EVENTUALITY.
WE HELPED ESTABLISH THE UNITED STATES GOVERNMENT.
EVENTUALLY, THE NEED FOR OUR INVOLVEMENT LESSENED, AND THE FOUNDERS DECIDED TO CHANGE OUR FOCUS.
TOLD YOU WHEN YOU ARRIVED, LT. CANDY.
I'M HERE BECAUSE I MADE A MISTAKE TRYING TO PROTECT A VALIANT MAN.
IN SHORT, WE'VE HAD A HAND IN PROTECTING ALMOST EVERY MAJOR EVENT IN UNITED STATES HISTORY.
SO...WHAT ARE YOU SAYING?
YOU'RE THE SECRET SERVICE AND THE ILLUMINATI, ALL ROLLED UP INTO ONE? THE UNHEARD-OF POWER BEHIND THE COUNTRY'S THRONE?
NOTHING SO MELODRAMATIC. OUR JOB HAS ALWAYS BEEN TO SECURE AMERICA. WE CHANGE TACTICS AND FOCUS WHENEVER WE NEED TO.
THERE ARE DANGERS YOU SHOULD KNOW ABOUT, THOUGH...

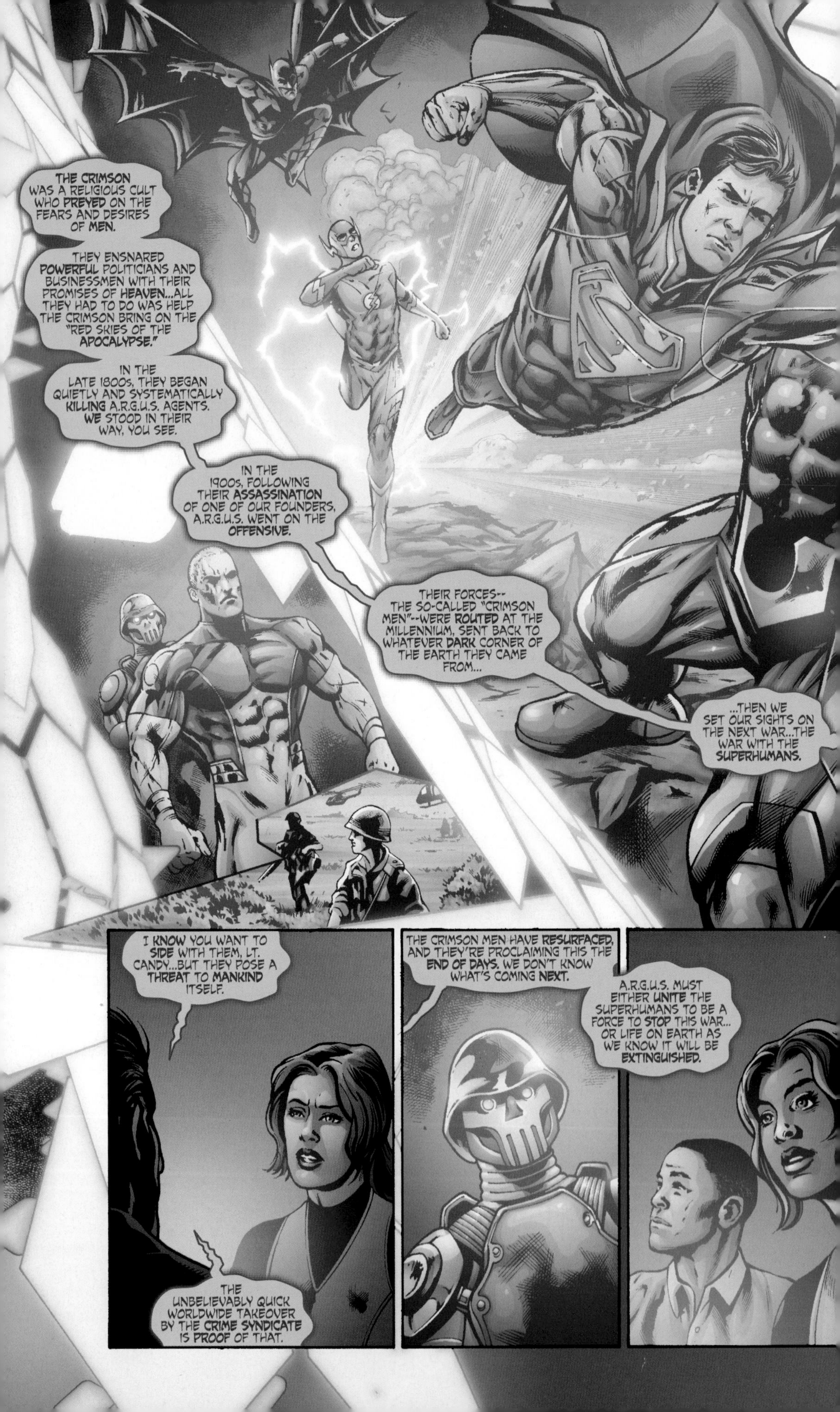
THE CRIMSON WAS A RELIGIOUS CULT WHO PREYED ON THE FEARS AND DESIRES OF MEN.
THEY ENSNARED POWERFUL POLITICIANS AND BUSINESSMEN WITH THEIR PROMISES OF HEAVEN...ALL THEY HAD TO DO WAS HELP THE CRIMSON BRING ON THE "RED SKIES OF THE APOCALYPSE."
IN THE LATE 1800s, THEY BEGAN QUIETLY AND SYSTEMATICALLY KILLING A.R.G.U.S. AGENTS. WE STOOD IN THEIR WAY, YOU SEE.
IN THE 1900s, FOLLOWING THEIR ASSASSINATION OF ONE OF OUR FOUNDERS, A.R.G.U.S. WENT ON THE OFFENSIVE.
THEIR FORCES--THE SO-CALLED "CRIMSON MEN"--WERE ROUTED AT THE MILLENNIUM, SENT BACK TO WHATEVER DARK CORNER OF THE EARTH THEY CAME FROM...
...THEN WE SET OUR SIGHTS ON THE NEXT WAR...THE WAR WITH THE SUPERHUMANS.
I KNOW YOU WANT TO SIDE WITH THEM, LT. CANDY...BUT THEY POSE A THREAT TO MANKIND ITSELF.
THE UNBELIEVABLY QUICK WORLDWIDE TAKEOVER BY THE CRIME SYNDICATE IS PROOF OF THAT.
THE CRIMSON MEN HAVE RESURFACED, AND THEY'RE PROCLAIMING THIS THE END OF DAYS. WE DON'T KNOW WHAT'S COMING NEXT.
A.R.G.U.S. MUST EITHER UNITE THE SUPERHUMANS TO BE A FORCE TO STOP THIS WAR... OR LIFE ON EARTH AS WE KNOW IT WILL BE EXTINGUISHED.

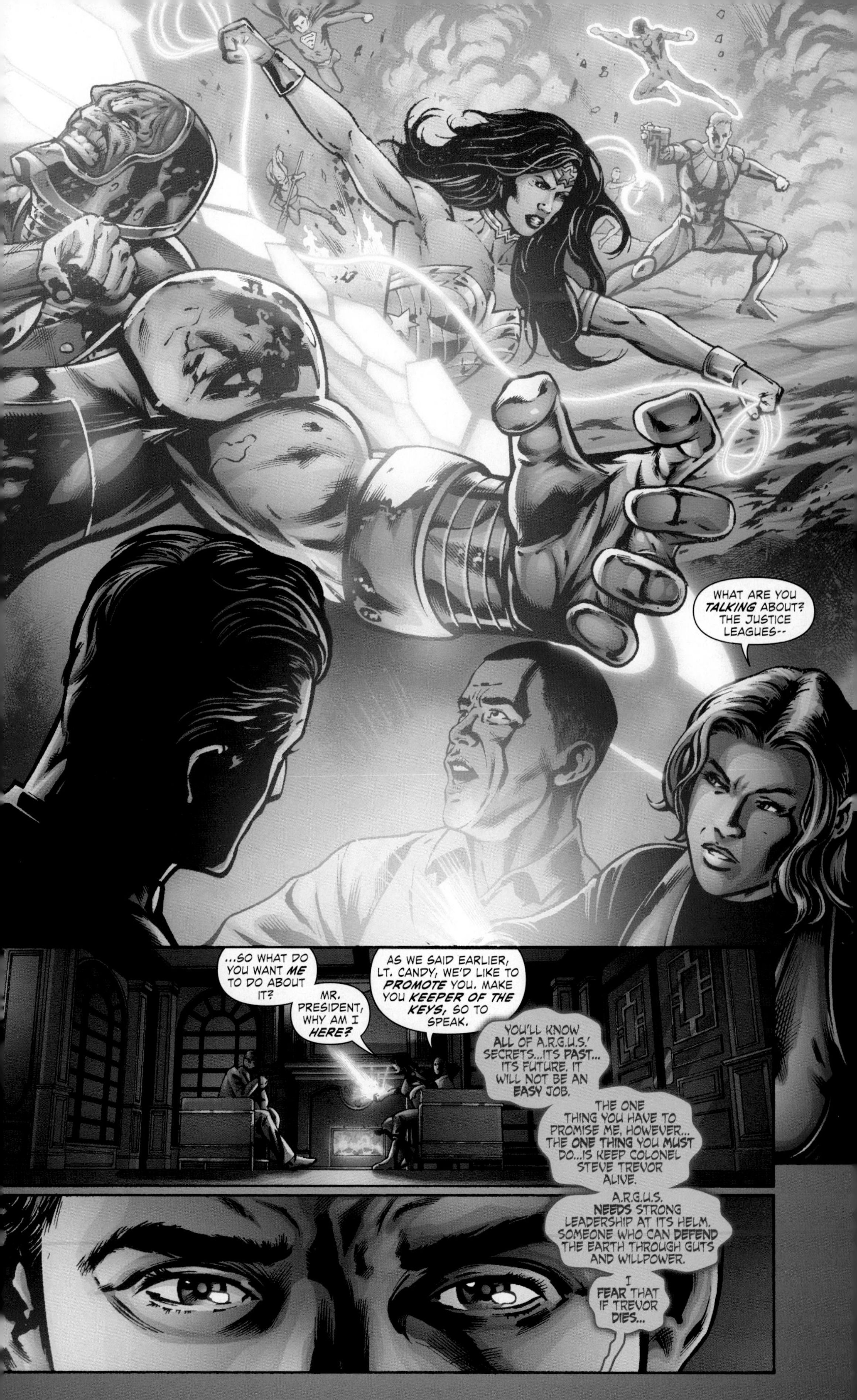
WHAT ARE YOU TALKING ABOUT? THE JUSTICE LEAGUES--
...SO WHAT DO YOU WANT ME TO DO ABOUT IT?
MR. PRESIDENT, WHY AM I HERE?
AS WE SAID EARLIER, LT. CANDY, WE'D LIKE TO PROMOTE YOU. MAKE YOU KEEPER OF THE KEYS, SO TO SPEAK.
YOU'LL KNOW ALL OF A.R.G.U.S.' SECRETS...ITS PAST... ITS FUTURE. IT WILL NOT BE AN EASY JOB.
THE ONE THING YOU HAVE TO PROMISE ME, HOWEVER... THE ONE THING YOU MUST DO...IS KEEP COLONEL STEVE TREVOR ALIVE.
A.R.G.U.S. NEEDS STRONG LEADERSHIP AT ITS HELM. SOMEONE WHO CAN DEFEND THE EARTH THROUGH GUTS AND WILLPOWER.
I FEAR THAT IF TREVOR DIES...

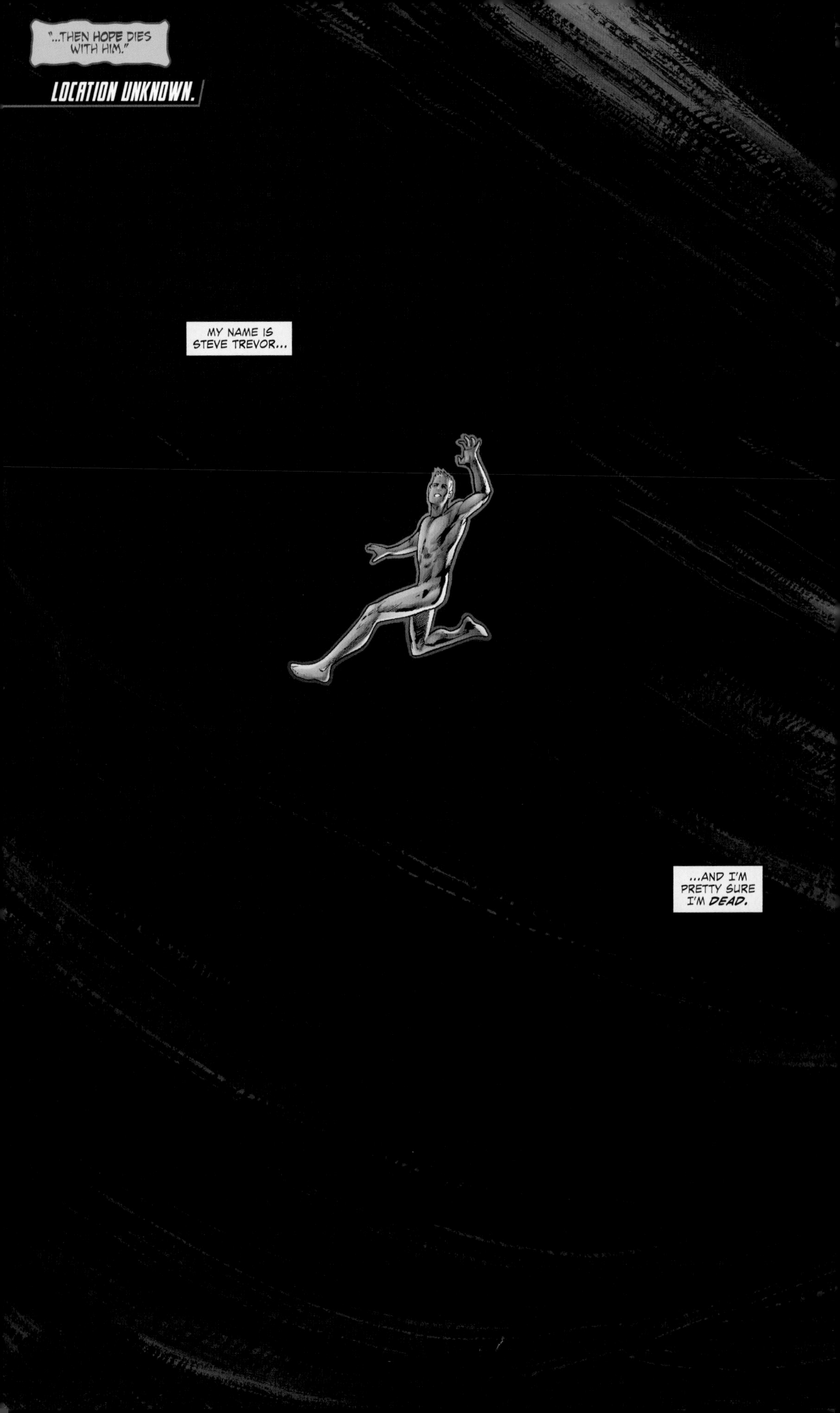
"...THEN HOPE DIES WITH HIM."
LOCATION UNKNOWN.
MY NAME IS STEVE TREVOR...
...AND I'M PRETTY SURE I'M DEAD.

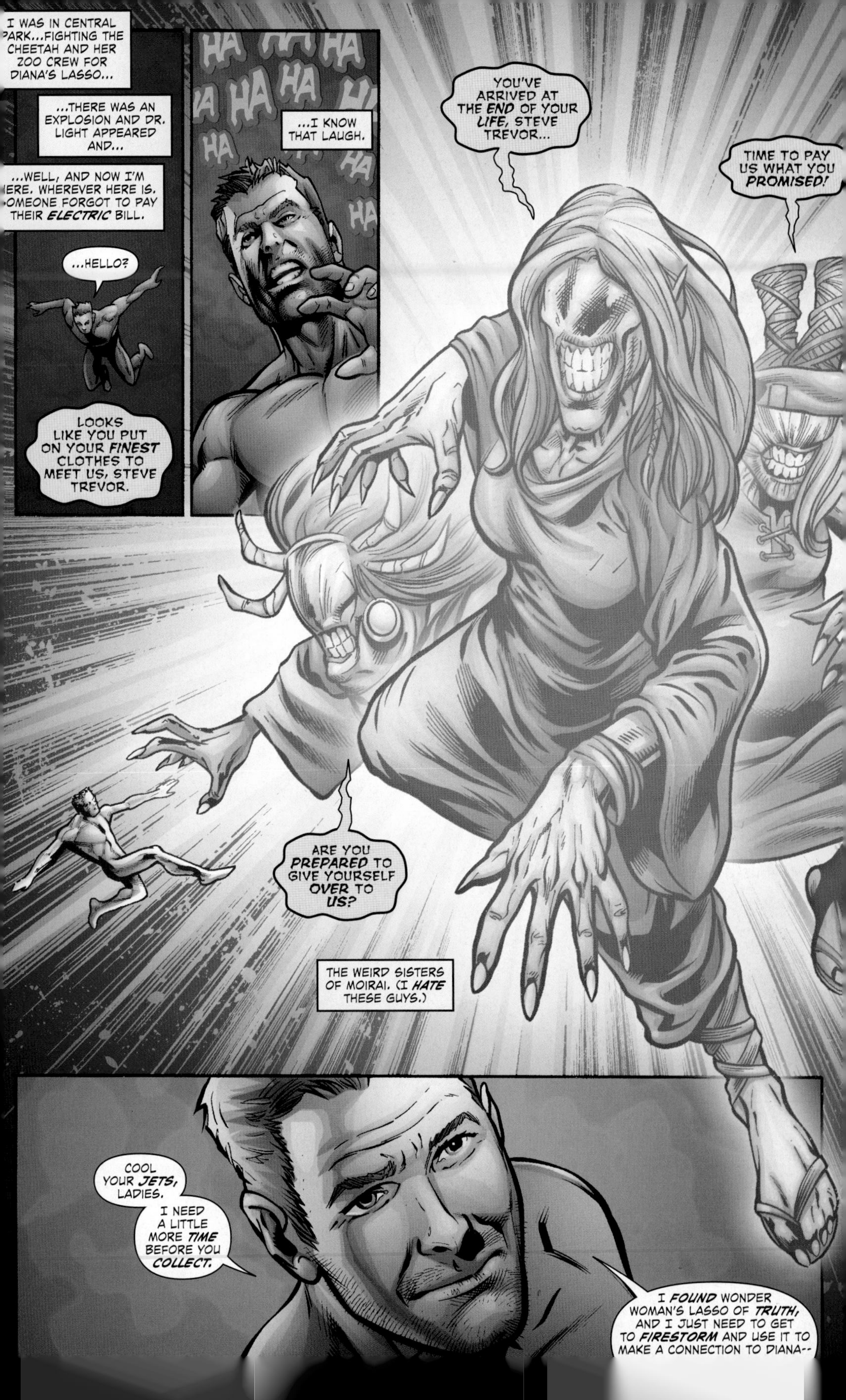

I WAS IN CENTRAL PARK...FIGHTING THE CHEETAH AND HER ZOO CREW FOR DIANA'S LASSO...
...THERE WAS AN EXPLOSION AND DR. LIGHT APPEARED AND...
...WELL, AND NOW I'M HERE. WHEREVER HERE IS. SOMEONE FORGOT TO PAY THEIR ELECTRIC BILL.
...HELLO?
LOOKS LIKE YOU PUT ON YOUR FINEST CLOTHES TO MEET US, STEVE TREVOR.
HA HA HA HA HA HA HA HA HA HA HA HA
...I KNOW THAT LAUGH.
YOU'VE ARRIVED AT THE END OF YOUR LIFE, STEVE TREVOR...
TIME TO PAY US WHAT YOU PROMISED!
ARE YOU PREPARED TO GIVE YOURSELF OVER TO US?
THE WEIRD SISTERS OF MOIRAI. (I HATE THESE GUYS.)
COOL YOUR JETS, LADIES.
I NEED A LITTLE MORE TIME BEFORE YOU COLLECT.
I FOUND WONDER WOMAN'S LASSO OF TRUTH, AND I JUST NEED TO GET TO FIRESTORM AND USE IT TO MAKE A CONNECTION TO DIANA--

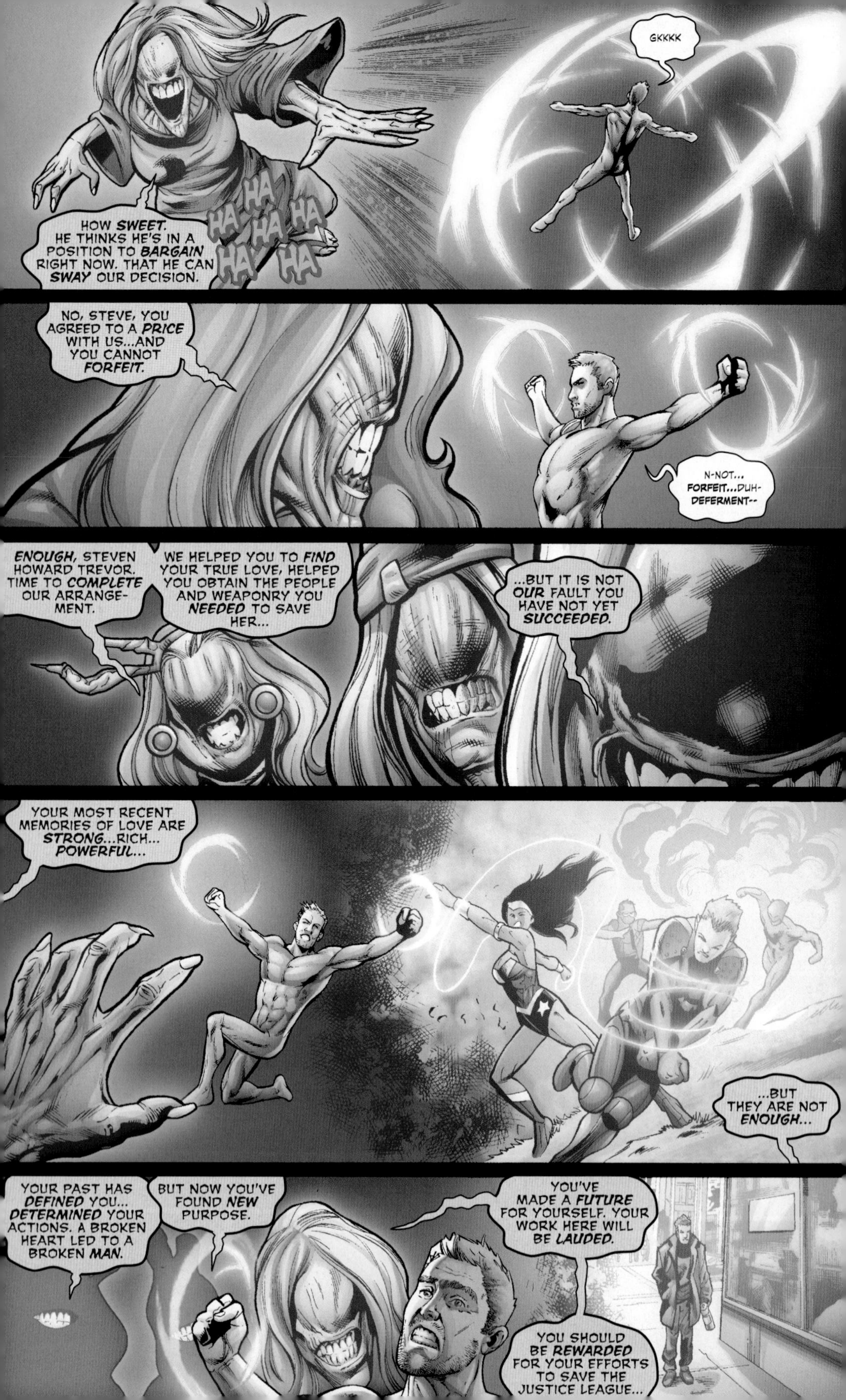
GKKKK
HOW SWEET. HE THINKS HE'S IN A POSITION TO BARGAIN RIGHT NOW. THAT HE CAN SWAY OUR DECISION.
HA HA HA HA HA HA
NO, STEVE, YOU AGREED TO A PRICE WITH US...AND YOU CANNOT FORFEIT.
N-NOT... FORFEIT...DUH-DEFERMENT--
ENOUGH, STEVEN HOWARD TREVOR. TIME TO COMPLETE OUR ARRANGE-MENT.
WE HELPED YOU TO FIND YOUR TRUE LOVE, HELPED YOU OBTAIN THE PEOPLE AND WEAPONRY YOU NEEDED TO SAVE HER...
...BUT IT IS NOT OUR FAULT YOU HAVE NOT YET SUCCEEDED.
YOUR MOST RECENT MEMORIES OF LOVE ARE STRONG...RICH... POWERFUL...
...BUT THEY ARE NOT ENOUGH...
YOUR PAST HAS DEFINED YOU... DETERMINED YOUR ACTIONS. A BROKEN HEART LED TO A BROKEN MAN.
BUT NOW YOU'VE FOUND NEW PURPOSE.
YOU'VE MADE A FUTURE FOR YOURSELF. YOUR WORK HERE WILL BE LAUDED.
YOU SHOULD BE REWARDED FOR YOUR EFFORTS TO SAVE THE JUSTICE LEAGUE...

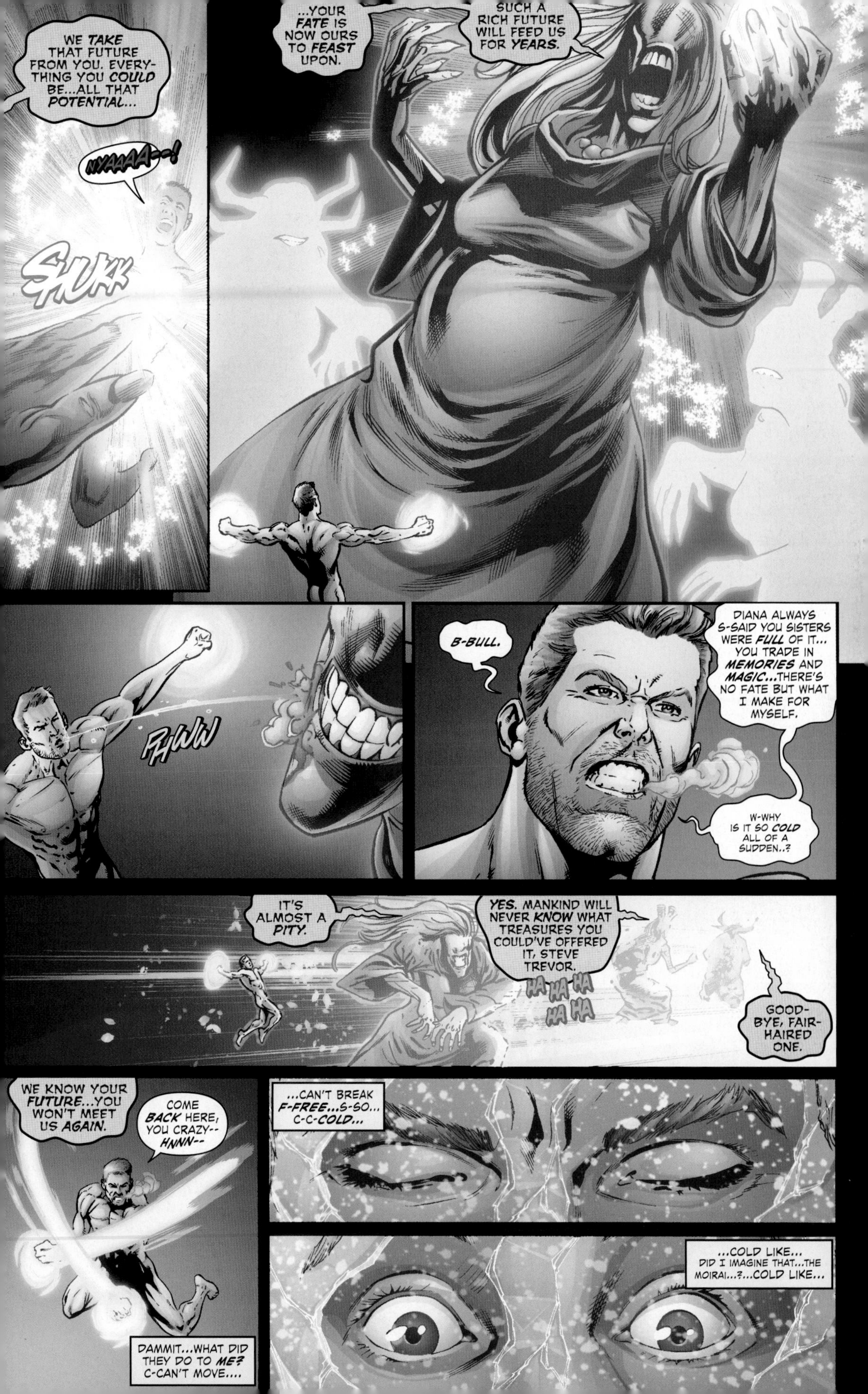
WE TAKE THAT FUTURE FROM YOU. EVERYTHING YOU COULD BE...ALL THAT POTENTIAL...
...YOUR FATE IS NOW OURS TO FEAST UPON.
SUCH A RICH FUTURE WILL FEED US FOR YEARS.
NYAAAA--!
SHUKK
PHWW
B-BULL.
DIANA ALWAYS S-SAID YOU SISTERS WERE FULL OF IT... YOU TRADE IN MEMORIES AND MAGIC...THERE'S NO FATE BUT WHAT I MAKE FOR MYSELF.
W-WHY IS IT SO COLD ALL OF A SUDDEN..?
IT'S ALMOST A PITY.
YES. MANKIND WILL NEVER KNOW WHAT TREASURES YOU COULD'VE OFFERED IT, STEVE TREVOR.
HA HA HA HA HA
GOOD-BYE, FAIR-HAIRED ONE.
WE KNOW YOUR FUTURE...YOU WON'T MEET US AGAIN.
COME BACK HERE, YOU CRAZY-- HNNN--
DAMMIT...WHAT DID THEY DO TO ME? C-CAN'T MOVE....
...CAN'T BREAK F-FREE...S-SO... C-C-COLD...
...COLD LIKE... DID I IMAGINE THAT...THE MOIRAI...?...COLD LIKE...

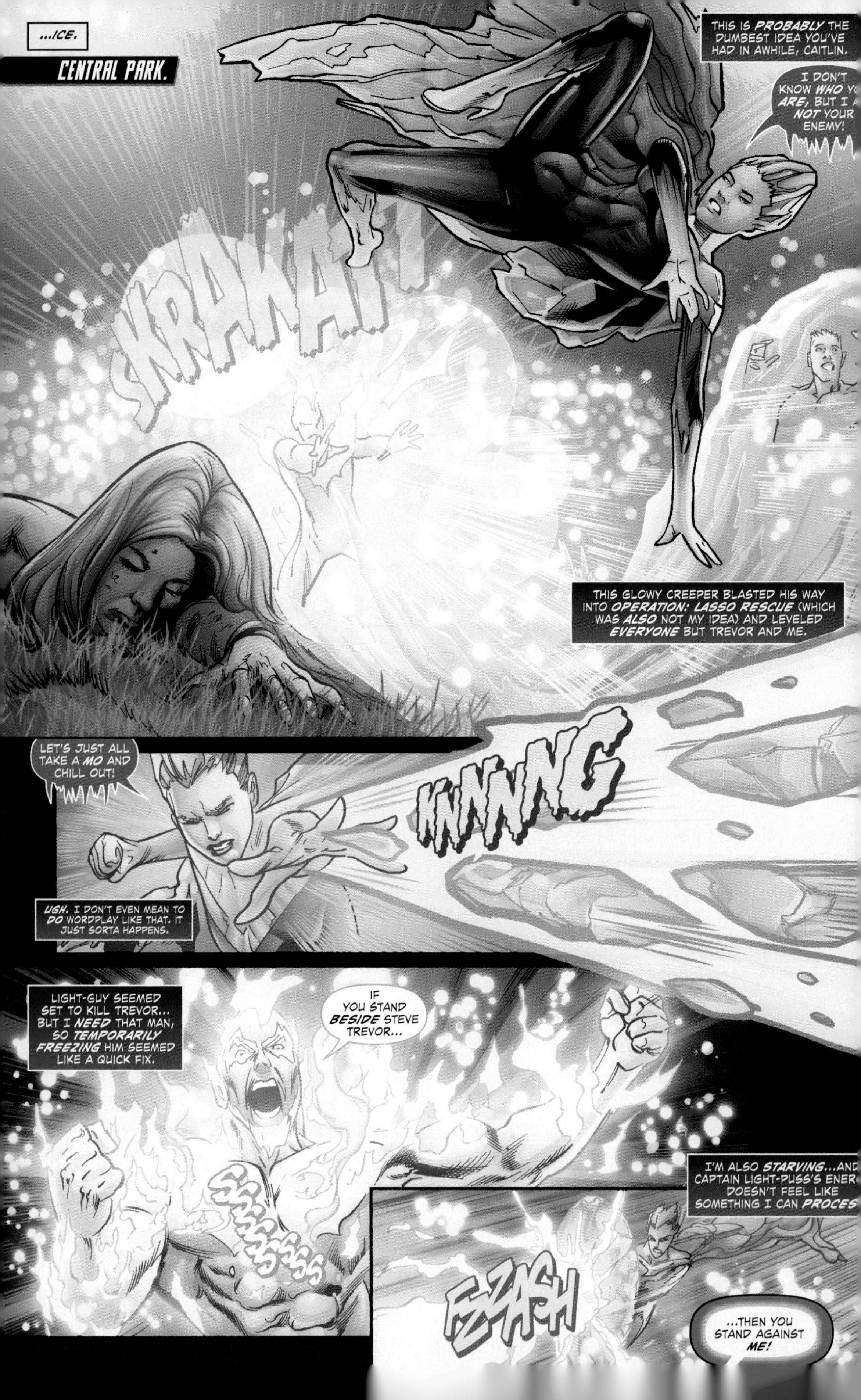
...ICE.
CENTRAL PARK.
THIS IS PROBABLY THE DUMBEST IDEA YOU'VE HAD IN AWHILE, CAITLIN.
I DON'T KNOW WHO Y ARE, BUT I NOT YOUR ENEMY!
SKRAKAT!
THIS GLOWY CREEPER BLASTED HIS WAY INTO OPERATION: LASSO RESCUE (WHICH WAS ALSO NOT MY IDEA) AND LEVELED EVERYONE BUT TREVOR AND ME.
LET'S JUST ALL TAKE A MO AND CHILL OUT!
KNNNG
UGH. I DON'T EVEN MEAN TO DO WORDPLAY LIKE THAT. IT JUST SORTA HAPPENS.
LIGHT-GUY SEEMED SET TO KILL TREVOR... BUT I NEED THAT MAN, SO TEMPORARILY FREEZING HIM SEEMED LIKE A QUICK FIX.
IF YOU STAND BESIDE STEVE TREVOR...
SSSSSSSSS
I'M ALSO STARVING...AND CAPTAIN LIGHT-PUSS'S ENER DOESN'T FEEL LIKE SOMETHING I CAN PROCES
FZZASH
...THEN YOU STAND AGAINST ME!

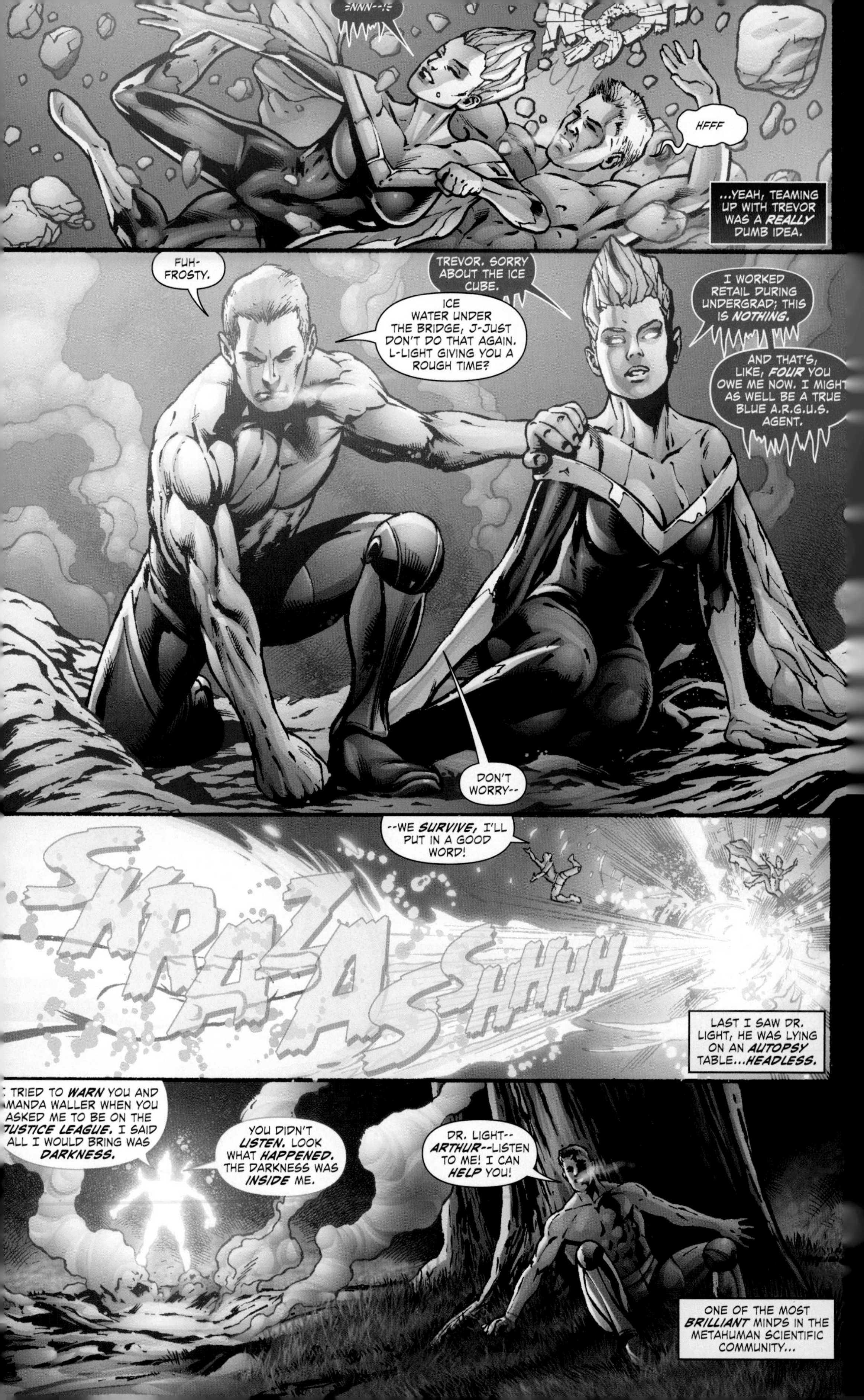

NNN--!
HFFF
...YEAH, TEAMING UP WITH TREVOR WAS A REALLY DUMB IDEA.
FUH- FROSTY.
TREVOR. SORRY ABOUT THE ICE CUBE.
ICE WATER UNDER THE BRIDGE, J-JUST DON'T DO THAT AGAIN. L-LIGHT GIVING YOU A ROUGH TIME?
I WORKED RETAIL DURING UNDERGRAD; THIS IS NOTHING.
AND THAT'S, LIKE, FOUR YOU OWE ME NOW. I MIGHT AS WELL BE A TRUE BLUE A.R.G.U.S. AGENT.
DON'T WORRY--
--WE SURVIVE, I'LL PUT IN A GOOD WORD!
SKRAZASHHHH
LAST I SAW DR. LIGHT, HE WAS LYING ON AN AUTOPSY TABLE...HEADLESS.
TRIED TO WARN YOU AND MANDA WALLER WHEN YOU ASKED ME TO BE ON THE USTICE LEAGUE. I SAID ALL I WOULD BRING WAS DARKNESS.
YOU DIDN'T LISTEN. LOOK WHAT HAPPENED. THE DARKNESS WAS INSIDE ME.
DR. LIGHT-- ARTHUR--LISTEN TO ME! I CAN HELP YOU!
ONE OF THE MOST BRILLIANT MINDS IN THE METAHUMAN SCIENTIFIC COMMUNITY...

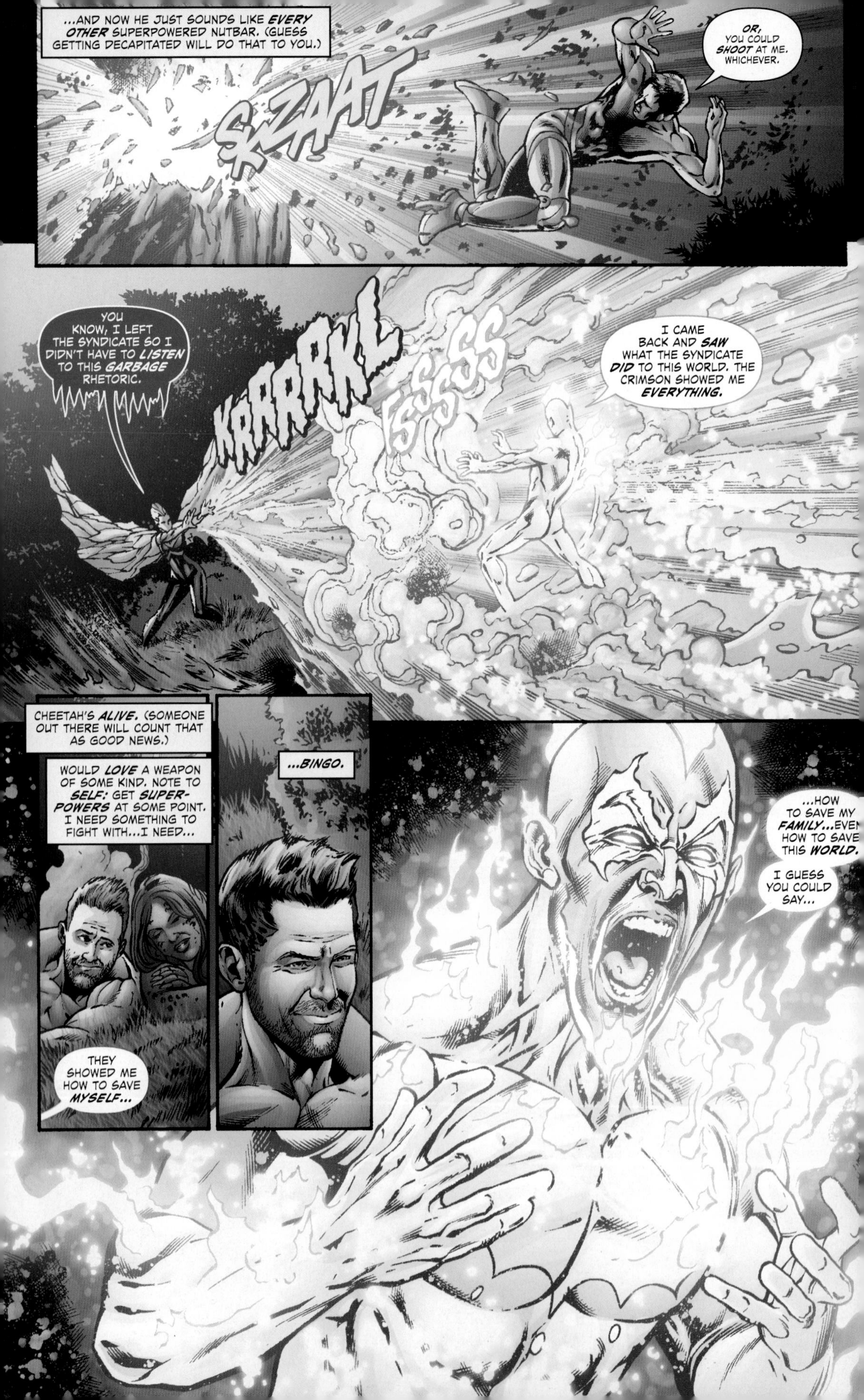
...AND NOW HE JUST SOUNDS LIKE EVERY OTHER SUPERPOWERED NUTBAR. (GUESS GETTING DECAPITATED WILL DO THAT TO YOU.)
SKZAAT
OR, YOU COULD SHOOT AT ME. WHICHEVER.
YOU KNOW, I LEFT THE SYNDICATE SO I DIDN'T HAVE TO LISTEN TO THIS GARBAGE RHETORIC.
KRARRKL
FSSSSSS
I CAME BACK AND SAW WHAT THE SYNDICATE DID TO THIS WORLD. THE CRIMSON SHOWED ME EVERYTHING.
CHEETAH'S ALIVE. (SOMEONE OUT THERE WILL COUNT THAT AS GOOD NEWS.)
WOULD LOVE A WEAPON OF SOME KIND. NOTE TO SELF: GET SUPER-POWERS AT SOME POINT. I NEED SOMETHING TO FIGHT WITH...I NEED...
THEY SHOWED ME HOW TO SAVE MYSELF...
...BINGO.
...HOW TO SAVE MY FAMILY...EVEN HOW TO SAVE THIS WORLD.
I GUESS YOU COULD SAY...

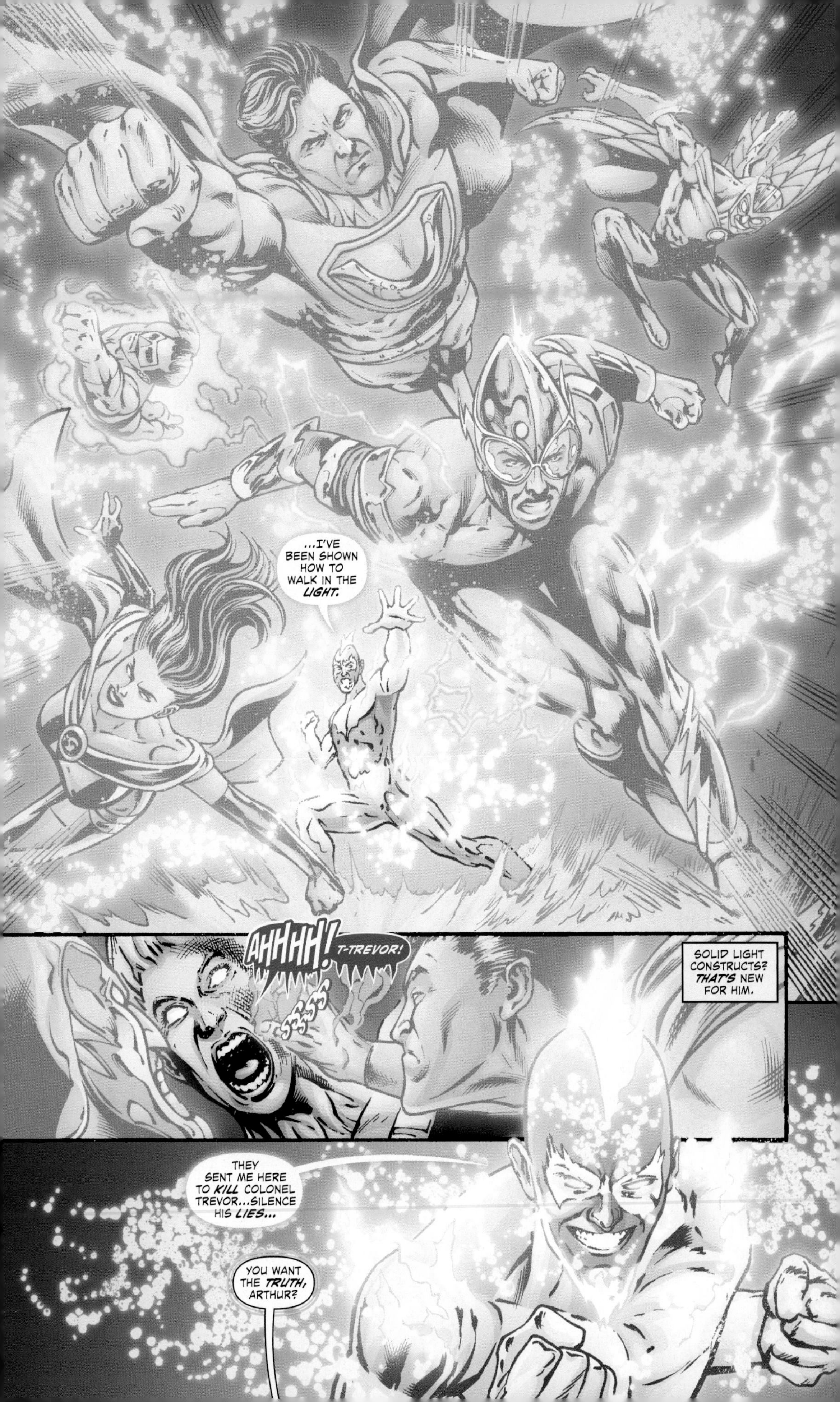
...I'VE BEEN SHOWN HOW TO WALK IN THE LIGHT.
AHHHH!
T-TREVOR!
SSSSSS
SOLID LIGHT CONSTRUCTS? THAT'S NEW FOR HIM.
THEY SENT ME HERE TO KILL COLONEL TREVOR...SILENCE HIS LIES...
YOU WANT THE TRUTH, ARTHUR?

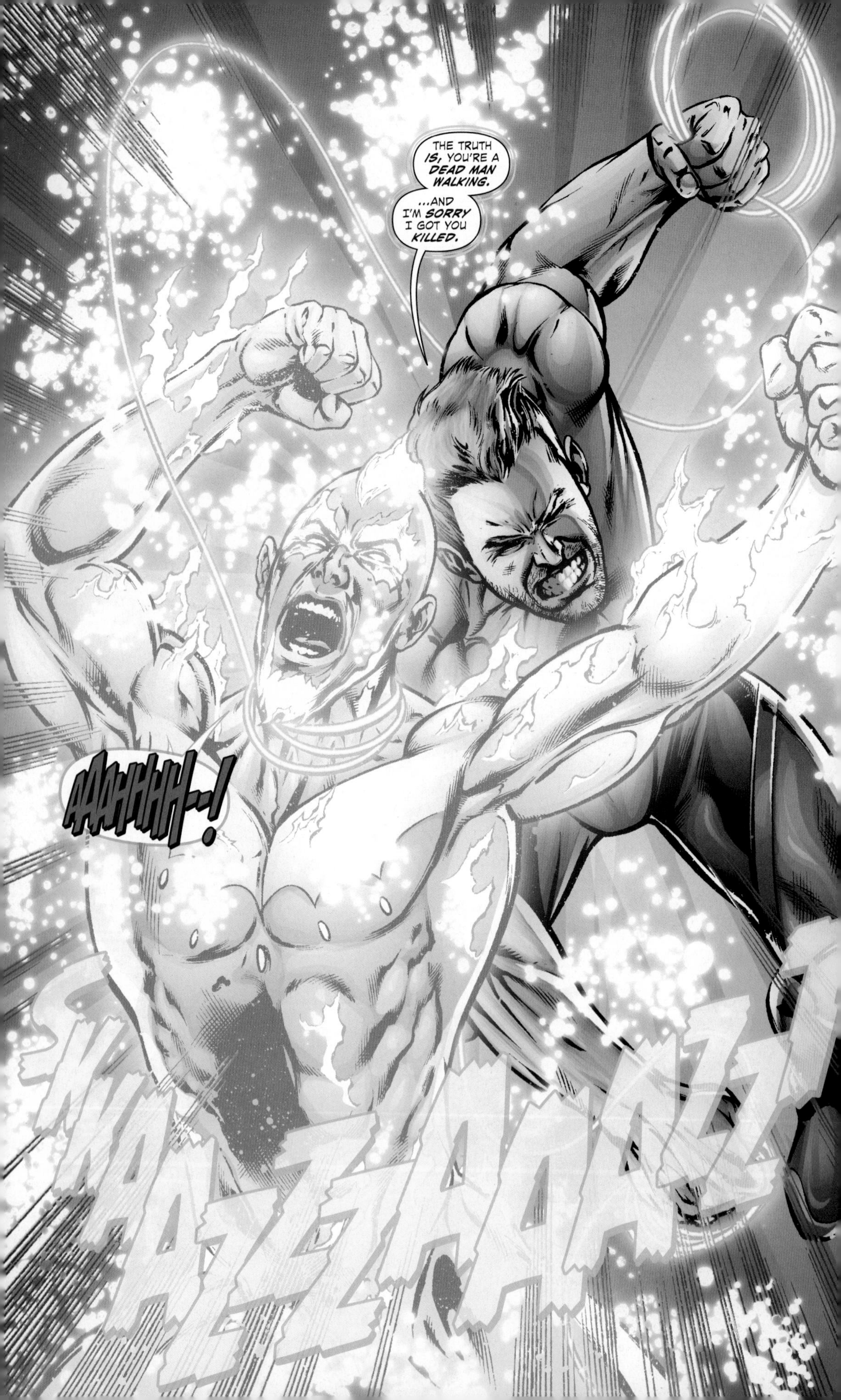
THE TRUTH IS, YOU'RE A DEAD MAN WALKING.
...AND I'M SORRY I GOT YOU KILLED.
AAAHHHH--!
KRAZZAAAZ!

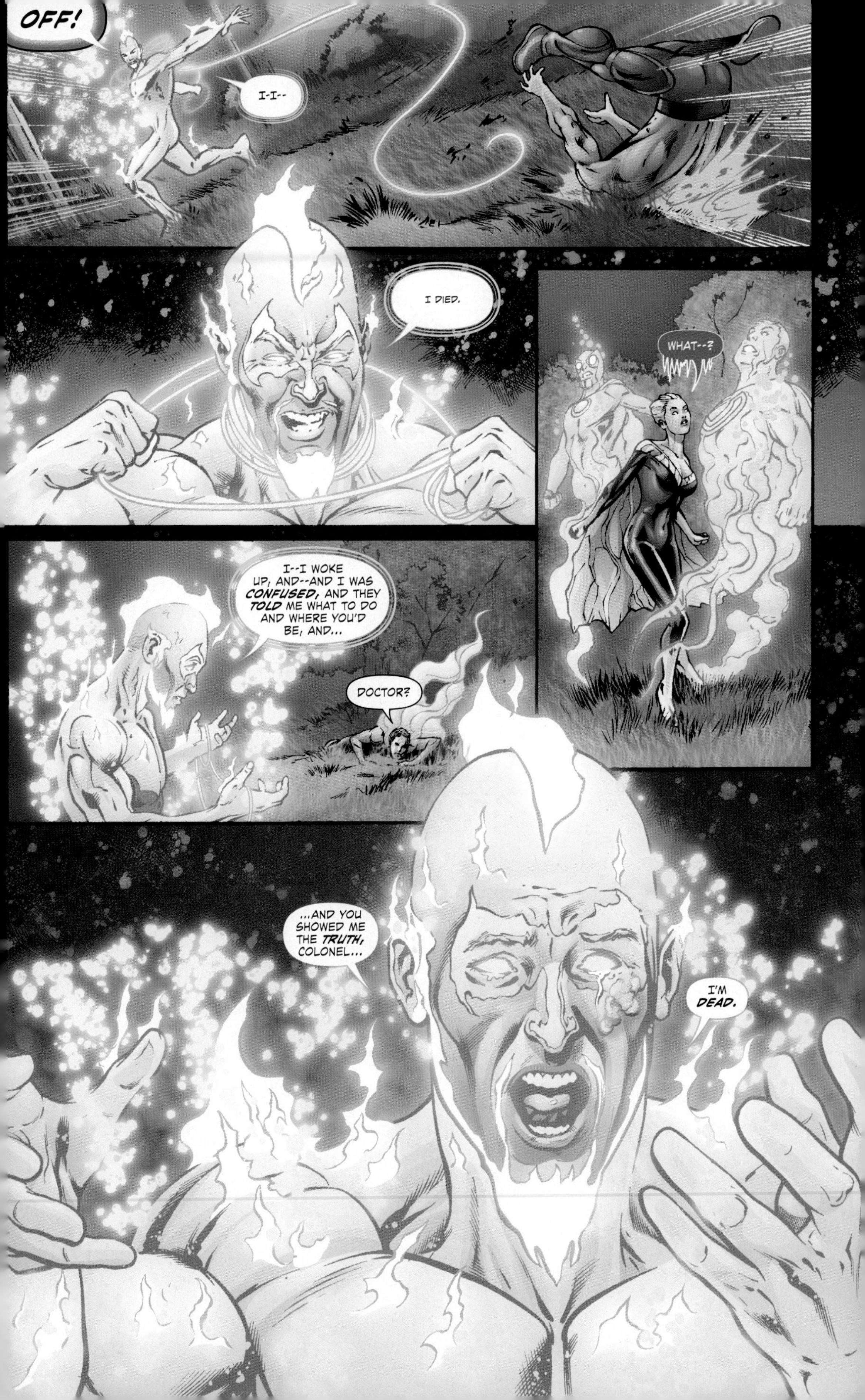
OFF!
I-I--
I DIED.
WHAT--?
I--I WOKE UP, AND--AND I WAS CONFUSED, AND THEY TOLD ME WHAT TO DO AND WHERE YOU'D BE, AND...
DOCTOR?
...AND YOU SHOWED ME THE TRUTH, COLONEL...
I'M DEAD.

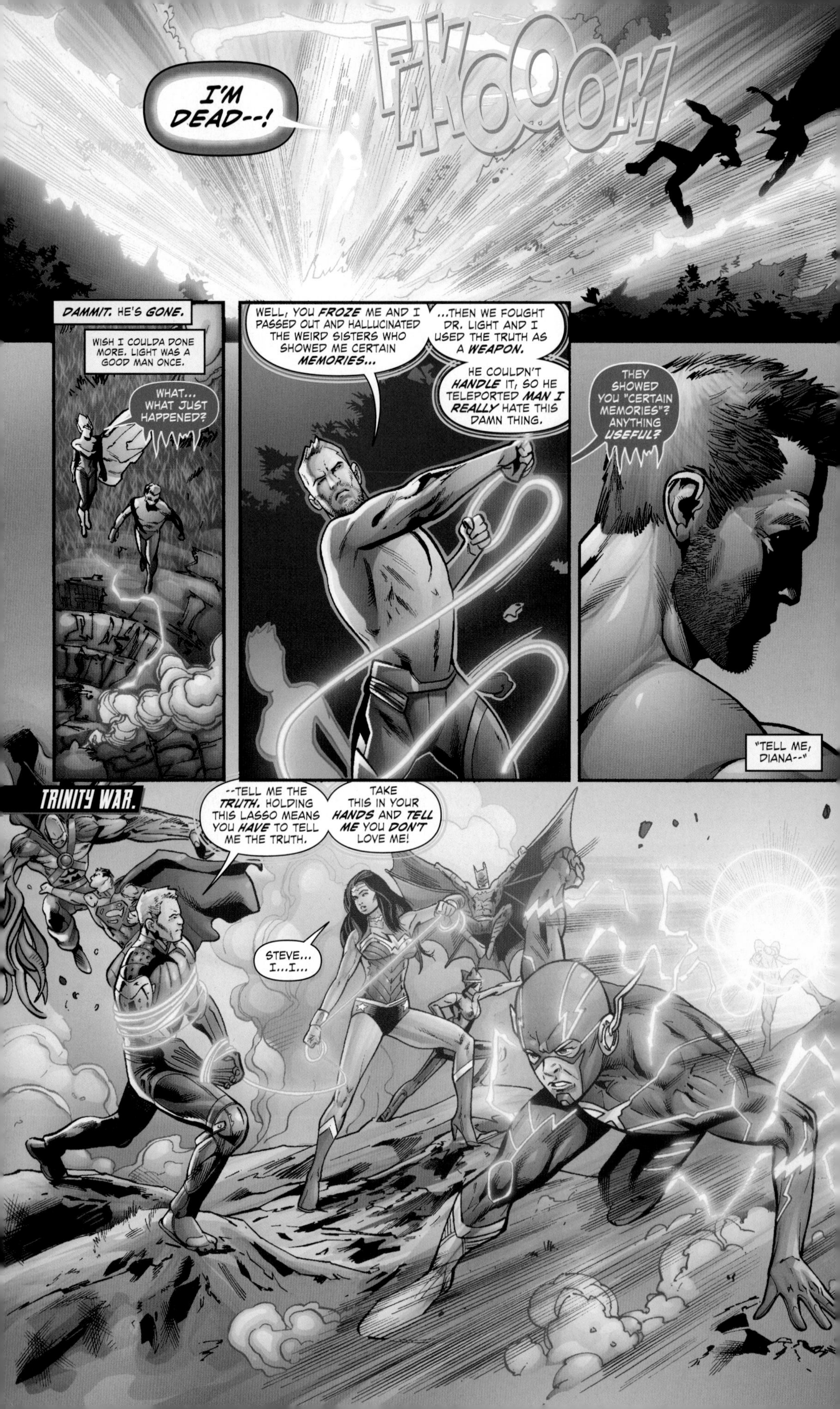
I'M DEAD--!
FAKOOOOM
DAMMIT. HE'S GONE.
WISH I COULDA DONE MORE. LIGHT WAS A GOOD MAN ONCE.
WHAT... WHAT JUST HAPPENED?
WELL, YOU FROZE ME AND I PASSED OUT AND HALLUCINATED THE WEIRD SISTERS WHO SHOWED ME CERTAIN MEMORIES...
...THEN WE FOUGHT DR. LIGHT AND I USED THE TRUTH AS A WEAPON.
HE COULDN'T HANDLE IT, SO HE TELEPORTED MAN I REALLY HATE THIS DAMN THING.
THEY SHOWED YOU "CERTAIN MEMORIES"? ANYTHING USEFUL?
"TELL ME, DIANA--"
TRINITY WAR.
--TELL ME THE TRUTH. HOLDING THIS LASSO MEANS YOU HAVE TO TELL ME THE TRUTH.
TAKE THIS IN YOUR HANDS AND TELL ME YOU DON'T LOVE ME!
STEVE... I...I...

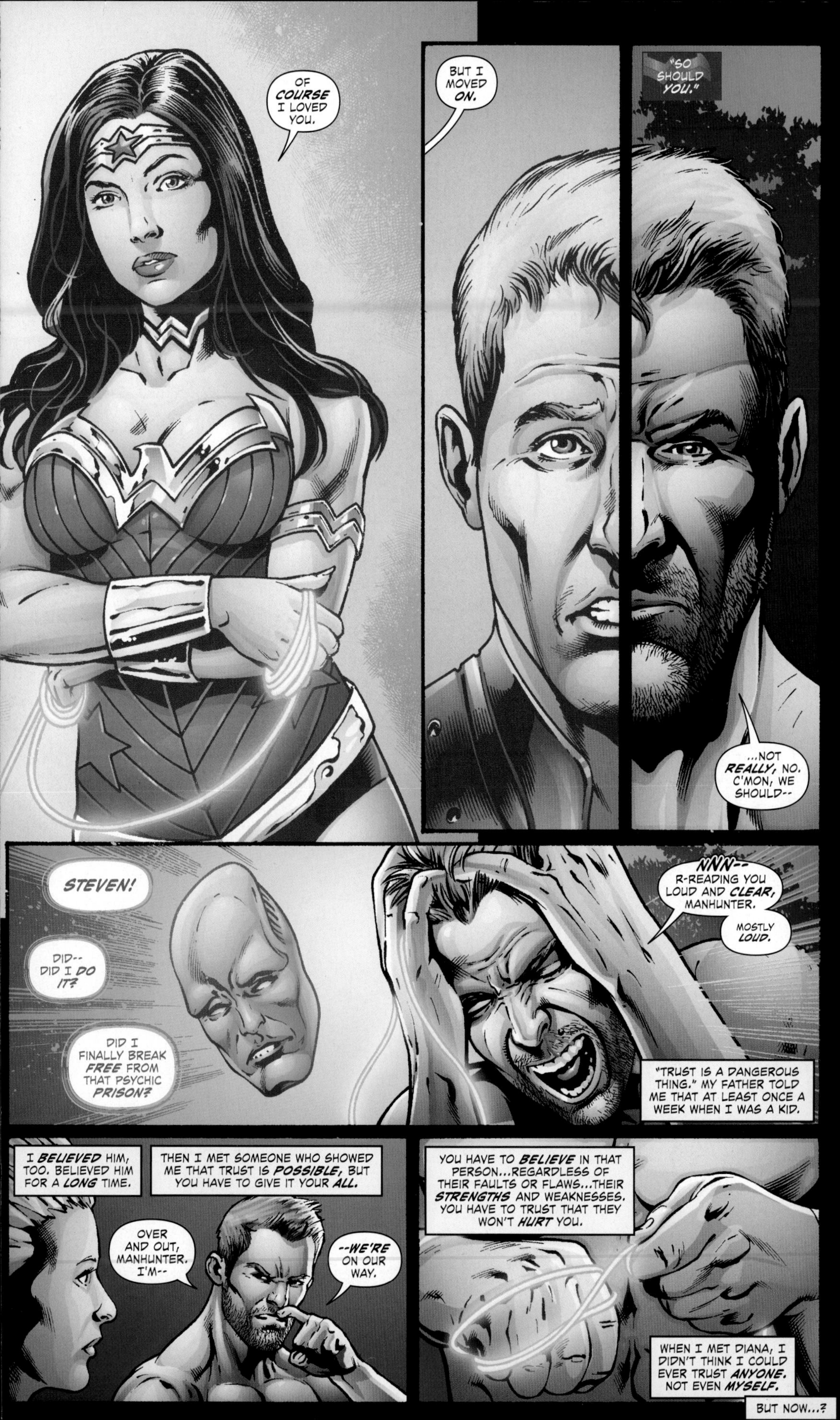
OF *COURSE* I LOVED YOU.
BUT I MOVED *ON.*
"SO SHOULD *YOU.*"
...NOT *REALLY,* NO. C'MON, WE SHOULD--
STEVEN!
DID-- DID I *DO IT?*
DID I FINALLY BREAK *FREE* FROM THAT PSYCHIC *PRISON?*
NNN-- R-READING YOU LOUD AND *CLEAR,* MANHUNTER.
MOSTLY *LOUD.*
"TRUST IS A DANGEROUS THING." MY FATHER TOLD ME THAT AT LEAST ONCE A WEEK WHEN I WAS A KID.
I *BELIEVED* HIM, TOO. BELIEVED HIM FOR A *LONG* TIME.
THEN I MET SOMEONE WHO SHOWED ME THAT TRUST IS *POSSIBLE,* BUT YOU HAVE TO GIVE IT YOUR *ALL.*
OVER AND OUT, MANHUNTER. I'M--
--*WE'RE* ON OUR WAY.
YOU HAVE TO *BELIEVE* IN THAT PERSON...REGARDLESS OF THEIR FAULTS OR FLAWS...THEIR *STRENGTHS* AND WEAKNESSES. YOU HAVE TO TRUST THAT THEY WON'T *HURT* YOU.
WHEN I MET DIANA, I DIDN'T THINK I COULD EVER TRUST *ANYONE.* NOT EVEN *MYSELF.*
BUT NOW...?

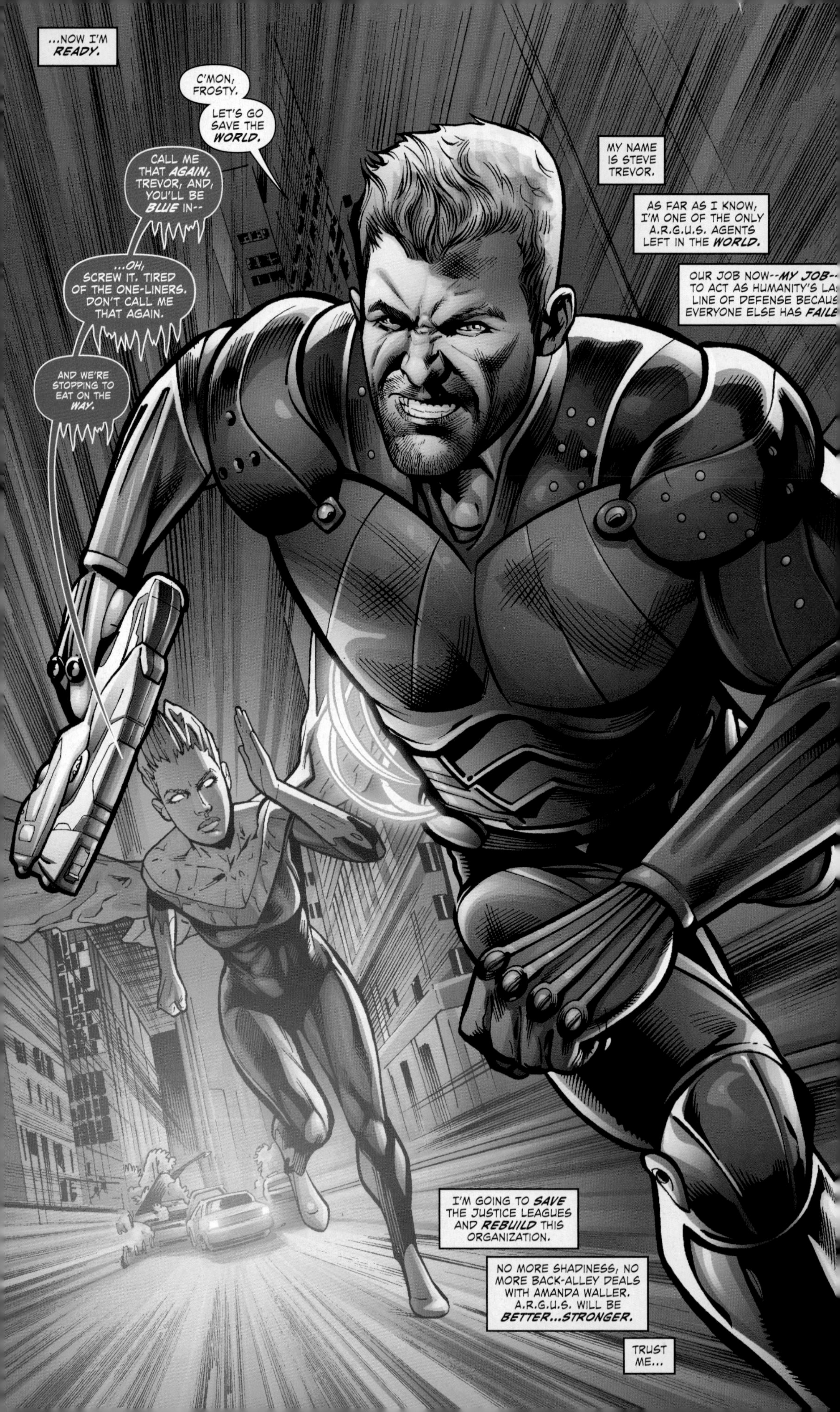
...NOW I'M READY.
C'MON, FROSTY.
LET'S GO SAVE THE WORLD.
CALL ME THAT AGAIN, TREVOR, AND, YOU'LL BE BLUE IN--
...OH, SCREW IT. TIRED OF THE ONE-LINERS. DON'T CALL ME THAT AGAIN.
AND WE'RE STOPPING TO EAT ON THE WAY.
MY NAME IS STEVE TREVOR.
AS FAR AS I KNOW, I'M ONE OF THE ONLY A.R.G.U.S. AGENTS LEFT IN THE WORLD.
OUR JOB NOW--MY JOB--TO ACT AS HUMANITY'S LA LINE OF DEFENSE BECAUS EVERYONE ELSE HAS FAILE
I'M GOING TO SAVE THE JUSTICE LEAGUES AND REBUILD THIS ORGANIZATION.
NO MORE SHADINESS, NO MORE BACK-ALLEY DEALS WITH AMANDA WALLER. A.R.G.U.S. WILL BE BETTER...STRONGER.
TRUST ME...

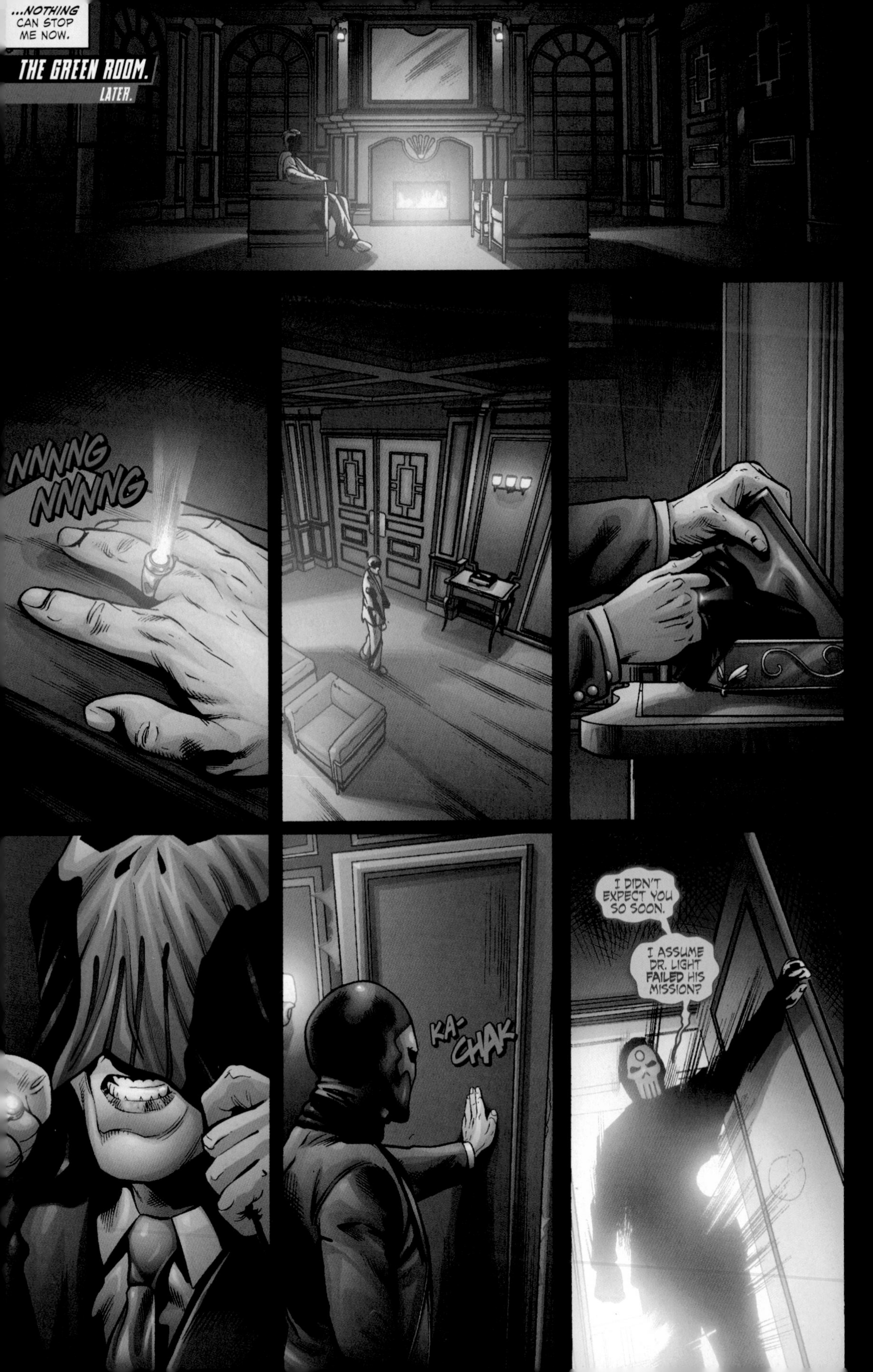
...NOTHING CAN STOP ME NOW.
THE GREEN ROOM.
LATER.
NNNNG NNNNG
KA-CHAK
I DIDN'T EXPECT YOU SO SOON.
I ASSUME DR. LIGHT FAILED HIS MISSION?

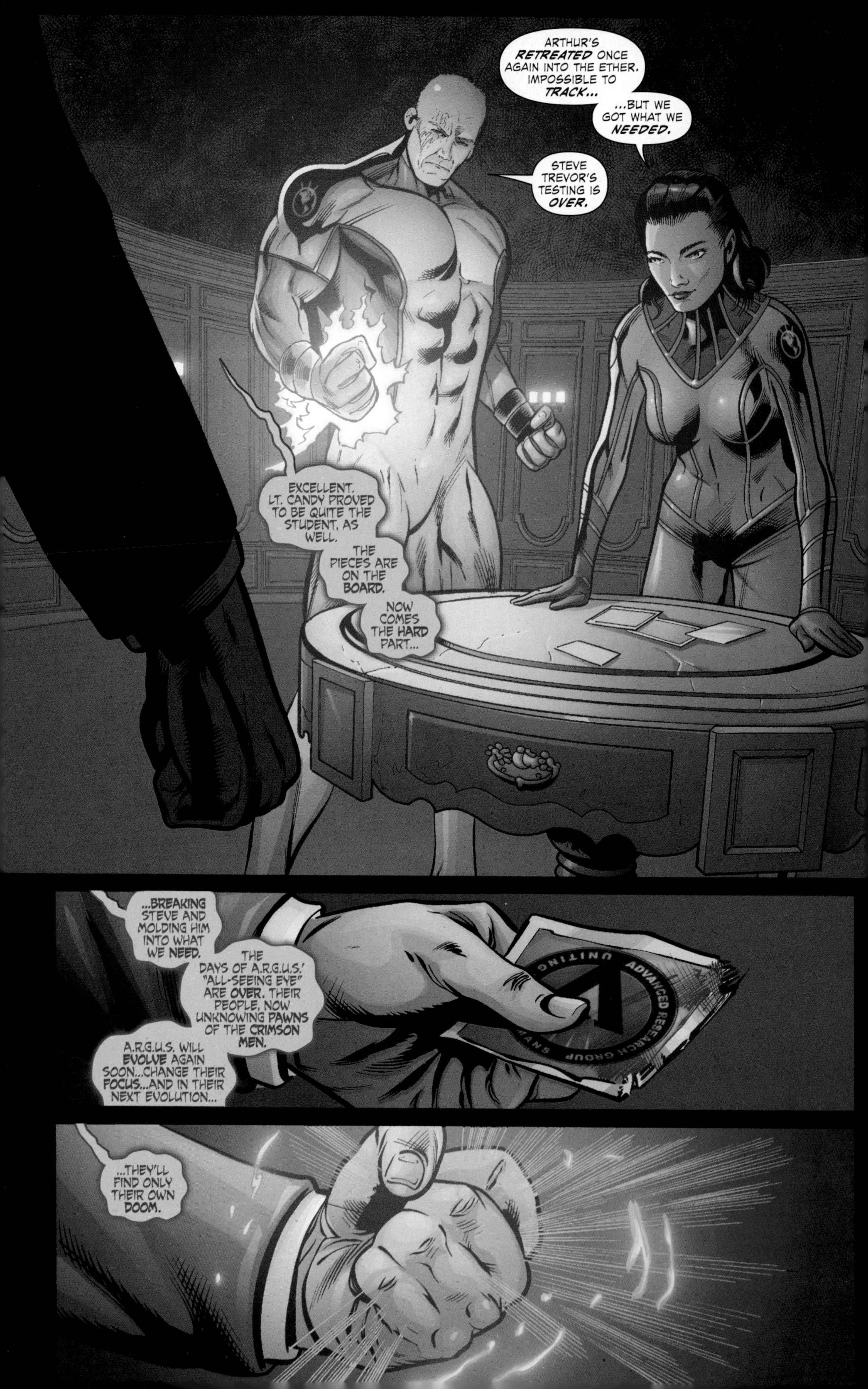
ARTHUR'S RETREATED ONCE AGAIN INTO THE ETHER. IMPOSSIBLE TO TRACK...
...BUT WE GOT WHAT WE NEEDED.
STEVE TREVOR'S TESTING IS OVER.
EXCELLENT. LT. CANDY PROVED TO BE QUITE THE STUDENT, AS WELL.
THE PIECES ARE ON THE BOARD.
NOW COMES THE HARD PART...
...BREAKING STEVE AND MOLDING HIM INTO WHAT WE NEED.
THE DAYS OF A.R.G.U.S.' "ALL-SEEING EYE" ARE OVER. THEIR PEOPLE, NOW UNKNOWING PAWNS OF THE CRIMSON MEN.
UNITING
ADVANCED RESEARCH GROUP
A.R.G.U.S. WILL EVOLVE AGAIN SOON...CHANGE THEIR FOCUS...AND IN THEIR NEXT EVOLUTION...
...THEY'LL FIND ONLY THEIR OWN DOOM.

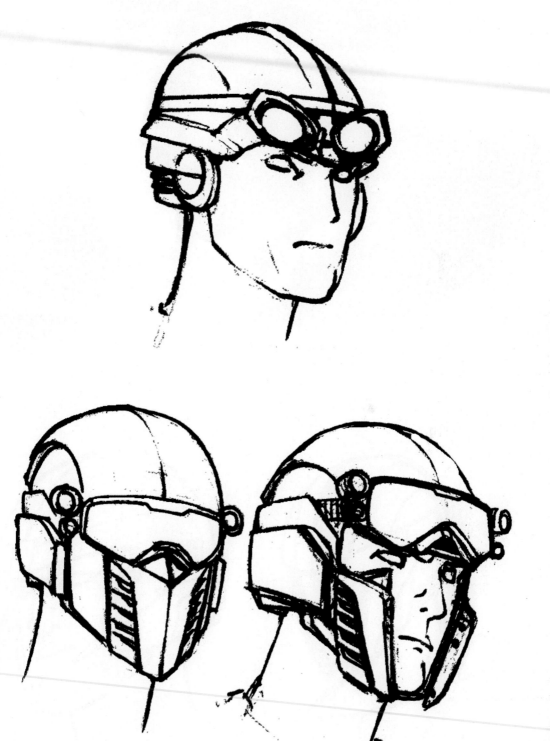

Helmet designs by Gene Ha

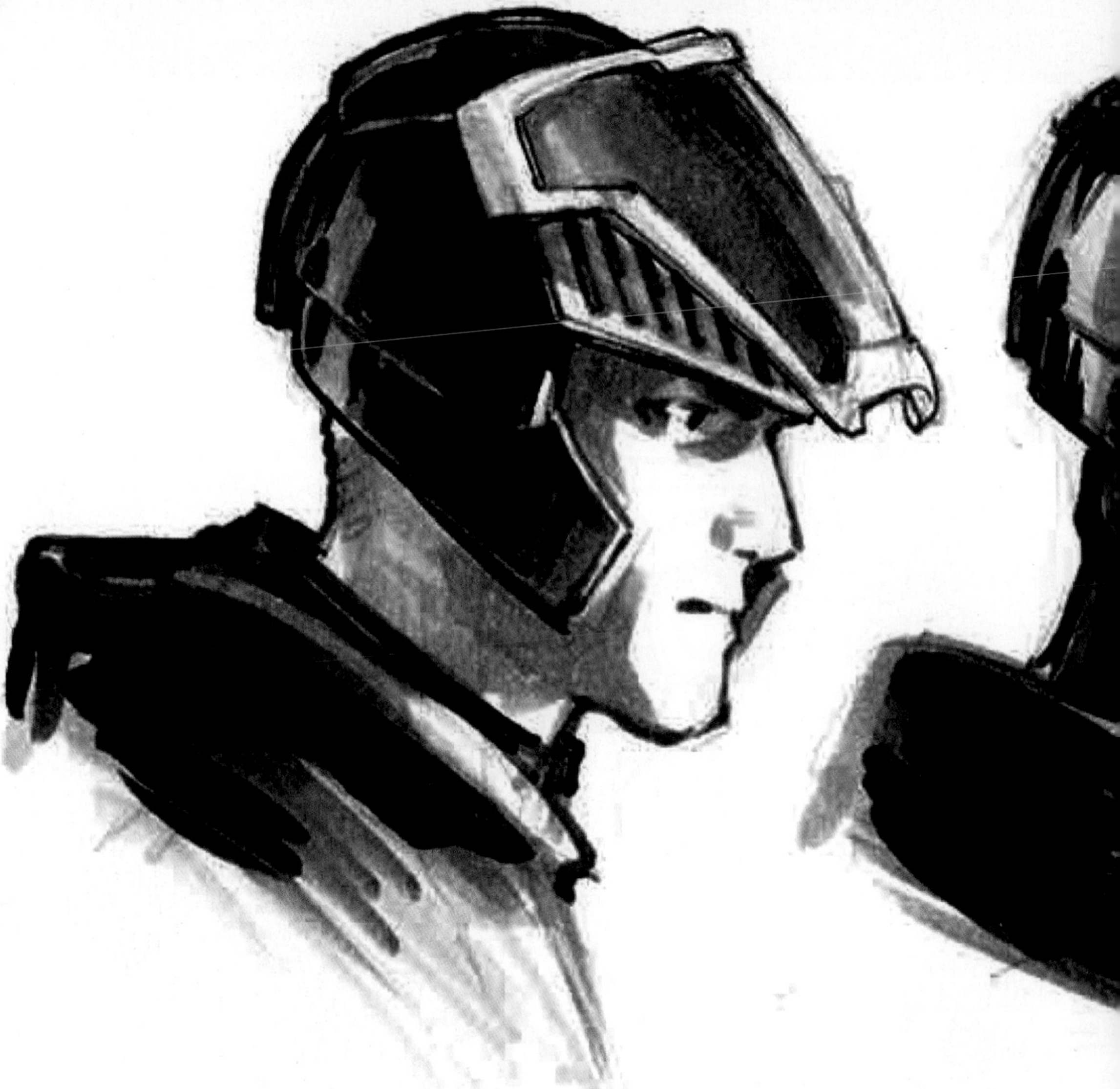

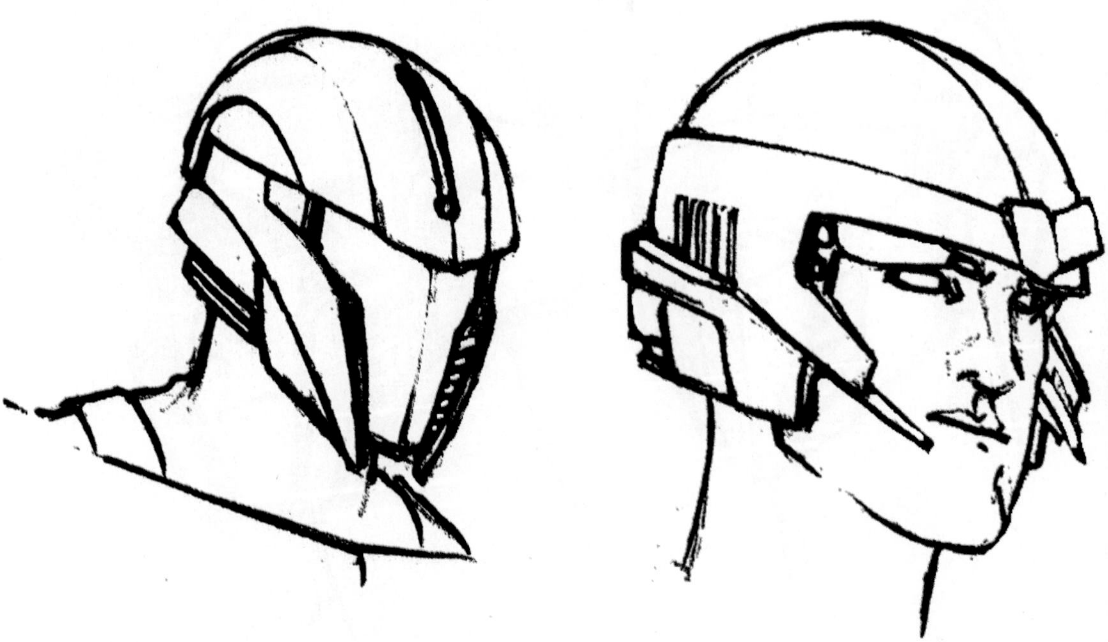

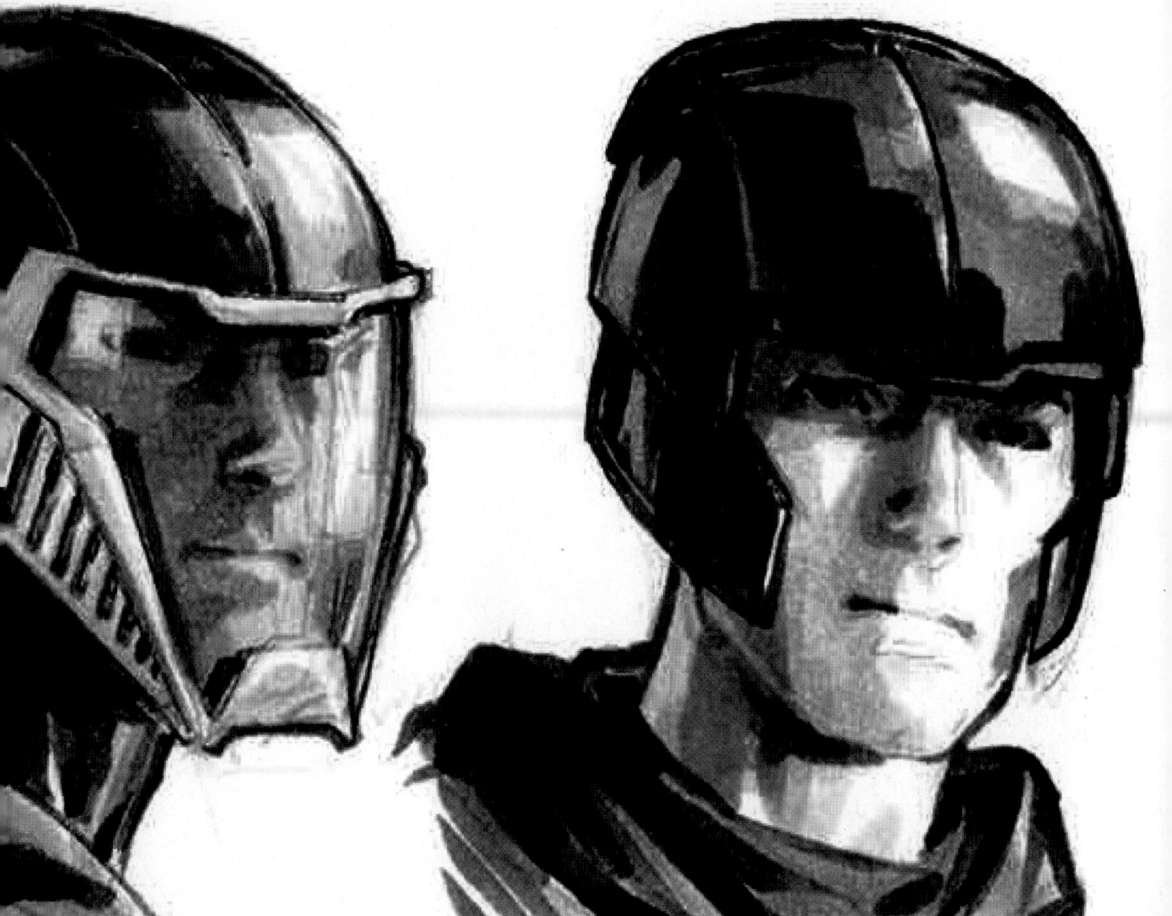

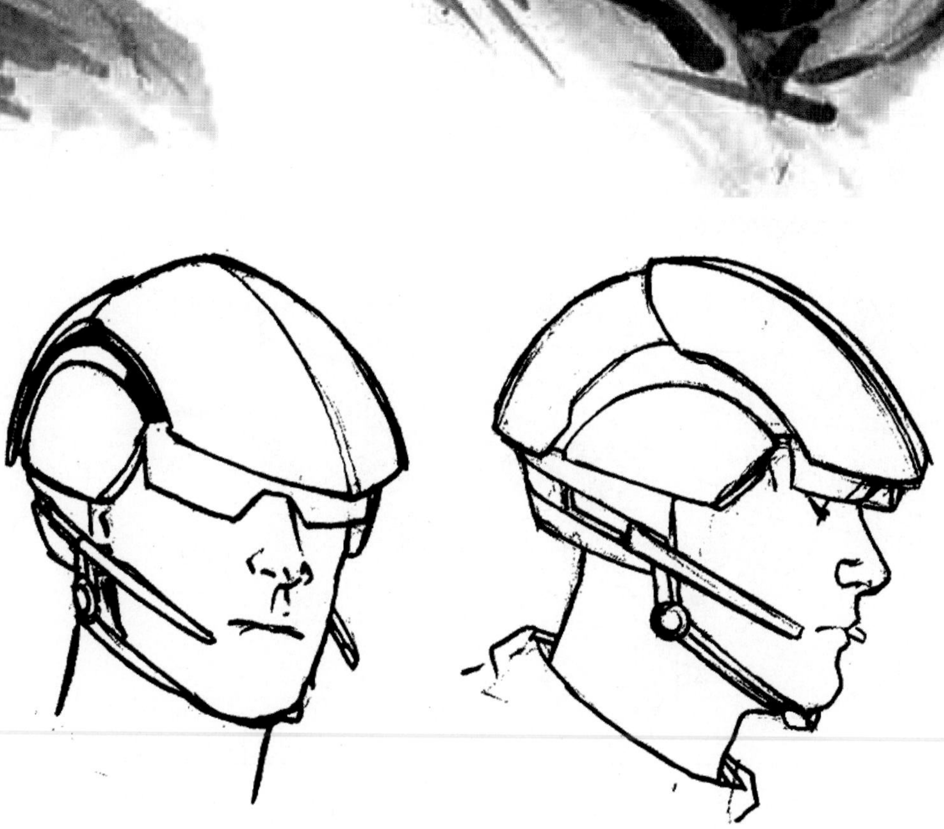

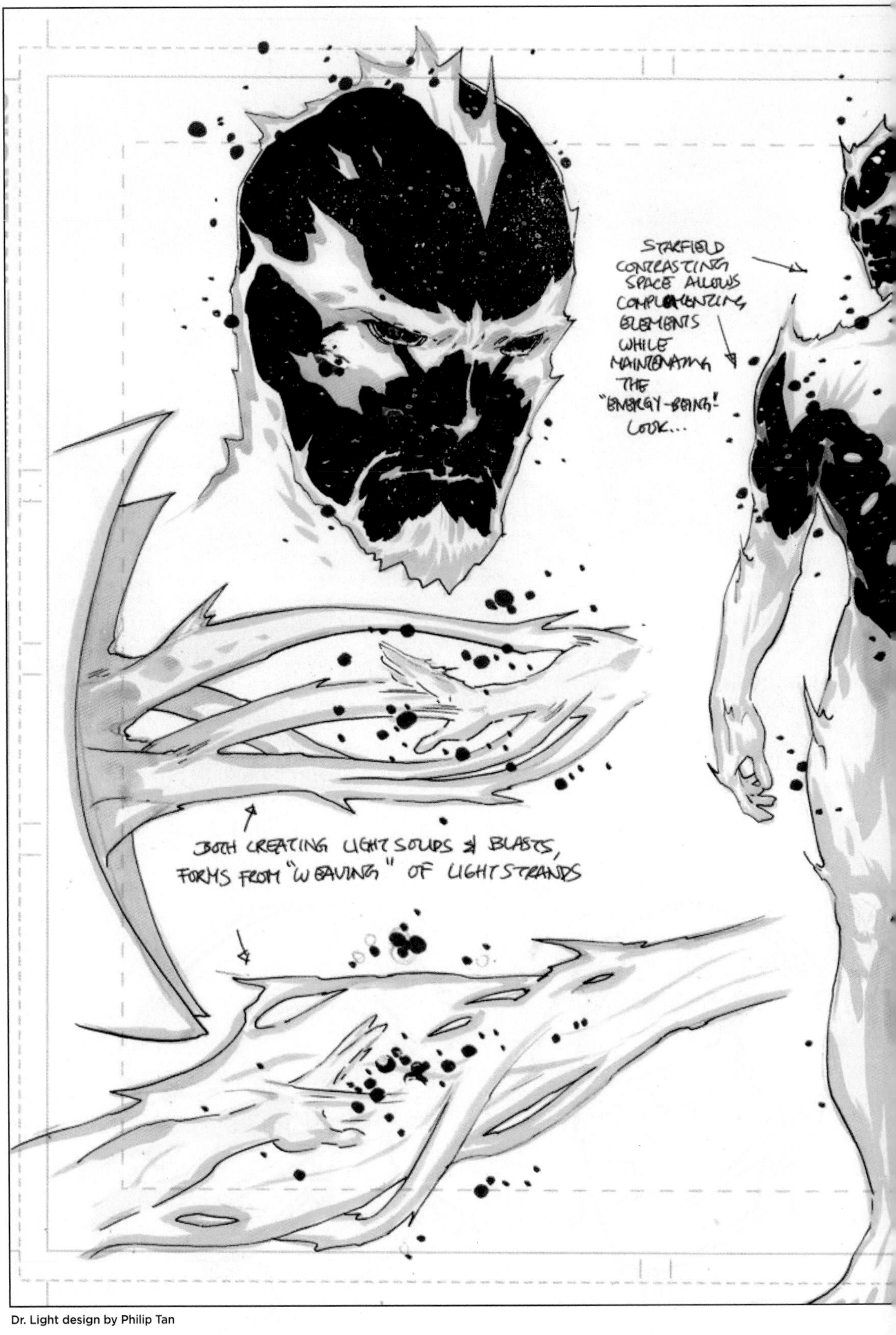

STARFIELD CONTRASTING SPACE ALLOWS COMPLEMENTING ELEMENTS WHILE MAINTAINING THE "ENERGY-BEING" LOOK...
BOTH CREATING LIGHT SOLIDS & BLASTS, FORMS FROM "WEAVING" OF LIGHTSTRANDS

Dr. Light design by Philip Tan

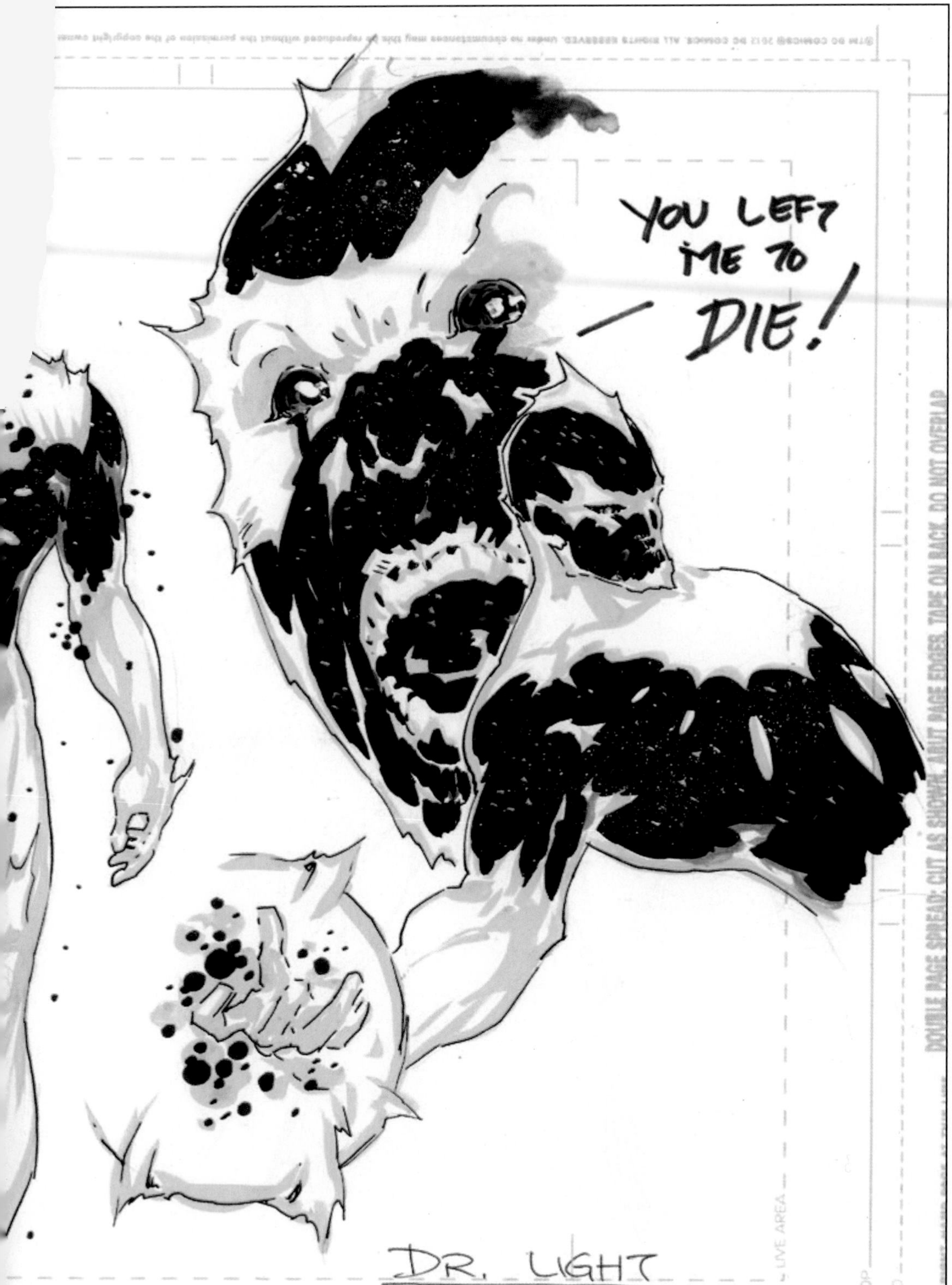
YOU LEFT ME TO DIE!
DR. LIGHT
PHILIP TAN 9/8/2013

A.R.G.U.S. Armor design by Brett Booth

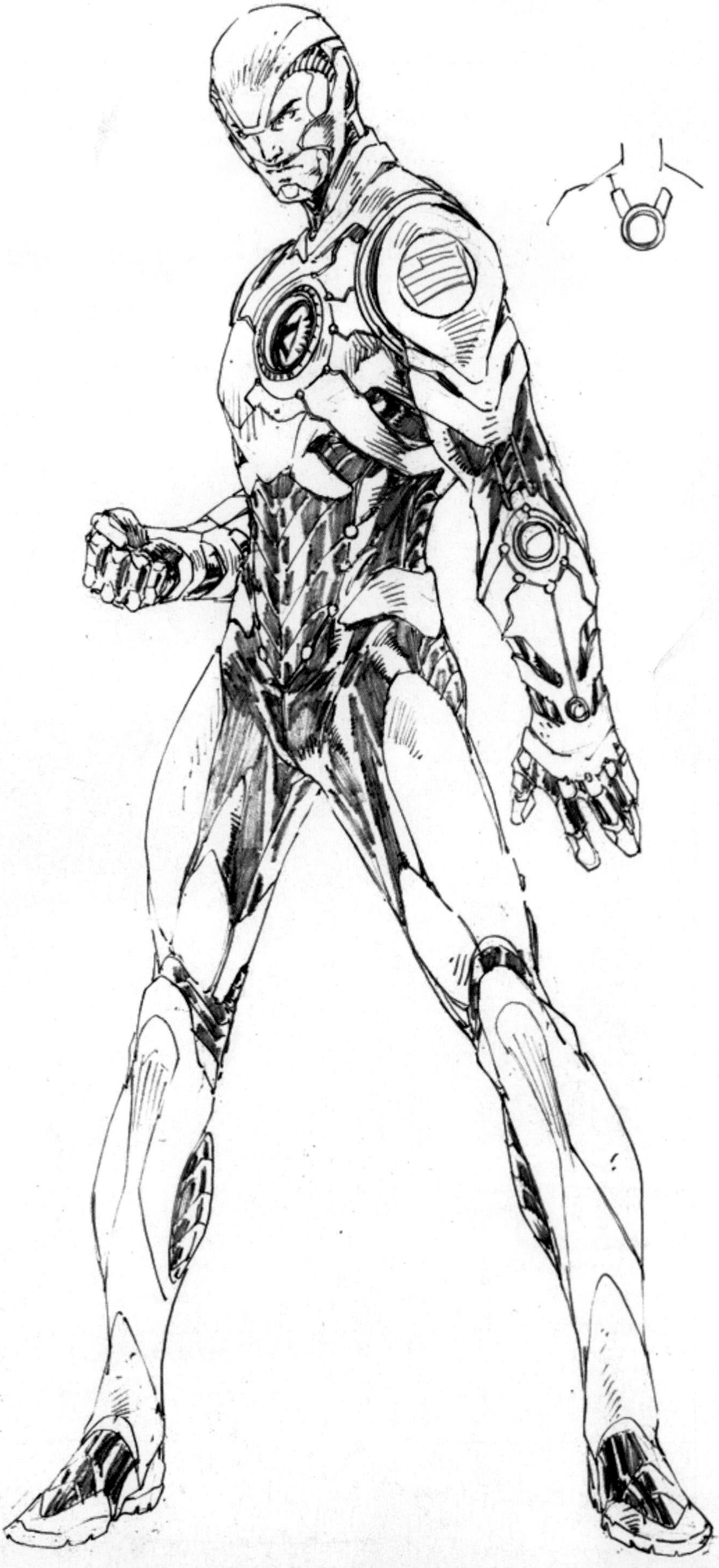

"A pretty irresistible hook. What if the good guys assembled a bunch of bad guys to work as a Dirty Dozen-like superteam and do the dirty work traditional heroes would never touch (or want to know about)?"—THE ONION/AV CLUB

START AT THE BEGINNING!

SUICIDE SQUAD
VOLUME 1: KICKED IN THE TEETH

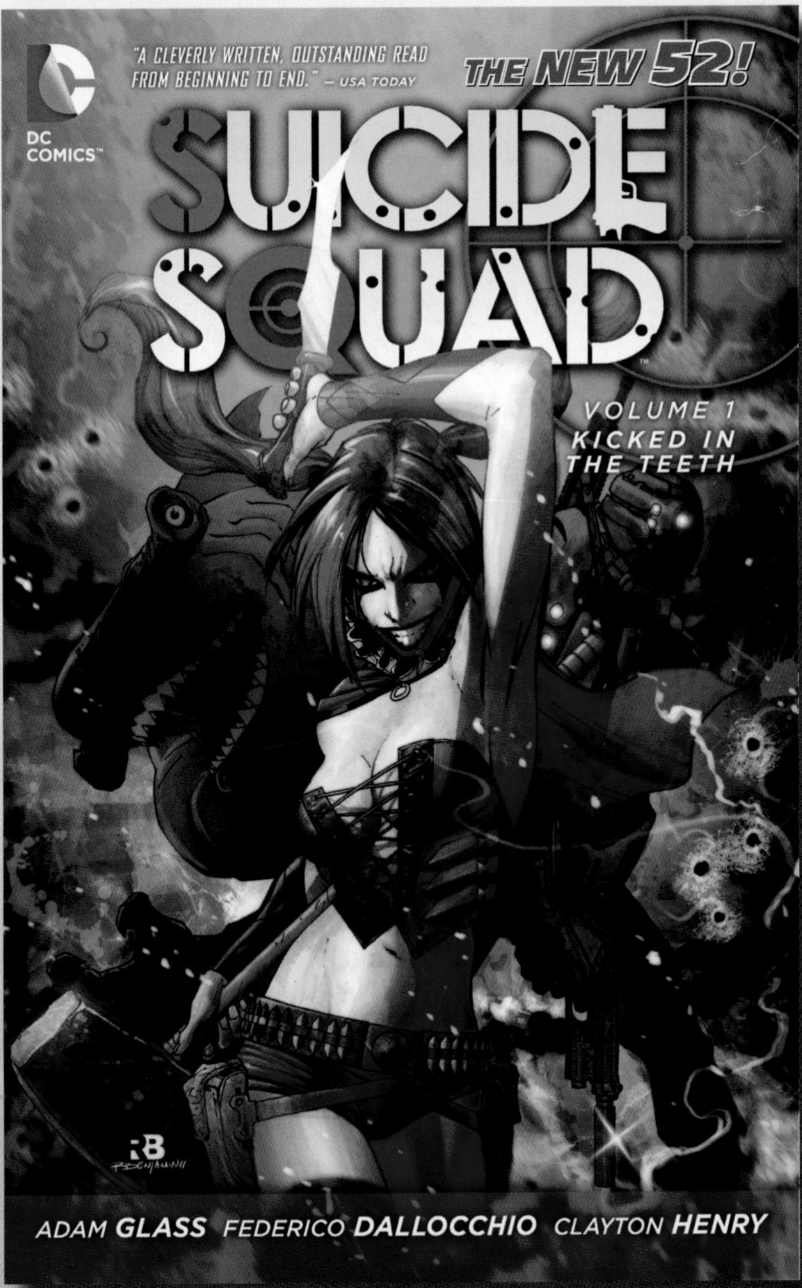
DC COMICS
"A CLEVERLY WRITTEN, OUTSTANDING READ FROM BEGINNING TO END." — USA TODAY
THE NEW 52!
SUICIDE SQUAD
VOLUME 1 KICKED IN THE TEETH
ADAM GLASS FEDERICO DALLOCCHIO CLAYTON HENRY

SUICIDE SQUAD VOL. 2: BASILISK RISING

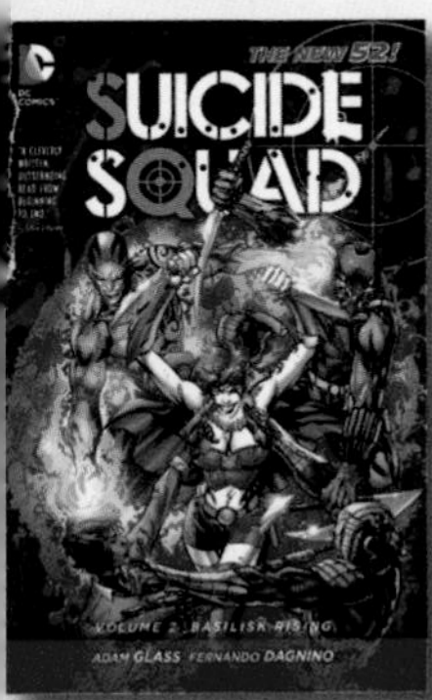
THE NEW 52!
SUICIDE SQUAD
VOLUME 2: BASILISK RISING
ADAM GLASS FERNANDO DAGNINO

SUICIDE SQUAD VOL. 3: DEATH IS FOR SUCKERS

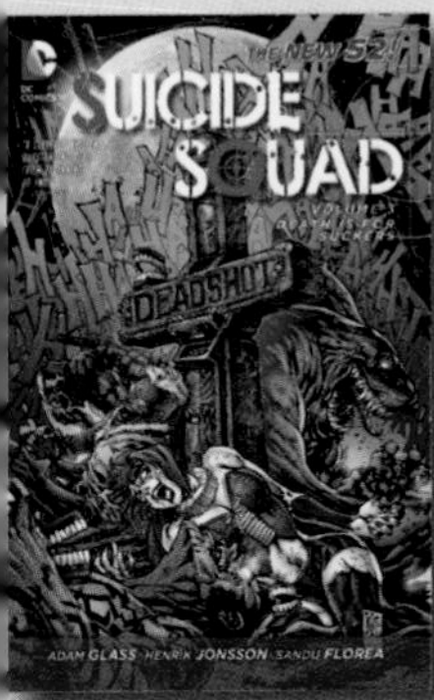
SUICIDE SQUAD
DEADSHOT
ADAM GLASS HENRIK JONSSON SANDU FLOREA

DEATHSTROKE VOL. 1: LEGACY

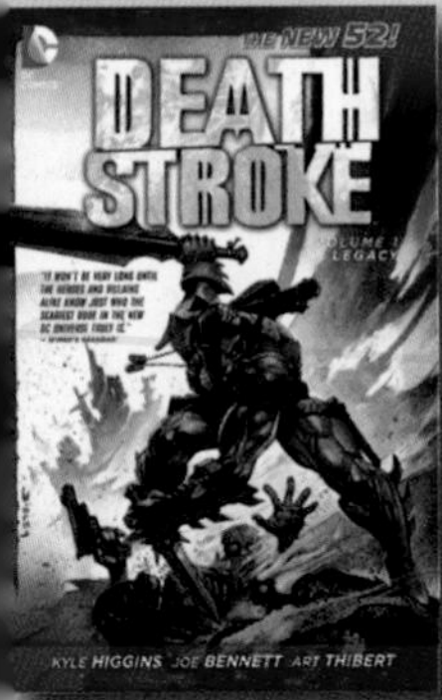
THE NEW 52!
DEATHSTROKE
KYLE HIGGINS JOE BENNETT ART THIBERT

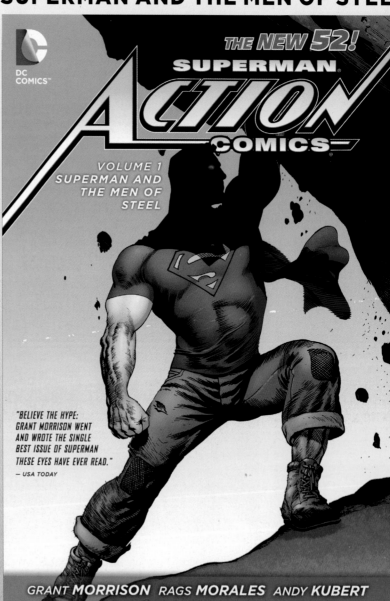